Dag Øistein Endsjø is a professor of religious studies at the University of Oslo, Norway, specializing in gender, human rights and death studies. His books – published in thirteen languages – include *Flesh and Bones Forever: A History of Immortality*; *Primordial Landscapes, Incorruptible Bodies* and *Greek Resurrection Beliefs and the Success of Christianity*.

SEX AND RELIGION

Teachings and Taboos in the History of World Faiths

Dag Øistein Endsjø

SPEAKING TIGER

SPEAKING TIGER BOOKS LLP
125A, Ground Floor, Shahpur Jat, near Asiad Village,
New Delhi 110049

First published in English by Reaktion Books 2011
This edition published in India by Speaking Tiger Books 2024

This book was first published in Norwegian in 2009 by Universitetsforlaget, Oslo, under the title *Sex og Religion: Fra jomfruball til hellig homosex* by Dag Øistein Endsjø

English translation by Peter Graves

ISBN: 978-93-5447-822-2
eISBN: 978-93-5447-748-5

10 9 8 7 6 5 4 3 2 1

Printed at Chaman Enterprises, New Delhi

Contents

Preface

Entering the sacred garden of sex and religion, we soon encounter seemingly countless variations. Whereas some Christian teenage girls attend purity balls where they promise God to abstain from sex until marriage, there are Buddhist monks who consider sex between men a sacred mystery. There is no simple key to the relationship between sex and religion. Religious discussions on homosexuality dominate the media headlines, and believers ponder whether the death penalty should be the punishment for certain forms of heterosexuality, whether promiscuity leads to hurricanes and nuclear holocaust, whether God condones marriage between people of different faiths and whether there is sex in heaven.

Our society is apparently obsessed with sex – and so are our religions. Whether we are supposed to have it or not (or hardly at all), sex plays a prominent role in most religious world views. Various creeds both condemn and glorify sex; they prohibit us from having sex and force us to have it; they punish us for our sexual activity and reward us for it. Your sexual behaviour does not only have consequences in this life, but in the hereafter. The gender, marital status, colour, religion, caste and number of your sexual partners are all factors that may seal your fate for eternity.

But how is it that the same form of sex can lead you to perdition, according to some, and to salvation, according to others? The apparently countless ways in which sex and religion may be combined does not mean that there is any lack of logic in doing so. But the logic is of a particular kind, found in complex patterns that reflect our relationship with the divine and with human nature, which is explained differently in each and every religion.

Focusing particularly on Judaism, Christianity, Islam, Hinduism and Buddhism, this book tries to explain some of the background, motivation and general beliefs behind the complex landscape of religious attitudes towards sex today, employing sacred texts, ancient myths, doctrinal statements, historical material, surveys on sexual behaviour, and a great variety of other sources.

The very variety in this field is more than just titillating. In a time when we repeatedly encounter religious claims of eternal – and universal – truths about sex, it is even more important to be aware of how historically and religiously limited so many of these claims really are. It is equally relevant to see how some of the most profound religio-sexual demands today were originally intimately connected with beliefs that may even seem embarrassing to many of those who now advocate these rules. Strict pious control of *female* extramarital sex is traditionally often found combined with a pronounced tolerance of *male* extramarital affairs; the religious logic explaining the harsh condemnation of sex between *men* simultaneously connects with the tacit acceptance of sex between *women*; claims by the faithful about how God's creation invalidates same-sex unions are mirrored in similarly creationistic arguments against marriages between people of different skin colour.

Just as sex is hardly ever just about sex, the topic of sex *and* religion is about much more than just a combination of the two: it is about politics and identity, it relates to language and economics and is intimately tied to the general social fabric of our society. Regardless of whether we are believers or not, sex and religion connect with how we lead our lives in general and with how we think of ourselves as human beings.

Introduction

Hippolytus was a young man with very little appreciation of sex. He was simply not interested: 'He shuns the bed of love and wants nothing to do with marriage.' The only thing he enjoyed was running round hunting wild beasts in the forests around the Bronze Age Greek city of Troezen.

Aphrodite, the goddess of love and sexuality, hated Hippolytus. By preferring life in the wilderness to sex the young man was demonstrating that he found the goddess of love utterly irrelevant, that he considered her to be 'the worst of the gods'.

But Aphrodite would not allow Hippolytus to go unpunished for ignoring sexual life, her domain. The handsome young man ended up as a mutilated corpse, hurled from his chariot when his horses were frightened by a monster the gods had sent for that very purpose.

This story is more than a fascinating tale from the world of Greek mythology.[1] The fate of Hippolytus reflects an authentic religious conviction that the gods not only desired but demanded that we should be sexually active. Sexual abstinence was quite simply disgraceful.

Religion For and Against Sex

The story of Hippolytus and Aphrodite does not conform to the usual image we have of the relationship between sex and religion. News headlines today can easily give the impression that religions are more preoccupied with sex than ever before, but the picture is almost invariably the opposite to the one given in the story of Hippolytus. Most religions are usually seen as opposing and condemning sex – sex with the wrong people, in the wrong way, at the wrong time, in the wrong place. They are angry that sex is written about too much and talked about too much; they are exasperated because sex is written about and talked about in the wrong way. The condemnation is often so absolute that many people are left with the impression that religion utterly rejects sex in all its forms.

How can it be that one religion condemns people who abstain from sex whereas another religion condemns the majority of people who have sex? There is no simple answer to the question, and the question itself is perhaps too simple. Not even the ancient Greek religion of Hippolytus and Aphrodite preached complete acceptance of all forms of sexuality, and unless an individual followed a whole series of complicated rules as to what kind of sex was religiously acceptable the consequences could be serious. Even though the tragic fate of Hippolytus reflects important religious beliefs in ancient Greece, it is no more than one piece of the complex puzzle that makes up the picture of the relationship between sex and that particular religion.

Even today the picture is a good deal more complicated than the headlines would have us believe. The one-sided concentration on religious opposition to various forms of sex does not make it easy for us to pick out the nuances. We fail to see that much of the condemnation simultaneously implies that religion is giving its blessing to sex – as long as it is the 'right' sort of sex, of course. The condemnation and blessing of sex go hand in hand. In looking at the relationship between sex and each individual religion it is important to focus on where the borderlines run between what is accepted and what is rejected, what is sacred and what is condemned.

The Basic Rules of the Game

No known society has ever existed without rules about sex. From time to time happy sailors, artists and social anthropologists have believed they have discovered an utterly sexually liberated society on some South Sea island paradise, a society without any sexual checks at all. This has always proved to be an illusion. These long-distance travellers simply found themselves in societies with few if any of the sexual restrictions they knew at home, but were unable to identify the local sexual restrictions because they were so alien to them.

It is difficult if not impossible to discover which came first – cultural patterns of sexual behaviour or religious rules about it. Did the various prohibitions and directives about sex originally arise independently of religion, only to be given a religious significance later? Or did the religious regulation of sexual life come into being independently of what people were actually doing and then, at a later stage, guide sexual behaviour in new directions? Was it a case of religions merely sanctioning sexual patterns that already existed in human society, or did religions step in and change our sexual practices right from the start?

Our ancestors were having sex well before they had religion. We have been having sex ever since our ancestors were no more than small bundles of cells hundreds of millions of years ago. On the other hand, it is impossible to be sure whether we had rules about sex before we had religion. Zoologists have shown that even animals have a variety of behavioural patterns that govern much of their sexual activity, but whether such patterns can be considered as *rules* is less certain. All known human societies, however, have rules about sex, though we have no idea when they arose. We are dealing with something that took place so long ago that it is impossible to draw any valid conclusions.

Animals do not have religion. Ancient cave paintings and elaborate burials demonstrate, however, that religion goes far, far back into human history, perhaps as far back as humans have existed as a species. The question then is whether religions have always attempted to regulate human sexuality. What we do know is that we can find religious sanctions on and condemnations of various forms of sexuality even in the earliest written sources on religion – and the same thing holds true in all known non-literate cultures. In both the ancient written sources and in the traditions of pre-literate societies we can see that there is, on the whole, conformity between religious rules for sex and the more general rules for sex – the prohibitions and injunctions that exist are, as a rule, religious as well as secular.

Regardless of how the relationship between religion and sexuality originated, it is clear that the unbelievable diversity and intricate religious sexual structures we find in all societies have been formed and developed through a complex cultural and religious process. There is no single standard for how religion relates to human sexuality: a form of sex held up as the ideal or even as sacred by one religion may be rejected as an abomination by another. But all of these patterns have one thing in common: not one of the models of sexuality advocated by different religions represents a natural limitation of sex. What we are dealing with in every case is a cultural construct.

Why Sex and Religion?

The fact that religion focuses primarily on belief and faith is a relatively new phenomenon. We can see that religion was originally perhaps more concerned with correct behaviour, and correct sexual behaviour was a central part of that. The conviction that performing certain actions is fundamental to the practice of religion has never lost its power – and the continuing religious focus on sexuality provides a good example of that.

But even among religious actions sex seems to occupy a rather special position. There are religious rules about how you should behave, what you should eat, how you should wear your hair, how you should wash and how you should conduct yourself at religious services, but people rarely kill each other because of these rules. On the other hand, quite a lot of people are killed because of other people's religious attitude to their sex lives. Sex is more likely to inflame emotions than most other things in the religious context. While the Spanish Catholic church peacefully accepted almost forty years of Franco's systematic suppression of the most fundamental human rights, it immediately organized huge demonstrations of hundreds of thousands of the faithful when a democratically elected government proposed the legalization of same-sex marriage.[2]

Most present-day religions have abandoned the idea that they can force everyone to follow the one true faith. Many of those same religions nevertheless aim to impose certain aspects of their beliefs on society at large; and sex tends to be at the top of the agenda.

What is it about sex that makes it such a central issue, sometimes the *ultimate* issue, for so many religions? It is impossible to give a conclusive answer to a question of that sort, and any answers will, of course, vary depending on which religion we are talking about. In many religions sex looms as an enormously powerful phenomenon, not least because heterosexual vaginal sex is the only way human beings can create new life. For many faiths sex – or abstaining from sex – represents an important way in which we can imitate the behaviour of the gods or of those perfect human beings back at the beginning of time. In the view of many religions certain kinds of sex will make salvation impossible; some maintain that *all* sex will prevent us from achieving our full potential; whereas others again see certain kinds of sex as *necessary* to placate the gods. Not all religions, however, are equally preoccupied with sex.

If we look at the consequences of sexual control, we can perhaps suggest another fundamental answer as to why so many religions are keen to control our sexual behaviour. The implications of regulating sexual behaviour go well beyond direct control of the most intimate sectors of people's private lives: they have a very significant impact on many major parts of their lives. Prohibitions and injunctions as to when, how and not least *with whom* you may have sex do not define just your sexuality but also who you can associate with in the most personal of all spheres, who your children and grandchildren will be; they play a role in deciding your social circle, your alliances and how you live your whole life. Sex is thus often a key to how the religions want you to be in your very essence – so that you can achieve salvation and redemption.

Even though the use of homosexuality and heterosexuality as identity markers is a relatively recent phenomenon, sexuality has always played a part in defining human identities. Sexual rules preserve and reinforce identities and categories within many religions. Sex, marital status, religion, ethnicity, caste – all these are important religious identity markers. By regulating human sexuality, religions uphold and strengthen these sacred categories. If you reject the religio-sexual injunctions and prohibitions you are simultaneously rejecting your whole identity. Since religio-sexual beliefs are likely to define your identity as a human being, anything that falls outside the religio-sexual frames of reference can be considered unnatural. If you fail to behave in the expected religio-sexual manner, you are not even a proper human being.

So when the religions regulate your sexual life they are also controlling your life, your identity and even your understanding of what it is to be human. And when religions strive to make secular authorities enforce their religio-sexual beliefs, they know that this means that some of their most central religious rules are being made to seem natural and self-evident. They may not succeed in making a convert of you, but by controlling your sexual life they can make you live as if you were a believer. They have thus put you on the road to salvation and to what they consider to be human perfection.

This makes it easier to understand why so many religions put such emphasis on sex. It is particularly apparent in the case of those religions that have come to recognize that they can no longer control all aspects of society: if they can succeed in having their sexual rules accepted as general principles, major structural elements of their ideal religious society will nevertheless have been put in place.

The Central Idea and Structure of the Book

A complete presentation of all aspects of the relationship between sex and religion would require a multi-volume work of encyclopaedic length. The aim here, then, is rather to identify the most important and typical features of the religio-sexual landscape.

In this book I try to point out some of the most important sexual patterns to be found in the major religions and I have also included a number of examples which, although not equally representative, are all the more important precisely because they show other ways in which sex and religion may be combined. Even when dealing with the major religions it is important to look at some of the more marginal phenomena since these can often provide a corrective to such general statements as 'Judaism has always . . . ' or 'Islam has always . . .'.

This religio-sexual diversity brings us back to our starting point. There is nothing natural or self-evident about the ways in which the various religions prescribe or proscribe, bless or condemn different types of sexuality. Whether sex becomes either sacred or abhorrent depends entirely on whether the particular religion defines it as such.

There is no single and obvious way of structuring the contents of a book about sex and religion. I could have given a chronological presentation of how the relationship between sex and religion has changed throughout history, or I could have presented each religion individually. I have, however, chosen to work thematically, with each chapter reflecting some of the most significant problematic areas in the relationship between sex and religion. It will include such things as what people mean by sex in a religious context, who you may have sex with, sex as a directly religious activity, and what religions state to be the consequences of sex – both for the individual and for society at large.

In the first chapter I shall examine the definitions of sex and religion: how can we decide whether something is religious or not; how can we say that certain rules are typical of such and such a religion when every single religion includes a wide variety of views about many different kinds of sex? Religious perceptions of what sex actually is also vary widely. It is by no means a naturally defined category:

to the extreme conservative Muslims in the Taliban a woman showing her ankles is committing a sexual crime worthy of punishment, whereas in some Christian circles unmarried youth practising mutual masturbation do not believe they are having sex. The definitions of what is considered to be sexual vary from one group of believers to another, which demonstrates again that our understanding of sex is fundamentally a cultural construct.

In the second chapter we shall see that many believers do not think we should have sex at all: the theme there is the religious ideal of absolute abstinence.

The third chapter examines solitary sex. Even though sex is mainly a social activity, it is not only that. Solitary sex is not only possible but is also the subject of differing interpretations by different religions.

The fourth chapter, the longest in the book, deals with heterosexuality. But this is no clear-cut category: there are great differences between various forms of heterosexuality and the religious attitudes towards these. Given the religious tendency to condemn homosexuality, it is frequently forgotten that few if any religions give their unconditional blessing to heterosexuals who want to be free to have sex with anyone they choose. Condemnation, eternal damnation and the death penalty are just some examples of what is in store for those who fail to limit themselves to the *correct* heterosexual partner, the *correct* context and the *correct* orifices. The chapter is divided up into sections dealing with premarital sex, marriage as an institution, mandatory sex, procreative sex, polygamy, extramarital sex, divorce and, finally, other prohibitions and bodily orifices.

The fifth chapter deals with homosexuality. Many present-day religions seem almost fixated in their condemnation of homosexuality, but there are others that view sex between people of the same sex as either unproblematic, divine or, at least, as superior to heterosexuality. But homosexuality itself is not a straightforward category: many religions accept some forms of homosexuality as natural at the same time as condemning others.

The overwhelming concentration on gender in modern religious debates about sex leads us to overlook the numerous other human categories that can give rise to both prohibitions and injunctions. This forms the subject of the sixth chapter. Whereas skin colour has been an important factor to many Christians, some other religions are more concerned about regulating the possibility of believers having sex with someone of a different faith. And in Asia, for instance, we find caste as a deciding factor in the sexual behaviour of Hindus and other believers.

Whereas religions constantly have to fight for their territory in the physical, empirical world, they are on much firmer ground in other parts of the human universe. Heaven, hell and the other regions we may end up in after death are still primarily the domains of religion. These are also places where sex is practised and regulated according to a variety of religious rules. And the beings that belong to these places – gods, angels and demons – are not exempt from the religious urge to regulate sexual behaviour. This is the subject of the seventh chapter.

Our sexual practices in this life are often seen as the key to what will happen to us after death, but the consequences of sex can easily be wider than that. Not only can the gods punish you as an individual while you are still alive, but your sexual behaviour can affect the way the divine powers treat the whole of your community. This is the subject of the eighth chapter.

The ninth chapter deals with how sex is used, in the most literal sense, in a religious context. We shall, for example, visit places of worship and see what kind of sexual displays are sometimes to be witnessed in these places. The use of ritual sex is not necessarily alien to the masters of religious ceremony.

The tenth chapter is concerned with the examination of religio-sexual priorities. Various prohibitions and injunctions are either downgraded or elevated in relation to each other and in relation to other aspects of religion. Why, for instance should some prohibitions and injunctions be effectively ignored at certain periods whereas at other times the same prohibitions and injunctions are regarded as among the most vital elements of the religious world view?

I
Defining Sex and Religion

How can we define the proper Christian relationship to sex? Or the correct Muslim one? Or the proper Hindu? We are constantly hearing that this or that is forbidden to Christians or Buddhists or Jews, and then, just as often, we hear people saying something quite different. Then comes the argument about who is right and who is wrong. In other words, confusion can set in the moment we enter the field of religion and sex. But perhaps it is in this very disunity that many of the answers lie.

All believers like to see themselves as true Christians, true Muslims, true Hindus, true whatever it may be. No one can argue with that. Yet because of the multiplicity of traditions, the perception that one can be a true Christian, Muslim or Hindu poses a dilemma. If Mona, who is a proper Jew, believes such and such, what is Hanna, who perhaps does not believe such and such? Is she not just as much a Jew? We find exactly the same dilemma when it comes to what religious believers understand as constituting correct sex. Each religion is so diverse in itself that it becomes difficult to draw any absolute conclusions about its relationship to any form of sex.

Many religious people like to speak on behalf of all their fellow believers, making statements that this or that is forbidden to Christians, Muslims or Hindus; what they overlook, consciously or unconsciously, is the huge diversity that exists within every religion. And it is not only the current state of affairs they are overlooking: it is also their history. All the great religions both condemn and defend homosexuality, for instance, in spite of claims that it has always been condemned by most religions.

Within any given religious tradition there will always be a host of different authorities a believer can fall back on – authorities that frequently say different things, and will not necessarily give unambiguous answers. The extent to which individual believers will follow what an authority says will depend partly on the choices the individuals make for themselves and partly on the level of compulsion and sanction that they are subject to. But as long as individuals consider themselves to be members of one religion or another, or at least retain formal membership in a denomination, they still have to be considered as Buddhists, Christians, Muslims and so on. The fact that so many people behave in ways that are different from the way their religious authorities want them to behave does not mean they have broken with the denomination as such but that they are expressing their religion in a new way. Given the permanent disunity within religions about the relationship between sex and religion, the answer to the question of what is truly Muslim, Christian or Hindu sexual behaviour is always going to be open to multiple responses.

Not everything is relative, however, and some authorities – certain sacred writings and leading religious figures, for instance – are more central than others. There are also clear trends visible in the interrelationship between authorities, with certain of the prohibitions in the sacred writings being given much more weight while others may be virtually ignored. It is important to examine both what is emphasized and what is ignored because this can demonstrate how much of expressed religion is the result of conscious or unconscious choices. We can also see that there are clear tendencies with regard to how or whether believers obey or ignore one or another prohibition or injunction. We shall look more closely at some of these issues when we attempt to map the religio-sexual landscape.

There are many people who select their sources carefully in order to come up with absolute claims. They pick out specific sections of the Bible or the Koran and use them to prove that Judaism, Christianity or Islam takes such and such a view of a particular sexual variant. This kind of selection shows how even core sources cannot be used to give conclusive answers about a religion, even though such claims may frequently represent religious convictions and traditions. In the Gospels Jesus totally prohibited divorce but the majority of Christians nowadays think differently. This does not, however, make either the supporters of divorce or its opponents any less Christian.

This leads us on to the question of which sources we should rely on when investigating the relationship between sex and religion.

We cannot use, for instance, sacred texts alone for the simple reason that believers themselves choose to interpret them in such different ways. In attempting to paint a picture of the relationship between sex and religion it will therefore be necessary to use a variety of sources. The reading of religious texts will have to be set against what members of the various faiths believe today and what they have believed through the course of history. Statements made by religious leaders cannot be understood without considering the extent to which believers act according to such injunctions. Religious ideals will have to be compared with what is actually practised and tolerated, and what emerges in terms of sanctions and reactions when people find themselves in the border zone of the acceptable.

It is also essential to ask what the limits of religion actually are. For many religious people, particularly today, sex is not included in what they would consider to be religion. There are others, however, who see certain rules about sex as central to their religion whereas other rules are seen as culturally determined. And there are things that started off as *religious* injunctions and prohibitions that have since become so internalized that they are now perceived as being 'natural'. Even when religious people define the whole or parts of their sexual lives as completely outside the sphere of religion, their attitudes to sex will nevertheless remain relevant to a study of sex and religion simply because such people still view themselves as religious.

Huge cultural and regional differences further complicate the picture – both within any particular religion and between different faiths. In the whole of the Mediterranean area, for instance, there is a common traditional pattern in sexual matters whereby men, more or less, can do whatever they like, whereas women's sexuality is subject to strict controls. This pattern remains essentially the same whether we are talking about Christianity, Judaism, Islam or other religions. The question then is whether this is a matter of religion, culture or both. Since this is a general pattern that has survived for thousands of years and through many religious changes, there is good reason for thinking that it represents a fundamental cultural trait that goes beyond religion. But if you ask individual Christians, Jews or Muslims about it, you are likely to get different answers: even though very few of them would argue that there is a religious explanation for men being permitted to generally do what they like, most would see the strict control of female sexuality as closely associated with religious beliefs. Once a pattern of this kind becomes internalized in a specific religion, it becomes part of it.

There are some countries in which, for religious reasons, the state attempts to impose strict controls on the sexual behaviour of its citizens. This will inevitably affect the degree to which citizens adhere to the traditional religious rules governing sexual conduct. Though an increasing number of states are permitting citizens to make their own choices in sexual matters, the actual ability of the state to impose controls has increased as its apparatus becomes ever more extensive and effective. Generally speaking, it would seem that religious injunctions and prohibitions were stricter in the past than they are now, but religious and state authorities had much less power to ensure that they were adhered to.

In other parts of the world we shall find cultural patterns that cross religious boundaries: the patterns of sexual behaviour among young Jews, Christians and Muslims in New York or Berlin will have more in common with one another than with those of their young co-religionists in villages in Kerala or Ethiopia. Economic and other non-religious factors are involved here: it is obvious that the levels of social and religious control are very different in situations where an unmarried individual can operate independently and in places where being rejected by one's family means economic and social ruin. The small, economically independent nuclear family capable of moving to another part of the country provides a very different set of circumstances for an individual than the extended family in which, even as an adult, you cannot escape the scrutiny of parents, grandparents, aunts and uncles. It is factors of this kind that explain why more Muslims and Hindus live in accordance with traditional religio-sexual rules than Christians and Jews: fewer Muslims and Hindus live in societies in which individuals have the opportunity to exist independently of their families and other tight-knit social networks. There is little or nothing in any of these religions themselves to account for such major statistical differences. In all religions we can find the whole spectrum of sexual behaviour, from extremely strict rules to relaxed attitudes.

All in all it is difficult to provide conclusive answers with regard to how any particular religion relates to sex. Religions are not clearly defined units: they are categories whose boundaries are often notably unclear. The various beliefs have also changed greatly through the course of history. And each of these faiths embraces a wide spectrum

The expulsion from Eden.

Nakedness, or merely the suggestion of nakedness, represents another border area that has been strongly sexualized within many religions. In the biblical account of the Garden of Eden, Adam and Eve were ashamed of their nakedness and covered themselves with plaited fig leaves as soon as they had eaten from the tree of wisdom 'and the eyes of them both were opened'.[12] When Noah in his drunkenness was seen naked by his son Ham, Ham and his sons were cursed for generations.[13] Anthony the Great, the first of the legendary Christian desert fathers, was praised for never having allowed anyone to see him naked while he was alive. To be on the safe side, the holy man gave up washing for life, and as a good model for Christians, he would not even place 'his feet in water unless he had to'.[14]

The Christian attitude to nakedness has, however, undergone changes. Pope Julius II at the start of the sixteenth century had no problem with the many naked biblical figures Michelangelo painted in the Sistine Chapel whereas Pope Paul IV a few decades later was horrified by all the nudity and planned to destroy the paintings. It was only the strength of the resultant protests that made him give up his original plan and instead commission one of Michelangelo's pupils to paint clothes on the indecent biblical figures.[15] In the modern age

Christians have devoted seemingly endless efforts to attempting to limit the depiction of nakedness in films and in print. Even today the issue is still current. While ever more football teams and women's institutes publish naked calendars of themselves, the American Chad Hardy was excommunicated by the Church of Jesus Christ of Latter-day Saints in the summer of 2008 because he published a calendar of male Mormon missionaries with naked torsos.[16]

Ideally speaking, Islamic adults should not show themselves naked, even among those of their own sex, but practice has varied considerably, especially at public baths.[17] The prohibition against nakedness is related to the Koran's exhortation to women to dress modestly, particularly when in contact with men outside the immediate family.[18] Decent women should remain well-covered, whereas the rules are less strict for men: this is noticeable, for instance, on European beaches where fully dressed Muslim women can often be seen sitting alongside their male relations and husbands who

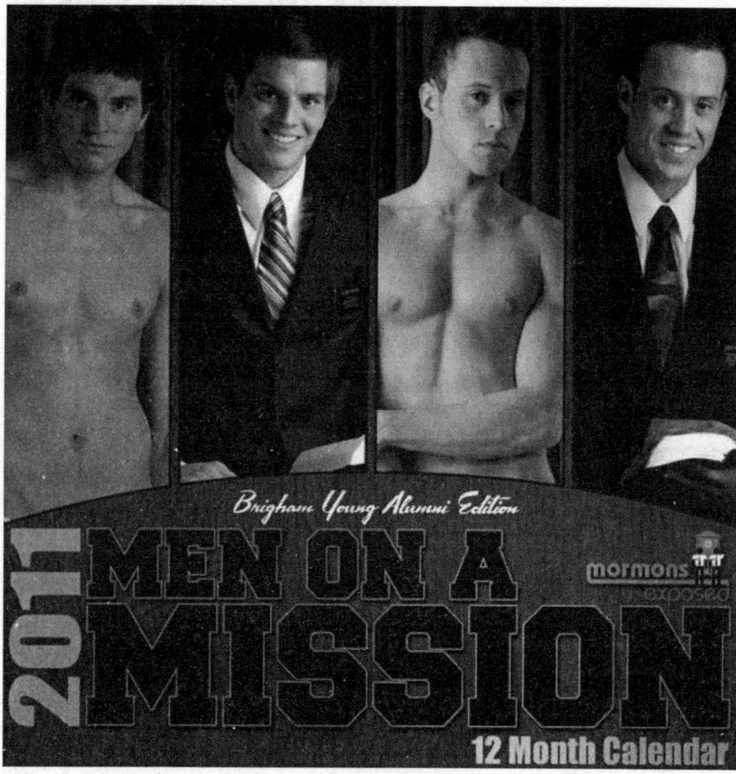

'Men on a Misson', Mormon calendar, 2011.

are wearing minimal swimming trunks. But men do not always get away with it. Since the 1979 revolution in Iran men are no longer able to dress as they like, while in 2009 Hamas patrolmen in the Gaza Strip began to admonish men who walked around the beach bare-chested.[19]

Clothes alone are not always sufficient to cover women's nakedness. Abu Hurairah, one of Muhammad's closest disciples, warned against 'women who are naked even though they are wearing clothes'. Such women 'go astray and make others go astray'. According to Abu Hurairah, dress habits of this kind will exclude the wearer from entering paradise.[20] The exhortation to dress modestly is what lies behind the increasing use of the hijab and niqab we see today, even though Muhammad himself did not demand either. It was Caliph Umar who is supposed to have been divinely inspired to invent the hijab shortly after the death of the Prophet.[21] There is, however, a huge difference between fashion-conscious women in Tehran wearing neat designer hijabs on top of elaborate hairdos, and the habit of being completely covered by clothes and dark veils that is normal for almost all women in Sana'a, the capital of Yemen. In the autumn of 2008 the leading Islamic judge in Saudi Arabia declared that the showing of scantily clad women and other 'great evil' justified killing the owners of the television companies in question.[22] Rather similarly, right up until the 1980s conservative families in the United Arab Emirates would not allow their sons to marry a girl who had been seen by anyone – male or female – outside her immediate family circle.[23]

If we go to the other extreme we can occasionally find religion revealing a rather more limited understanding of what constitutes sex than the one held by people in general. A 2003 US survey showed that 27 per cent of a group of college students who had signed conservative Christian pledges to refrain from premarital sex considered they had kept their promise a year later, even though they had indulged in oral sex during that year. They did not consider this to be sex.[24] A study of women who grew up in the environment of the Norwegian low-church movement and the Ten Sing movement shows that, in practice, a ban on sex before marriage often means that 'anything apart from having intercourse was permitted'.[25] Heterosexual couples are quite able to 'touch each other to the point of orgasm and things like that' without this being considered sex.[26] A young Christian woman, who makes it quite clear that she did not want to have sex before marriage, says that her boyfriend 'was surprised when I sucked him off, for example . . . almost straightaway, you know'.[27] The perhaps surprising boundaries as to what unmarried Christians in a conservative environment will or will not do with the opposite sex while insisting that they will not have sex before marriage are, however, 'quite normal' in their particular society.[28]

Sexual attitudes like these create a conceptual apparatus that is often rather confused, and the American internet pastor Bill McGinnis provides a good example of the kind of confusion that arises. He explains, for example, when outlining the normal American conservative Christian understanding of sex, that 'dating with petting to climax may be an option' for unmarried Christians who wish to stick to the Christian prohibition against premarital sex. There is nothing new about this in a Christian context and McGinnis points out that the same basic understanding was widespread in his own youth around 1960. As he states from his own experience: 'Both parties had a climax; nobody lost their virginity.' So as long as there is no penetration involved, there can be no question of it really being sex.[29] In other words, Bill Clinton's explanations in the Monica Lewinsky case were not conjured up out of thin air but reflected fundamental ideas held by the same conservative Christian circles that were condemning him. What Clinton seems to have overlooked, however, is that the boundaries of what constitutes sex seem to change once people get married. The very same acts that are accepted as harmless petting *before* marriage become impermissible sex *after* marriage if performed with anyone other than one's spouse. Furthermore, for it not to be thought of as sex, this kind of heavy petting must clearly be restricted to people of the opposite sex, irrespective of marital status. When young people in conservative Christian circles are told that they should not 'touch each other *too much* or pet *too* heavily',[30] the statement certainly does not imply that it is permissible to touch or pet in moderation with people of the same sex. Despite the countless passionate heterosexual kisses shown on US network television, just one clearly filmed homosexual kiss, shown on the TV series *Relativity* in 1997 – the first ever – led Tim Wildmon, vice-president of the conservative Christian American Family Association, to declare that 'the television industry continues to push the homosexual agenda with increasing fervency'.[31] According to the very different scale of values operative in some conservative Muslim and Hindu regions, two men can walk hand in hand with no sexual connotations or problems at all – but if an unmarried woman and a man were to do the same thing this act would have clear sexual associations.

The notion that sex primarily has to do with vaginal penetration is by no means unique to certain conservative Christian groups. Sex between women is commonly disregarded by many religions on the basis that it is simply not considered to be sex. Neither the Judaic Hebrew Bible nor the Koran contain prohibitions against sex between women, even though anal sex between men is considered deserving of capital punishment in the former, and of a less specified punishment in the latter. Rabbinic literature frequently refers to *mesolelot*, 'women who rub', that is, women who rub their sexual organs against one another's. According to most of the religious authorities who discuss this practice in detail, it does not mean that the women cease to be virgins.[32] Similarly, Hincmar, who was archbishop of Reims in the ninth century, insisted that sex between women was only possible with the use of penetrative objects,[33] and women in Aragon who were accused of lesbian sex in 1560 were acquitted precisely because they had not penetrated one another with artificial phalluses.[34]

But even penetration is not necessarily an absolute criterion of a religion's concept of sex. Among some young unmarried Catholics in various countries in Africa and the Americas, for instance, one can find the practice of heterosexual anal sex as a method of 'protecting the woman's virginity'. In Puerto Rico in 1998 44 per cent of sexually active male students were mainly practising heterosexual anal sex rather than vaginal sex.[35] It is unlikely that many of these young people would claim they were not involved in sex, but since they believe that the female partner does not lose her virginity in anal sex, they are quite clearly operating in a sexual borderland in which religion represents one of the most important factors in defining their behaviour. Once again, however, we find an enormous difference in attitude depending on whether the sex is between people of different sexes or between people of the same sex: men who have passive anal sex with other men are certainly not excluded by definition from what is understood as having sex.

The moment one begins to examine the field of religion and sex, it quickly becomes obvious that distinctions are rarely straightforward. But not everything can be relativized, even though the sexual borderland is often unclear. However reprehensible it may be to sit beside a member of the opposite sex on the bus, even the most zealous advocates of such regulations will nevertheless admit that there is a distinction between such an act and having vaginal sex. In a similar way, certain kinds of behaviour that are often defined as non-sexual in other conservative religious surroundings are nevertheless considered sexual if the parties involved are no longer single, or if they are of the same sex.

2
No Sex, Thank You

'It were better for you, foolish man, that your male organ should enter the mouth of a terrible and poisonous snake, than that it should enter a woman . . . It were better for you, foolish man, that your male organ should enter a charcoal pit, burning, ablaze, afire.' This was the message the Buddha gave to the monk Sudinna after he had gone back to his wives for a short time and made one of them pregnant in order to ensure the continuation of his lineage. As Buddha points out, both snakes and burning coals can lead to death but sex can lead to even worse things *after* death: 'you would pass to the waste, the bad bourn, the abyss, hell.'[1] There has rarely been a clearer statement in the religious context that sex is something to be avoided than this one, attributed to Buddha some time during the fifth century BC. But the absolute condemnation of sex in this episode is by no means unique.

One of the more common preconceptions is that religion in general is anti-sex. There is a grain of truth in this, as there is in many other rather simplistic notions. Much religious belief is, on the whole, against all sex, but – as we have already seen – far from all religions take this view. There is a major distinction to be made between the great religions in this respect. On the one hand, Judaism, Islam and Hinduism are certainly not against sex in general – quite the reverse, as we shall see in more detail in the chapter on heterosexuality. But many people often forget how utterly negative Buddhism and Christianity have been to all forms of sex. The Buddhist portrayal of heterosexuality as worse than associating with poisonous snakes and burning coals does not only refer to the monastic life but implies a general view of sex as something incompatible with eventual liberation from passion. And when we turn to Christianity we find that both Jesus and St Paul emphasized sexual abstinence as the best way by far.

In early Buddhist texts marriage is presented as a source of suffering, *dukkha*,[2] which is why Siddhartha, the future Buddha, left his wife and child on his road to enlightenment. Sexual abstinence is necessary in order to finally break the evil circle of reincarnation.[3] Sexual desire, like all other desire, is synonymous with passion, which more than anything else is what prevents us from achieving ultimate enlightenment. Heterosexual intercourse is therefore often portrayed as the worst possible act from the karmic perspective, because it not only leads to bad karma for the individual but also means that passion is passed on to others by the simple fact that the individual produces children.[4]

Siddhartha's action in leaving his wife is not the only way in which Buddha's actions show the absolute necessity of sexual abstinence if perfect salvation is to be achieved. When Siddhartha was approaching perfect enlightenment, the evil demon Mara attempted to use sex to keep him a prisoner of passion, by sending his three daughters to seduce Siddhartha. In order to be absolutely certain of coming up with what Siddhartha had earlier found most arousing, the three demon daughters created first the illusion of one hundred wondrously beautiful maidens, then of one hundred women who had not yet borne children, then one hundred women who had borne one child, next one hundred women who had borne two children, and finally one hundred old women. Siddhartha, however, remained so perfectly untempted by woman in all her forms that Mara compared

Mara's temptation of Buddha.

Sculpture of a Buddhist monk on a four-legged base.

his attempt to seduce Siddhartha with sex 'to crushing rocks with lotus stalks and destroying iron with teeth'.[5]

The sexual abstinence of Buddhist monks and nuns is part of the process of assigning them a markedly higher position in the religious hierarchy than lay people. The original rule was quite clear: the monk who lies with a woman or the nun who lies with a man is no longer a true monk or nun. In spite of Buddha's fairly unambiguous words that sex was something to abstain from, there are nevertheless major differences within the Buddhist monastic world. In China and Japan it is only the monks who live in monasteries who need to be celibate, whereas those who serve in temples are often married.[6] There are also married monks in Tibet, Korea and Indochina, but there are no corresponding exceptions in the case of nuns.[7] Monks who are celibate are, not surprisingly, usually ranked higher.[8]

According to tradition Buddha only allowed women to become nuns after he had been urged to do so by one of his leading male disciples. Even though sexual abstinence is one of the criteria necessary for the achievement of enlightenment, the possibility of abstinence was originally denied to women. Similar sexist attitudes to those behind Buddha's original scepticism about ordaining women ascetics are reflected by the fact that the focus on lifelong abstinence by women is generally less strong than that on abstinence by men. The duty of women to subordinate themselves to men often stands in the way of any desire they may have to live a life of complete abstinence because it is their duty to be the spouses of men who may not desire to practise abstinence. Buddhism has an ambivalent attitude to chaste women who stand their ground, and the concept of the 'obstinate virgin' who refuses to marry and sometimes even chooses death instead is a widespread one. Buddhist nunneries are sometimes places of refuge for such women but, in practice, Buddhism often gives primacy to a woman's duty to the family rather than to her need to achieve salvation.[9] The fact that the road of eternal virginity was often closed to women was nevertheless recognized as a misfortune. In Chinese Buddhism marriage is often viewed as suffering for women. The transgendered bodhisattva Guan Yin[10] plays an interesting role in this context. In the 'Pure Land' texts Guan Yin is a divine saviour figure who liberates mankind in six areas of spiritual passion and leads them to the Pure Land, where they are assured of enlightenment. She also rescues people from hopeless situations in this world – imprisonment, drowning, attacks by wild animals and robbers and the like[11] – and in a number of traditional legends she also saves women from the hopeless state represented by marriage.[12]

As with Buddhism, there is no mistaking the original sexual teaching of Christianity: the best path is abstinence. The great emphasis that much contemporary Christianity puts on heterosexual marriage as an ideal may easily lead us to assume that Christianity has always taken this view. That is not the case: if we go back to early Christianity we find that hetero-marriage was initially viewed as no more than a solution dictated by necessity.

St Paul's greatest desire was that 'all men were even as I am myself': sexually abstinent.[13] He was nevertheless sufficiently realistic to recognize that an absolute prohibition of that kind would seriously reduce the number of his followers, so his message to people in general was: 'I say therefore to the unmarried and widows, It is good for them if they abide even as I. But if they cannot contain, let them marry.'[14] In other words, heterosexual activity is ideally something to be abstained from, but if one cannot control oneself, it is better to get married because that permits sex to be practised in a manner that will not lead directly to damnation. Marriage is not at all a goal in itself, simply a last resort, a practical arrangement 'to avoid fornication'.[15]

In spite of a good deal of modern religious, literary and cinematic speculation on the topic, there is little or no evidence to suggest that Jesus was married or sexually active. Jesus lived without lovers, wives and children, and even renounced his father, mother and brothers.[16] So there is no way in which he can stand as a model for sex, marriage or family. His closest disciples also gave up sex and family to follow him and it is quite clear that he did not consider marriage as one of life's top priorities: 'If any man come to me and hate not his father, and mother, and wife, and children, and brethren, and sisters, yea, and his own life also, he cannot be my disciple.'[17]

When seeking guidance in various areas of their lives, more and more of today's Christians ask the question 'What would Jesus do?' The answer to this question is not clear in all aspects of life but it certainly is as far as sex is concerned. The answer to the question, '*Who* would Jesus do?' is very simple: no one. If one is to do as Jesus did, one must refrain from all sexual activity.

The virgin birth, which the great majority of Christian churches believe Jesus to be the product of, further emphasizes Christian scepticism about sex in general. But this was not the original Christian understanding of the conception of Jesus. Neither the epistles of Paul, the oldest surviving Christian texts, nor the Gospel according to Mark – the oldest of the Gospels – say anything about Jesus having been conceived without sex. Paul was of the opinion that Jesus was 'declared to be the Son of God with power, according to the spirit of holiness, by the resurrection of the dead' – he was not, then, born as the son of God. He was 'made of the seed of David according to the flesh',[18] and since there is nothing in the Bible to suggest that

The Annunciation, by Eliseo Fattorini after Fra Angelico, 1869.

Mary was of that lineage, only Joseph could lay claim to that line of descent.[19] The belief in the virgin birth appears first in the Gospels written after Mark's, probably partly in order to emphasize Jesus's status as the son of God and partly because of the thoroughly negative view of sex held by early Christianity. The Gospel according to Matthew tells us that Mary found that she was 'with child of the Holy Ghost', even though the genealogy of Jesus is once again traced back to David through Joseph.[20] In the Gospel according to Luke, Mary receives the following message from the angel Gabriel: 'The Holy Ghost shall come upon thee, and the power of the Highest shall overshadow thee; therefore also that holy thing which shall be born of thee shall be called the Son of God.'[21] Nevertheless, in spite of the lack of consistency in the Bible, the virgin birth is a central dogma of almost all Christian churches. Many believers doubt it, however: a survey in 2007 showed, for example, that 21 per cent of Protestants and 28 per cent of Catholics in the US do not believe in the virgin birth.[22]

The idea that abstinence is better than marriage was not only promoted by Jesus and Paul but was also the consistent standpoint of the early church fathers. Augustine of Hippo, the great father of the Western church, believed that heterosexual intercourse was a continuation of original sin. Paul, too, had recognized that mankind must suffer because of the sin of Adam, the first man,[23] but Augustine was the first to maintain that original sin was sexual in its nature. It is not genetics that accounts for the fact that original sin affects all of us, but the sexual desire that is involved in the very act of procreation.[24] This desire, even within marriage, is to be regarded as a sin, though it is a sin that could be forgiven.[25] A married couple must therefore recognize that sex, even in marriage, is sinful and something for them to feel ashamed of.[26] Thus in Christian tradition the Fall is closely linked with sex, but this is something that God is in the process of rectifying by means of sexual abstinence. Christianity's hostility towards sex is not, however, synonymous with a hostility towards the body. Rather the opposite: sexual abstinence contributes to *preserving* the body and is one of the many elements involved in the reachievement of the original sin-free and immortal state we had in the Garden of Eden. Seen in this light, sexual abstinence helps to anticipate the physically perfect body all true believers will receive at the Resurrection, at the end of history.

In original Christian tradition those who abstained from sex were clearly better people than those who did not. The fact that Jesus referred to himself as a divine bridegroom[27] has contributed to a special emphasis being put on virginity in women. Perpetual virgins became brides of Christ and even today women in the process of becoming nuns go through ceremonies resembling marriage. Tertullian, the North African church father, proclaimed to female virgins: 'you are married to Christ, you have given your bodies to Him.'[28] This special focus fitted in well with earlier beliefs that were common in the Mediterranean region, where the regulation of female sexuality was quite clearly more important than the regulation of male sexuality.

According to early Christianity, virginity did not only lead to salvation for the virgin but was also beneficial to those around her.[29] Ambrose explained some of the wonderful consequences of female abstinence: 'One virgin may redeem her parents, another her brothers.'[30] So much the worse for a family without a daughter to be kept in a state of virginity. Many women consequently chose to live their lives in a state of sexual abstinence or were forced to do so by their families. Such virgins seem originally to have remained living in the family but with the foundation of convents they began to live as communities. Even though there were many male virgins in the towns and villages around the eastern Mediterranean, little attention was paid to such men until they began to leave civilization and go out into the desert from the fourth century on. In the Hellenistic world view, wild and uninhabited terrain of this kind represented a geography considered to be particularly sexually challenging, which consequently made the abstinence practised by the desert monks even more impressive.[31] The ascetic hermit, sexually tempted by various natural and supernatural beings out in the desert, quickly became a prototype of what a pious monk should be.

The emphasis on sexual abstinence was even stronger in Christian Gnosticism than in the version of Christianity that emerged triumphant. In the Gospel of Pseudo-Matthew the Virgin Mary is horrified at the very thought of sex since 'God is worshipped in chastity'.[32] In the Acts of Thomas all sex is defined as abominable and even sex *within* marriage endangers one's hope of salvation.[33] The fact that Gnosticism was even more negative to sex than Christianity in general is connected to the Gnostics' repudiation of all material creation as evil. The worst aspect of sex was that it perpetuated the imprisonment of the human soul in matter. Similar views were held by the Cathars, who were numerous during the twelfth century in what is now the south of France: the material world was created by Satan and reincarnation ensured that we remained imprisoned in it. Among the Cathars, believers were divided into two groups: the 'perfect', who were ascetic and sexually abstinent, and the rest, who were not. Only the 'perfect' – those who abstained from sex – had the possibility of breaking out of the evil cycle of rebirth.[34] The Cathar 'perfects' carried their resistance to sex to the point that they were forbidden to eat anything that resulted from sex because any kind of procreation led to the imprisonment of the soul in the material: in practice, this meant that they did not consume meat, eggs or milk. Fruit and vegetables were permitted because the Cathars did not believe that anything sexual was involved in the propagation of plants.[35]

The emphasis on virginity also continued in the forms of Christianity that emerged victorious. The whole of the Christian monastic system, which still exists within the Catholic and Orthodox churches, is based on the idea that sexual abstinence is part of the way to achieve closeness to God. Various kinds of segregation have been practised in order to emphasize sexual abstinence. On Mount Athos, the Greek monastic republic on the easternmost of the Halkidiki peninsulas, all women and female domestic animals have been banned since the eleventh century. In some situations religio-sexual abstinence has clearly been motivated by rather more social factors. In Catholic Brazil during the seventeenth century so many upper-class families felt that there were insufficient available men of acceptable social status that the majority of their daughters ended up in convents. In seventeenth-century Bahia, for instance, 77 per cent of the daughters of leading families entered convents and only 14 per cent got married.[36]

While the monastic system is based on the principle of abstinence, it has never been absolutely clear whether Christian priests should also abstain from sex. People who protested against married priests in early Christian times were sometimes threatened with excommunication.[37] The principle of clerical celibacy has never taken root in the Eastern churches, even though bishops must be celibate. When a married priest became a bishop, the traditional solution was to send his wife to a convent.[38] The fact that many Orthodox bishops, including many of the patriarchs of Constantinople, were eunuchs made the prohibition of sex in the top levels of the church hierarchy easier to comply with.[39]

The notion of clerical celibacy had greater support in the West than in the East from a very early date. One of the first formal attempts to introduce celibacy for priests was made on the initiative of a Spanish bishop at the First Council of Nicaea in AD 325, but it was rejected precisely because of resistance from the East.[40] Interestingly, the concept of clerical abstinence did not always imply that the clergy should be unmarried – instead, they should 'abstain from their wives'.[41] Not until the First Lateran Council of 1123 was a final decision taken with regard to the celibacy of Catholic priests, and even then the decision may well have been reached largely to safeguard church property against clerics who were using it to enrich their offspring.[42] In practice, the Catholic decree on celibacy frequently meant that priests should abstain from marriage, not from sex. It was generally accepted in most Catholic countries well into the twentieth century that priests would have concubines with whom they cohabited, even though the central authorities of the Church reacted against this from time to time by threatening exile, the death penalty or slavery on the galleys.[43] Nor were priests unfamiliar with prostitutes, a situation that the church tacitly accepted. When church leaders gathered for the Council of Constance in 1414, a swarm of prostitutes flocked into the little town – at least 700 of them, according to contemporary sources.[44] Indeed, many of the popes are not only known to have been sexually active but also to have fathered children. Innocent VIII in the fifteenth century was the first pope to publicly acknowledge his children, conceived and born as they were in breach of all the dictates of the church. Innocent's successor, Alexander VI, a member of the Borgia family, appointed his son Cesare a cardinal and organized a magnificent wedding in the Vatican for his daughter Lucrezia.[45]

Even though the present-day Catholic Church formally demands celibacy of its priests, it recognizes that a not inconsiderable number of priests are in fact married: this is true, for instance, of many of the priests in the Eastern Catholic churches of the Ukraine and of Lebanon. And in addition to this, many formerly Anglican or Lutheran priests who have converted to Catholicism have been permitted to remain married.[46] There is also much resistance within the church itself to the rules concerning celibacy: a 1999 survey, for instance, revealed that only 27 per cent of Catholics in the USA considered clerical celibacy to be an important part of their Catholic faith.[47]

A new version of the Christian demand for sexual abstinence has developed because of the distinction conservative Christians are keen to make between what they like to refer to as 'homosexual inclination' and 'homosexual practice'. Increasing numbers of Christians have become convinced that many people are born homosexual, that is, *created* that way by God. But since many of the conservative Christians who accept this also believe that sex between people of the same sex is in conflict with Christian beliefs, they argue that those who are 'born homosexual' should practise total sexual abstinence. Since such people are homosexual by nature and therefore not sexually attracted to people of the opposite sex, heterosexual marriage on their part would imply deceiving their marital partner. The only possible solution, according to this particular line of Christian thinking, is total abstinence. This can have very direct consequences. The leader of the Dutch party ChristenUnie (Christian Union) declared in 2010 that the party's only openly gay parliamentary candidate would not have been nominated if he had been in a relationship. The candidate, Jonathan van der Greer, had announced that he had chosen to be sexually abstinent for his entire life.[48]

From time to time new Christian movements have emerged that demand absolute abstinence. The Shakers, for instance, members of a denomination founded in England in the eighteenth century and most widespread in the USA in the nineteenth century, considered sexual abstinence a prerequisite for salvation. Since sex was the root of all evil – religious, economic, social and political – it was only by abstaining from it that man could hope to re-establish the perfect human condition that existed before the Fall.[49] According to Mother Ann Lee, the founder of the movement, sexual abstinence was also necessary to re-establish the original equality between men and women that had existed in the Garden of Eden.[50] The Shakers, for obvious reasons, did not produce offspring, which

Shakers, separated by gender, performing a step dance in the meeting hall at New Lebanon, New York, *c.* 1830.

meant that the movement was dependent on constantly finding new converts: as converts became fewer in number, overall numbers fell, and there are only a handful of Shakers left today.

Even though, as we shall see later, abstinence was generally rejected by Judaism, there was some tendency towards the idea within Hellenic Judaism, although it disappeared again with Rabbinic Judaism. According to Josephus, the first-century Jewish historian, the Essenes were a group of male ascetics who lived without either marriage or sex.[51] The Essenes, the group usually identified as having written the Dead Sea Scrolls, were convinced that they were the last generation of the last generations and that all their attention and energy should be devoted to preparing for the final battle against evil, which in their view was imminent.

The Jewish philosopher Philo referred to what he called the *therapeutai*, a group of Jewish men and women who were also said to be sexually abstinent.[52] Once again, abstinence was seen as necessary in order to enable these people to concentrate utterly on God, but they did not share the Essenes' conviction that they were living at the end of time. The existence of these *therapeutai* is not proven, but the fact that Philo wrote of them demonstrates at the very least that he recognized abstinence as a religious ideal. In spite of these ascetic experiments in antiquity, however, Judaism did not subscribe to the idea that permanent sexual abstinence was something to be aimed at.

Hippolytus, as we have seen, was punished by the gods for attempting to remain a virgin. Even though the ancient religions normally demanded people to be sexually active, there were nevertheless exceptions. Some Greek priestesses were required to be abstinent either for life, like those of Artemis Hymnia in Arcadia or of Hercules in Thespiaie, or for as long as they were in the service of the god, such as the priestesses of Poseidon on Kalaureia.[53] Many different injunctions and prohibitions applied to priests and priestesses, but the fact that some of them involved sexual abstinence should be seen in the general context that religious specialists were governed by rules that did not apply to ordinary people. When sexual abstinence was demanded of people in particular religious positions, the sanctions for breaking the rules were notably severe. The Vestals, the Roman priestesses charged with tending the sacred flame of the goddess Vesta in Rome, had to remain virgins for the whole of their thirty-year period of service, although they were free to marry when they had completed it as middle-aged women. If, however, a Vestal had sex while still a priestess, a small underground chamber was prepared, furnished with a bed and a small quantity of food and drink, in which the Vestal was entombed. There she would die from hunger, thirst or suffocation.[54]

Islam, too, continued to accept the idea that Jesus was the result of a virgin birth[55] but did not view the concept of lifelong abstinence as an ideal. There were, however, certain parts of Islam in which celibacy was promoted, as for instance in sections of the mystic Sufi movement, which believed in turning away from all else but the search for God. But even here we can find the more traditional Islamic attitude that sexual abstinence is not something to be strived for.[56]

In Hinduism, too, complete abstinence gradually began to be seen as a positive thing. According to *Manusmriti*, the Laws of Manu, written some time between 200 BC and AD 200, a Brahmin man who has practised total sexual abstinence is assured of a place in heaven even though he will obviously not have ensured the continuance of his family.[57] The term *brahmacharya*, which actually refers to abstinence in general, is often used in Hinduism and also in Buddhism to refer specifically to the positive aspects of sexual abstinence.[58] Avoiding sex is considered a way in which men can successfully transcend ordinary human limitations, both physical and spiritual. The lifelong practice of celibacy is associated in particular with the numerous male ascetics present in many holy places. There are virtually no women among such lifelong ascetics since there is no parallel tradition of treating permanent abstinence among women as a virtue. A woman's most important function is to marry.[59]

The idea that religion is fundamentally against all sex is, like the majority of other rather simplistic suppositions about religion, both true and untrue. While early Christianity and Buddhism propose an ideal of total sexual abstinence as something that would automatically lead man closer to the ultimate condition, Hinduism, Judaism, Islam and many other religions imply the opposite. The general condemnation of all sex by Christianity and Buddhism has continued to characterize these faiths, although today it is disregarded to an ever-increasing extent. Yet this general opposition to sex is still the most important reason why particular and special religious groups within these two faiths are not permitted to have sex. Every sexually abstinent priest, monk or nun serves as a permanent reminder of the fundamental Christian and Buddhist belief that abstinence is superior to sex.

3
Solitary Sex

At the end of the nineteenth century, John Harvey Kellogg, the Seventh Day Adventist and inventor of cornflakes, was worried that sexual lust perpetuated the biblical Fall. He was particularly concerned about the 'solitary vice', masturbation, which was not only a dangerous introduction to other sexual lusts but also an act that could lead to a variety of diseases of the sexual organs as well as to epilepsy and madness. The conviction that such maladies could result from masturbation was widely held even in the medical world until well into the twentieth century.

Preventing people from touching themselves is difficult but Kellogg was not short of ideas. He focused in particular on preventing children and young people from doing so. Not only were his cornflakes nutritionally designed to suppress sexual desire in the young but a whole series of other practical measures he recommended also proved to be effective. Putting small cages over the sexual organs was a good method but, for boys, circumcision was particularly recommended: 'The operation should be performed by a surgeon without administering an anaesthetic, as the brief pain attending the operation will have a salutary effect upon the mind, especially if it is connected with the idea of punishment, as it may well be in some cases.' The main reason for the practice of circumcision in the USA throughout the nineteenth century was to discourage masturbation. In the case of girls who masturbate, Kellogg had found that rubbing pure carbolic acid on the clitoris was 'an excellent means of allaying the abnormal excitement'.[1]

Kellogg's pious advice reflects both the religious and the medical attitudes of his time, and it is sometimes difficult to separate the two. As far as the Seventh Day Adventists were concerned there was a clear connection between them. The idea that certain kinds of food suppress the sexual urge and consequently the incidence of masturbation was something that Kellogg took directly from his Adventist beliefs. And the belief that masturbation in itself is morally and religiously sinful was also a central tenet of the Adventism of the period.

The ban on having sex with oneself has a long tradition within both Judaism and Christianity, although this stricture has no direct basis in the Bible. Even the original biblical story associated with Onan does not actually have anything to do with onanism: God slew Onan because he had *coitus interruptus* with his wife, not because he was practising masturbation.[2] There is actually no prohibition of masturbation as such in the Bible, though the Torah does state that all ejaculation of sperm is unclean.[3] The story of Onan has nevertheless frequently been used as the basis for the proscription of onanism – a view reinforced by the fact that all sex other than marital heterosexual intercourse was originally totally prohibited within Christianity and partially forbidden within Judaism.

The condemnation of male masturbation within the Judaic tradition should not only be seen in the context of Onan 'spilling his seed on the ground' but also in the light of Rabbinic interpretation of the prophet Isaiah's criticism of child sacrifice.[4] Male masturbation is condemned not only because it does not lead to procreation but because, in theory, it *prevents* procreation. Spilling one's seed on the ground is – if the interpretation is pushed to its extreme – equivalent to taking the life of one's future offspring. The classical Hebrew expression for masturbation is *hashchatat zara*, which means 'the conscious destruction of seed'. The Rabbinic tradition even saw Isaiah's enigmatic references to 'your hands are full of blood' as a metaphor for how reprehensible male masturbation was. Following the same reasoning, however, there was no condemnation of female masturbation – it was considered to be irrelevant since it did not have any consequences for procreation.[5] An unmarried woman who masturbated in such a way that she penetrated her hymen could, however, be open to strong condemnation, not because she had masturbated but because what she had done might lead to suspicions that she had had premarital sex with a man. Present-day liberal Judaism takes a fairly relaxed view of masturbation and in the 1980s some rabbis publicly defended this form of sex.[6]

Within the Christian tradition masturbation was normally condemned quite simply because it is a sexual act outside the framework

A monk masturbates as he hears the confession of a woman, *c.* 1679–81.

of marriage. But it was only with the growth of the monastic system that onanism began to figure prominently in religious discourse. While the majority of people were permitted to be sexually active within the context of marriage, it was important to prevent monks and nuns from sabotaging their sexual abstinence by masturbating.[7] Some Christian writers were more negative towards masturbation than others: Thomas Aquinas, for instance, classified masturbation as 'unnatural' sex because, like anal sex, oral sex, bestiality and homosexuality, it precluded procreation. Even though he conceded that masturbation was better than these other kinds of 'unnatural' sex, it was nevertheless worse than other forms of 'natural' sex such as premarital sex, adultery, rape and incest.[8]

Many conservative Christians continue to condemn masturbation even though some, as we have seen, take a positive view of *mutual* masturbation between unmarried heterosexual couples. The Catholic Church has mounted a direct and official attack on the more modern understanding of masturbation as a 'normal phenomenon of sexual development especially among the young': 'Even if it cannot be proved that Scripture condemns this sin by name, the tradition of the Church has rightly understood it to be condemned in the New Testament when the latter speaks of "impurity", "unchasteness" and other vices contrary to chastity and continence.'[9]

Liberal Christians usually take a more relaxed view of solitary sex as something that is neither especially damaging nor particularly to be recommended. There are even some evangelical Christians who take a more positive view of masturbation and save their political energy for the struggle against homosexuality and premarital heterosexual sex. James Dobson, founder of the very conservative Christian lobbying organization Focus on the Family, thinks, for example: 'It is my opinion that masturbation is not much of an issue with God . . . Jesus did not mention it in the Bible. I'm not telling you to masturbate, and I hope you won't find the need for it. But, if you do, it is my opinion that you should not struggle with guilt over it.'[10] There are, however, relatively few Christians who actively support masturbation as a phenomenon. In 1994, when Joycelyn Elders was American Surgeon General, the top official in the US health system, she commented that it might be a good idea to promote masturbation in order to prevent young people from having risky sex; she was immediately sacked by President Bill Clinton following strongly negative Christian reactions.[11] Liberal Christians did not step forward to defend her suggestions.

In Islam, too, masturbation is often considered to fall under the general prohibition of sex outside the framework of marriage.[12] The Koran, for instance, emphasizes that people should guard against using their sexual organs in any other context than marital sex.[13] According to the hadiths, the narrations of the Prophet's deeds and statements collected during the first centuries after the death of Muhammad, the Prophet thought that diet had an effect on sexual urges. As he said to 'you young people': 'whoever is unable to marry should fast, as fasting diminishes his sexual power.'[14]

There is, however, some disagreement among modern Muslims with regard to masturbation. Generally speaking, Shia Islam condemns the practice, but there is disagreement between various schools of thought as to whether it is forbidden or merely unimportant. Some Sunni scholars, for instance, consider that masturbation is permissible if one is single, in danger of committing fornication or suffering from such powerful sexual pressure that there is no other way of releasing it. Others stress that masturbation may be tolerated if there is no possibility of fasting or of getting married.[15]

Buddhism's generally critical attitude to sex and desire means that masturbation is not regarded as commendable. Although solitary sex cannot lead to procreation, it is clearly associated with sexual desire, which in itself is a problematic area for Buddhists. But since Buddhism generally is less preoccupied with regulating the sexuality of people who have chosen not to be chaste, direct injunctions against masturbation are only to be found in monastic rules. The *Vinaya*, for instance, a text from the first century BC, specifies such rules, including references to acrobatically inclined monks capable of having oral or anal sex with themselves. Buddha considered this, as with all other solitary sex, to be an offence against the monastic code.[16]

Since Buddhism traditionally considered women to have stronger sexual urges than men, masturbation was particularly problematic for nuns. Nuns are thus explicitly forbidden from using a variety of vegetables such as cucumbers, onions or radishes on themselves, and when they wash their intimate parts they must ensure that it is not done in a way that provides them with satisfaction. Nor should they apply sanitary pads too tightly when they are menstruating, and they should not swim against the current.[17]

Among the world religions Hinduism has traditionally taken by far the most relaxed view of masturbation. There are examples of male and female masturbation depicted in a religious context in temple art, for instance in Khajuraho in Madhya Pradesh, Konark in Orissa and Bhaktapur, Kathmandu and Patan in Nepal. But the traditional and contemporary idea that men will become stronger if they do not spill their seed nevertheless implies an indirect call for moderation.[18] There are also restrictions on masturbation for people who are meant to be sexually abstinent, which means that masturbation is included in the category of acts that are considered to be sexual.[19] Some Hindu male ascetics go to great lengths to avoid becoming sexually aroused and having erections – they may, for instance, wear a tight iron ring around the penis.[20]

There are four main religious attitudes to masturbation: that it is quite acceptable or even recommendable irrespective of whether you are also having sex with other people; that it is permissible only for people who are sexually active anyway; that it is deplorable even if you are permitted to have other kinds of sex; or that it is forbidden in the same way as all other kinds of sex.

In situations where there is no religious injunction against masturbation, this kind of sex is often considered to be in a border

Hindu depiction of male and female masturbation performed while watching heterosexual intercourse. From the walls of the 10th-century Lakshmana Temple, Khajuraho, Madhya Pradesh, India.

area in that it is a solitary activity, whereas sex proper is something that can only take place with someone else. Rather less frequently, the permissibility of masturbation implies a more general positive sanctioning of most forms of sex.

When masturbation is only forbidden to people who should not be having sex anyway, we find that there is no fundamental distinction being made between solitary sex and other forms of sex. It is the sexual act itself, the conscious manipulation of the sexual organs resulting in arousal, which is the central point, not whether it is done alone or in the company of others.

When *all* sex is condemned, there is little point in looking closely at how this general prohibition works in relation to masturbation. But when masturbation is forbidden while other forms of sexual activity are tolerated, the focus on masturbation becomes very different. In such a situation masturbation either represents a religio-sexual category of its own, or it is taking centre position in a larger religio-sexual category defined as impermissible. Kellogg's Adventist efforts to limit masturbation provides one of the best examples of how solitary sex as a phenomenon can play a very central role in a religio-sexual worldview. More frequently we find masturbation being condemned because it does not fulfil various fundamental demands for what constitutes permissible sex: masturbation will, quite logically, be condemned if sex is something that should only occur within marriage or in circumstances that can lead to procreation.

Masturbation also presents a particular challenge to sexual control mechanisms in that it only involves one person. Unlike other forms of sexuality, it cannot be regulated by laying down rules as to who can marry whom or by preventing individuals meeting without chaperones. Since it is so difficult to prove and to control, masturbation has never been the target of great religious persecution. In so far as there have been direct efforts to control masturbation, these have usually concentrated on enclosed communities such as monastic institutions, or have targeted children, who are the subjects of a much higher level of control than other people.

What puts masturbation into a class of its own is that it lacks the social aspect that is fundamental to all other kinds of sexuality. The religious regulation of masturbation therefore has rather different consequences to other sorts of sex. Whereas the regulation of sexual activity usually involves a high degree of regulation of social interaction and identity, the religious regulation of masturbation – unless you are caught in the act – impacts only on your private life and self-image to the extent that you are influenced by the religious attitudes of the society around you. If and when a religion succeeds in controlling an individual's solitary sexual urges, it implies an extremely high level of influence over the whole of his or her being. Seen in this light, the control of solitary sexuality can be an important step in a religion's efforts to achieve salvation for a particular individual.

It is, of course, a fact that masturbation is very widespread. Statistics indicate that women masturbate much less than men, even though part of this difference may be explained by the fact that women usually tone down reports of their sexual activity when responding to surveys.[21] A 2009 survey from Iran shows that

26 per cent of women and 73 per cent of men say that they have masturbated.[22] A 1994 American survey shows that about 42 per cent of women and 53 per cent of men had masturbated in the course of the past year and that 7.6 per cent and 26.7 per cent respectively masturbated weekly.[23] Figures from 2002 show the same proportion among American women.[24] We do not find any significant changes if we go farther back: Alfred Kinsey, in his studies of male and female sexuality around 1950, found that 92 per cent of American males and 62 per cent of females had masturbated to orgasm.[25] Religious affiliation does, however, influence the practice of solitary sex. The 1994 American statistics revealed that non-believers masturbate considerably more than Christians, or at least admit to it more readily. Whereas 37.6 per cent of non-believing men and 13.3 per cent of non-believing women said that they masturbated weekly, the figures for Christians were just over 20 per cent for men and about 6 per cent for women. Among Christians, moderate Protestants masturbated slightly more than Catholics, while fundamentalist Protestants masturbated by far the least.[26] Even though many Christians who have been taught that they should not have sex with themselves do so anyway, the figures seem to show that the generally negative attitude to masturbating among Christians means that they do so to a lesser extent.

Thus, even though it has proved to be a pretty vain effort in practice, attempts to discourage people from masturbating have been a significant element in the religio-sexual control project. The prohibition on sex with oneself also serves to emphasize the belief held by many religions that clear limits on sexual behaviour may bring people closer to the divine.

4
The Blessings and Curses of Heterosexuality

Heterosexuality has never been uncomplicated. Its complexity from a religious point of view shows up particularly clearly, when it appears in situations in which many do not believe it should be present at all. Some of the Christian reactions to the presentation of a heterosexually active Jesus provide a good example. When Martin Scorsese's film *The Last Temptation of Christ*, with its rather modest Hollywood portrayal of Jesus as a sexually active married man, was shown in the autumn of 1988, conservative French Catholics did not restrict themselves to verbal protests. In cities such as Paris, Lyon, Nice and Grenoble, Christian activists attacked cinemas with tear gas and stink bombs and cinemagoers were knocked down. The cinema Le Saint-Michel in the Latin Quarter in Paris was fire-bombed on 22 October and fourteen people were injured, four of them seriously.[1]

There is scarcely a cinema anywhere at any time that is not screening one or more films depicting discreet heterosexual sex and these productions are for the most part left in peace. But the specific context may turn people who normally think of themselves as religious defenders of marital heterosexuality into angry protesters against the very same phenomenon. There are some Christians who feel that the fact that some people choose to go and see a production in which Jesus is portrayed as a sexually active married man is sufficient justification for violence and arson.[2] In other words, the heterosexual religious landscape may easily become a complicated minefield.

The major debate of our times about religion and homosexuality might easily lead us to assume that the relationship between religion and heterosexuality is mainly problem-free. This is far from being the case. It is not just the general hostility to sex found in some religious traditions that complicates heterosexuality. There are certain religions that constantly try to impose their understanding of *correct* heterosexuality on society as a whole. People who desire to practise their heterosexuality in ways that this or that religion do not believe to be proper can easily find themselves with problems. It is not only believers who are faced with a host of demands and prohibitions governing their heterosexual inclinations: there are some religious groups that constantly attempt to make the authorities compel the population at large, irrespective of its religious convictions, to follow whatever that sect believes to constitute the correct kind of heterosexuality. The problem is not made any less complex by the fact that there is a great variation in the extent to which religious groups themselves expect people to adhere to all the regulations.

There are many similarities visible between the different religions but there are no absolute lines. Some religious dictates will always come into collision with others and it would be impossible to live in accordance with the rules of what every religion believes to be correct heterosexual behaviour. Heterosexuals, those of a more ecumenical tendency at least, have good reason to lose heart.

Limited Virginity

A magnificent ball was organized at the Broadmoor Hotel in Colorado Springs in May 2008, at which middle-aged men danced with very young girls. This spring ball, equivalents of which are held in many other places across the United States, is as sexually innocent as it is possible to be. All of the girls are virgins, and the men are their fathers, stepfathers or, hopefully, their future fathers-in-law. After a formal dinner, at which the men mostly talk among themselves while the girls concentrate on the food, the men read out a text over dessert in which they promise 'before God to cover my daughter as her authority and protection in the area of purity'. Later in the evening couple after couple go forward and lay flowers at the foot of a gigantic cross prettily decorated with yards of tulle. Many of the girls make silent promises – one of them, sixteen-year-old Katie Swindler, pledges: 'I promise to God and myself and my family that I will stay pure in my thoughts and actions until I marry.' The ball we are witnessing here is called a *purity ball*, organized by evangelical Christians to encourage girls to remain virgins until they marry.[3]

Purity balls are actually just one element in an all-encompassing programme, ranging through rock music, sex education, pledges and political propaganda, aimed at convincing people to abstain from premarital sex. It is reckoned that about 12 per cent of American young people in 1995 had made virgin pledges similar to those made at purity balls.[4] A 2005 survey reveals that they are for the most part empty promises: 88 per cent of all those who make public or written virgin pledges will have sex before marriage.[5] These balls, formal purity pledges and rock music promoting virginity may be recent trends but they reflect a religious ideal that can be traced back into the mists of time. The majority of religiously inspired demands for sexual abstinence are time-limited, not demands for lifetime abstinence of the kind we saw in the previous chapter. The aim is quite simply to abstain from sex before marriage.

The starting point for Christians has always been that there should be no sex outside marriage. Full stop. Preferably, there should be so sex at all but, as St Paul pointed out, marriage is a necessity for those who cannot manage to be sexually abstinent. Sex *before* marriage is not a possible choice for a Christian, he stated, and 'fornicators' will certainly not 'inherit the kingdom of God'.[6]

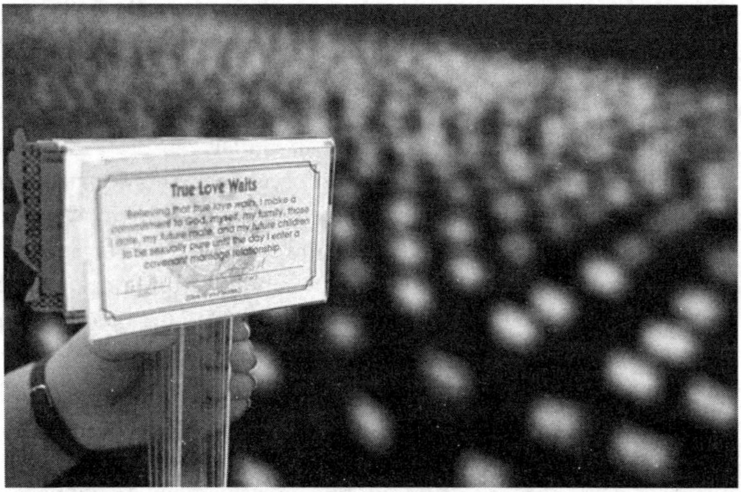

A Christian banner delaring 'Believing that true loves waits, I can make the commitment to God, myself, my family, those that I date, my future mate and my future children to be sexually pure until the day I enter a covenant marriage relationship', July 1994.

Paul's unequivocal demand for complete abstinence before marriage was, however, a novel idea to most people in the ancient world. A more common pattern was for there to be different demands for men and women: whereas any woman who hoped to get married had to remain a virgin until she married, an unmarried man could, on the whole, do what he liked. Such views are by no means restricted to the ancient world; they are still current in many religions even today. This gender-biased view of premarital sex is often combined with women marrying at a very early age, not unusually at around the time of puberty, which in itself minimizes the chances of them having premarital sex. The custom of marrying off women very young because their virginity is more important than that of men puts an extremely effective control on female sexuality. Even though Christianity in principle upheld a complete ban on premarital sex for both sexes, it soon became apparent that in practice Christians lived according to the more traditional view that female virginity was more important than male. This pattern has persisted. The purity balls of the present day reflect the same sexual bias, since there are no equivalent arrangements for boys.

It is normal in most religions for women to be punished more than men in connection with improper heterosexuality. Physical differences between men and women have clearly contributed to the different ways men and women are treated in many religions. The female hymen as supposed evidence of virginity often means that there is a quite different focus on female virginity than on male. And should premarital sex lead to pregnancy, the woman bears living proof of what she has done. Even in those situations where, according to religious dictates, men and women are on an equal footing, the loss of the hymen or the possibility of pregnancy mean that unmarried women are kept under much stricter control than their unmarried brothers. In Islam, for instance, the strict demand for the provision of proof means that it is easier to punish women than men for unlawful sex.

The fact that it is not always easy to demonstrate who is the father of a child has contributed to the way many religions are concerned to prevent women from having more than one male partner – at the same time, at least. The fact, too, that most religions usually give men higher status than women has no doubt contributed further to the way most religions have in practice guaranteed men control over women's sexuality and over who fathers their children.

The cliché that sex always involves an active and a passive partner is to be found in many cultures and seems to have defined how most people think a good male or female Muslim, Christian or Hindu should behave sexually. While the 'active' male makes conquests that only serve to increase his social standing, women have a 'passive' sexuality that has to be protected against such male conquests. The same young man will gladly have sex with the unmarried sister of a neighbour at the same time as doing everything he can to prevent other men having sex with his own unmarried sister. In a sexual landscape of this kind it is often difficult to distinguish between what people think of as religious rules and what is actually governed by less religious considerations such as honour and shame. The boundaries are often fluid. But generally speaking, a man with many female sexual partners does not present a moral problem to many faiths, whereas a woman who has sex with men other than her husband presents a major challenge to many – and often the very same – religions.

In the Hebrew Bible, the Christian Old Testament, there is no general ban on sex before marriage. Gender and marital status are the deciding factors in whether premarital sex is permissible or not. A man is only forbidden to have sex with women who are married or engaged to other men: sex with unmarried women is permitted.[7] Whether the man himself is married or not is irrelevant. Even the prohibition against rape is limited to women married or engaged to other men, since in the case of rape, the perpetrator has 'violated another man's woman'.[8] If, however, a man is caught in the act with a virgin who is not engaged to someone else, he must give the woman's father fifty silver shekels and marry her.[9] Taking a woman's virginity is synonymous with damaging her marital chances significantly and thus also diminishing her market value. And since an unmarried woman is the property of her father, he is the one who receives the compensation.

An engaged woman, like a married woman, may be sentenced to death if she has sex with anyone but her future husband. Even an engaged virgin who is raped within the city walls should, in principle, be stoned together with her violator.[10] Like men, in principle at least, women who are neither married nor engaged will not be punished for having sex. If, however, a woman wanted to find a husband, she would be taking an enormous risk if she had sex before marriage: her husband might claim that he had found 'no sign that she was a virgin' when he married her and it would be up to her parents to produce 'a sign that she was a virgin and bring it to the elders at the town gate'. She would be in a rather difficult position if they were unable to provide such evidence: 'If the accusation is true and if there is no sign that the woman was a virgin, they shall take her out before the doors of her father's house and the men of the town shall stone her to death. For she has performed a shameful deed in Israel in that she has committed fornication in her father's house. Thus shall you rid yourself of evil.'[11] In practice this meant that women who were sexually active before marriage could never get married unless they could find a husband who thought it better to have a living, non-virgin wife than a dead one. This kind of severity did not apply to prostitutes and other unmarried women who had already lost their virginity and were not planning marriage: such women had a greater degree of sexual freedom.

The Judaic rules for heterosexual activity before marriage have changed since Old Testament days. Pointing to the practice of concubinage in the Hebrew Bible, a number of rabbis in the Middle Ages were of the opinion that a stable and faithful sexual relationship with a woman outside marriage was permitted by Judaic law – the important thing was to avoid promiscuity. The self-evident premise for such a relationship was that the woman would be unmarried whereas the marital status of the man was, as before, irrelevant. This kind of extramarital relationship did not, however, achieve any general recognition among medieval Jewry[12] and in practice a prohibition on premarital sex for women was generally upheld. Furthermore, as originally in Christianity, there was an increasing tendency to view male premarital sex as being in conflict with Judaic law.[13]

There are enormous variations between modern-day Jewish communities depending on whether they are in ultra-Orthodox neighbourhoods in Jerusalem or in the secularized suburbs of Copenhagen or Chicago. Surveys reveal that 60 per cent of Jews in the United States think it is fine for unmarried heterosexual couples to have sex if 'they really like one another'.[14] Attitudes to premarital sex have become significantly more liberal in recent decades, even among Orthodox Jews. The ultra-Orthodox, on the other hand, have retained the traditional restrictions to a much greater extent and young unmarried women in Jerusalem risk being physically assaulted by ultra-Orthodox men if they are simply seen together with men in the street.

Christian attitudes to premarital heterosexual behaviour have also shown enormous variation. While church authorities have often taken a strict line in principle, the level of obedience has not usually matched it. Once again, the male/female distinction is central and in most Christian countries it was tacitly accepted that unmarried men would have their sexual initiation with prostitutes rather than when they got married. Prostitution was openly regulated and taxed even in the Papal States.[15] During the Reformation, however, prostitutes were expelled from many Protestant and Catholic towns in Central Europe.[16] That was certainly not the end of prostitution, however, which has continued to exist, constantly oscillating between tacit acceptance and open persecution. Typically, given that female heterosexuality was considered much more problematic than that of men, it was usually the prostitutes themselves who were persecuted and discriminated against. There were periods when prostitutes were imprisoned, suffered corporal punishment, were deported and sometimes even – after repeat offences – executed.[17] Their male customers were rarely subjected to any serious sanctions. During the nineteenth and twentieth centuries Christian activists led extensive campaigns against prostitution, which they viewed as legalized sin, but whatever the level of persecution, prostitutes rarely ran short of Christian customers.[18]

The institution of slavery in the Americas created a very particular Christian attitude to premarital sex. In many areas slaves lacked the legal right to marry and any ceremonies they themselves used to bond with one another had no legal status; this solved any ethical dilemmas slave-owners may occasionally have had when they split up heterosexually bonded couples and sold them separately. By dint of only acknowledging marriage when it was between free people, Christian authorities made it impossible for significant sections of the population to practise heterosexuality within the framework of marriage. Slaves, the majority of whom were Christian, were left with no alternative but to have sex outside marriage. The legislation in many of the states of the US took the logical consequences of this into account and ruled that slaves could not be punished for fornication or adultery. It was not only the authorities who found this situation unproblematic: churches in the southern states did little or nothing to give slaves the right to marry.[19]

At times when sanctions grow milder, there is an accompanying tendency for people to treat official religious sexual morality with greater freedom while retaining their Christian faith. There are good examples of this in Western Europe in the period around the Napoleonic Wars, a time when legislation controlling sexuality became less strict in a number of countries.[20] Legal protection of illegitimate children and their mothers was also enhanced, something which indirectly implied a greater degree of tolerance of premarital sex.[21] The abolition of the strict laws governing sexual conduct and reflecting Christian sexual morality led to changes in sexual habits, particularly among the lower social classes. When a young Catholic woman in Bavaria in the early nineteenth century was asked why she kept on having children even though she was unmarried, she answered: 'It's OK to make [illegitimate] babies . . . the king has OK'd it!'[22] If God was no longer ensuring that the authorities punished extramarital sex, what was the problem? Clergymen complained that there were hardly any virgins left. One can see a similar change in Ireland at the end of the twentieth century. A liberalization of the laws leads to a revolution in attitudes. There are, nevertheless, very wide attitudinal differences depending on the degree of religious activism. In 1974 71 per cent of the Irish population thought that premarital sex was *always* wrong but by 1994 that figure had shrunk to 32 per cent. But even though the majority of the Irish are Christian there are nevertheless clear differences of attitude discernible within these figures: of those who condemned premarital sex, 43 per cent went to church weekly, whereas of those who went to church once a month or less, only 5 per cent condemned it.[23]

Many Christians still hold the view that premarital sex does not accord with Christian teaching, although there are only a small number who seek to convince the state to forbid it. Even so, many attempt to use legislation to discourage it in other ways, for example by attacking sex education in schools. Christians in the USA have focused on abstinence-only educational programmes, which promote total premarital abstinence rather than offering general sex education. In 2006 alone the conservative Christian authorities in Washington granted $200 million to these programmes and state governments provided almost as much.[24] Yet statistics suggest that though such methods may possibly change *attitudes* among some young people, they fail to change *behaviour* to anything like the same extent. The practical results are certainly not that young people have less sex, and sometimes they have more: they are, on the other hand, less inclined to use contraceptives and thus more likely to experience sexually transmitted diseases and unwanted pregnancies.[25]

Young Christians who take the religious prohibition against premarital sex to heart do seriously try to abide by it but, as we have already noted, there is a tendency to come up with creative solutions, such as categorizing mutual masturbation, oral sex and anal sex as not really sex. It is thus hardly surprising that statistics suggest that young Christians who have made abstinence pledges actually have more heterosexual oral and anal sex than other young people.[26] These other forms of sexual activity are not seen as completely problem-free by many of those who practise them, because they blur the boundaries and may consequently lead to vaginal intercourse.[27] But the interpretative boundaries can be blurred even further with regard to what constitutes premarital sex: whereas many set the boundary at vaginal penetration, some young Norwegian Christians believe that 'entry without ejaculation is permissible'[28] and others again think that only 'having intercourse with many partners is the real breach of the norms'.[29]

Heterosexual experience before marriage is no longer regarded as a sin by the majority of Christians; it is just something most people have. In 2005 the proportion of adults who felt it was important to encourage young people to abstain from premarital sex was just 1 per cent in the mainly Orthodox Bulgaria, Greece and Serbia-Montenegro; 4 per cent in Ireland, 2 per cent in Italy and 6 per cent in Poland – predominantly Catholic countries; and 2 per cent in the mainly Lutheran Iceland and Sweden. In the USA, which has a more mixed and more conservative Christian population, 14 per cent of respondents believed that premarital abstinence was an important message to send to young people.[30] A good indication of changing attitudes is provided by the statistics for children born out of wedlock. Statistics from largely Christian countries show that the proportions of 'illegitimate' children have increased, especially since 1980. In the present member states of the EU (excluding Romania and Bulgaria) the proportion was about 5 per cent in 1970[31] but there was a sixfold increase to 31.4 per cent by 2004. The lowest figures in Europe are to be found in certain Orthodox countries like Greece and the Republic of Cyprus (4.9

and 3.3 per cent respectively), whereas other Orthodox countries such as Bulgaria, Georgia and Romania have 48.7, 44.6 and 29.4 per cent respectively.[32] In the US the proportion rose from 3.8 per cent in 1940 to 11 per cent in 1970 and 33 per cent in 1999,[33] while in Chile the proportion grew from 30 per cent to 62 per cent between 1990 and 2007.[34] Attitudes reflect these changes. In 1997 in Colombia, Guatemala and Mexico, 87 per cent, 67 per cent and 57 per cent respectively did not consider it immoral to have children outside marriage, while the figures for Germany and Iceland were respectively 90 per cent and 95 per cent.[35] The number of marriages has also declined. In the 25 member states of the European Union there were 8 marriages per 1,000 inhabitants in 1964 but the figure had gone down to 4.8 by 2004. Even though there has been an enormous increase in the number of Christians having children out of wedlock, it is necessary to recognize that actions and attitudes are not always in agreement. In the United States 97 per cent of those who have had sex at all have also had premarital sex; even among women born in the 1940s and 1950s the proportion is 88 per cent.[36] Nevertheless, in 1997, 47 per cent of the population still considered having children before marriage to be wrong.[37]

Islam, like Christianity but in contrast to Judaism, takes a general prohibition of sex before marriage as its starting point.[38] There is, however, no absolute agreement between the Koran and tradition on what the appropriate sanctions against premarital sex should be. The Koran states: 'And as for those who are guilty of an indecency from among your women . . . confine them to their houses until death takes them away or Allah opens some way for them.'[39] It is not only women, however, who should be punished, since the Koran also states: 'the two who are guilty of indecency from among you, give them both a punishment', but it is not made clear how the men are to be punished.[40] One of the injunctions in the Koran that is rarely followed is that those who have sex before marriage may only marry other 'fornicators' or 'idolaters'.[41]

The hadiths provide instructions about how free unmarried people are to be punished for having sex – they should be whipped, usually a hundred lashes. Additionally, they should be expelled, usually for a year.[42] Unmarried slaves who continue to have sex even after being punished three or four times (the man reporting Muhammad's words in this case could not remember the precise number recommended by the Prophet) should be sold, 'if only for a rope'.[43]

In practice, however, Islam has shown much greater tolerance of male premarital and extramarital sex.[44] This can be seen, for instance, in Islamic attitudes to prostitution. The only thing the Koran says about prostitution is that slave girls should not be forced into prostitution if they desire to remain chaste.[45] Even though Muhammad said, 'There is no prostitution in Islam',[46] buying sex has often been tolerated in Islamic countries[47] and frequently regulated and taxed by the Muslim authorities themselves. The existence of prostitution opens the way for an institutionalization of male sexuality outside the confines of marriage and, simultaneously, prostitutes stand in clear contrast to other women, who are utterly forbidden to have sex before marriage. Because of the strict restrictions imposed on the sexuality of unmarried women who are not prostitutes, prostitution frequently provides the first heterosexual experience for many Muslim men in conservative countries, just as it did in the past in many mainly Christian countries.[48] There have, however, been periods of considerable opposition to prostitution and, as in Christian countries, this has usually been directed at those who sell sex rather than at their customers.[49] After the Islamic revolution in Iran, for instance, many prostitutes were executed after summary trials.[50]

Many Muslim countries such as Afghanistan, the United Arab Emirates, Iran, Saudi Arabia and Sudan retain the traditional legal prohibition of premarital sex. The fact that other Muslim countries permit premarital sex should not be taken to mean that the authorities in those countries consider the issue to be unproblematic from a Muslim point of view. The lack of a ban merely means that the state considers the issue to belong to the sphere of private life. There are, however, some people who argue that Islam does not forbid premarital sex: the American Muslim feminist Asra Q. Nomani goes so far as to say that Muslim women (and consequently men, too) have the right to decide for themselves whether to have sex before marriage.[51] There are few Muslims who would state this quite so categorically. In Norway the Muslim Labour Party politician Saera Khan believes that 'Islam forbids this' but goes on to emphasize that 'all women have the right to control their own bodies'.[52] She is thus maintaining a balance between religious freedom and other human rights. At the same time as professing that she herself believes that Islam forbids sex before marriage, thereby avoiding contradicting her more conservative fellow believers, Khan is saying that it is up to people to decide for themselves. As she knows, any legal prohibition would conflict with the human right to respect for the private life of the individual. On the other hand, there are conservative Muslims who want to use legislation to limit premarital sex in a more indirect way, for instance, by allowing only minimum access to contraception[53] or sex education in schools.[54] A practical little Chinese device a woman can put in her vagina that will release a suitable quantity of blood-like liquid so that the man will believe her to be a virgin caused a furore in Egypt in 2009. Conservative Muslims immediately demanded that the sale of such fraudulent virginity devices should cease. The sales blurb that accompanied the devices – 'No more worry about losing your virginity' – was not the message the Muslim Brotherhood wanted to send to its sisters and daughters.[55]

When Muslims are asked whether and in what circumstances premarital sex is permissible, the answers may well be different if the question is posed in a form less directly related to religion. A 2002 survey of female university students in Tunisia showed that 45 per cent thought it was acceptable for women to have premarital sex as long as they were 'prepared for the risks, both societal and medical'.[56] In Turkey in 2005 only 9 per cent said it was important to tell young people to abstain from premarital sex, whereas 79 per cent thought it was more important to encourage them to have safe sex.[57] It is interesting that Muslims in some parts of Western Europe seem to be more conservative: figures from 2008 suggest that 38 per cent, 30 per cent and 11 per cent of the Muslims in Berlin, Paris and London respectively believed it was 'morally acceptable' to have sex before marriage.[58] And Muslims, like other believers, are also involved in changing their religion by behaving in ways that differ from those their religion has traditionally demanded. Even though it is rarely discussed in public, health workers in Tunisia are certain that the average age at which women have their first sexual experience is falling, whereas the average age of marriage has risen to 26.[59] It is estimated that 70 per cent of women in Morocco have sex before marriage.[60] But there is still a significant difference between the sexes among modern Muslims and women's sexuality is still the prime focus of attempts to impose controls. A 2005 internet survey in Norway revealed that 37 per cent of all unmarried Muslims had had sex, but the figure was only 17 per cent for Muslim girls. When asked to rank their parents' possible reactions to a list of issues, 48 per cent of the young people surveyed also said that their parents would react most strongly to finding out that they had been having sex.[61]

In some traditional Muslim areas, as in many other conservative religious societies, girls marry at a very young age, a practice partly designed to ensure they are virgins when they marry. In rural Yemen in 2008, for instance, the average age of marriage for girls was under thirteen, and 57 per cent of all girls in Afghanistan marry before the legal age of sixteen, according to figures from 2007.[62] Women are the ones who face strict sanctions whereas young unmarried men are permitted, by and large, to do what they like, not least with non-Muslim Western women. One and the same family can encourage its sons to be sexually active – even with prostitutes – while vehemently demanding that its daughters preserve their virginity.[63] An unmarried woman's virginity is often an absolute requirement whereas virginity in an unmarried man is frequently seen as a sign of a lack of manliness.[64] The demands placed on male and female sexuality in some Muslim environments are so utterly different that is practically impossible to compare them. The simple fact that a young girl goes out 'alone or with girl friends in the evening' can be enough for 'a girl to have her reputation ruined', something 'that will be remembered for seven generations', according to a group of Norwegian-Pakistani women in their fifties and sixties. In that case, 'Death is better than dishonour.' The heterosexual doings of young men, on the other hand, are not called into question and Norwegian-Pakistani boys can to a great extent do whatever they like. Even sons who have served prison sentences are preferable to daughters with a 'ruined reputation', since a boy can always start 'attending the mosque' and 'people will be pleased that he has pulled himself together'.[65]

It is women, not men, who are murdered by their own families in so called 'honour killings' for unacceptable heterosexual behaviour. About forty Palestinian women are killed by their own families every year as a result of this, and this type of killing accounted for about two-thirds of all the murders in Palestine in 1999. It is estimated that there were about 400 murders of this kind in Yemen in 1997, the majority of the victims being women.[66] It is important to recognize that rumour alone can be sufficient to spark an 'honour killing', and the family is not necessarily interested in proving that premarital sex actually occurred. In Jordan, for instance, a majority of the women killed by their own families proved to be virgins.[67] Even women who have been raped are at risk of being killed by their families in order to restore the family honour. When men are murdered in hetero-related 'honour killings', it is usually the woman's family that instigates the murder. The person who carries out an 'honour killing' is usually regarded as a hero. Just as the 'loose' woman 'destroyed' the honour of the family, the murderer 'restores' it.[68] It would, however, be completely mistaken to associate 'honour killings' with just Islam as such – many Christian women in the Middle East and elsewhere are murdered by their families for the same reason. In Brazil, right up until 1991, the 'upholding of honour' was grounds for the acquittal of a man who had killed his wife – as thousands of men did. Between 1980 and 1981 in the federal state of São Paulo alone, 722 men accused of murdering their wives claimed to have done so to defend their honour after their wives had been accused of adultery.[69] What all such so-called 'honour killings' have in common is that they represent a religious defence of the fundamental right to regulate female sexuality. In Jordan, in 2003, conservatives and Islamists joined forces to form an overwhelming majority in parliament to defeat the introduction of a law that would have made the punishment for 'honour killing' more than symbolic: they argued that the new law 'would encourage vice and destroy social values'.[70]

Hinduism, too, joins many other religions in prohibiting premarital heterosexual relationships and again, in practice, it is mainly unmarried women who are faced with sanctions if they have sex before marriage. The Hindu epics frequently present premarital chastity as a virtue, particularly for young women.[71] But according to traditional Hindu teachings about the stages of life, the first adult stage for men should also involve sexual abstinence.[72] Hindu nationalist movements have consequently not only stressed the importance of the chastity of unmarried Hindu women but have also demanded pledges of chastity from specially organized groups of young male members. This modern emphasis on male abstinence is also motivated by the idea that men can enhance their spiritual and physical strength by saving their sperm.[73]

The worldwide changes that have led to increased sexual freedom have also had an impact on Hinduism. Premarital sex is frequently one of the zones of conflict, since young people to a larger degree see an opportunity to live their lives free from traditional restrictions. This is particularly apparent in immigrant communities, since on occasion there is little correspondence between what is acceptable to the immigrant minority and what is acceptable to society at large. A survey carried out among Indian immigrants in southern Florida reveals that there are great differences between the attitudes of first- and second-generation immigrants to issues like dating and premarital sex.[74] Thirty per cent of second-generation respondents stated unequivocally that they would like to have premarital sex.[75] This was inconceivable to their parents, who were, however, afraid of being too strict because they would risk losing any chance of regulating their children's behaviour if they alienated them.[76] Some of the attitudinal changes that occur, however, do not happen without reference to tradition: when the Supreme Court of India removed all legal restrictions on cohabitation between unmarried adults in 2010, it pointed to the Hindu belief that Krishna had cohabited with Radha.[77]

The fairly common practice of abstaining from sex at a later stage of life is rather peculiar to Hinduism. Widows are not expected to remarry and consequently not be sexually active. Nevertheless, it has been more common for women of low caste to remarry,[78] and what is called the *darewa* or *karewa* system opens the way for exceptions in that a woman is permitted to marry a brother of her dead husband.[79] But this has never been an ideal. According to conservative Hinduism, the most pious widows of all commit *sati*, that is, they lie on their husband's funeral pyre – or, as is often the case, are forced to burn together with their dead husband. This is a very rare occurrence these days, not least because it is strictly forbidden in India. When the eighteen-year-old widow Roop Kanwar, willingly or unwillingly, was burned together with her dead husband in the village of Deorala in Rajasthan in 1987, it did not only cause loud protests from the authorities and liberal Hindus, but also excited great enthusiasm among the traditionalists. Between 200,000 and 300,000 pious Hindus came to the village for the religious celebrations that followed the *sati*.[80]

A Hindu man should ideally begin and end his life in a state of sexual abstinence. According to the Hindu doctrine of the stages of life or *ashrama*, the period as a husband and provider is followed by a period of gradual withdrawal from the world, during which there are different opinions about whether a man should abstain from sex. Finally comes a stage of complete renunciation of the world, during which a man should leave his home and family – and celibacy is clearly one part of this.[81] The abstinence is voluntary and its purpose is to give him a better existence after death. Sexual abstinence at the end of one's life was seen in many Hindu traditions as necessary to final redemption, but a man is not punished if he chooses not to follow this path or if he dies before reaching this stage of life.[82] Seen in this light, a man has more to gain by abstinence than a widow, whose only alternative to abstinence is automatic damnation and a terrible *karma*.[83] Even though they are less visible than men, there are nevertheless abstinent women ascetics who have left a normal life and live more closely to the ideals of the male stages of life.[84]

Buddhism takes a generally negative view of heterosexual behaviour, but even there heterosexual activity is preferable within marriage rather than outside it. Buddha accepted marriage for lay people who were not striving for liberation in their present lives.[85] In practice, sanctions against women for sex before marriage are once again more severe than for men, although in some Buddhist areas abstinence for unmarried young men also has an important part to play: in South-East Asian Buddhism, for example, young men are expected to spend a period – usually a year – as monks before getting married. Most men only stay as monks for a few weeks but this still serves to underline the central importance of sexual abstinence. The proportion of young Thai men who enter monasteries is still significant, even if the number is declining.[86]

The call for limited sexual abstinence often means something quite different from the call for absolute abstinence, the latter usually implying an overall condemnation of sex and a perception that virginity brings one closer to the divine. Abstinence that is only limited by the need to be married first can imply one of two things: either that sex can, at most, be tolerated within the framework of marriage – as was the case originally in Christianity and Buddhism; or that marital sex is actually regarded as having a positive value – as in Hinduism, Islam and Judaism. In these cases, from the religious point of view, it is marriage itself that is the factor that defines whether one and the same sexual act is utterly abhorrent or merely acceptable or a blessing.

The call for limited virginity also means that sex is kept within the limits of the clear-cut and more easily controllable framework of heterosexual marriage, irrespective of whether the marriage itself is or is not a religious institution. If it is perfectly acceptable to have sex before marriage it becomes much more difficult to control both the number and the status of the partners than when the only legal sex is that which occurs within marriage. Better control is achieved even if it is only women who are actually punished for premarital sex. But the fact that marriage opens the way to a greater degree of religio-sexual control leads us on to consider precisely how the individual religions try to control heterosexuality within that framework.

The Complications of Marriage

Marriage was 'instituted of God in the time of man's innocency', as the 1662 English *Book of Common Prayer* puts it.[87] As such, marriage is a sacred institution that has remained essentially the same since the beginning of time, the argument often goes. If things had been that simple there would be little to write about, but we know that is not the case. Many people, both Christians and those of various other faiths, have, as we have seen, considered marriage evil, or as no more than a last resort for those utterly incapable of fully abstaining from sex.

The perception that marriage as an institution has remained unchanged for thousands of years is a core element in the belief structure of many people – even though there is no historical basis for it. If a Hindu, Jew or Christian says that marriage is sacred to her or to him because it has never changed, that represents a theological truth, a witness of faith of the same sort as a religious person makes when confessing to belief in a god. There is a difference, however, in that no one has yet clearly disproved the existence of some sort of deity, whereas the claim that marriage has remained unchanged is a historical statement which is quite simply untrue. When, for example, the Vatican states that 'society owes its continued survival to the family, founded on marriage',[88] that too is a witness of faith, but it is certainly not an objective truth because we know that many societies have managed perfectly well without the Catholic concept of marriage, and many still do.

Ideas about the unchanging nature of marriage have constantly been used as arguments for what God considers to be acceptable or unacceptable sex. In such a context it might be useful to bear in mind that it was only about 200 BC that anyone started using the myth of Adam and Eve to defend various fundamental attitudes and values.[89] Irrespective of what actually happened in the Garden of Eden, it is quite clear that heterosexual marriage has not remained the same within any of the religions that refer back to the biblical narrative of creation.

It seems obvious to us that we should be free to choose our own marital partner – it is even one of the human rights.[90] But the idea that young men and women should be permitted to choose their own spouses is a fairly recent phenomenon that could even be described as a social revolution. Marriage was originally a business deal arranged by the family and almost all religions share that position; what the potential partners themselves thought was more or less irrelevant. Men did sometimes have a say in the decision, however, because age differences were often so great that men tended to be fully adult before they were in a position to get married and in some cases that gave them sufficient authority to make their own choice. Situations where women were allowed to choose for themselves can only be classified as social-anthropological rarities.

It is a widespread traditional religious rule that the woman shall be subordinate to the man in a marriage. In biblical Judaism it is clear that the woman is usually considered to be the property of the man: you (that is, the man) shall not, for instance, 'covet thy neighbour's wife, nor his manservant, nor his maidservant, nor his ox, nor his ass, nor anything that is thy neighbour's'.[91] According to Paul in the New Testament, 'the head of the woman is the man' just as 'the head of every man is Christ'.[92] Augustine declared that marriage is 'a friendly and true union of the one ruling, and the other obeying'.[93] The Koran describes how the man is the woman's protector or maintainer, her *qawwam*.[94] Many religions, including biblical Judaism and traditional Christianity, understood woman's subjection to man to be so complete that a man had the right to rape his wife. Religion did not condemn it and it was an accepted part of the religiously inspired laws on sex. By 2003 only just over fifty countries had made marital rape a criminal offence.[95] In the USA, for instance, rape within marriage was still legal in all states until 1975, when North Dakota became the first state to make it illegal.[96] It is still not against the law in most Muslim countries.

Arranged marriages are still a common practice in many religions. The continued existence of forced marriage remains a serious breach of human rights in many parts of the world, including Western countries, and underlines the fact that marriage as it has traditionally been arranged in most religions conflicts with the modern understanding of human rights. Those who argue for the eternally unchanged nature of marriage are not keen to remind us of that kind of unpleasant fact.

What about changes in our ideas about marriage? In Christianity, for example, marriage has gradually moved from the ritual periphery into a central position in the religious world view of many believers. Initially Christians did not even regulate entry into marriage – that was left to the pagan authorities of the Roman Empire. There is no evidence for Christian weddings before the fourth century. Even though marriage was and remained the only legal Christian framework for sex, marriage was nevertheless not viewed as a particularly important or sacred institution. It was during the Middle Ages that marriage developed from being an institution with little church or canonical involvement to being something in which the church was deeply involved.[97] It was not until the thirteenth century that marriage became a sacrament.[98]

In spite of marriage becoming a sacrament many people continued to marry outside the church. From the legal point of view, a marriage vow alone was sufficient, irrespective of where it was made. The church wedding did not become the only legally binding way to marry in England and Wales until 1753.[99] When various religious congregations like the Catholic Church formally state that 'marriage is holy',[100] they are absolutely right from their own theological understanding of their position, but this has not always been the case either within the Catholic Church or in the rest of Christendom.

A different concept of Christian marriage argues that people should practise sexual abstinence even within marriage. This, for instance, was argued by a number of the early church fathers. Priests, in particular, who were allowed to be married in Western Christendom until 1123, were exhorted to 'abstain from their wives'.[101]

A totally different kind of sex-free marriage is to be found among Hindus. In certain special circumstances, Hindus do not get married to other people but to animals or even to physical objects. A man by the name of Nandi Munda from the Indian village Ghatshila in the state of Jharkand married a mountain called Lakhasaini in 2007. The goddess of the mountain had come to him in a dream and told him that attacks by the local Maoist guerrillas would cease if he married the mountain. His fellow villagers supported his decision and celebrated his marriage to the mountain with a traditional wedding feast and hundreds of guests.[102] In the state of Tamil Nadu in 2007, P. Selvakumar of Manamadurai married a dog in order to atone for killing two dogs fifteen years before. After killing the dogs he had been afflicted by a whole string of misfortunes and, according to an astrologer, marrying a dog was the only way of turning his fate round. The wedding was celebrated following all the usual rules, including a ritual bath at the local Hindu temple. His bride, a bitch called Selvi, was chosen by the bridegroom's family in the same way as they would have chosen his bride for a traditional Hindu human marriage.[103] In the village of Pallipudpet, also in Tamil Nadu, there is a tradition of arranging weddings between frogs and little girls in order to protect the latter from mystical diseases. The custom has its origin in a myth about how the god Shiva was once turned into a frog. As two seven-year-olds, Vigneswari and Masiakanni, experienced in 2009, there is no sex involved in this kind of marriage: the little girls went straight back to their earlier lives and their husbands, two frogs, were allowed to return to the pond they had come from.[104]

Another version of sexless marriage has had a renaissance in Chinese religion. A fundamental rule for Chinese married couples is that they should be buried together. There are consequently occasions when an unmarried man dies and his parents do not want their son to be buried alone, so they procure a female corpse, marry the two corpses and bury them together. It is not always easy to find an available corpse when it is needed and this has created a market opportunity. There are grave robbers who make good money by stealing women's bodies – the fresher the corpse, the higher the fee. There have been occasions when grave robbers have found it easier to murder living women and sell their corpses to parents looking for a bride for a dead son rather than go to the trouble of digging up a dead body.[105]

Buddhists do not view marriage as a central religious institution. Indeed, it is often the non-religious perspective that is stressed and according to tradition monks should not be in attendance. Unlike Christianity, which has generally lost its original ideal of total abstinence and is happy to bless heterosexual marriage, Buddhism has never viewed marriage as an end in itself. Some branches of Buddhism, however, have developed a greater level of religious symbolism that involves active participation by religious authorities. In Western Buddhism, wedding ceremonies have been developed on the model of Christian ceremonies[106] and some Thai hotels offer package deals which include Buddhist wedding ceremonies adapted to Western tastes, with monks, bridal bouquets, wedding cake and local dancers.[107]

If we are hoping to find a simple and uniform picture of marriage as a religious institution, Islam is not the religion to turn to either. Islam has always been quite certain that there are several quite distinct kinds of marriage. Normal lifelong marriage, which can only be dissolved by death or formal divorce, is supplemented by several other varieties. *Mutah*, fixed-term marriage with clear time limits, is one legally recognized form of heterosexual relationship and it can be negotiated to last for anything from a couple of hours to a couple of years. The primary aim, here, is quite simply to give the partners the chance to fulfil their desires while sparing them from having sex outside marriage. After such a marriage, women have to menstruate three times before they are allowed to enter another marriage – this is to ensure that there can be no doubt about any future paternity. The Koran's reference to when men are legally permitted to have sex with women who are slaves or were captured in war[108] is often taken as a reference to this kind of *mutah*-marriage. Most Sunni Muslims no longer consider *mutah* to be permissible: the hadiths state that it was legal in Muhammad's day but that it was banned later by Caliph Umar.[109] *Mutah* is, however, still practised within Shia Islam and is legal in Iran.

Misyar is another form of marriage with reduced commitments. In this case the man does not have to live with the woman or support her financially. This kind of marriage is practised either because the couple are unable to enter ordinary marriage with its respective economic commitments, or as an alternative to what might otherwise be an extramarital relationship – in which case the husband will very often have other wives. There is, however, no agreement as to Islam's position with regard to such marriages. Nor is there any agreement among Muslim scholars about the legality of so-called *urfi* marriages. These are secret marriages whose only proof is a written declaration signed by witnesses; if the declaration is destroyed there is no other proof of the marriage. In spite of that, there has been an increase in the number of such secret marriages, particularly among young people who cannot afford to set up home or who use it as a religiously sanctioned alternative to premarital sex, the latter being categorically condemned in the Koran.[110]

The widespread perception that marriage has always existed as a more or less unchanged religious institution is thus simply a matter of religious faith. Marriage has been seen as something that conflicts with religion, or something not specifically religious, just as often as it has been perceived as having a central role in a range of religions. In addition, there is also the idea that there are clearly distinguishable types of marriage, some of which are more valuable than others. There are also some very fundamental differences about such matters as who can marry whom.

Even though different regulations exist with regard to marital heterosexual behaviour, there are certain patterns that cut across religious boundaries. With the exception of those religions which condemn all sex, the majority of religions tend to agree that heterosexual activity within marriage is acceptable to some extent – though it may not always be absolutely commendable. Yet as we shall see, this by no means holds true for all kinds of heterosexual activity.

Sex Whether You Want It or Not

The sexual organs are 'the visible signs of a mandate received from the gods', explained the prominent Japanese Shintoist Miyahiro Sadao in 1831. His view was that 'Men are born equipped with male sexual organs and these . . . are organs that should be used to do what they are designed for – that is, procreation, for increasing the number of people in our land.'[111] The penis is 'in truth . . . a tool by which to honour the generation of descendants'. Any attempt to prevent anyone from using his male organ is sacrilege.[112]

So it is not only poor Hippolytus, whom we met in the introduction, who has reason to fear the gods because he does not want to have sex. The ancient Greek religion is not alone in its insistence that its followers have sex, and Japanese Shintoism is among the religions that preaches the gospel of heterosexuality most explicitly. When a religion takes this view of sex, allowing men to be abstinent becomes a problem and many Shintoists openly criticized Buddhism, arguing that its anti-sex message was blasphemous. Miyahiro Sadao went so far as to say: 'To transform unenlightened young lads into Buddhist priests is itself a sin before our gods.'[113] Whereas Buddhists, Catholics and many others do whatever they can to promote the celibacy of priests, Shinto priests, logically enough, have a duty to get married.[114]

The ambivalent attitude to marriage visible in some parts of Christianity and Buddhism is thus not the only way in which religion attempts to regulate heterosexual behaviour: sex and marriage can also be seen as a religious duty. Judaism, which is the starting point for Christianity, is among the religions with a very different understanding of heterosexuality and marriage from the one we find in Buddhism or in the teachings of St Paul. In Judaism, men and women were not just expected to marry; they had a duty to do so. The story of Jephthah's daughter in the Book of Judges provides a good example of the central role of marriage in the most ancient times. When Jephthah went out to war against the Ammonites he promised God he would sacrifice the first person to come out of his house to meet him should he return from the battle unharmed. After defeating the Ammonites he was met by his daughter, his only child, who came dancing out to greet him playing the drum. His daughter recognized that his vow to God meant that she must die and her only request to her father demonstrated what was considered most important in existence: 'Let me alone two months, that I may go up and down upon the mountains, and bewail my virginity, I and my fellows.'[115] To be killed by one's father was one thing, but to die unmarried was a tragedy.

If she had had time to marry before her father took her life, Jephthah's daughter would have had to have sex, because sex became obligatory as soon as one was married. God made this obligation clear to Adam and Eve right back in the Garden of Eden: 'Be fruitful, and multiply, and replenish the earth.'[116] Some centuries later, on leaving the ark, Noah and his sons were given the same instruction after God drowned all other human beings in the Flood.[117]

Throughout its history Judaism has taken a generally negative view of celibacy. Sex and fruitfulness are closely linked. If one thinks of one's descendants as a reward from God, to abstain from heterosexual intercourse is equivalent to saying no to God. As we can read in the Book of Psalms: 'Lo, children are an heritage of the Lord: and the fruit of the womb is his reward.'[118] God's promise to the Jewish people is identical to the promise he gives to Abraham: 'And I will make of thee a great nation, and I will bless thee, and make thy name great; and thou shalt be a blessing.'[119] By means of marriage and obligatory marital sex aimed at procreation, all Jews are contributing to the promise God made to Abraham. Fruitfulness is a sign that the faithful have God with them: 'there shall not be male or female barren among you'.[120] When God commands Jeremiah – the only figure in the Hebrew Bible to whom it happens – not to take a wife, the episode arises in the context of him being given the task of showing the Israelites that they have turned away from God.[121] Jeremiah's unmarried state is the tragic symbol of an Israel that has deserted God.

A woman's right to be made fruitful went so far in biblical Judaism that she had the right to marry her husband's brother if her husband died before she was pregnant. In Genesis we meet Tamar, who first marries Judah's eldest son, but he soon dies because he 'was wicked in the sight of the Lord'. Then she marries Judah's second son, who also dies without giving her children. When she sees that her father-in-law will not give her his third and youngest son as a husband, she dresses as a prostitute and tempts Judah himself into making her pregnant. When her pregnancy becomes apparent and she is accused of fornication, she proves that it was her father-in-law who made her pregnant. As a God-fearing man (and a notably relaxed customer for sex) Judah's conclusion is as follows: 'She hath been more righteous than I; because that I gave her not [as a wife] to Shelah my [third] son.'[122] The story functions as an exaggerated mythic demonstration of how important a duty it was for the husband's family to ensure that a wife conceived.

Rabbinic Judaism retained this duty-bound view of sex and the *Mishnah*, the oral Torah written down around 200 AD, states categorically that sex is a man's marital duty: 'A man should not abstain from the performance of the duty of propagation of the race unless he already has children.' Even after ten years of childless marriage he must not abstain: 'If a man took a wife and lived with her for ten years and she bore no child, he may not abstain.' 'He who does not engage in propagation of the race is as though he sheds blood.' It is, then, a man's duty to reproduce but, according to the *Mishnah*, a woman does not have the same duty: 'A man is commanded concerning the duty of propagation but not a woman.'[123] Maimonides, writing in the twelfth century and one of the most influential Jewish scholars, thought that women also had a duty to have sex: if a wife refuses her husband, he must separate from her. This particular demand on women did not receive much support, since one of its implications was that women might easily get a divorce.[124]

The thirteenth-century *Zohar*, one of the most important Jewish cabbalistic texts, places the male duty to have procreative sex in a cosmic perspective. The sixth commandment – you shall not commit adultery – is redefined to mean that you *shall* reproduce. A refusal to reproduce by a man is equivalent to rebelling against God.[125] Sexually abstemious men are even more clearly condemned in the *Shulhan 'Aruch*, a sixteenth-century legal work by the Palestinian rabbi Joseph ben Ephraim Caro and the Polish rabbi Moses Isserles. Caro argues: 'Anyone who does not engage in being fruitful and multiplying is as if he spills blood . . . and causes the divine presence to depart from Israel.' Isserles follows on: 'He who does not marry is not allowed to make a blessing or to engage in Torah and he is not called a man, and when he marries a woman his sins are forgiven, as it is said [in Proverbs]: "One who has found a wife has found goodness and obtains favour in the eyes of God."'[126]

In spite of his fundamental belief that marriage was an institution founded to prevent fornication, even St Paul recognized sex as a duty for the sexually incontinent once they had found a haven for their lusts in marriage. It is acceptable for a couple to abstain from sex within a marriage only if 'it be with consent for a time'.[127] It is not enough for only one partner to have lost the desire, have a headache, or whatever it might be. On the contrary, one should give oneself to the more eager partner irrespective of how little desire one has: 'Let the husband render unto the wife due benevolence: and likewise also the wife unto the husband. The wife hath not power of her own body, but the husband: and likewise also the husband hath not power of his body, but the wife.'[128] It was an ancient Judaic tradition that the wife had a right to sex in a marriage. That this also meant that the wife had power over the husband's body was unprecedented and was something that was rarely stressed by later Christians.

While there were some church fathers who considered it better not to have sex even within marriage, the medieval Christian view of marriage was that a true marriage would necessarily involve sex. Most canonical laws made a distinction between entry into a marriage and the consummation of that marriage by sexual intercourse. A marriage could be dissolved without difficulty as long as the couple had not had sexual intercourse, but if they had had sex, the marriage was thereby made indissoluble. The first occasion of marital sexual intercourse was thus an act with serious legal and theological implications.[129] This is why it was usual for the whole bridal party to accompany the bride and bridegroom to the marital bed and literally put them to bed, with the priest even blessing the bed in which they lay. The couple were, however, normally permitted to consummate the marriage in private once the guests had left the room.[130]

Even though the Catholic Church has not persisted with the idea that sex within marriage is a duty, it still insists that the *ability* to have vaginal sex is a demand. Catholic canon law states that if a man or a woman lacks the ability to have sex on entering into marriage, the marriage is annulled.[131] Many marriages have been dissolved by the Church precisely because the woman has discovered that the man is impotent. The Brazilian Hedir Antonio de Brito was the victim of a less well-known consequence of this sacred regulation. In 1996, when de Brito was to marry the woman in his life, Elzimar Serafim, he sent out all the wedding invitations, but forty days before the planned wedding he was informed by the Catholic church in his town that it was going to refuse him permission to marry because he was in a wheelchair and therefore, according to the church, unable to have sexual intercourse.[132] The Catholic church has also refused to marry other people with disabilities for the same reason.[133]

While many Christians have felt some general social pressure to get married, there have been times when the element of duty has been much more prominent. The Herrnhuters in the eighteenth century took to casting lots to decide on marriages, believing that Jesus would decide who should marry whom.[134] The custom survived among Herrnhuters who emigrated to the Danish West Indies, although eventually it was decided that the practice should just apply to missionaries; it was only finally abolished in 1836.[135] A different view is taken by the Christian Moonie movement led by Pastor Sun Myung Moon, among whom the notion of sex as a duty is traced back to the traditional reading of the Fall. God's original plan was that Jesus would reverse the Fall by getting married, being heterosexually active and thus creating a new generation of mankind who would be free of sin. Unfortunately Jesus was crucified before this could take place and God has now sent the Reverend Moon instead so that a new and sin-free generation can be produced by him and his descendants. Followers of the Reverend Moon view marriage as a duty and, thanks to the pastor's blessing, these marriages can be notably free of sin. During the sect's well-orchestrated mass weddings the Reverend Moon himself frequently decides who shall marry whom, thus ensuring divine intervention right from the start of the marriage.[136]

Islam shares the Judaic tradition of viewing marriage and marital sex as a duty. God says in the Koran: 'And marry those among you who are single and those who are fit among your male slaves and your female slaves.'[137] When a man marries he must have sex and if his wife complains of his abstinence he has an explicit duty to have intercourse with her before a year has passed.[138] He may not abstain from marital sex for more than four months at a time after that.[139] If he continues to abstain, he must divorce.

In Hinduism the most important role for a woman is to marry, have marital sex and produce children. Even though sexual abstinence is held up as a duty for young girls and for widows, the opposite is the duty of married women. Marriage is actually the only Vedic sacrament for women,[140] and consequently women who abstain from sex and marriage are in breach of one of the most fundamental sexual concepts in Hinduism.

Various duties are incumbent on a Hindu man depending on the stage of life he has reached. At the age of twenty-four he is considered to be at the ideal stage to enter the phase of being a husband and during this stage he should strive for sensual pleasure and material welfare.[141] When a man first enters marriage there is a clear understanding that he has a duty to have sex. The *Laws of Manu*, for instance, state that a man should have sex with his wife when she is fertile and should always achieve satisfaction with her.[142] A man who does not have sex with his wife at the time she is most likely to conceive is to be censured.[143] Procreation is of the utmost importance and producing a son virtually guarantees a man a place in heaven.[144] Even though the majority of Hindus even today have not read the *Laws of Manu*, the principle of a man's duty to be sexually active and to produce male descendants persists. It is considered to be a great misfortune not to have managed to produce a son to light one's funeral pyre when the time comes.

Thus, while there are many people who are convinced for religious reasons that we should on the whole abstain from sex, there are also plenty of religious ideals that insist on the opposite – that we have a duty to have sex. Viewed in this light, it is possible to draw parallels with other practices demanded of us by religion, such as prayer, making sacrifices or following the correct forms of rites of passage like baptism or burial, so we see that sex suddenly stands right at the heart of religious observance. When the demand to have sex is absolute, it is obvious that neither prayers nor sacrifices are sufficient: sex then becomes essential, as Hippolytus and others have discovered so painfully.

The reasons for having sex are, however, many and diverse. Mankind's duty to the gods to procreate is one reason that turns up repeatedly – in Judaism, Shintoism, Hinduism and elsewhere. There is frequently a clearly sexist element in this concept of sexual duty: in traditional Hinduism, for instance, marital sex is of little avail if it only produces daughters. At one extreme, not having sex is a crime against the gods. In other contexts, it is your duty to be sexually available to your spouse when first married – we find this, for instance, in Judaism, Christianity and Islam. Some of these religious rules may fill many people with trepidation: not only are you required to enter into a heterosexual marriage whether you want it or not, but you must also be sexually available to your partner for as long as he or she demands.

Only for Procreation

Defining a particular kind of sexuality as inhuman is a well-known strategy for controlling other people's sex lives. The Catholic Church probably has one of the most restrictive definitions of what constitutes proper human sex: 'Sexual relations are human when and insofar as they express and promote the mutual assistance of the sexes in marriage and are open to the transmission of new life.'[145] Any kind of sex other than heterosexual, contraception-free sex within marriage is therefore defined as inhuman. As we have seen, religious encouragement of sex is often linked to sex in the service of procreation. The Catholic Church, however, is saying something quite different: there is no duty to have sex, but if you do have sex it should *only* be of the kind that can lead to procreation. All other kinds of sex are objectionable, wrong and essentially inhuman. But this official insistence dating from 2003 is in no way exceptional: it represents a long tradition going back to the beginnings of Christianity and with roots traceable back into Judaism. It is also possible to find similar ideas in other religions.

The story told in Genesis about Onan, Tamar's second husband, provides a dire example of what can happen when people dabble in non-procreative sex. When his brother died, Onan took over his brother's wife Tamar as a way of creating descendants for his brother. Any child Onan had with Tamar would legally count as his brother's. Having little desire to produce children simply to provide descendants for his brother, Onan 'spilled [his seed] on the ground' every time he had intercourse with his wife/sister-in-law. But this 'displeased the Lord' and God punished Onan by killing him.[146]

God did not continue to eliminate people who refused to procreate but there are nevertheless strict rules about birth control in canonical Jewish texts. The use of both contraception and coitus interruptus were generally forbidden, although other Jewish sources show that both methods were widespread among Jews even in ancient times.[147] The Talmud openly permits contraception when it is a matter of the health of the woman.[148] These days contraception is generally accepted by the majority of Jews[149] but it is still not absolutely straightforward: many rabbis accept the use of the contraceptive pill within marriage but only after the couple have had at least two children.[150] Ultra-Orthodox still adhere to the older precepts and consider the wasting of seed to be impermissible. Understandably enough, the size of ultra-Orthodox families reflects that position.

Modern Christian teaching on contraception also has a history independent of Judaism. Even though marriage in itself represents a 'loving union' in which 'one governs and the other obeys', Augustine tells us that children are the only 'virtuous fruit' of marital sexual life.[151] If a married couple has sex and excludes the possibility of having children, the church father finds it difficult 'to see how this can be called a marriage'.[152] Having marital sex while attempting to avoid procreation is, in his view, equivalent to fornication within marriage.[153]

The emphasis on the procreative side of sex in early Christianity shows yet again the extent to which Christianity focused on the physical aspects of this world. The more people born, the more there were to save for eternity. Augustine knew also of the opposite view, having been a Manichean in his youth. According to the Manicheans, if you were going to have sex at all, it should be heterosexual, but preferably during the woman's infertile periods in order to prevent yet another soul from being 'entangled in flesh'.[154]

As a more extreme form of birth control, the classical tradition of exposing unwanted infants continued well into the Christian period and none of the early Christian emperors banned the practice.[155] But the church gradually began to condemn both the exposure of infants and less dramatic forms of birth control more strongly. In a decree issued in 1230, Pope Gregory IX declared that 'he who does sorcery or gives potions of sterility is a murderer'.[156] In 1588 Sixtus V repeated that contraception and abortion were murder but in 1591 Gregory XIV made a distinction between abortion and contraception, deciding that the latter was a less serious crime.[157]

The Catholic Church has reiterated its opposition to birth control time after time. Pope Pius XI maintained that anyone attempting to have marital sex in a manner that deliberately prevented conception was guilty of a 'grave sin' and was breaking both God's law and a Catholic 'law of nature' – a set of dogmatic rules of conduct that has nothing to do with Newton's ideas or any other kind of elementary natural science.[158] In 1951, however, Pope Pius XII took a radical step forward when he permitted married couples to try to limit the number of children by restricting their sexual activity to safe periods – 'periods of natural sterility'.[159] All of a sudden Catholic married couples were given permission to have vaginal sex just for the sake of sex. This did not lead to any further liberalization and, at the same time, many Catholic couples complained publicly that the calendar method ruined their sex lives and broke the link between love and sex.[160]

The introduction of mass-produced and cheap forms of contraception, above all the Pill, brought about a much more marked separation between sex and procreation. The fact that it was now much simpler for people to have sex without having to worry about pregnancy increased the level of active resistance to religious decrees that tried to limit sex in general. The challenges facing religious authorities if they were to avoid getting on to a collision course with their own followers became considerable.

At the time of the Second Vatican Council at the beginning of the 1960s there were signs that the Catholic Church was willing to permit contraception. Pope John XXIII, for instance, expressed his growing concern about the population explosion, and immediately before he died of cancer in 1963 he appointed a six-person commission to examine the issue of contraception.[161] The fact that the issue was addressed at all was a strong indication that Pope John wished to officially change the Catholic position. Meanwhile the popular Dutch bishop Willem Bekkers of 's-Hertogenbosch stated that contraception was a matter for the married couple to decide on[162] and Catholic nuns in Congo-Léopoldville, where there was a civil war raging, were given permission to use contraceptives if they were in danger of being raped.[163] When Pope Paul VI, John's successor, nevertheless opposed all forms of contraception and sterilization in his 1968 encyclical *Humanae Vitae*, there were massive protests from many believers. Numerous Catholic theologians voiced their disagreement[164] and newspapers all over the world were inundated with thousands of protest letters from Catholics.[165] Both church attendance and monetary donations declined dramatically in the first years after *Humanae Vitae*. In 1969 alone, church attendance fell by a third.[166] The moral authority of a large section of the church leadership went up in smoke when they moved against the wishes of their followers so obviously. The decline has not continued at the same pace but the relationship between the flock and its shepherds has never been the same again. In 1999, for instance, only ten per cent of the Catholics in the USA believed that the Church had sole authority to judge what was moral in relation to birth control.[167]

The Vatican position has not eased in the years since then. In 1993 Pope John Paul II defined contraception as 'intrinsically evil' under any circumstances[168] and Pope Benedict upheld the ban on it in October 2008.[169] The attitude of the Catholic Church to sex and procreation provides a good example of how the attitudes of the religious leaders can often differ very significantly from those of the majority of their followers. Whereas the Vatican still condemns the use of all contraception, the view farther down the hierarchy is very different. The Vatican continues to believe that sex with contraceptives is not a 'human' act,[170] but 73 per cent of American Catholics in 1993 said it was possible to use contraception and still be a good Catholic.[171] The statistics for the use of contraception from a whole series of primarily Catholic countries also reveal how little support the official Vatican position has among the faithful. The use of contraception among sexually active people in the middle of the 1990s was as follows: Brazil 76.7 per cent, Bolivia 72.2 per cent, Peru 64.2 per cent, the Philippines 48.3 per cent and Guatemala 31.4 per cent.[172] Figures such as these also have to be viewed in the light of other factors, such as knowledge about contraception and access to reasonably priced contraceptives.

Other church communions have undergone great changes in the course of the last century. The Anglican Church accepted contraception within marriage in 1930, although abstinence was regarded as preferable even here.[173] During the 1950s the most important of the Lutheran churches decided that contraception within marriage was acceptable, stressing simultaneously that procreation was not the only purpose of sex – the union of love and physical satisfaction also had their part to play.[174] The majority of Protestant church communions now permit contraception, although there is still significant opposition among conservative Christians to contraceptives being available to the unmarried. Present-day religious resistance to contraception seems to represent opposition to premarital and extramarital sex rather than to non-procreative sex. This emerges particularly in the significant opposition to the use of condoms to stop the AIDS epidemic. Those who adhere firmly to the Christian ideal of sexually faithful husbands and wives who did not indulge in premarital sex are, of course, at little risk of becoming HIV-positive. By systematically opposing the distribution of the condoms that can make the difference between life and death to people having sex outside the confines of a heterosexual marriage, many Christians have the pious hope that they will convert these people to their own Christian sexual ideals, if for no other reason than that the alternative is to die of AIDS.

Resistance to contraception in Christian circles can lead to some peculiar consequences. Some young, unmarried Protestants are worried about using contraception because they feel it would give them an excuse 'to fall into sin' and 'live in sin'. The use of contraceptives seems to legitimize having a sex life, whereas sex without contraception is not premeditated in the same sort of way.[175] A young unmarried woman, for instance, talks about contraceptive pills being even worse than condoms because taking them would make her 'actively responsible' for what she thinks of as her 'sinful sexual life'.[176] But this is not the only perspective conservative Christians may have on birth control: the generally socially conservative Norwegian Christian People's Party proposes free contraceptives for young people in order to reduce the number of abortions, since they consider abortion to be a greater evil than premarital sex.[177]

Islam has had a notably simpler relationship with contraception from the start because, as Muhammad points out, God is so omnipotent that no human action can change his decision about who will be conceived and born.[178] Consequently the Prophet did not see coitus interruptus as a problem.

Islamic jurists began discussing the use of various contraceptive methods as early as the ninth century.[179] The majority of Muslim leaders today support the right to contraception.[180] Surveys have revealed that about half of the sexually active people in Bangladesh, Indonesia, Egypt and Jordan use contraceptives, and by the end of the 1990s the figures were 20.8 per cent and 11.8 per cent for Yemen and Pakistan respectively.[181]

In spite of Muhammad's conviction that man can do nothing to alter God's plan about who will be conceived, there are nevertheless many Muslims today who do oppose contraception. Some Muslims argue that contraception may only be used in certain circumstances, such as when a married couple do not want children because they themselves are still in education or when there is a chance of a disabled child.[182] The Ulama Council in Saudi Arabia, the highest religious authority in the country, condemned the 1994 United Nations Conference on Population and Development in Cairo as a 'ferocious assault on Islamic society' and told Muslims not to attend. The great majority of Muslim countries went ahead anyway and participated, although Sudan, Iraq and Lebanon (which is half Christian) fell into line and boycotted the conference.[183] Since Islam has taken a relaxed view of contraception from the start, it is actually very clear that Muslim objections are motivated primarily by the desire to discourage sex outside the confines of heterosexual marriage.

Birth control has been a problem for Hinduism from the start because of the traditional emphasis on the high importance of procreative sex. But even in the earlier Ayurvedic writings from the centuries before Christ, there are a number of recommendations about contraception and abortion.[184] Similar advice is repeated in Hindu texts of recent centuries.[185] These traditional methods of contraception have largely been replaced by newer and more secure methods but statistics from the beginning of the 1990s show that only just over 40 per cent of those sexually active in India (of which the great majority will be Hindu) use contraception.[186] Part of the explanation for this rather low figure is probably to be found in the extreme poverty in which a large part of the Indian population lives, which means that they cannot afford to buy contraceptives. There is the additional factor that

Hinduism sets great store on having a son and it would be seen as problematical for a couple to use contraception unless they already had a son.[187] The selective abortion of female foetuses by those who can afford to do so, and the widespread killing of girl babies in some poorer regions, are further consequences of this focus on producing a son.[188]

A number of Hindu nationalists have come out against birth control primarily because they are afraid of a decline in the proportion of Hindus in the Indian population. To add support to their case, many Hindu activists since the 1970s have claimed that Muslims oppose birth control and that statistics show the birth rate among Indian Muslims to be somewhat higher than among Hindus.[189] In the New Age Hare Krishna movement, however, there is a more straightforward religious resistance to birth control. The movement, considered by many Hindus to be a particularly conservative form of Hinduism, only permits sex within marriage when there is the possibility of procreation.[190]

The Buddhist Pali texts from the first centuries before the Christian era stress that contraception is acceptable as long as nothing living is lost.[191] A survey in Sri Lanka in the 1990s showed that better educated monks did not find any contradiction between Buddhism and birth control and did not see the issue as particularly important from a religious perspective. Less educated priests in rural areas, on the other hand, believed that birth control did conflict with Buddhism because preventing something from being born was considered to be tantamount to killing it. Even this latter, more negative group did not really consider contraception to be a serious religious issue.[192] The use of contraceptives in Thailand has multiplied many times over during the last decades and Buddhists in the north of the country have actively encouraged the use of premarital contraception, even though premarital sex is not viewed with favour by Buddhists.[193]

It seems fairly clear that access to contraception generally leads to more sex, as was demonstrated by the role of the Pill in the sexual revolution. Of course, contraception reduces the risk of pregnancy resulting from casual sex and this, rather than the prevention of new life, seems to be more upsetting to many opponents of contraception. The fact that there are groups of Muslims who are anti-contraception, even though contraception is traditionally not a problem for Islam, points in the same direction: the issue is less about contraception than about restricting sex of a kind that is disapproved of. This also seems to be the case with the Catholic Church: ever since 1951, when it recommended having sex during a woman's safe periods, the Church has acknowledged the possibility of married couples having sex just for the sake of sex. Many conservative religious groups are even against the use of contraception as a way of preventing the spread of AIDS. The repeated lie that condoms do not prevent HIV infection gives us good reason to suspect that many religious conservatives consider their war on extramarital sex to be more important than fighting the AIDS catastrophe.[194]

How many Husbands or Wives do you Want?

In 1524 Martin Luther stated that he could not in principle forbid a man marrying several wives because there was nothing in the Bible to prevent it.[195] In a letter he wrote in 1540 to Landgrave Philip of Hesse, one of his most important supporters, Luther explicitly acknowledged the landgrave's right to take wife number two.[196] Luther did not, however, take the concept of Christian polygyny any further than that and thus polygyny did not become part of the general practice of Lutheranism. Probably the most important lesson we can learn from the case of Philip of Hesse is that Luther thought there was an essential difference between people in general and a powerful monarch and supporter in particular. If other powerful men had followed Philip's example, this peculiar episode from the time of the Reformation might have led to polygyny being acceptable in some quarters of Protestantism. Now, however, Luther's biblical defence of polygyny has largely been forgotten, although his argument demonstrates that there is nothing self-evident in religious terms about only having one spouse.

The number of permissible partners is one of many variations in the religious sanctioning of heterosexuality. From a historical perspective monogamy does not rule supreme. Christianity, in fact, is the only world religion that seems to have taken a stance in favour of monogamy the moment the question arose,[197] although it is important to bear in mind that neither Jesus nor Paul addressed the issue of polygyny or forbade it. Their lack of interest may be connected to the fact that Roman law only permitted one wife at a time, and that this was also the normal rule in contemporary Palestinian

Judaism. So it might well be that Christianity simply accepted monogamy as a religious rule because it was the norm in the society in which the religion arose.

Monogamy was not, however, entirely problem-free for Christians since even the early church fathers recognized, as Luther did later, that the Bible presented them with a challenge in this matter. How are we to tally the church's demand for monogamy with the fact that so many of the men held up as models by the Bible had a number of wives? Augustine tried to defend the polygyny of the patriarchs by arguing that they did it simply for the sake of procreation and that sexual desire had nothing to do with it. At that time, Augustine went on, there were neither laws nor customs that stated that there was anything wrong with having several wives.[198] His argument is fine as a defence of polygyny in the Old Testament, but it made it harder for him to argue that men of his own day should be satisfied with one wife each.

In the Bible, which provides the starting-point for both Judaism and Christianity, women are never offered the possibility of having several husbands. This, of course, is related to the principle of property reflected by Old Testament marriage: women belonged to *one* man at a time as a matter of principle. For one woman to belong to several men at the same time could lead to a number of intractable problems. If a woman had several husbands, for instance, which one should she obey? And – in those days long before DNA testing – how could anyone be sure whose child she was bringing into the world?

As both Luther and Augustine point out, polygyny was originally legal in Judaism. The Hebrew Bible not only tells us that the patriarchs and the kings of the Israelites often had a number of wives, but also provides rules as to how a man should rank his wives.[199] Even if he no longer likes his first wife, he cannot remove her son's rights as the first-born son.[200] A king, given his wealth, could take as many wives as he wanted, but he was advised not to have too many, not to 'multiply wives to himself'.[201] Just how many he should not 'multiply' is not defined more closely.

Two traditions developed within Rabbinic Judaism, one in favour of polygyny and one against; one in the Babylonian Talmud, one in the Palestinian Talmud. This distinction was clearly influenced by the acceptance of polygyny in Persian society as opposed to the ban on polygyny among Romans, Greeks and Christians.[202] For the same reason, it was easier for polygyny to survive in the east because the Middle East was taken over by polygynous Muslims; some Jews in certain Muslim countries have retained a polygynous tradition right up to today.

Islam, like Judaism and Christianity, insists that women must be monogamous, whereas Muslim men may have up to four wives. Muhammad, who had a special position as the Prophet, had fourteen or fifteen wives. Other Muslim men have sometimes had more wives but it is difficult to defend this on the basis of religion, and it can lead to sanctions. The Nigerian man who appeared in the media in 2008 talking about his 86 wives was quickly told by his national Islamic authorities to divorce 82 of them or risk being condemned by the sharia court in the federal state in which he lived.[203] Since men have a duty to care for the needy – fatherless children, for instance – the Koran exhorts them to marry widows with children, even 'two, three and four' widows.[204] If a man has several wives, Islam makes it quite clear that he is duty bound to treat them all equally, including the women he may have married in order to protect their fatherless children.[205] And since the Koran also demands that a man should have a certain minimum economic standard before he marries,[206] it is obvious that he has to have fairly healthy finances if he wants more than one wife.

Islam did not originally set a limit on the number of concubines a man could have, nor on his sexual behaviour with his slave women.[207] There were periods when concubinage existed on a very large scale among the more affluent members of Muslim societies.[208] In the ninth century, for instance, Caliph Al-Mutawakkil was famous for supposedly having 4,000 concubines, all of whom shared his bed.[209] Given such a fabulous number, it is hardly surprising that Al-Mutawakkil's harem figures in the *Thousand and One Nights*. But harems probably figure more prominently in the oriental fantasies of the West than they actually did in the historical social organization of Muslim life. The object of a harem was not to collect as many wives and concubines as possible but to segregate the women in more affluent households and, among other things, prevent them from coming into contact with men from outside the family.[210] The harem was a place that was *haram* – forbidden – to men, and it was certainly not a place into which male guests were brought. Many of the women who ended up in harems were slaves, but they might also end up as wives or formal concubines of the men in the family. At the end of the nineteenth century the imperial

Ottoman harem in Constantinople had between 400 and 500 slaves, many of them from the north Caucasus regions. The harem was not necessarily the end of the road for all of them, however, and many of the women left the harem by marrying powerful government officials.[211]

The acceptance of polygyny today varies from one Muslim country to another and even in the countries where it is permitted different limits are set on the practice. In Sunni Islam, for instance, a man does not traditionally need the agreement of his existing wife or wives before he takes a new wife, whereas in Shia Islam he does. In Iran in 2008 a legal change was proposed to enable a man to take a second wife without the agreement of his first wife. This was criticized by a senior ayatollah as being 'harem, a sin, a religious offence contrary to the concept of justice prescribed by the Koran'. Parliament subsequently rejected the proposal.[212]

The *Kamasutra*, written in the second century AD and probably the most important Hindu text on sex and love, also lays down rules as to when a man may take another wife: if his first wife is frigid, promiscuous or unlucky in love, if she cannot provide him with children, or if she only bears him daughters. This whole catalogue of reasons was in any case superfluous since not liking his existing wife was reason enough in itself.[213] The possibility of polygyny also survived in other Indian religions. Among the Jains, the possibility of taking a second wife is one of the issues that divides the two most important branches of the faith: whereas Svetambara Jainism permits the taking of a new wife if the first is infertile, Digambara Jainism forbids this.[214] Up until the nineteenth century a man who was a Parsee – a member of the Zoroastrian community in India – could take an extra wife if the first could not give him children.[215] Polygyny also exists among the Sikh upper class.

The practice of polygyny no longer survives in Hinduism, however. Marital rights in modern India are linked to the individual's religion. The common marriage law for Hindus, Buddhists, Jains and Sikhs forbids polygamy, as do the specific marriage laws for Parsees and Christians.[216] The Indian personal law for Muslims, on the other hand, refers to sharia, which means that, in accordance with the Koran, a Muslim man may take up to four wives.[217]

In spite of its rather ambivalent attitude to heterosexuality, polygyny is not unknown in Buddhism. Padma Sambhava, the founder of Tibetan Buddhism, happily accepted a wife as a present

The art of love in a Hindu illustration.

from the Tibetan king even though he already had at least one main wife.[218] King Jigme Singye of Bhutan, who abdicated in 2006, also has four wives. Farther east, in Chinese Taoism, it was also possible for a man to take multiple wives.[219]

It has historically been much less common for a religion to allow a woman to have multiple husbands, although Tibetan Buddhism has traditionally permitted women to be married to several men simultaneously. The usual procedure in such a case is that the woman marries several brothers at the same time, which means that any uncertainty about the family membership of her children is obviated.[220]

Polygyny has been common in a whole range of traditional African religions although its religious significance has varied. Rastafarians in Jamaica and elsewhere have taken up polygyny on the grounds that it is allegedly an important part of original African culture and must thus be carried on.[221] Although Christian missionaries and colonial administrators systematically worked against polygyny in African countries, this has not prevented many modern African Christians from believing that polygamy and Christianity are compatible. They base their arguments on the fact that polygyny was legal in the Old Testament and there is nothing in the New Testament to forbid it.[222] Statistics from 1994 reveal that 13 per cent of women between the ages of fifteen and fortynine live in polygamous relationships in Namibia, 18 per cent in Zambia and 17 per cent in Zimbabwe, all three of which countries are mainly Christian.[223]

Polygyny presents some legal difficulties in Western, mainly Christian countries, partly with regard to the status of the extended family and partly in relation to the diplomatic status of second, third or even fourth wives. There is less of a problem with the children of polygamous households because human rights legislation forbids a state to discriminate against children on grounds of their birth:[224] it is irrelevant whether they are born in monogamous or polygamous marriages, or, for that matter, outside marriage altogether.

Christian polygamy is to be found in certain parts of the world where the practice exists as a continuation of earlier religious practices. In the first years after the Spanish conquest of Latin America, the indigenous upper classes resisted the Catholic prohibition on polygamy. This resulted in men making their first marriage according to Catholic ritual and then using traditional rituals for marriage number two or three.[225] There were some traditional priests who proposed polygamy as a particularly effective way of protesting against Catholicism.[226]

Monogamous marriages were the norm in Norse religion, though kings and other powerful men were keen to have several wives. In the early tenth century the Norwegian King Harald I Finehair had six wives and a number of concubines as well. Keeping concubines and 'housekeepers' continued to be a widespread habit in early Catholic Norway even though the clerical hierarchy was less than enthusiastic about such arrangements.[227]

A number of Christian groups have attempted to practise polygamy since then. The radical Anabaptists who held power in Münster in 1534–5 practised polygyny according to the model of the Old Testament, but when a woman proposed that women too might have several husbands, she was quickly executed for her un-Christian suggestion.[228] The Anabaptists' marital experiment did not last long in any case: within a short time the town was captured by a Catholic army which then massacred the majority of the faithful.

The Christian Oneida Community in the northern part of New York State in the middle of the nineteenth century operated what they called 'complex marriage': that is, all the men and all the women were married to each other. If a couple wanted to have sex only with each other, they would be forbidden to see each other for a specified period since exclusive and emotionally laden sex was regarded as both egotistic and idolatrous. Believers should reserve such emotional attachment for God only, not other people. Monogamous marriage was viewed as incompatible with true Christianity and the Oneida followers pointed out that 'There is no place for such in the Kingdom of Heaven.'[229]

The Mormons are perhaps the most important example of Christian polygamy. Joseph Smith, the founder of the Church of Jesus Christ of Latter-day Saints, told fourteen-year-old Helen Mar Kimball, one of the many women he married in the spring of 1843, that 'If you will take this step [polygamous marriage], it will ensure your salvation & exaltation and that of your father's household & all your kindred.' Other women were given similar assurances about the connection between polygamy and salvation.[230] After Smith's death it became an established article of faith that a woman who became wife number two guaranteed a place in the heavenly kingdom not only for herself but also for her husband and for wife number one.[231] For every man to have several wives proved to be a problem from a purely practical point of view, and there were many Mormon men who did not wish to do so anyway. Nor was there any compulsion on men to have a number of wives simultaneously – the same principle of salvation operated if a man took a new wife after the death of his first wife. Some men entered a formal marriage with unmarried dead women or with older women with whom they never actually cohabited.[232] Not everyone, however, saw any reason to limit themselves and Brigham Young, Smith's successor, married more than fifty women.[233]

The only kind of marriage that was significant from the point of view of salvation was what the Mormons defined as heavenly marriage; other marriages did not have the same eternal consequences. The result of this was that, in principle, a woman could be married to several men at once. In 1846 Cordelia Morley entered a heavenly (and consequently eternal) marriage with Joseph Smith a year and a half after the latter had been killed, at the same time as she married another man in a marriage that was restricted to their time on earth.[234]

Mormon polygamy normally met with severe disapproval from other American Christians and in 1862, in the middle of the Civil War, Congress approved a ban on polygamy in 'a Territory of the United States, or in other places over which the United States have the exclusive jurisdiction', a careful definition specifically targeting the Mormons, who lived mainly in what was then Utah Territory.[235] President Abraham Lincoln allowed the Mormons to continue as before despite the law he had signed, but pressure on the Mormons steadily grew stronger as the years passed. In 1887 Washington approved a motion to dissolve the Mormon church and confiscate all its property. Polygamists could be sentenced to up to five years in prison; children born to any women other than the husband's first or only wife lost all rights of inheritance; only men who swore an oath renouncing polygamy were permitted to vote or hold public office; and women's right to vote – which had existed since 1870 – was abolished for all women in the Utah Territory because polygamous wives were perceived as being a political menace.[236] More than a thousand men were sentenced for polygamy[237] and almost 200 pregnant women in polygamous relationships were arrested for fornication.[238] Federal pressure was so strong that Wilford Woodruff, president of the Mormon church, refused to give church permission for new polygamous marriages after 1889. The whole affair was nevertheless resolved when God appeared to Woodruff in a vision on 23 September 1890 and told him that he no longer supported polygamy. The new doctrine was published in a manifesto two days later and immediately afterwards the leadership of the church unanimously approved it as their official teaching.[239] The church did, however, continue to recognize any earlier polygamous marriages and most such relationships lasted until death brought them to a natural end.

In spite of the new doctrine, many Mormons continued to enter polygamous marriages after 1890, including a number of prominent individuals within the church.[240] The Mormon church did, however, take the new doctrine seriously and in 1904 it passed a motion to excommunicate all those who married polygamously.[241] Since taking this step it has been particularly careful to prevent polygamy. When it was discovered in 1943 that one of the twelve apostles of the church – one of the most prominent figures in the organization of the church – had a woman he treated as wife number two, he was dismissed from all his key posts and excommunicated.[242]

Over time, however, a number of breakaway Mormon fundamentalist churches developed, claiming – with considerable theological justification – that they represented the true tradition of Joseph Smith and Brigham Young. They follow traditional polygamous practices, which they still associate with salvation. Since there is no longer a legal ban on having sexual partners in addition to one's legal wife, these groups are no longer persecuted for practising polygamy, though in one case in Utah in 2001 a polygamous man was sentenced for bigamy, in addition to being found guilty of insurance fraud and the rape of minors.[243]

The polygamous marriages in these breakaway Mormon churches are not given legal recognition. In rather the same way as gays and lesbians in many countries are campaigning to have legal recognition of same-sex marriages, some of the Mormon fundamentalists are lobbying for polygamy to be recognized in the United States.[244]

The religious sanctioning of polygamy has an impact on many aspects of the general relationship between sex and religion. Polygamy, as Luther and Augustine discovered, is a good example of the kind of problems people face when their sacred sources tell them something very different from what they themselves consider to be the true faith. In a number of ways, both the nineteenth-century Mormons and the Mormon fundamentalists of the present day have had and continue to have harsh experiences of people's insistence on trying to regulate the sex lives of others according to their own religious convictions. Given that polyandry, as the reflex of polygyny, is so rare, the religious sanctioning of polygamy also highlights how extreme the differences are between religious rules for men and those for women. It is absurd to talk of equal status for men and women within religion if absolute monogamy is demanded of women whereas men are allowed a number of wives. This remains a problem in spite of efforts to find a solution that gives the sexes equal status. How can a woman be given the right to take multiple husbands if all the sacred sources forbid it? And on what basis can a man be forbidden to have multiple wives if the same sources permit it?

Most importantly, perhaps, polygamy represents a corrective to the claims that monogamous heterosexual marriage is self-evidently natural – claims that are voiced particularly commonly in Christian contexts. But Christian sources themselves do not actually give monogamous heterosexual marriage that kind of unique status.

Outside Marriage

On 5 July 2007 in the town of Aghche Kand in north-eastern Iran, Jafar Kiani had his hands tied behind his back before being buried up to his waist. In this position, with his upper body above the ground, he was stoned to death with stones that were not too big, so they would not kill him too quickly. The 'crime' that Kiani had been found guilty of was that he had had extramarital heterosexual intercourse with a married woman some ten years earlier.[245]

There is no contradiction between the generally positive Islamic views on heterosexuality and Jafar Kiani's tragic fate. What we can see here is an example of one of the clearest boundaries within the acceptance of heterosexuality that is by no means unique to Islam, but found in the great majority of religions: the boundary between heterosexuality within marriage and heterosexuality outside marriage.

Jafar Kiani was found guilty according to Iranian law, which is mainly based on sharia – Islamic law. But the notion of stoning people for extramarital heterosexuality is also enshrined in a book found in the shelves of many Western homes. The Bible tells us, in Deuteronomy, that 'If a man be found lying with a woman married to an husband, then they shall both of them die, both the man that lay with the woman and the woman.' The rationale for the death penalty is given immediately afterwards, when God declares: 'so shalt thou put away evil from Israel.'[246] If the writers of the

Pentateuch did not receive this message directly from God himself, they may possibly have been influenced by the oldest extant legal work, the Code of Hammurabi. This Mesopotamian work from 1700–1800 BC, reportedly also a divine composition, declares that an unfaithful woman should be drowned along with her lover.[247]

In considering that stoning is recommended in the Bible for a variety of extramarital sexual acts, we need to pay particular attention to the sex of those involved. Even though every heterosexual act by its very nature involves both sexes, the religious rules applied to men certainly do not always conform with those applicable to women. We have already noted this in connection with premarital regulations. A married woman risks being stoned if she has sex with any other man than the man she is married to: the law demands the death penalty even if she is raped.[248] Men, on the other hand, are free to have sex with unmarried women both before and outside marriage. The fact that the Pentateuch does not prohibit prostitution is relevant in this context,[249] and the Bible contains references to quite a number of female prostitutes. Thus the commandment 'Thou shalt not commit adultery'[250] does not apply in practice to all extramarital sex. Men are only forbidden to have sex with women who are married or engaged to other men. Whether a man himself is married or not is irrelevant when it comes to punishment for illegal sex. Thus it is not marriage itself that is being protected by the law codes, but the husband's sole right to his wife. The law is ensuring that a man's honour is protected from the injury that would result from her having sex with someone else.[251]

Judaism ceased to have a death penalty for sexual crimes after antiquity: this was not just because Jewish communities, being minority groups, were not usually in a position to impose the death penalty, but because Rabbinic literature reveals a fairly consistent aversion to the death penalty.

The Koran does not include a commandment that people should be stoned for extramarital heterosexuality even though Caliph Umar, who knew Muhammad, claimed that there had originally been a commandment to that effect in the holy book.[252] Nevertheless, Islam follows the basic biblical principle that extramarital sex is properly subject to religious law. According to Islam all extramarital sex is sinful – *zina* – and conflicts with true teachings. Since it is evil and abhorrent, extramarital sex can lead to even worse things[253] and thus be a threat to the whole Islamic order. Therefore, according to the Koran, anyone guilty of being unfaithful should be punished with a hundred lashes.[254]

Although the Koran itself makes no mention of the death penalty for heterosexual adultery, tradition shows that Muhammad demanded it, and many different hadiths bear witness to this.[255] There is not necessarily a contradiction between the Prophet's command and the fact that the Koran has nothing to say about capital punishment for extramarital heterosexuality. Muhammad linked his own call for the death penalty for illegal sex to the Pentateuch,[256] which Islam also considers to represent divine tradition. Muhammad himself saw to it that a Jewish man and woman who had committed adultery were stoned in accordance with the Bible. The event is described by Umar, the later caliph: 'I was one of those who stoned them, and I saw him protecting her with his body . . . leaning over the woman to protect her from the stones.'[257]

Muhammad commands that those condemned for adultery should be given a hundred lashes, as the Koran prescribes, but the Prophet also makes it clear that the adulterous individuals should be stoned after the whipping.[258] Even though stoning is the normal punishment for adultery, there are certain measures to be taken before the sentence can be carried out. On one occasion a woman came to the Prophet, admitted to adultery and said she was pregnant. He told her to return when she had borne the child, which she did. Then he told her to return when she had weaned the child, which she also did. Then he told her to give the child away to other people. When she returned for the third time, no longer pregnant and with no child, the Prophet had her buried up to the chest and 'commanded people and they stoned her'.[259]

Yet there is still hope for people condemned to death for adultery because if one dies praising none but Allah, one will still gain entry to paradise. So said the Prophet.[260]

At the same time as demanding such severe punishment for those having extramarital sex, Islam demands very firm proof of the crime. Before anyone may be punished there must either be a confession or four male witnesses.[261] The following account reveals how firmly Muhammad insisted on this. A man asked the Prophet what he should do if he found another man lying with his wife at home: 'Should I leave him there until I had brought four witnesses?' 'Yes', answered the Prophet.[262]

People are warned against making accusations based on insufficient evidence. Anyone who falsely accuses a slave of adultery will be punished on the day of resurrection.[263] Those who make false or unfounded accusations can also expect more immediate punishment: 'Those who accuse chaste women and cannot produce four witnesses, whip them with eighty lashes.'[264]

The strict demand for proof also left a rather original opening that many Muslims have taken advantage of, more or less consciously. In the thirteenth century, for instance, the Tunisian Ahmad Ibn Yusuf al-Tifashi wrote a book, *The Delight of Hearts, Or What you will not Find in any Book*, on how one might enjoy various forms of forbidden sex without being disturbed. Among much practical advice on the topic, we can find tips on how to recognize a willing woman at a distance or behind her veil.[265]

Even though the Islamic code on adultery is the same for both sexes, equal status does not really enter the picture. Since the rules permit men to have up to four wives and also to have sex with slave women and concubines,[266] the notion of what constitutes male infidelity is a rather more limited one from the outset. Because women can become pregnant, female infidelity is often easier to prove, which in turn means that more women than men are found guilty of sexual offences. Men, however, are not exempt from the harshest punishments once they *are* found guilty – as we can read in the hadiths and as the Iranian Jafar Kiani discovered so painfully in 2007.

Rape presents Islam with a particular challenge since, in common with other illegal sex and as a matter of principle, either a confession or four male witnesses are required to obtain a conviction. A rape victim who reports the attack can end up being charged with illegal sex if the rape occurs outside marriage. The very act of reporting the crime is a confession on the part of the victim that she or he has had either pre- or extramarital sex or been involved in a male homosexual act. If the victim cannot prove the rape, she or he is at risk of being punished as a result. A United Nations study in Afghanistan showed, for example, that around half of the women in prison in 2006 were there because they had been charged with pre- or extramarital sex, but the real reason was that many of these women were the victims of rape.[267] In Pakistan, until the rape laws were changed in 2006, it was also the case that many rape victims were charged with immorality or adultery. When the law was changed, the Islamic six-party alliance protested vehemently because it meant that rape was no longer subject to sharia law.[268]

It would, however, be too easy to conclude that the current Islamic view of sex is identical to the one we meet in the Koran and in tradition. There are huge differences in the extent to which Muslims really believe these laws to be relevant. Many people reject them altogether and believe that God is not particularly concerned with the way people practise their sexuality. Others consider that individuals should not be punished for consensual sexual activity while still believing that extramarital sex is not compatible with Islam. Nevertheless, many Muslims really believe extramarital sex to be so fundamentally in conflict with Islamic principles that it is impossible to ignore the traditional demand for severe punishments.

The extent to which Muslims relate to the ban on extramarital sex shows great variation. A 1992 survey revealed, for instance, that as many as 45 per cent of the mainly Muslim inhabitants of Uzbekistan thought it was quite acceptable to have a lover as well as a spouse. Statistics from its equally Muslim neighbour Tajikistan, on the other hand, showed that only 14 per cent of the population considered infidelity of that kind to be acceptable.[269] Popular literature, too, reveals divergent attitudes, as we can see in the classic love story *Heer Ranjha*, written by the Indian Sufi Muslim poet Waris Shah in the eighteenth century. In this story a woman leaves her husband and elopes with her lover. When they are caught and brought before the ruler, they curse the city for its injustice. God listens to the prayers of the adulterous couple and immediately sets fire to the city.[270] It may not be common but, as here, it is possible for Muslims to conceive of God ranking true love above the institution of marriage.

Christianity did not originally have such clear-cut judicial rules about extramarital heterosexuality. Quite the opposite. The Jesus of the Gospels intervened directly to prevent the execution of the woman taken in adultery. However, it was not that he considered adultery excusable, for he said to the woman: 'Go, and sin no more.'[271] On another occasion he declared that those who commit adultery would go straight to hell.[272] But since he prevented the stoning of the adulterous woman, it seems that Jesus believed that a matter of this kind was not for human justice to judge, while simultaneously making it clear that extramarital sex will lead to eternal damnation. According to Jesus, then, it is God, not our fellow man, who will be the judge of our sexual behaviour.

Given that St Paul considers marriage an emergency refuge for those who cannot manage to be sexually abstinent, it follows logically that he believed that infidelity conflicted with God's teaching. But not even Paul proposes punishment in this world for those guilty of adultery; he simply emphasizes that they will not 'inherit the Kingdom of God'.[273] The tone of his condemnation is thus milder than that of Jesus. The Epistle to the Ephesians, which many believe was not written by Paul, similarly stresses that 'no whoremonger . . . hath any inheritance in the kingdom of Christ and of God.'[274] While Paul focuses on the exclusion of sexual sinners, the Epistle to the Hebrews puts more weight on explicitly negative sanctions and states 'but whoremongers and adulterers God will *judge*.'[275] Thus these other biblical sources seem to accord with Jesus; both regard adultery as synonymous with damnation and state that it is not for people in this world to punish it. In spite of Jesus and Paul both recognizing that illicit sex was something that only God should punish, when Christians came to power they quickly began using the legal system to ensure that the population followed the proper sexual course. Since the Bible made the point that adultery resulted in going to hell, it seemed right to have laws to frighten people away from it. People quickly forgot that Jesus himself did not want such matters to be in the hands of human justice.

In Christianity, too, there was traditionally a wide divergence between the treatment of adulterous men and adulterous women, though there is no basis for this in the New Testament. The attitudes to women prostitutes frequently provide us with telling examples of this. The early medieval books of penance recommended that prostitutes be excommunicated, whereas nothing was proposed for their male customers even if they were married men.[276] In general, prostitutes tended to be tacitly accepted as an outlet for extramarital male sexuality. Both Augustine and Thomas Aquinas defended the existence of prostitution as a means of preventing what they thought of as greater sins, such as men having sex with other men's wives.[277] Martin Luther, however, rejected the tacit acceptance of prostitution.[278]

The definition of what constituted adultery was frequently more limited for men than for women. In Orthodox Russian tradition men were only defined as having been unfaithful if they produced children outside marriage, whereas for women the sexual act alone was sufficient.[279] Early Protestant Europe also provides us with examples of wide differences. Women were not only found guilty of heterosexual crimes much more frequently than men, but the law itself often made a consistent distinction between men and women. In colonial New England a man was only punished severely if the woman he was with was married or engaged – the woman, on the other hand, faced a harsh punishment anyway.[280] A law introduced in Geneva in 1566 made a married woman liable to the death penalty for adultery whereas a man would get away with twelve days in jail. The English law on adultery of 1650 made both parties liable to the death penalty for adultery if the woman was married, but if only the man was married the punishment was a mere three months in prison.[281]

In Hinduism, gender is a consistently decisive factor in religious attitudes to infidelity. In epic literature and Hindu classical texts, extramarital sex is presented quite simply as part of a man's life.[282] The *Kamasutra*, for instance, describes how men are free to have sex with low-caste women, with women who have lost their caste or with prostitutes, but cannot marry any of these. Sex with women of this kind is just for pleasure.[283]

Female prostitution was widely accepted in Hinduism and the prostitute had a position in society that was determined by her karma.[284] Upper-class men had educated and precious courtesans while more common prostitutes were available to other men.[285] Whereas a wide range of sexual possibilities is open to men, unfaithful women, according to the *Laws of Manu*, deserve to be devoured by dogs.[286] The *Kamasutra*, however, does concede a woman the right to be 'mildly offended by her husband's infidelities', though she should not complain too much. A wife should not scold her husband, rather she should 'rebuke him with conciliatory words, whether he be in the company of friends or alone'.[287]

But men do not have it all their own way in Hinduism. They should not commit a crime against other men – that is, sleep with other men's wives. To sleep with the wife of one's teacher is particularly deplorable.[288] The injunctions against adultery and the bad karmic consequences that result from it give rise to some creative solutions for people who find too little excitement in sexual fidelity. The sixteenth-century erotic text *Ananga Ranga* takes as its starting point the fact that extramarital sex can easily lead to disaster and then goes on to describe so many sexual positions that the married couple will feel as if they had had thirty-two partners.[289]

The Dalai Lama, commenting in 2010 on the effectively public extramarital affairs of a fellow Buddhist, the golf star Tiger Woods, stated that 'all religions have the same idea' about adultery.[290] Yet as we have seen this is not the full story, and a blanket condemnation of that sort is not so simple even in Buddhism. The generally negative view of sex taken by Buddhism does not prevent some kinds of sex as being perceived as worse than others, and adultery quite clearly comes into this category. Adultery is frequently compared with killing, lying, drunkenness and theft but, along with these, it is also one of the worst deeds one can commit in relation to both ethics in general and karmic consequences. As the classical Pali text *Sutta Nipata* stated in the first century BC: 'If a man is unable to lead a celibate life, he should not go to another's wife.'[291] The choice of words is not accidental in that the ban on adultery is as much about not doing injury to another as it is about the sex itself. The person affected by adultery is, of course, the man who is deceived.[292] The underlying premise here, as in so many other religio-sexual contexts, is that the sexuality of women is subordinate to men – it is the husband she belongs to who will suffer injury if she sleeps with someone else. The laws in Buddhist countries were consequently correspondingly gender-biased in that a woman's infidelity to her husband had legal consequences whereas a husband's infidelity to his wife did not.

What relatively few people realize is that a number of Christian countries have retained the ban on adultery even though they rarely use it. The constitutional court in Uganda abolished the legal ban on adultery in 2007 because it discriminated against women – only adulterous women could be punished, not men.[293] The general secretary of the Ugandan joint council for the Catholic, Anglican and Orthodox churches immediately asked the authorities to institute a new law against adultery, this time punishing men as well as women.[294]

A number of American states still have laws against adultery, although in practical terms all such laws are dormant. Even the state attorney in Michigan was surprised to discover in 2007 that the state law on adultery could lead to a life sentence.[295] As recently as 2004, John R. Bushey Jr was sentenced to twenty hours community service in Virginia for adultery.[296] David Scott from Britain and Cynthia Delfino from the Philippines discovered in 2008 that there are still Christian countries where adultery laws are anything but dormant. Since Delfino's divorce from her husband was still not final, she and Scott were charged with adultery, arrested and thrown into jail in Manila. The fact that they already had a child together was sufficient proof of what they had done. According to the laws of that strictly Catholic country, the couple were liable to up to seven years in prison. Instead of waiting to find out how the Philippines' courts would interpret the law in their case, they absconded from prison, fled to Thailand and from there home to Britain.[297]

It is difficult to find any really accurate figures on the frequency of adultery in the various religions today. There are often marked differences between groups belonging to the same religion but living in different countries. A 2005 survey showed, for instance, that 10 per cent of adults in Poland, which is overwhelmingly Catholic, admitted to having had extramarital sex whereas in equally Catholic Italy the figure was 26 per cent. Similar variations are visible in mainly Muslim countries, with Turkey showing 58 per cent whereas Indonesia only shows 16 per cent.[298] Another reason for the difficulty in coming up with accurate figures is that surveys can only base themselves on what people say. From surveys in the US it would appear that the level of an individual's involvement in institutionalized religion is a factor that lessens the likelihood of adultery.[299] But because of the strong condemnation of adultery in precisely these religious circles, it is difficult to take the results of such surveys as absolute facts since they are based solely on people's own responses. There is, after all, no shortage of politicians and religious leaders – particularly in the United States – who have publicly and vehemently condemned extramarital sex only to be exposed for adultery themselves.

Adultery, like any other consensual sex between adults, is protected by the human rights legislation for private life.[300] However, it is among the few forms of consensual sex not to have found serious advocates either within or outside the sphere of religion. Although sexual infidelity may be no more and no less than one among the many varieties of consensual sex, it is nevertheless a form of behaviour that involves others apart from those actively participating in it. By its very nature, adultery means that at least one of the parties is married, which means in turn that she or he – frequently only she – has entered an agreement that includes sexual fidelity. The breach of promise adds an extra dimension. Even if a state does not have the right to punish those who commit adultery, the deed can nevertheless have judicial consequences, and since adultery usually involves a breach of contract, it often gives the injured party certain rights when it comes to divorce.

The specifically religious condemnation of adultery is paralleled by a more general lack of acceptance of marital infidelity in many societies. Only the harshest punishments hit the headlines. It is not only in Iran that men and women are still being sentenced to death for improper heterosexual activity: the same situation pertains in the United Arab Emirates, Nigeria, Pakistan, Saudi Arabia and Sudan. A number of other Muslim countries have less severe punishments for adultery. Western politicians and human rights advocates in general have sometimes become very involved on behalf of individuals, particularly women, who are waiting to be executed or have been executed. What is interesting is that their involvement is not motivated by the fact that adultery is banned but by the fact it carries the death penalty. Not many people have lobbied for countries to remove the ban on adultery, even though such a ban conflicts with the human rights protection of all consensual sex between adults.

The EU's sharp protest to the governing Islamic party in Turkey when it tried to reintroduce the ban on adultery in 2004 is to some extent an exception. The earlier law had been removed by the constitutional court in 1996, not because of a general human rights principle against punishing consensual sex but because it punished women more severely than men and was thereby counter to the human rights principle of gender equality.[301]

The fact that women are the most frequent targets of the religious ban on adultery both strengthens and weakens the parallels between religious precepts and more everyday ethics, depending on how widespread the differing standards for the sexes are in any given society. The ever greater emphasis on gender equality means that the religious practice of punishing adulterous women more than adulterous men is causing a problem that many religions are finding difficult to explain away. As we saw in the cases of Turkey and Uganda, the very fact that religion-inspired laws often punish women alone – or punish them more harshly – has caused those laws to be repealed as being contrary to the legal principle of gender equality.

Getting out of Marriage

Two Orthodox Jewish women – Michelle, mother of three, and Dani, mother of four – were left by their husbands at the end of the 1990s. The men, however, had no wish to get divorced even though both were having open affairs with other women and had fathered children with them. According to Orthodox Judaism, only men have the right to apply for divorce, so Michelle and Dani had no choice but to remain married.

Marriage and divorce in Israel are regulated by religious – not secular – authorities. All Jews, irrespective of the branch of Judaism they belong to, are automatically subject to the Orthodox Jewish courts as these are the only courts Israel recognizes in the sphere of Jewish family law. The only way to avoid the jurisdiction of the religious authorities is to get married abroad. The cases of Michelle and Dani, which are depicted in the 2004 documentary film *Mekudeshet* or *Sentenced to Be Married*, are by no means unique and many Jewish women in Israel live in a similar situation. Even if Michelle and Dani's husbands openly admitted to their relationships with other women, the Orthodox religious courts would not allow the women a divorce unless the men agreed to it. Meanwhile Michelle and Dani are not permitted to meet or marry other men whereas the men who deserted them can effectively do what they like so long as they don't remarry.[302]

The rules governing divorce form an important element of religio-sexual regulation, not least because they offer an effective way for religions to limit the number of sexual partners people may have. Adultery, the alternative to divorce, is one of the few acts of consensual sex still disapproved of by the majority of believers, whatever their faith. Those religions that succeed in limiting access to divorce thus also limit the possibilities for married people to have sex with anyone other than their original spouse.

Since the majority of religions generally put more emphasis on controlling the sexual behaviour of women, it hardly comes as a surprise to find that the mismatch between the religio-sexual rights of men and those of women is frequently reflected in the religious rules pertaining to divorce. At the same time, we can see that divorce is one of the areas in which religions have had to surrender control over their own followers to a great extent over the course of the last century. It is also worth noting that some religions have traditionally viewed divorce as completely unproblematic, both for men and for women.

If we go to the Pentateuch we find a fairly straightforward rule regarding divorce. When a man marries a woman and 'it comes to pass she find no favour in his eyes', perhaps 'because he hath found some uncleanness in her', then all he has to do is to 'write her a bill of divorcement and give it in her hand, and send her out of his house'.[303] If the husband changes his mind, he is free to remarry the same woman, but only if she has been not married to another man in the interim. Should the first husband remarry her in that situation, it is considered an 'abomination before the Lord'.[304]

There was, however, one kind of woman a man could not divorce. If a man was caught red-handed with a virgin who was not promised to another man, he must not only pay the virgin's father fifty shekels, but must also marry her, and 'he may not put her away all her days'.[305]

The wife's view of being divorced and thrown out of her home on the whim of her husband was irrelevant. Women did not have any comparable right to divorce although some certainly took the law into their own hands. In Judges we hear of a concubine who became angry with her Levite husband and 'went away from him to her father's house to Bethlehem'.[306] The concubine would never have been given a formal divorce, however, unless her husband gave it to her, and the only real hope for women wanting a divorce was that her husband would find 'some uncleanness in her' or quite simply get tired of her.

Rabbinic Judaism continued to allow men to divorce and to deny that right to women. As it says in *Mishnah*, 'a woman may be divorced with or without her consent, a man can be divorced only with his full consent'.[307] Once a woman is divorced, her sexuality is no longer governed by the rules for married women. The formal declaration of divorce that a husband is legally bound to give his wife includes confirmation that she is now 'permitted to any man'.[308] Shortly after the Islamic conquest of Mesopotamia, Jewish scholars gave women the right to divorce but this right was abolished in the course of the thirteenth century.[309]

In the eleventh century the famous Talmudic scholar Gershom ben Judah successfully proposed to the Ashkenazi Jews that a husband must have his wife's agreement to a divorce, a significant limitation of the man's original right,[310] but most Sephardic Jews have never accepted this limitation.[311] When national divorce laws in Western countries were liberalized and Jews could legally divorce irrespective of the stricter religious regulations, Jews who remarried according to the civil law were considered to be living adulterously and any children they had were considered illegitimate.[312] Modern Reformed Jews now accept a common right to divorce and see no mismatch between religious and civil divorce laws but, as we have seen, many Orthodox Jews still stick to the traditional gender-biased right to divorce.

Islam starts from the same position as Judaism: a man has the right to divorce, a woman does not. Islam, however, has operated with more comprehensive divorce regulations right from the beginning: the whole of Chapter 65 in the Koran is devoted to the topic and, indeed, is known by the name *al-Talaq*, 'divorce'. The husband is explicitly forbidden to simply drive his wife out of her home in the manner of the Pentateuch and a period of separation is compulsory.[313] According to the hadith, both Caliph Umar and Muhammad's nephew Ali thought that the period of separation should begin with the husband swearing an oath to abstain from sex with his wife. The separation should last four months.[314] Once the period of separation is over, the husband should either take his wife back 'with kindness' or divorce her 'with kindness'. Should he decide that divorce is what he wants, he cannot simply put a letter into his wife's hands. He must have two male witnesses to his declaration of divorce.[315] The man is also duty-bound to support his ex-wife according to his economic ability, especially if she is pregnant.[316]

The better-known and widespread custom of the husband repeating three times 'I divorce you' is legally binding within Islam but there are many Muslims who see it as a sinful misuse of male rights and in conflict with the Koran.[317] Very many countries with Muslim populations do not consider such a declaration of divorce legally valid within their national legislative systems and they consequently compel Muslim men to follow a more comprehensive divorce procedure.[318]

Muslim women, like their Jewish sisters, did not originally have any right to demand a divorce, but there are considerable regional differences in this. There is traditional acceptance of women taking out divorce on their own initiative in Western Sahara, for instance, a territory largely occupied by Morocco.[319] Many Muslim countries today allow women to divorce for a whole range of reasons, many of the legal changes being based on interpretations of the Koran.[320] Turkey and Sudan both gave women the right to initiate divorce proceedings at the beginning of the twentieth century.[321] Women in Iran have a number of divorce possibilities, often depending on what is stated in their marriage contracts.[322] In 2004 Morocco introduced a law enabling women to sue for divorce.[323]

Christianity has taken a very different view of divorce to Islam and Judaism right from the start. Jesus pronounced that all those who remarry after divorce are by definition committing adultery and will be cast into hell. Even if a divorced man himself remains single, it will be of no avail, because he will be guilty of the adultery that is being committed by his ex-wife if she remarries. In the view of Jesus, fornication was the only legitimate grounds for divorce, but even this exception may be a later interpolation in the text rather than something Jesus actually said.[324]

The fact that Jesus did not say a great deal about sexuality has often been perceived as a problem since it has forced Christians to try to draw conclusions from other things he said. But Jesus is crystal clear about divorce: it is forbidden and leads straight to damnation.

It is no good going back and trying to moderate Jesus's statements by showing that men in the Old Testament had the right to do what they wanted. The starting-point for Jesus's discussion of divorce was precisely the Pentateuch rules under which a man had the right to leave his marriage: Jesus rejects them out of hand and says they are not strict enough.[325] There is nothing else in the New Testament on which one can base an argument that Christians should have the right to divorce. Paul permits a *non-Christian* to take the initiative to divorce, in which case the Christian half of the partnership, whether male or female, is no longer 'under bondage'.[326] But a Christian has no right to leave a non-Christian spouse. The starting point for Christianity, then, is totally indisputable: divorce is strictly forbidden.

Given that it is impossible to interpret Jesus's teaching and the rest of the New Testament as anything other than a complete ban on divorce, it is particularly interesting to observe the extent to which divorce is either fully accepted or not regarded as a problem by the majority of modern Christians. Even many otherwise quite conservative Christians find divorce acceptable. The first and so far only divorced president to occupy the White House was Ronald Reagan, who was elected with massive support from the conservative

Christian right. John McCain, the 2008 presidential candidate supported by the great majority of American Christian conservatives, was also divorced without it ever becoming a significant issue.

When Per Oskar Kjølaas, Bishop of North Hålogaland, became the first Norwegian bishop to start divorce proceedings, there were only a few conservative Læstadian ministers who demanded that he demit office. Bishop Olav Skjevesland, primus of the Church of Norway, did not even find Jesus's total ban on divorce to be a problem. Indeed, rather the contrary, he considered 'this to be a private matter which does not concern the public at large'. It is 'perfectly possible to be a divorced bishop', he argued. According to the primus of the church, the bishop's divorce did not have any 'aspects that affected his official role' – in spite of the total ban in the Bible.[327]

A number of the early church fathers believed that even where a divorce resulted from adultery the innocent party did not have the right to remarry.[328] Tertullian, for example, was utterly clear when he stated that a second marriage 'can be called nothing other than a form of fornication'.[329] But the traditional gender biases soon surfaced again. The Council of Elvira in Spain at the beginning of the fourth century, for instance, demanded that the husband *must* divorce if his wife was unfaithful, but if the husband was unfaithful the wife would have no divorce rights at all.[330] In the Orthodox Byzantine Empire a man had the right to divorce his wife not only for adultery but also if she frequented notorious locales like race-tracks or public baths. In the case of the husband, however, adultery alone was not sufficient grounds for divorce; the adultery needed to be particularly public or directly disruptive in terms of society.[331]

As well as the gender difference there was also the social difference between high and low. Charlemagne himself, whose civil law banned remarriage after divorce, married and divorced a number of times.[332] But as we all remember from our history books, it was not always so easy for monarchs to escape from their marriages either by divorce or annulment. The pope refused to allow King Henry VIII of England to leave his first wife, a refusal that contributed to the break between the Catholic and Anglican churches.

The Reformation did not open the way for divorce to become more common even in England. Adultery was the only grounds for divorce accepted by the Anglican Church up until 1857. It was not easy to get out of a marriage even if you had an adulterous spouse: only sixteen divorces were ratified between 1670 and 1749.[333] In other Protestant countries divorce could be sanctioned if there was proof of adultery or impotence and sometimes if the spouse had an infectious disease, changed religion or was found guilty of a serious crime. Even then, in many countries the divorce rate in the early modern period ran at only about two a year per 100,000 inhabitants,[334] compared with 350 per 100,000 in the usa in 2008.[335]

In formal terms the Catholic Church has retained its zero tolerance of divorce, and although it circumvents its own ban by annulling marriages in quite significant numbers, it has consistently opposed most efforts to legalize divorce in Catholic countries. The Catholic Church resisted strongly, for instance, when the Span ish republic legalized divorce in 1932 but fortunately from the Catholic point of view, Franco reversed this decision when his Fascists took power a few years later.[336] The Vatican succeeded in torpedoing a divorce law proposal in Italy in 1921[337] and also did what it could to convince Italians to vote against a new law legalizing divorce in a referendum in 1974: 59 per cent of the overwhelmingly Catholic Italians, however, voted to retain their new right to divorce.

The Lutheran state church in Denmark has created a ceremony for divorce,[338] but that kind of Christian institutionalization of divorce is still rare. The most important evidence for the complete change of attitude to divorce among Christians is quite simply the number of people who go ahead and divorce. The proportion of marriages that end in divorce in European Protestant countries runs at between 40 and 50 per cent. In Catholic countries we not only find that very many people live in direct opposition to the official teachings of the Catholic church but that religious affiliation is not the only deciding factor. There are significant variations between different European Catholic countries: in Belgium, Liechtenstein, Lithuania, Luxembourg, Hungary and Austria the divorce rate is over 40 per cent, whereas in Italy, Croatia, Poland and Spain it is less than 20 per cent.[339]

Buddhism's initial position with regard to divorce is one of neutrality, which is clearly related to the fact that neither sex nor marriage are ranked very high in that religion. Divorce has traditionally been accepted and easy to get in Buddhist countries such as Sri Lanka, Burma and Thailand,[340] but when we look at Buddhist practice in a number of other countries, it is apparent that there have often been difficulties, particularly for women. Confucian beliefs, as well as those of other religions, have contributed to the situation being more of a problem for women in countries like Vietnam and China.[341] In Japan, where Buddhism shares first place with Shintoism among the country's religions, it was virtually impossible for a woman to get a divorce before 1947 unless she had the agreement of her husband, whereas a husband, or even the husband's family, could gain a divorce for no other reason than that they no longer liked the wife. If a wife did not become pregnant, the husband's family could push through a divorce even if the husband himself had no desire for one. Adultery on the part of the husband did not give the wife grounds for divorce whereas adultery by a wife was clear grounds for divorce.[342]

The only way a Japanese Buddhist woman could get a divorce on her own initiative was by becoming a nun,[343] but of course this meant that there was no possibility of her remarrying; and women who became nuns in this way were considered to be of lower status than other nuns.[344]

In its origins Buddhism is an offshoot of Hinduism but there are few parallels in their views on divorce. Divorce is highly problematic for Hinduism since marriage is viewed as an eternal union which will endure through several lives and in heaven. This explains why women should not remarry if they are widowed; men did not have the same problem because they were permitted to take several wives.

There are, however, plenty of exceptions – as so often in Hinduism. People who are casteless or members of the lowest castes have traditionally had easier access to divorce, as have India's many tribal peoples. It is rather more surprising that divorce was even practised by the very highest castes in parts of the Punjab and Maharashtra.[345] The rules on divorce were to a large extent dependent on which caste an individual belonged to and in many castes divorce was traditionally permitted if both parties agreed.[346] In some castes, however, the man has the right to divorce his wife whatever she herself might want.[347] In some castes there did exist some possibility for a woman to get a divorce on her own initiative, either by paying the husband all the wedding expenses,[348] or if the husband was impotent, had disappeared or had become an ascetic.[349]

The modern Indian family legislation applicable to Hindus was adopted in 1955 and makes divorce generally available as well as putting women and men on an equal footing as far as divorce and the annulment of marriage are concerned. A number of high-caste spokesmen declared this to be a symptom of religious and cultural decline.[350] A marriage may, for example, be annulled if the husband turns out to be impotent or if the woman was pregnant by another man at the time of the marriage. Adultery, cruelty, leprosy, venereal disease, desertion, becoming an ascetic, entering a religious order or no longer being a Hindu all became grounds for divorce for both men and women.[351] Kenya and Uganda introduced very similar laws for Hindus in 1960 and 1961 respectively.[352] And since 1976 Indian Hindus have had the right to divorce for no other reason than that one or both parties, after one year's separation, desire to do so.[353]

It is not possible to categorize religious attitudes to divorce simply on the basis of whether the particular religions permit it or not. Examined more closely, there are a whole series of factors that govern these attitudes. In Christianity and Hinduism there is the underlying principle of the indissolubility of marriage, which obviously means that their starting-point is that divorce is unacceptable. In Buddhism, on the other hand, the main factor is the essential irrelevance of marriage. Entry into marriage is not fundamentally considered a religious issue – consequently, neither is exiting from it. In Judaism and Islam, again, the starting-point was neither a complete prohibition nor a general acceptance of divorce. The guiding principle instead is the right of men to control the sexuality of women. Only men have the right to initiate a divorce, which means that men's right to control women is clearly ranked higher than marriage as an institution.

The more modern religious attitudes to divorce, particularly within Christianity, offer a good example of the way in which religions are capable of turning a blind eye to what they normally hold up as absolute authorities. The possibility of divorce has become so self-evident in the lives of so many Christians that most of them do not even recognize Jesus's absolute condemnation of divorce as any sort of problem. The Christian attitude to divorce is thus a very clear example of how absolute religious bans can be totally ignored if they are no longer felt to be relevant by the believers themselves.

Other Prohibitions and the Orifices of the Body

'And the Lord spake unto Moses, saying . . . "And if a man shall lie with a woman having her sickness, and shall uncover her nakedness; he hath discovered her fountain, and she hath uncovered the fountain of her blood: and both of them shall be cut off from among the people."'[354] There is little point in questioning this biblical ban on sex during menstruation: God's ban is total and those who commit this 'abomination' should be killed. This might sound more than a little extreme perhaps, but according to the Bible it is extremely important.

The point here is not to come to any final theological conclusion about what should be done to those who have menstrual sex, but to show that religious rules for heterosexual behaviour cover very much more than whether people are permitted to have sex inside or outside of marriage. The rules about sex during menstruation exemplify just one of many similar sex rules. But if we look more closely at the specific phenomenon of sex during menstruation, we quickly realize that this rule alone represents an area of some complexity.

Even though the biblical call for the death penalty for menstrual sex was absolute, there is not much to suggest that it was acted on. A little earlier, the same text – rather confusingly – refers to quite different sanctions. If a man has intercourse with a menstruating woman during the seven days she is regarded as unclean, he must merely ensure that her 'flowers' do not come upon him. Should they do so, however, he himself 'shall be unclean seven days; and all the bed whereon he lieth shall be unclean'.[355] This is also something 'the Lord spake unto Moses',[356] so it is a little difficult to know exactly what to do with people who have sex during menstruation. What is quite clear is that sex during menstruation is forbidden and perhaps it is up to the individual believer to decide whether these sexual criminals deserve the death penalty or not.

In Judaism the ban on menstrual sex is connected to a wider understanding of ritual and religious purity that includes many other sexual and non-sexual elements. Those that are best known are the rules regarding what may and may not be eaten – the latter includes pork, hares, camels, ostriches, shrimps and certain kinds of grasshopper (other kinds of grasshopper are quite acceptable).[357] Similar injunctions about uncleanliness refer to skin diseases, birth and mould on the clothing.[358] *All* sex that involves bodily fluids is unclean: 'The woman also with whom man shall lie with seed of copulation, they shall both bathe themselves in water'; and even after a ritual bath they will both 'be unclean until the even'. The same principle of uncleanliness holds for a man whose seed 'go out of him' when he is not having sex with a woman, and is not restricted to those whose seed is released with or without sex: 'every garment and every skin, whereon is the seed of copulation, shall be washed with water, and be unclean until the even'.[359] When a menstruating woman is defined as being unclean for seven days, it is hardly surprising that the combination of that level of uncleanness with sexual activity – which is also unclean – sometimes leads to fairly extreme sanctions.

Menstrual sex, however, does not stand alone as a particularly unclean variety of sex worthy of the death penalty, since the same penalty is recommended for adultery, bestiality, anal sex between men, incest and sex with those who have married into the family. All these kinds of unclean sex, along with cursing one's parents, being a wizard and eating unclean animals, are disgusting acts that both the Egyptians and 'the nation which I cast out before you' are reported to have practised.[360] Whether these things were actually practised to any extent by other peoples in the region is rather doubtful, but the *perception* that they did such things is important in the religion of the Bible. The point is that the Israelites believed it, and since God said to them, 'I the Lord am holy, and have severed you from other people, that you should be mine', the Israelites needed to take care not to imitate the peoples that lived around them.[361] If they committed such acts, the holy land itself would be 'defiled'.[362] So when the Israelites killed those who indulged in menstrual sex or ignored any of the other sexual prohibitions, they were performing a sacred act that stressed the unique nature of their relationship with God.

As with many other aspects of the biblical injunctions on ritual purity, the ban on menstrual sex was retained by Rabbinic Judaism. Even though they ignored the demand for the death penalty, the Mosaic ban on sex during the seven days a woman was 'unclean' had 'seven clean days' added to it – in other words, sex was prohibited for two whole weeks every month because of menstruation.[363]

The ban on menstrual sex was taken over by the other Abrahamic religions although the violent divine implications seem to have been largely forgotten. The Koran upholds the ban but says nothing about punishment, simply saying that men should not have sex with menstruating women because they are unclean.[364] Medieval Christianity not only banned sex during menstruation, but also during pregnancy and the period of breastfeeding. Anyone found guilty of any of these sins had to do forty days' penance.[365] The Irish Penitential of Cummean from the seventh century went a step further and forbade sex on Wednesdays, Fridays, Sundays and Saturday nights. The married couple should also abstain from sex for three forty-day periods each year – all of which leaves them with about ninety days a year when they may have sex.[366] Later in the Middle Ages embargoes of this kind were seen as less important[367] and there are very few modern Christians who would imagine that any of these things might be seen as problems from a religious point of view.

Moving east, we find that sex during menstruation is forbidden by the *Laws of Manu*.[368] These ancient texts also contain numerous other sexual prohibitions that very few modern Hindus would support. It is, apparently, a sin to have sex in the water and a man who does so must atone by doing *samtapana kricchra*,[369] that is, taking a dose of cow urine, cow dung, milk, sour milk, butter and a decoction of *kusa*-grass, after which he should fast for 24 hours.[370] Men of the three highest main castes may not have intercourse with a woman during the daytime or in a cart pulled by oxen: should he do either of these deplorable things he must pass fully clothed through a cleansing ritual bath afterwards.[371] Prohibitions of this kind seem absurd to most of us but they do demonstrate very clearly how few limitations there are on the kinds of sex that can be subject to religious regulation.

Once upon a time the Greek heroine Atalanta and her husband Melanion had sex in a temple dedicated either to Zeus or to the mother goddess Cybele. It is unclear whether they just happened upon the temple during a hunting trip or whether they were driven to it by a fit of wild desire incited by the love goddess Aphrodite, who was enraged because they had failed to make a suitable sacrifice to mark their gratitude to her. Whichever it was, they should have known better – Greek religion usually forbade people to have sex in temples. According to Ovid, the many ancient wooden images of the gods turned their eyes away from the couple copulating in the holy place. Atalanta and Melanion did not go unpunished for their sexual misdemeanour. Their necks became bent and covered in fur, their fingers curved into claws, their arms became forelegs and they sprouted tails. Suddenly they were no longer human beings, they were transformed into lions.[372]

To be transformed into animals for having sex in Greek temples was no doubt the exception but it does underline the extent to which sex was forbidden in these sacred places. The Pentateuch also forbids sex in the temple,[373] a ban that has been continued and applies to all Jewish sacred places. When the sons of Eli had sex with the women serving in God's sanctuary, their father received a message from God that, as punishment, 'in one day they shall die both of them', which indeed they did.[374] Christianity has the same general prohibition although it is more of an implicit one. The Christian ban on sex in sacred places is, however, perhaps best exemplified by the many Christian fantasies about satanic and other un-Christian rituals being performed in churches. These often involve sex in the church itself or rituals that consciously reverse church rituals.

In 1481 Giovanni Furlan was beheaded and burnt in Venice for having sex with his wife. But this was not an extreme expression of the general doubts about heterosexuality that have troubled Christianity throughout its history. Furlan's problem was that he had the *wrong* kind of sex with his wife – he had used an inappropriate orifice. The death sentence was the result of repeated sodomy or, more accurately, anal intercourse with his wife.[375] In 1578 a Frenchman in Catalonia was sentenced to lifelong slavery in the galleys for having anal sex with his wife, and men were executed in 1583 and 1619 in Saragossa for the same crime.[376] Thus the view held in certain Christian circles today that heterosexual anal sex is acceptable in that it preserves the virginity of the female partner certainly does not occupy an undisputed position in Christian sexual theology.[377] The Christian ban on anal sex was connected with the notion that sodomy and anal sex were synonymous and that it was not something men and women should be doing with each other. Anal sex was also seen as problematic because it was defined as unnatural sex; in other words, it cannot lead to procreation.

There is nothing in the Bible about anal sex between men and women. The Christian ban on anal sex is therefore based on no more than the Christian interpretation of what God believes to be proper sexual morality. The Jewish Rabbinic tradition comes up with a different interpretation: anal sex is permissible in marriage.[378] When discussing permitted sexual positions, the Islamic hadiths forbid married couples to have anal sex – but no explanation of the ban is given.[379] As in Christian thinking, however, a number of Sunni jurists draw a parallel between heterosexual anal sex and the kind of sex reportedly practised in Sodom.[380]

In the year 342 the Christian emperors Constantius and Constans prohibited all sexual relations within marriage other than vaginal sex.[381] This is not just an example of Christian concern about anal sex; it also includes oral sex. As we have seen, many conservative Christians of the present day consider oral sex a good and practical alternative for those who do not want to have sex before marriage.[382] It is obvious, then, that this is not a view that all Christians have always held – and, indeed, oral sex has frequently been considered to be rather worse than anal sex.

Augustine held that it was better for men who liked 'unnatural sex', such as anal or oral sex, to do it with prostitutes rather than their wives, the reasoning being that it was better to do such morally deplorable things with women whose salvation was already in doubt rather than endangering that of their pious wives.[383] Gratian, whose twelfth-century collection of canonical law is one of the most important works of its kind in Western Christendom, believed that this kind of 'unnatural sex' in marriage was worse than fornication and adultery.[384] Other church fathers bemoaned the fact that these appalling varieties of sexual behaviour were very difficult to prove and they had little to go on unless people confessed.[385]

Even though it is hardly an issue at the forefront of the minds of most Christians, the Christian proscription of anal and oral sex is not just ancient history. These kinds of sex quite clearly fall outside the procreative marital sex that the Catholic Church defines as being the only permissible and truly human type of sex.[386] Heterosexual anal and oral sex have also remained crimes in some modern Christian legislation. It was not until 2003 that the US Supreme Court overruled the last state laws forbidding anal and oral sex between men and women.[387] Anal sex, incidentally, provides another good example of the frequent mismatch between what people actually do and what is banned either by direct religious injunction or by laws inspired by religion. Statistics from 2005 suggest that 47 per cent of all adults in the US have had anal intercourse. In Italy, despite nine out of ten of the population being members of the

Catholic Church that harshly condemns anal sex, 50 per cent of the population admit to having had it anyway.[388]

The religious rules governing when, where and how people can have sex encompass many different ways of regulating sexuality. The restrictions on when people can have sex are concerned with rules about purity and with the desire to put strict limits on sexuality within marriage. Even in the days when the private life of married people was a good deal less private than it is now (only the very rich had their own bedrooms), regulations attempting to set time limits on sexuality were very difficult to enforce. Nor, with the exception of menstrual sex and injunctions to have sex when the woman is most fertile, have the attempts to time-limit people's sex lives been particularly well-grounded either in common sense or in religious sources. No doubt these factors go some way to explaining why religio-sexual time limitations have had such little success.

The zealous religious regulation of which orifices may be used in sex is another area that is very difficult to enforce since it involves a profound intrusion into the sex lives of partners who in other respects have a right to have sex with one another. Religio-sexual regulations have nevertheless come to focus more on defining which orifices are permissible than on time restrictions, although, once again, there are a number of different aspects involved. The heterosexual use of any orifice other than the vagina automatically means that the sex is non-procreative and consequently any religion which teaches that sex should be restricted to the purposes of procreation will condemn the sexual use of these other orifices. Once the heterosexual use of non-vaginal orifices is tolerated, however, we begin to move into a heterosexual borderland. If the definition of sex is restricted to the act of the penis penetrating the vagina, any sex but heterosexual acts is automatically defined as not 'natural'; but if the use of other orifices is tolerated, the question then arises as to why people should not permitted to do the same thing with people of the same sex.

The ban on sex in holy places and at certain other locations has been more common than temporal restrictions, but it has never been of major significance, possibly because it coincides with the basic everyday rule in most cultures that the sexual act is not something to be performed in public. Restrictions as to place have therefore seldom been widely opposed either in principle or in practice.

These religious rules for where, when and how sex may occur can act as a last reminder of how complicated heterosexuality can be from a religious point of view. At the same time, they provide good examples of the central role played by sexual matters in the various religions; there are notably few, if any, areas of sexual behaviour that religion has not tried to regulate.

It is above all the diversity of regulations that typifies the religious approach to heterosexuality. So much of the present-day debate would seem to suggest that it is only homosexuality that religions may consider problematic, but it is important to recognize clearly that various forms of heterosexuality – indeed, heterosexuality in itself – can be just as problematic from a religious viewpoint.

Even working with heterosexuality as a category per se within the various religions can itself be problematic. The rules for men and for women are so different in many religions that heterosexuality itself becomes meaningless as a category for discussing what is permitted and what is forbidden: it would be more accurate to treat female heterosexuality and male heterosexuality as separate categories.

The focus on the marital framework for sex is so absolute in some of the religions that it would be meaningful to operate with marital and non-marital sex as the most important categories. In an approach of this kind, the question of whether the sex was heterosexual or some other kind of non-marital sex would be less than relevant: anything other than marital sex is equally condemned.

There are other religions that classify sex on the basis of whether it can lead to procreation or not, and they bless or condemn it accordingly. The sex of the partner and the choice of orifice are clearly relevant factors here, but these would not in themselves be the factors that would determine which kind of sex was considered correct in terms of religion.

There is a clear tendency, observable in perhaps the majority of today's religions, to give greater recognition to heterosexuality as a category per se. This, to a great extent, is the result of homosexuality being so clearly defined as a category in its own right, both by the religions and by society in general. Once the sex of the partner has become the major factor in defining sexuality, it follows that heterosexuality, too, becomes the focus of greater attention as a meaningful category. When we look, for instance, at the usual Christian attitudes to sex between heterosexual partners in large parts of Europe, it becomes obvious that for many people it is no longer an issue whether the sex is performed within the framework of marriage or outside it. Marital sexuality has thus largely been replaced by heterosexuality as the dominant category in religio-sexual discourse.

5

Homosexuality: Expected, Compulsory, Condemned

At the end of the sixteenth century a frustrated man by the name of Mitsuo Sadatomo was wandering in the wilderness in Japan. He was hoping to receive miraculous inspiration from the Buddhist monk and holy man Kobo Daishi, who had lived in the ninth century. Mitsuo sat for sixteen days praying in isolation without anything happening. But his efforts were not to be in vain. On the seventeenth day the holy and long-dead monk revealed himself to the patient Mitsuo and guided the pious man in all 'the mysteries of loving young boys'.

The story of Mitsuo Sadatomo and his encounter with the Buddhist saint who had such wondrous insight into sacred homosexuality was written by Mitsuo himself. It is the introduction to his *Kobo Daishi's Book*, published in 1598. The rest of the book contains detailed advice from the holy Kobo Daishi (also known as Kukai) on how monks can interpret various hints from male novices, how to seduce them, and what kinds of sexual techniques and positions monks should use once they have got the attention of the young boys.[1]

Kobo Daishi's view that sex between men was a sacred mystery is not exactly typical of religious attitudes to homosexuality. It does, however, offer an important corrective in that there is so much concentration on religious condemnation of same-sex sexuality that one might easily conclude that that is the only view. The fact that the majority of religions are more negative towards homosexuality than to married heterosexuality does not, however, mean that there is a fundamental clash between religion and homosexuality. As Mitsuo's visions reveal, homosexual sex can just as easily be seen as sacred as damned. There is nothing in the nature of religion that means it must be homophobic.

As a number of scholars have pointed out, homosexuality is by no means unproblematic as a category. Just as we saw in the case of heterosexuality, the idea of homosexuality as a single uniform classification is alien to many religions and cultures. In many religious and cultural contexts, for example, it is not the sex of your sexual partner that is significant but what you actually do with him or her. In many other religious contexts, on the other hand, we have seen that gender is even more important than is normally the case today, because male and female sexuality are simply not considered to be parallel phenomena; that is also true of homosexuality.

Another important factor to bear in mind when looking at the relationship between religion and same-sex sexuality is that the gay or lesbian individual is to some extent a modern construct. The concept of homosexuality was invented in the nineteenth century. People have had sex with others of the same sex since the beginning of time, but the notion that same-sex sexuality represents a part of your identity in the way it does in modern Western society has not always been the case. At the same time, though it is difficult to find counterparts of the modern gay man or lesbian woman far back in history, there have nevertheless been very widespread ideas about people who prefer to avoid sexual relations with people of the opposite sex.

The global middle class of today tends to talk of three main categories of human sexual identity: heterosexuals, who identify themselves as being attracted to and having sex with people of the opposite sex; gays and lesbians, who identify themselves as being romantically and sexually attracted to people of the same sex; and bisexuals, who identify themselves as being romantically and sexually attracted to people of both sexes.

But these categories are not clear-cut even today. Most of the people who have sex with others of the same sex would still not define themselves as gays, lesbians or bisexuals: these are people who live mainly heterosexual lives but have or have had sex with people of the same sex, and still define themselves as either heterosexual or as nothing at all in terms of sexual categorization. A survey from 2007 reveals that slightly over 97 per cent of Australian adults would define themselves as heterosexual but 8.6 per cent of men and 15.1 per cent of women said that they were sexually attracted to others of the same sex. As many as 6.9 per cent of the men surveyed and 13.2 per cent of the women had had sexual experiences with people of the same sex.[2] Another survey suggests that as many as 22 per cent of adult Australians have had homosexual experiences.[3] In

Norway, 14 per cent of those who identify themselves as heterosexual say they are open to sex with people of the same sex, and 4 per cent have already had it. Three out of ten heterosexual women under thirty could imagine having sex with a partner of the same sex.[4] A number of surveys in Pakistan reveal that the great majority of men who have sex with men are married. Figures from 2000 show, among other things, that 49 per cent of male Pakistani lorry drivers had had sex with other men even though 83 per cent of the drivers were heterosexually married.[5] According to an Iranian survey carried out in 2009, 24 per cent of women and 16 per cent of men have had homosexual experiences.[6] Alfred Kinsey's research in the US in 1948 revealed that 37 per cent of all men had had sex with other men, whereas the equivalent figure for women was 14 per cent.[7] In a Moscow survey, 42 per cent of the mainly Russian Orthodox medical students questioned responded that they had 'discovered masturbation . . . through someone else'; that is, other men and boys.[8] A survey in 1963 showed that 44 per cent of all male students (both Muslim and Christian) at the American University in Beirut admitted to having had sex with other men.[9]

It is worth keeping some of this in mind when we look more closely at the changing religious attitudes to homosexuality. When working in this kind of terrain, it is a challenge to find working categories that are meaningful both to ourselves and also in different religious and cultural contexts.

Sacred Homosexuality

Mitsuo Sadatomo's Buddhist visions of sacred homosexuality do not stand alone in the religious landscape, even though they cannot be said to represent the dominant view. None of the great religions takes an unequivocally positive view of homosexuality but in all of them we find more positive views from time to time. If we look at modern religious landscapes we will find believers within every religion who argue that their religion must be regarded as taking a positive view of homosexuality.

Mitsuo is, in fact, fairly representative in the context of Japanese Buddhism. Buddhist monasteries in Japan were widely known as places where homosexual love affairs took place, usually between men of different ages and status. Some men entered monasteries precisely because of their love for other men.[10]

Buddhism and male homosexuality were seen as closely associated with each other in Japan. The bodhisattva Kobo Daishi, who instructed Mitsuo in the field of sex between men, was often credited with being the man who introduced both esoteric Buddhism and male homosexuality to Japan during the ninth century.[11] A specific narrative genre, *chigo monogatari*, telling of the relationships between monks and young novices (*chigo*), flourished from the fourteenth to the sixteenth century. These stories usually end with the monk losing his beloved novice but, through the loss, the monk achieves a higher plane of consciousness. It frequently emerges that the young novice is actually a manifestation of a great bodhisattva, a Buddhist saint, who endows the monk with deeper insight by means – among other things – of homosexual acts.[12]

Kitamura Kigin, a scholar and counsellor of the Tokugawa shoguns, published his *Rock Azaleas* in 1667. It is a collection of homoerotic poems, once again with Buddhism at its core. Most of the poems are declarations of love written by monks to different novices, the oldest verse being from the tenth century and reputedly penned by a pupil of Kobo Daishi.[13] Kigin is even more explicit in his coupling of homosexuality and Buddhism. He writes in the preface:

> As relations between the sexes were forbidden by the Buddha, priests of the law – being made of neither stone nor wood – had no recourse but to practice the love of boys as an outlet for their feelings . . . [T]his form of love proved to be deeper than the love between men and women. It afflicts the heart of aristocrat and warrior alike. Even the mountain dwellers who cut brushwood have learned of its pleasure.[14]

We meet the old homosexual saint Kobo Daishi again in *The Mirror of Manly Love*, written by Ihara Saikaku in 1684. According to this book, 'Kobo Daishi did not preach the profound pleasures of this love [between men] outside the monasteries because he feared the extinction of humanity.'[15] In the preface to his book Saikaku does not only associate sex between men with Buddhism, but also with Shintoism, the national religion of Japan. Saikaku tells us that male homosexuality arose, according to Shinto mythology, at the beginning of time: 'In the beginning when the gods illuminated the heavens, Kuni-toko-tachi was taught the love of boys by a wagtail bird living on the dry riverbed below the floating bridge of heaven . . . Even the myriad insects preferred the position of boy love. As a result, Japan was called "The Land of Dragonflies".' Heterosexuality and 'the cries of wailing infants' first entered the world because 'the god Susa-no-wo, no longer able to enjoy the love of boys in his old age, turned to the princess Inada for comfort'.[16] In other words, as Saikaku points out, there was a religious basis for Buddhist temples and Shinto shrines functioning as favoured meeting places for men who desired other men. Legendary priests might write thousands of love letters to their male lovers without causing a stir, but one single letter to a woman could destroy a man's reputation for ever.[17]

Homosexuality enjoys nothing like the same level of acceptance in modern Japan as it did in the past; this is largely because of outside influences and the desire of the Japanese authorities to modernize their country on a Western model once they had opened up to the outside world in the middle of the nineteenth century. In 1873 the Japanese introduced a legal ban on sex between men based on a German model. Although the ban was lifted ten years later on the advice of French jurists, policies of this kind meant that homosexuality no longer enjoyed the same social acceptance and consequently lost its central role in religion.[18]

Leaving Japan and crossing the Yellow Sea, we can see that Chinese society accepted sex between men in a similar way for a long period. Buddhism also played a central role in China from the second century BC on, and just as Buddhism was closely linked with Shintoism in Japan, it is difficult to disentangle Buddhist, Taoist, Confucian and other more ancient Chinese religious beliefs from each other. Male homosexuality was, however, accepted at the very highest levels of society, which gives an indication of the level of acceptance in the religious world view in China. These views go back beyond the arrival of Buddhism. An account written in the third century BC by the philosopher Ha Fei Zi tells of the ruler of Wei and his male lover Mizi Xia at the end of the sixth century BC. Xia picked a peach and, when he discovered how wonderful it tasted, he gave the rest to the ruler rather than eat it himself. 'The half-eaten peach' then became an expression associated with absolute love between men.[19] There is thus a clear line of continuity from the most ancient Chinese times down to the period when the influence of Buddhism began to make itself felt. Sima Qian devoted a whole chapter to the various male lovers of the emperors of the early Han dynasty in his great work on Chinese history written around 100 BC.[20] Emperor Wen, for instance, became the lover of a boatman in the imperial palace after dreaming that the boatman had helped him reach the dwelling of the immortals.[21] A later emperor, Wu, was buried together with his lover even though both men were married.[22] Being buried together and finding a path to the land of the gods demonstrates how positively same-sex love was viewed in a religious context, and this positive attitude lasted until after the time of the first Han emperors. Emperor Ai Di, who ruled in the years just before the birth of Christ, was so taken with his lover, whom he had appointed commander-in-chief of the army, that he chose to cut off the sleeve of his precious tunic rather than wake his lover who had fallen asleep on it. This became a recurring story in Chinese literature and because of this episode love between men was often referred to as 'the passion of the cut sleeve'.[23] Under non-Chinese dynasties like the Mongols and Manchus, there was usually less enthusiasm for sexual relations between men.[24] As with Japan, Chinese opposition to homosexuality increased further under Western influence, but it was not until the Communists came to power that homophobia really took over in China, though there was never a formal ban.[25] There were periods of active persecution under Mao's rule, and homosexuality was defined as 'non-existent'.[26]

The positive relationship between religion and male homosexuality in the traditions of Japan and China should also be seen within a wider Buddhist context. As Kitamura Kigin pointed out, the homosexuality that was widespread in the monastic world can be seen in the light of Buddhism's overall opposition to heterosexuality.[27] Since, according to Buddhism, the worst aspect of sex was procreation, homosexuality was often seen as better than heterosexuality. So we should not be surprised to find a greater degree of acceptance of same-sex sexuality in other parts of Buddhism too.

An excess of desire is a problem irrespective of who the sex partner may be. A number of early Buddhist texts, for instance, paint a less than positive picture of what they called *pandaka*; that is, more feminine men who were accused of being voracious in their desire for non-*pandaka* men. It is not the same-sex aspect that causes the problem here, but the limitless desire. *Pandakas* are consequently likened to female prostitutes or lustful young girls. It was said that Buddha refused to ordain *pandakas* as monks.[28]

Having sex with a feminine *pandaka*-man was, however, a less serious misdemeanour for a monk than having sex with a woman. Having sex with a non-*pandaka* man, that is, someone not afflicted by the limitless desire ascribed to women and *pandakas*, was less serious again.[29] What we have here is an interesting and quite clear ranking of varieties of sex and an indication of the variety that is least harmful to a monk. If a monk had to have sex, sex with an 'ordinary' man was very much to be preferred, followed by sex with feminine *pandaka*-men, leaving heterosexual sex as by far the worst kind.

The situation in Tibet was that discreet relationships between monks were common.[30] There was also, however, a particular order of monks notorious for their desire for other men. The *ldab ldob* monks were ultra-masculine, spoiling for a fight and given to wearing dark eye-shadow to make them look even more fierce. The *ldab ldob*, who were frequently used as bodyguards because of their fighting skills, did not only have affairs with younger monks but were reputed to kidnap men they were attracted to.[31]

The Theravada Buddhism widespread in Sri Lanka and Southeast Asia does not practise the same absolute tolerance of monastic homosexuality that was traditional in Japan and Tibet, but the punishment for heterosexual activities is more severe than for homosexual activities. Whereas a heterosexual misdemeanour leads to exclusion from the monastery, sex between men usually only leads to a minor penitential exercise.[32] Discreet sexual relationships between monks are fairly common in practice and are not usually punished.[33] Unlike heterosexuality, homosexual behaviour is not regarded as a challenge to monastic life since it does not involve family duties or loyalty to anyone outside the monastery.[34]

It would, however, be wrong to see Buddhism as taking a positive view of homosexuality per se. All the examples we have looked at only involve sex between men. Sex between women was thought of quite differently and generally seen in a more negative light. Whereas sex between men was not only tolerated but sometimes even seen as sacred, sex between women was not. The great problem with sex from the Buddhist perspective is the presence of desire. It is this that makes female sexuality more troublesome since, in the Buddhist view, women are considered to be creatures governed by their sexual desires.[35] It is therefore impossible to equate sex between women with sex between men and there are much stricter rules regulating relationships between nuns than between monks. Not only are nuns barred from sleeping two to a bed unless one of them is ill, but they are not permitted to undress in front of each other, to talk about sexual matters, massage each other or use the same water when bathing. Adult nuns may not sit down on a young girl's bed, nor inspect her clothes.[36]

That sex between men was widespread and accepted in ancient Greece is a well-known fact. What is less well known is that it was also closely associated with religious beliefs. Religion did not condemn male homosexuality and there were, in fact, many religious precedents for it. Most of the male gods had relationships with young mortal men. Zeus fell so much in love with young Ganymede that he carried him to Olympus. Apollo was deeply in love with the beautiful Hyacinthus, and a rejuvenated Pelops was abducted by a love-smitten Poseidon. A number of works of art show clear parallels between the way men try to seduce one another and the way the gods try to seduce mortal men.[37] According to the poet Pindar in the fifth century BC, the love of older men for younger men was directly inspired by the gods.[38]

Sex may have been forbidden in temples but they were nevertheless used as meeting places. There are a great many pieces of ancient graffiti on temple walls telling us things like 'Jason lay with Hector here'.[39] Sometimes it is not only the location itself that places the sex in a religious context. In the Temple of Apollo on Santorini the following confession from the seventh century BC tells us: 'By Apollo Delphinius, here Crimon penetrated the son of Bathycles.' Alongside it is another inscription: 'Here Crimon penetrated Amotion.'[40]

In the Greek city-states, sexual relationships between men were institutionalized in a variety of ways. As a general rule, there was an older and, ideally speaking, active partner and a younger man who was expected to be the passive partner – a pattern that reflected the relationship between male gods and mortal men. Just as in the heterosexual context, in which the woman was always the inferior partner, homosexuality should not normally occur between equals. Sex between socially equal partners was not only seen as essentially un-Greek: at times it was also seen as verging on the non-human.[41]

In Thebes, younger and older men often lived as couples, in parallel with being married to women.[42] This practice clearly had religious aspects and in 378 BC the city founded the 'Sacred Band', a military unit consisting of 150 male couples.[43] This sacred homosexual band contributed to Thebes achieving a short but firm period of hegemony over the rest of Greece. In classical and Hellenistic Sparta there were strict rules for how male couples should behave towards one another, which included the older partner being responsible for the behaviour of the younger lover.[44] In Crete the ritual abduction by young men of younger men they were attracted to was part of the formal rite of passage from boyhood to manhood. A youth was considered to be disgraced if no one found him attractive enough to abduct. Once again, this ritual reflected religious beliefs about young men being abducted by the gods, and a sacrifice to Zeus was considered appropriate when the young man returned home.[45]

Even though the Romans did not share the Greeks' view of sacred sex between men, the young and beautiful Antinous was nevertheless declared a god (essentially because he was the lover of Hadrian, the Roman emperor) after he drowned in the Nile in AD 130.[46] Although the majority of deified individuals in the imperial family usually enjoyed no more than formal cult status, this handsome homosexual god became a popular figure throughout the eastern Mediterranean and his cult survived several decades after the death of the Emperor Hadrian.[47] The worship of him was even compared to the worship of Jesus[48] and many Christians were deeply concerned by the endurance of this cult of the emperor's divine young lover.[49]

Rather as in the Buddhist and Shinto traditions, sex between women never had the same sort of position in ancient Greek religion as sex between men. We find instead that sex between women was usually considered to be abnormal and unnatural, since normal sexuality was understood to involve one partner penetrating another. This meant that sex between men could be perceived as natural whereas sex between women could not.[50]

The poet Sappho, who lived on Lesbos and Sicily during the sixth and seventh centuries BC, is famous for her love poems to her younger female pupils, but her poems are virtually unique during the thousand years and more of Greek religion. It is worth noting, however, that she appeals to Aphrodite for divine assistance in her love for women, just as she would have done if she had been in a heterosexual relationship.[51]

The Greeks were well aware that women could fall in love with other women but the sexual fulfilment of that kind of love was seen as a physical challenge, since it did not match their perception

A Greek amphora depicting men courting boys, *c.* 540 BC.

of sex as being an activity that necessarily involved an active and a passive partner. The Greek tale of Iphis, a young Cretan woman brought up as a boy, tells us something about their ideas. Iphis, in love with the girl she is engaged to (everyone thinks Iphis is a man), despairs of her love because she sees it as being against nature: 'Cows do not burn with love for cows, nor mares for mares.' (Iphis is obviously ignorant of recent research results which point to a significant amount of lesbian sex in the animal world.) The gods, however, apparently agree with Iphis's conclusion that lesbian sex is unnatural sex, but instead of condemning her they take pity on the unfortunate woman. When the gods intervene, they do so by operating within the normal framework of what they consider to be natural sex: the goddess Isis transforms Iphis into a man so that her love for the girl may be consummated in a way the Greeks considered natural.[52]

The patterns of acceptance of same-sex sexuality we have today do not, however, reflect the patterns visible in Buddhism and Shintoism and the religion of the ancient Greeks. Although sex between men was accepted, the expectation was that it would not happen between men who were similar in age or social status. If we go on to consider the ways in which these three religions viewed sex between women, we can see that their approach to male homosexuality never actually saw or dealt with same-sex sexuality as a general category. What it was actually concerned with was the religious acceptance of a particular kind of *male* sexuality.

These examples of situations in which male homosexuality is well integrated into the religious framework have all been taken from history. Historical circumstances have meant that these particular religious traditions have not continued unchanged through to the present day. The religious convictions we have been discussing here may be *ancient* religious convictions, but that does not detract in the least from their demonstration of the fact that religion as a phenomenon can be gay-friendly. On the contrary, for the majority of religions the very fact that something is *ancient* imbues it with authority. After all, the *ancient* opposition to homosexuality in many other religions is used as an argument for continued hostility to homosexuality today. Even in those mythical ancient times that religions tend to consider so important, it emerges that religions can be gay-friendly, which is why it is important for us to be aware of these historical examples.

Other Sexual Borderlines

Various types of transsexualism are often associated with the religious acceptance of same-sex sexuality. In many religions an individual can – or could – at least partly leave the traditional male or female role and take on different gender roles. Such people are often expected to have sexual relations with people of the same biological sex. This pattern of behaviour means that those who remain within their traditional male or female role may have same-sex sex with people who challenge these gender roles without actually having to step outside their own sexual role.

This pattern of sexuality is particularly widespread in a number of widely differing societies that have remained relatively untouched by the major religions. The descriptors used for this phenomenon

The Ceremonial Dance to the Berdashe, Sauk and Fox (Meskwaki) Indians by George Catlin, 1830s. The two-spirit person stands to the right, while his fellow tribesmen tease him but also vie for his attention, which is deemed an honour.

vary widely but anthropologists have often referred to it as the third sex or as *berdache* (originally a Persian word). Modern Native Americans refer to such individuals as *two-spirits people*. Transsexuals or transgendered are other collective terms used to describe people who stand to one side of traditional male or female sexual roles.

In many North American indigenous religions individuals are called to two-spirit status as a result of divinely inspired dreams and visions.[53] Among the Osages, Lakota and Omaha, for instance, a goddess appeared to young people in visions linked to their rites of passage and gave them a choice between objects associated with men and with women. Those who were to be initiated sometimes deliberately chose the objects associated with the opposite sex, in which case they had to live accordingly. At other times the goddess tricked them into choosing the objects. Thus the call for them to live as two-spirits people was sometimes a divine imposition rather than something they chose for themselves.[54] Two-spirits people played a pivotal part in many traditional North American religions since they were thought to be sacred individuals in particularly close contact with the gods.[55] This, for instance, was the situation with many peoples – the Cheyenne, Hidatsa, Kiowa, Lakota, Meskwaki, Mohave, Navajo,

Sauk, Tohono O'odham, Yokut, Yurok and Zuni peoples all came into this category.[56]

Some North American religions permitted marriage between two people of the same biological sex if one of the partners was a two-spirits person. The famous political and religious Lakota chief Crazy Horse had, for instance, two two-spirits or *winkte* wives.[57] A two-spirits or *koskalaka* woman could likewise take a wife with the blessing of the Lakota goddess Double Woman.[58] In a few other peoples, on the other hand, marriage was either uncommon for two-spirits people or not permitted. This did not, however, mean that same-sex sex was forbidden to them and two-spirits people were often expected to be sexually promiscuous.[59] This was not a pattern of sexual behaviour without religious significance and young men among the Sauks and Meskwaki had to have sex with a two-spirits man before being ritually accepted into male society.[60]

A similar relationship between religion, same-sex sexuality and sexual expression is to be found in many African societies. In the Yoruba religion in south-west Nigeria all the priests involved in calling up the spirits are dressed as women irrespective of their biological sex.[61] Sex between men is also associated with magic – in one way or another it is seen as helping reduce the distance between the human and the divine dimension in the cosmos.[62] In a similar way, among the Dagara people on the border between Ghana and Burkina Faso, men who have sex with men are seen as gatekeepers between this world and the spirit world.[63] Transgender men who have sex with men also play a central role in the pre-Islamic *Bori* cult among the Hausa people in the Sahel.[64]

Farther south in Africa, among the Ovambo people on the border between Angola and Namibia, most men who dressed as women traditionally functioned as healers and shamans. These men also married other men.[65] Homosexual men among the Ila people in Zambia often function as prophets.[66] The Meru people in the Kenyan Highlands have their *mugawe* men, who dress as women and sometimes marry other men. The *mugawe* men, like their equivalents in many other cultures, also have a special religious role.[67] In the Haitian Voodoo religion, which also has its roots in African culture, the goddess Èzili Freda has a particularly close association with feminine men who have sex with other men and she is often considered to be their patron goddess.[68] Even though Haitian society in general is not notably gay-friendly, men who live openly homosexual lives are usually accepted both by the congregations and by the priests of the Voodoo religion.[69]

There are numerous other examples of different kinds of institutionalized structures for same-sex sexuality in African societies but it is not always easy to determine the extent to which religion is involved in them. It is sometimes possible to see how religion becomes involved when people are active in the border areas of what is generally considered acceptable in relation to sex and sexuality. The British social anthropologist Brian MacDermot gives an account, for example, of how a local prophet among the Nuer people in Ethiopia reacted to a man who started to wear women's clothes. The prophet consulted the spirits, who declared that the man was now to be considered a woman and should be referred to as 'she'. She should now dress as a woman and should be permitted to take a husband.[70]

There were some religious ideas associated with sex between men in the pre-Christian Norse religion too. The Norse *seið* -man, who had the ability to make contact with the superhuman dimension of existence, was associated with *ergi* – passive homosexuality[71] – though this did not equate with any general religious acceptance of sex between men. It was precisely the *violation* of ordinary sexual morality that contributed to the *seið*-man's supernatural abilities. To accuse other men of *ergi* was normally extremely problematic since it was considered a serious insult,[72] which meant that *seið*-men had a rather ambivalent role in Norse society. Ragnvald Rettilbeine, the son of the Norwegian King Harald I Finehair, was a famous *seið*-man in Hadeland in south-eastern Norway. When Ragnvald's brother, Eirik Bloodaxe, burned him and eighty other *seið*-men alive in his house at the instigation of their father, it was – according to the thirteenth-century Icelandic historian Snorri Sturluson – a 'work [that] was much praised'.[73] This episode tells us something about the exposed position *seið*-men had in Norse society, though we may suspect Snorri of allowing his Christian sympathies to colour his account.

The religious acceptance of same-sex sexuality in situations where one of the partners takes on an alternative gender role is not the same as acceptance of same-sex sexuality at large. Whereas a general acceptance of homosexuality will normally also include accepting same-sex relationships in which one partner lives outside traditional sex roles, the reverse is less often true. Those religions that are quite open to various alternative gender identities frequently exhibit little acceptance of homosexual sex when the partners remain within their traditional sex roles, and we very rarely find sexual relationships of this sort being institutionalized. In other words, the underlying view of gender is utterly different when a religious world view recognizes the existence of more than two sexes. Ideas about sex with people who are neither men nor women are not to be found in all religions. If we look at this phenomenon with modern western eyes and take it to be an example of religion sanctioning homosexuality per se, we would be wrong. At the same time, however, we should be clear that many people within such religions point to these traditions precisely in order to show a traditional acceptance of something other than heterosexuality – and they are quite right to do so.

Maiming, Throttling, Burning, Hanging

The 24th of September 1731 was no ordinary day in the Dutch village of Faan. The small community in the province of Groningen was full of soldiers sent to keep the peace among the local population during what was to be a public display of Christian justice. First of all, the corpse of a village man who had died in the local jail, probably as a result of torture, was hung from a gibbet. Then ten men and nine teenage boys – the youngest only fourteen years old – were marched in and bound to stakes, where they were garrotted one by one, strangled by the slow tightening of a thick rope around their necks. And then, while the soldiers were busy preventing the agitated crowd intervening on behalf of their sons, fathers, brothers, neighbours and friends, the twenty-two corpses were burned so that none of the condemned men could be given a Christian burial.[74]

The events in Faan were the culmination of what can best be described as a pious Christian witchhunt against men who had sex with other men. The whole business had started with a series of accusations and arrests in Utrecht a year earlier. At least 74 men were publicly executed in this first wave of religiously inspired persecution of homosexuals and a hundred more were sentenced to death *in absentia* after they had fled the country. Whereas the bodies of the men in Faan were burned, many of those executed in Utrecht were tied to heavy weights and thrown into the sea,[75] the intention being to annihilate all traces of the condemned men for all of eternity.

These bloody mass executions in the Netherlands in 1730 and 1731 are by no means exceptional; indeed, they exemplify a pattern typical of the religious persecution of people who have sex with others of the same sex. Even though condemnation of homo sexuality had been, and still is, found within parts of most religions, it is the Western religions – Judaism, Christianity and Islam – that have traditionally been the most negative and homophobic. Christianity emerges as by the far the most aggressive of the three, although the beginnings of this bloody history are to be found in the Hebrew Bible.

The Pentateuch states that 'If a man also lie with mankind, as he lieth with a woman, both of them have committed an abomination: they shall surely be put to death.'[76] There are, however, many things that suggest that the death penalty was not demanded for all sexual acts between men. The defining feature seems to be that a man has sex 'as he lieth with a woman', which implies that penetration must be involved before anyone has the right to put him to death with God's blessing. The fact that the Pentateuch does not contain any prohibition of sex between women points in the same direction. In a legal sense, then, sex was synonymous with penetration. It is important to notice that this means that there is no condemnation of homosexuality per se in the Hebrew Bible: it is only penetrative anal sex between men, that is condemned.

As we have already seen, there is nothing unique about demanding the death penalty for certain kinds of sexual behaviour – God also commands us to kill men and women who have sex during menstruation, adulterous women and men who have sex with women who are married or engaged to another man.[77] The prohibition of anal sex between men was also justified by the claim that this was one of the sexual habits of the neighbouring peoples and consequently something the Israelites should avoid.[78] Male anal sex must also be seen in the context of biblical decrees on ritual purity, the focus of which lay on upholding clear-cut categories: men who penetrate each other can easily be seen as confusing proper gender categories. God views men and women who wear the clothes of the opposite sex as an 'abomination'.[79] And it is not only sexual categories that must be kept pure: among its various sexual proscriptions, the Pentateuch also forbids the use of 'a garment mingled of linen and woollen', ploughing with an ox and an ass together, and sowing two kinds of seed in the same field.[80]

For two men to have sex with each other as they would with a woman also means that 'their blood shall be upon them',[81] possibly precisely because they are reversing the Judaic gender categories. This kind of reversal of social structures leads to blood-guilt in many contexts. Parents have a right to curse their children but children who curse their parents incur blood-guilt and must therefore be killed, just like men who have penetrative sex with other men.[82] The same holds true for people guilty of murder,[83] certain kinds of adultery, various forms of incest and sex with animals.[84] To this list we can add anyone who is possessed by 'a familiar spirit or that is a wizard'.[85]

It is nevertheless questionable how important this ban on anal sex between men actually was in the religion of the Israelites. Other sexual prohibitions in the Pentateuch are repeated extensively and exemplified elsewhere in the Hebrew Bible but nothing further is said about the prohibition of anal sex between men. When we are told of the love between King Saul's son Jonathan and the young boy David, who later became king, there is no problematization what sover of the close intimacy between the two men. The very first time Jonathan saw David 'the soul of Jonathan was knit with the soul of David, and Jonathan loved him as his own soul'.[86] Jonathan gives David weapons and clothes as signs of his love and saves him on a number of occasions from being killed by his father, King Saul. On his part, David desires that Jonathan make 'a covenant with the house of David'.[87] The two men like to kiss.[88] The relationship between the two men is also directly compared with a heterosexual relationship and when Jonathan is killed, David despairs and pours out his feelings: 'thy love to me was wonderful, passing the love of women'.[89]

St Paul's condemnation of both male and female homosexuality is specific to Christianity but, since he was a Jew, it cannot be seen without reference to the prohibition of male anal intercourse in the Pentateuch. St Paul condemned not only sex between men but also *lust* between men. His complete lack of acceptance of men having sex with men is probably a result of his Jewish upbringing but, unlike the Hebrew Bible, Paul believed that same-sex desire is a logical consequence of man turning away from God. Homosexuality is a punishment sent by God. According to Paul, 'those who changed the truth of God into a lie, and worshipped and served the creature more than the Creator . . . God gave them up unto vile affections.' The men, 'leaving the sex and religion natural use of the woman, burned in their lust one toward another.' It is, however, uncertain whether Paul's condemnation of women who did change the natural use into that which is against nature,' refers to sex between women or to

Miniature from a French Bible Moralisée of the early 13th century, showing two same-sex couples being encouraged by devils to indulge in forbidden love.

female desire in general, since any active desire was seen as contrary to women's supposedly passive nature.[90] If Paul really meant to set women having sex with women alongside men having sex with men, this would be a fairly new element brought into the religious discourse. The Jews traditionally had no legal restrictions on lesbian sex, whereas the Greeks saw sex between men as something blessed by the gods but sex between women as something fundamentally unnatural. This possible Pauline parity between male and female homosexuality has, nevertheless, rarely been followed in Christianity either, where sex between men has usually been much more fiercely condemned than sex between women. Before the twentieth century the two were generally not even considered as parallel phenomena.

To return to Paul's assertion that homosexuality was an automatic consequence of ungodliness: even though it is God who makes people homosexual as a punishment for no longer believing in him, it is those who God changes who themselves must take 'that recompence of their error'.[91] Paul goes on to compare homosexuality to 'all unrighteousness, fornication, wickedness, covetousness, maliciousness; [people] full of envy, murder, debate, deceit, malignity'.[92] And he concludes: 'Who knowing the judgment of God, that they which commit such things are worthy of death.' The majority of the actions Paul picks out do not, according to Mosaic law, qualify for the death penalty. To a great extent, then, Paul is not following the Hebrew Bible and he does not appear to make any reference to the strict judicial decisions about male anal sex in the Pentateuch. When he states that thieves, malicious people and those who have adulterous or homosexual sex deserve to die, he is almost certainly referring to divine justice in general rather than to human law. This point, however, has frequently been ignored and Paul's words have been used time and again to justify the execution of homosexuals, particularly male homosexuals.

Jesus, unlike Paul, said nothing about homosexuality. His clear condemnation of extramarital heterosexual activity is nevertheless a good basis for assuming that he also disapproved of male homosexuality since, as far as Judaism was concerned, this was to a certain degree identical to extramarital sex. But since Jesus opposed the human punishment of the adulterous woman, saying 'go, and sin no more',[93] we may assume that he also held that homosexuality should not be subject to human justice, effectively the same view as that held by Paul.

The story in Matthew's Gospel of the Roman centurion who comes to Jesus because his servant – *país* – is seriously ill complicates the picture, however.[94] *País* is the Greek word that is often used for the younger lover in a sexual relationship between two men. The immense tenderness the centurion shows for his *país* suggests that this is the case here – it is certainly not just a question of a mere haphazard servant or slave. Luke, when he tells the same story, uses both *país* and 'slave', which does not exclude the possibility of a close and sexual relationship between the two men.[95] The story of the centurion and his *país* means that Jesus may have healed a man in a homosexual relationship without admonishing either of them – indeed, he holds the centurion up as an example to be followed by others, both Jews and gentiles.[96] One could, if one were so inclined, go so far as to ask whether Jesus might have approved of same-sex marriage.

This, of course, remains hypothetical since he did not make any clear statements on the issue. Irrespective of what Jesus might have meant, almost two thousand years were to pass before that kind of gay-friendly reading of the words of Jesus had any real impact on Christianity. In the intervening period the great majority of people took it as given that Jesus condemned sex between men, even though there is no record of him doing so.

The violent condemnation of same-sex sexuality by Jews, Christians and Muslims alike thus begins with the death penalty for penetrative sex between men prescribed by the Hebrew Bible on the basis of religious rules on purity and other more general sex regulations. There is also another episode in the Pentateuch which, although originally having little to do with homosexuality, has come to take centre stage in forming the attitudes to homosexuality within these three religions. This is the story of Sodom.

After Abraham's nephew Lot has taken up residence in Sodom, he meets two angels at the city-gate one evening and invites them to his house. Soon the whole of the male population of the city gathers and demands that Lot 'bring them out unto us, that we may know them' or 'so that we can have sex with them'.[97] The translations of the passage vary but it is clear from the Hebrew original that the men's intention is to rape the heavenly visitors. The episode ends with the angels bidding Lot and his family to leave the city, after which God destroys Sodom and the neighbouring city of Gomorrah, wiping out all the inhabitants by raining down burning sulphur from heaven.

In spite of the obvious sexual intentions of the inhabitants of the city, it was not sex between men that was originally considered to be Sodom's great sin; as is made clear in other biblical passages, the original reason for the punishment of the Sodomites is their lack of respect for the rules of hospitality.[98] Elsewhere the reason for punishment is suggested as being the Sodomites' desire to have sex with non-human beings,[99] their ungodliness,[100] or their general sinfulness.[101]

In the Book of Judges we are presented with a situation that parallels the Sodom case quite closely: the male inhabitants of the Israelite city of Gibeah demand sex with a Levite man who is the guest of an elderly resident of the city. Once again we can see that the problem is not homosexuality but the breach of the rules of hospitality. The less than hospitable Gibeah men are not too bothered about the gender of their victim and are quite satisfied when they are allowed to rape the guest's concubine instead of the visitor himself.[102]

Jesus, too, did not connect the crimes of Sodom with homosexuality; he associated them with a lack of hospitality[103] and with an overall lack of true faith.[104] The Jewish philosopher Philo, writing around the time of the birth of Christ, was the first to refer to the Sodomites' desire to have sex with other men as one of the sins that led to the destruction of their city: 'They not only sinned against their neighbour's marriage in their wild lust for women but they also lay with men.'[105] It is worth noting here that Philo seems to be saying that the homosexual inclinations of the Sodomites are a result of them having no boundaries at all to their general sexual lusts – they will also sleep with other men's wives. Nevertheless, after Philo, the idea that male homosexuality was the sin of the Sodomites was repeated and emphasized by Jews such as Josephus and by early Christians such as Clement of Alexandria and Augustine.[106] From then on the connection between Sodom and male anal sex effectively became the standard interpretation of the cause of the city's destruction. The term 'sodomy', however, gradually came to be used for anal sex in general, heterosexual as well as homosexual.

The originally incorrect perception that male homosexuality was the cause of God's destruction of Sodom has had violent and often lethal consequences in the sexual history of religion. The idea that sex between men could draw down God's punishment so directly helped sustain negative attitudes to homosexual behaviour by men. While the equally strict ban on menstrual sex in the Pentateuch, along with a series of other misdeeds worthy of the death penalty, were either marginalized or completely forgotten by Christianity, the ban on sex between men was constantly reformulated to meet new circumstances.

The Jews did not retain the Pentateuch's demand for the death penalty for sex between men. Even though Maimonides thought it was the right punishment,[107] only a few others supported it and, in any case, Jews were not usually in a position to enforce a death penalty. Rabbinic Judaism, for the most part, paid little attention to homosexuality – just as was the case in Old Testament times.[108] The sixteenth-century Palestinian rabbi Joseph ben Ephraim Caro, for instance, did not make any reference to homosexuality

The Blinding of the Sodomites, after Nicolaus Hoy, 1583.

in general, though he did say that Jews were not usually suspected of sex between men. And since Jewish men were supposedly not inclined to homosexuality, it was permissible for two men to meet alone. To be on the safe side, however, such private meetings were not recommended, and the men should certainly not share a bedspread.[109] Later commentators resident in Christian countries thought that these cautious rules of conduct only applied to Jews living in Muslim countries (like Caro), since sex between men was said to be more widespread among Muslims than among Christians.[110] Jewish men in Muslim Spain, nevertheless, were assiduous imitators of Muslim men's love poetry to young boys, and their Muslim neighbours were far from being their only inspiration. Men in love often paraphrased parts of the Song of Solomon when they wrote in praise of the young men they were in love with. Even though Jewish love poems are rarely as explicitly erotic as Muslim poems, it is quite obvious that the Jewish men, too, were hoping for rather more than the kisses and embraces they limited themselves to writing about.[111] Not all Jews with writing abilities were afraid to be explicit: given that the Pentateuch only forbids anal sex between men, it is understandable that Rabbinic authorities discussed the exact degree of penetration that qualified as anal sex. Whereas the thirteenth-century Spanish text *Sefer ha Chinuch* claimed that the whole of the *glans penis* must be inside, others thought that 'just a little' qualified. Round about 1100 the respected Torah commentator Rashi stated that one had to push the penis in as deep as one pushes 'an applicator into a tube [of eye shadow]'.[112]

Although Rabbinic Judaism paid less attention to male homosexuality than the Pentateuch, sex between women is condemned on several occasions, which is not the case in the Hebrew Bible.[113] Maimonides, for instance, associates lesbian sex with sexual practices among the Egyptians and consequently with the Pentateuch's prohibition against doing what the people in Egypt do. The implication of this deduction is that lesbian sex must also deserve the death penalty but Maimonides thought that a whipping was sufficient for women practising such sex.[114] Other Jewish authorities maintained, as we have seen, that sex between women was not sex in any real sense.[115] Women who had lesbian sex were, however, expected to marry men and a number of medieval commentaries gave men the right to punish their wives if they caught them having lesbian sex;[116] the very fact that it was the husband, not society, that had the right to punish shows that this was normally seen as a private matter rather than as a serious sin. So, for instance, if a husband thought it was perfectly all right for his wife to enjoy herself with her woman friends, then this was the case.

Christian reactions to homosexuality were often complicated by the fact that there was a separation of powers between church and state. It was normally only the state that had the mandate to pronounce the most severe punishments and this frequently hindered the church in its desire to execute people. Yet again, Sodom is frequently mentioned in order to support the ban on sex between men and, very often, the fate of Sodom is referred to in order to justify the severity of the punishments.

Although it is difficult to argue that there was ever a period when Christianity generally accepted homosexuality, there were times when the fight against homosexuality was given lower priority. The Council of Elvira in Spain at the beginning of the fourth century paid little attention to same-sex sexuality. Sex between women was not mentioned at all, nor was sex between men in a general sense, although men who 'corrupt boys' should be punished with eternal exclusion from the church.[117] In other words, what is being attacked is the classical model of grown men having relationships with young boys and the attack is probably motivated by the central role played by relationships of that kind in large parts of pagan societies.

In 390 AD the Christian emperor Theodosius the Great introduced a law that stipulated death at the stake for anyone who 'changed' his male body 'into a female body by practising sexual acts reserved for the other sex'.[118] In other words, only the passive party to anal sex was to be condemned to death. In 538, however, Justinian ordered the arrest and execution of all men who had sex with men, irrespective of whether they were the active or the passive partner, but this was only to happen if they continued to practise homosexuality after first being warned.[119] The thrust of the law was thus more concerned with principle than with practice.

Initially, anyway, these decisions on the death penalty had few consequences in the Christian world and actual practice in the Western world remained a good deal milder during the centuries that followed. Early medieval church meetings and books of penance proposed various kinds of fasting and penance.[120] It was the act itself, not the intention, that was the serious issue and lack of consent was not always sufficient reason to escape punishment. There were also injunctions against sex between women though they were much less common than those against sex between men.[121] The lack of any great severity in the sanctions against homosexuality was probably also related to the fact that these were church ordinances rather than public law and consequently they had limited powers to impose punishments.

There is no mention of homosexuality in the early lawcodes of most of the Germanic peoples who had converted to Christianity, such as the Anglo-Saxons, Bavarians, Burgundians, Saxons and Lombards.[122] This was to change. In the Visigothic kingdom in Spain, where bishops became very closely involved in state administration after the king converted to Catholicism, both active and passive male homosexuality became punishable by castration in the seventh century.[123] The Council of Paris in 829 once again called for the death penalty for sodomy,[124] but since it was only canon law there was no legal basis for the penalty being put into practice. In order to ensure that people really would be executed, Benedict Levita (as he called himself) set about falsifying parts of the laws of Charlemagne of AD 779 by incorporating the later Council of Paris decision on the death penalty for sodomy into the Carolingian law code, with the result that the church decree immediately became public law. Benedict Levita's falsified version of Charlemagne's laws became widespread and had a very significant influ ence on secular legislation in Christian countries. It was accepted as genuine until 1836, when a German scholar finally uncovered the fraud.[125]

The combination of Christian conviction and secular law proved to be fatal for many men who had sex with men. In Norway, where the power of the state was not greatly developed, the Gulathing Law of around 1170 determined that men who had sex with men should be outlawed.[126] This meant that anyone had the right to kill them. In other parts of Europe amputation and torture were frequently combined with the death penalty. In the thirteenth century King Alfonso the Wise of Castile, for instance, went a step further than the old Visigothic law by deciding that sodomites should not only be publicly castrated but once that was done they should be hanged upside down until they died.[127] English laws of around 1290 stipulated that sodomites should be buried alive.[128] In Orléans during the High Middle Ages the condemned man would have his testicles removed for a first offence, his penis cut off for a second and be burned at the stake for a third.[129] In Renaissance Venice sodomites were liable to a range of punishments: they might be exiled, sold into slavery, shackled in prison for life or put in a cage until they died; others were whipped, had limbs amputated, were beheaded, hanged, burned or any combination of these things. But anyone who made false accusations could, on the other hand, also have their limbs amputated.[130] In Spanish cities such as Madrid and Almeria, men executed for homosexuality could be seen hanging upside down on the gallows with their amputated sexual organs tied around their necks.[131] There were periods when certain states even initiated active persecution, mounting systematic campaigns to identify and punish men who had sex with men. This happened in Perugia in Italy in the thirteenth century, in Spain during the time of Columbus and in the Netherlands in the eighteenth century.[132] After the foundation of the Inquisition by Pope Gregory IX in 1233, there were periods when the church itself had the right to punish 'offenders', and it made zealous use of that right. At times there were more sodomites than heretics at the stake.[133] The Inquisition in Aragon dealt with almost a thousand cases of sodomy between 1570 and 1630 and 170 men were executed.[134]

The persecution of men who had sex with men was paralleled from time to time by the persecution of women who had sex with women. The law in Orléans stipulated that women, like men, should have part of their genitals removed for a first offence, further amputation for a second offence, and be burned at the stake for a third.[135] Men and women found guilty of homosexuality in the northern Italian town of Treviso would have their sexual organs nailed to a stake, where they would have to stand for a whole day before being burned.[136]

In general, however, lesbian sex was more frequently ignored than male homosexuality. When a number of women were accused of homosexual offences in a town in Aragon in 1560, the judicial authorities ruled that formal charges should only be raised when women used artificial phalluses: female sex without penetration could not really be considered sex.[137] In his 1770 commentary on canon law, the Franciscan theologian Ludovico Maria Sinistrari argued that women could only be guilty of sodomy if one of the women had a clitoris large enough to penetrate the other woman. If this was suspected, the women should be examined and if it proved to be true, 'it is necessary to have recourse to torture, that the Judge may find out whether the unmentionable crime was committed.'[138]

The religious aspect of Christian persecution shows up very clearly in the way same-sex sexuality is associated repeatedly with religious heresy. The Bogomiles, the Cathars and the Templars were all accused of sodomy. Men who were condemned for homosexuality tended to be also condemned for heresy, even when there was nothing apart from their sexual behaviour to suggest any violation of Christian teachings.[139] In fourteenth-century Navarre homosexuality: expected, compulsory, condemned male homosexuality could be referred to as 'committing heresy with his body'.[140] This is clearly connected to St Paul's belief that God punished those who turned away from him by making them attracted to people of the same sex:[141] people who felt homosexual attraction must, then, necessarily hold false beliefs. Other commentators argued that demonic forces were involved: the laws of Emperor Justinian for instance, show that some people believed that it was the Devil who made men have sex with other men[142] (even though Paul, of course, believed it was God who made men do it).

Many Christians were particularly concerned about controlling homosexuality because they believed that everyone could be attracted to people of the same sex. The influential fourth-century church father Basil of Caesarea clearly recognized that young men could be particularly attractive to other men and the advice he gave monks was fairly comprehensive. They should be careful, for instance, to sit well away from a younger brother; when going to bed, they should take care that their clothing did not touch his – 'rather let an elder brother lie between you'. Basil believed that men's desire for young men was so prevalent that danger was everpresent: 'When a young brother talks to you or is face to face with you in the choir, answer with your head bowed so that you do not accidentally look him straight in the face, allowing the evil sower to sow the seeds of desire in you from which you will harvest damnation and destruction.'[143] Many of the Puritans in colonial New England believed that *all* human beings were filled with homosexual as well as heterosexual desire and that the good Christian should direct that desire into procreative sex within marriage.[144] The same conviction underlies many of the present-day efforts of conservative Christians to limit both equal status and positive references to homosexuality: the idea is that the greater the level of acceptance of homosexuality and the more positive statements that are made about it, the more people will give in to their latent homosexual lusts.

The proscription of sex between men did not only survive the Reformation but, as we saw in the Netherlands, was sometimes enforced even more severely than before. There was little persecution in England until the eighteenth and nineteenth centuries, during which several dozen men were executed, especially during the Napoleonic Wars.[145] The last execution was carried out in 1836.

The death penalty for sodomy existed in all the British colonies in North America except Pennsylvania.[146] The majority of those found guilty in North America were not executed, being punished with the lash and expulsion instead. A number of clerics vehemently opposed this moderation, pointing out that ungodly deeds of this kind deserved death.[147] There were other Christian countries that retained the death penalty even longer: South Africa, for instance, retained it for sex between men until 1907, though the last execution took place in 1831.[148]

Although the Nazis disapproved of Jews and people with disabilities from the start, they were initially not unduly concerned about homosexuality. When confronted in 1930 with complaints about the less than discreet affairs Ernst Röhm, the SA leader, was having with men, Hitler stated: 'The sole objective of any investigation must be to confirm whether an officer of the SA . . . is performing his official duties . . . His private life cannot be the subject of investigation unless it is in conflict with the fundamental principles of National-Socialist ideology.'[149] This kind of tolerance of homosexuality was, however, extremely difficult to hold in the face of the traditional Christian conservatives and the bourgeois and aristocratic elites of Germany. When the Nazis did a complete about-face and began their systematic persecution of homosexual men, the change should be seen in the context of a strategic adaptation on their part to the more traditional Christian attitude to homosexuality. In his speech to the Reichstag on 23 March 1933, Hitler laid great emphasis on the fact that 'the Government of the Reich . . . regards Christianity as the unshakable foundation of the morals and the moral code of the nation.'[150] The ability of the Nazis to convince the Christian right that their aim was to protect traditional Christian ideals of sexual purity was decisive in establishing and stabilizing the legitimacy and power base of the Nazi regime during the spring and summer of 1933.[151] In its first few years in power, both Protestant and Catholic reactions to the Nazi regime were positive.[152] Even the Vatican openly commended the way the Nazis immediately tightened up censorship of sexual content in the written and visual media.[153] This censorship was one of the things that provided the legal basis for the destruction of the gay rights pioneer Magnus Hirschfeld's Institut für Sexualwissenschaft on 6 May 1933.[154] New, stricter laws against all forms of sex between men were introduced in 1935 and they marked the start of more systematic persecution.[155] Christian spokesmen took a generally positive view of these legal changes, seeing them as a good initiative to enable the punishment of 'crimes against marriage' and 'attacks on marriage'.[156] The Nazi persecution of homosexuals may have started as a way of adapting themselves to Christian moral rules but this did nothing to moderate their own enthusiasm once the persecution was under way. The Nazi regime continued to arrest men for having sex with men right up until the very last days of the Second World War, when Berlin was surrounded by Soviet forces.[157]

While Christian ideas seem to have provided the Nazis with their starting-point for the persecution of homosexuals, some of the victims of the Nazis were to discover to their cost that those who defeated the Nazis were also Christians. A number of gay men in concentration camps were not freed after the defeat of the Nazis; instead, the Allies sent them straight to prison to serve out the remainder of the sentences passed on them under the Nazi regime.[158] Homosexuals may not have been the largest group of people persecuted by the Nazis but they were the only group whose persecution the Allies acknowledged as having been legal.

The traditional Christian view has been to condemn and persecute sex between men in the most lethal ways possible. On the basis of a few rather ambiguous verses in the Bible, Christianity constructed a tradition of repressing sex between people of the same sex, particularly between men. Whereas Judaism – starting from the same biblical foundations – has taken a more relaxed view of same-sex sex, Christianity has a history of persecuting men who have sex with men – a history that at certain periods has been notably bloodthirsty. The repression of homosexuality was considered to be central to the religion. When Christians castrated, burned, hanged, drowned and buried alive those they found guilty, they did so in the conviction that they were carrying out the will of God. As we shall see, however, there were also other voices.

Acceptance amid overwhelming Condemnation

If we return to the Dutch mass persecution of men who have sex with men in the 1730s, we can also see how varied the attitudes to homosexuality could be in a Protestant society. The persecution itself demon strates the close connection between church and state, since Christian beliefs were at the heart of it. The executions of all those found guilty of sodomy in various large cities bear witness to how little sympathy for them there was among the urban masses. Like most executions of the time, they were events with great entertainment potential and they attracted large crowds.

The arrests in Utrecht and other cities, however, also revealed a homosexual sub-culture in which – before they were arrested – the members seemed to have had a good and fairly relaxed understanding of what they were doing and of what the Christian doctrines were.[159] A different kind of religious and sexual landscape emerges in the village of Faan, where the legal documents do not reveal any sort of homosexual sub-culture or, indeed, any understanding at all of sex between men as a particular sexual category. What the documents record are more or less casual sexual meetings in farm buildings or out in the fields.[160] The heavyweight religious dimension of the actions seems only to have entered the picture when official persecution began. The loud protests voiced against the persecution by other villagers show that they did not share the official religious view of sex between men as something that must be eradicated at all costs. The Christian villagers remained adamant that their men should be set free even after the trials had given them a clear insight into what their equally Christian superiors thought about homosexuality.

The Dutch farmers, authorities and city-dwellers in the eighteenth century were all Calvinist Christians. But we can clearly see in this case the great variations in the way different parts of society understand and practise one and the same faith. As a result of the extreme levels of persecution and the absolute condemnation in speech, writing and practice, history books may be dominated by the official, strictly religious view of homosexuality, but the simultaneous presence of alternative Christian views of homosexuality is evidenced by the existence of an urban homosexual sub-culture, the unproblematic acceptance of homosexuality among male farmers and the opposition of the villagers of Faan to the persecution. While the urban homosexual sub-culture indicates some degree of *conscious* opposition to contemporary religious views, rural homosexuality and the villagers' resistance represents something different. It does not reflect anything approaching modern principles of equal status or human rights for gay people but it does bear witness to recognition that sex between men was not really that serious an issue and was certainly not seen as any great threat within this rural Calvinist environment.

Throughout the whole of Christian history, people of both sexes have taken part in homosexual activities without feeling that it conflicts with their Christian faith. While the Russian Orthodox church tried to prevent homosexuality in its monasteries, it was generally more tolerant of homosexuality than other churches in society.[161] Many of the travellers and diplomats who have visited Russia since the fifteenth century have reported that open homosexuality was more widespread and more tolerated than in Western Europe. On his visit to Moscow in 1568 the English poet George Turberville was more shocked by the homosexuality he saw among Russian peasants than by the numerous executions ordered by Ivan the Terrible.[162]

The Russians did not ban sex between men until 1832 and even then the law was seldom invoked. Sex between women was never banned.[163] Russia was by no means unique. Sex between boys was so widespread and, to a great extent, accepted in English boarding schools in the nineteenth century that various kinds of unofficial institutionalization existed.[164] Male transvestites who had sex with other men were traditionally accepted in a few Christian areas – they were common among Amharic Orthodox believers in Ethiopia, for instance, where they were known as *wandarwarad*.[165] Different patterns are visible in countries where there was less tolerance of homosexuality. The most usual situation, as in the Dutch village of Faan, was that people performed homosexual acts without thinking that they were particularly problematic from a theological perspective. Elsewhere we can find an outspoken defence of homosexual sex that includes a direct religious reference: a Franciscan monk in Sicily around the year 1600 stated that sex between men was 'something holy and just', a statement that led to the honest monk being whipped in public and jailed for a year. A nobleman in Catania was given a five-year prison sentence for stating that anyone who says no to the chance of being sodomized 'commits a mortal sin'.[166] The Venetian ambassador to the Papal States in 1578 told of a Catholic priest who carried out marriage ceremonies for several Spanish and Portuguese male couples in a church near the Lateran Basilica in Rome. The authorities arrested as many of the men involved as they could catch and burned them all.[167]

In their different ways, these individuals did not see any conflict between Christianity and homosexuality and had they been more powerful figures they would have escaped more lightly. Many Christian rulers had a taste for sex with others of the same sex and lived accordingly, without needing to fear punishment. We might, for instance, mention the Byzantine emperors Nicephorus I, Michael III, Basil I, Constantine VIII and Constantine IX; King Magnus Eriksson of Norway, Sweden and Scania; the English kings William II, Richard the Lionheart, Edward II, Richard II, James I and William of Orange; the French kings Henri III and Louis XIII; the Holy Roman Emperors Frederick II and Rudolf II; the Swedish Queen Christina, the Russian Tsar Peter the Great and the Prussian King Frederick III. In 1617 King James VI of Scotland and I of England defended his relationship with George Villiers, Duke of Buckingham, with the following words: 'Jesus Christ did the same, and therefore I cannot be blamed. Christ had his John, and I have my George.'[168] King James did not leave it at that and, in practice, male homosexuality was encouraged at his court.[169] In her many letters, Louis XIV's sister-in-law Elisabeth Charlotte not only mentioned the numerous relationships her husband Philip of Orléans had with other men but noted that many of the men at the French court maintained that sex between men had only been a sin in the days when there were so few people that the earth needed to be populated. As they pointed out, God had not punished anyone for homosexuality since Sodom and Gomorrah.[170]

Despite the Christian convictions that underpinned the persecution of homosexuals in Christian countries, the Catholic Church itself, as well as many Orthodox churches, often functioned as a refuge for men who were sexually attracted to other men. Discreet sex between clerics was often tolerated. In the Middle Ages even Muslim poets commented enthusiastically that love between men was common in Orthodox monasteries.[171] Catholic priests suspected of homosexuality could not be punished under secular law unless the Church defrocked them, which it frequently refused to do. The Church usually preferred to send guilty priests into monasteries, which themselves were not free of homosexuality.[172] When the philosopher Jean-Jacques Rousseau complained about a male guest making sexual advances to him, the head of the Catholic lodging-house he was staying at reprimanded the philosopher and told him he could hardly complain if someone found him attractive;

as to the sexual act itself, any fear Rousseau might have was just vanity on his part.[173] The tacit toleration of discreet homosexuality went right to the top of the hierarchy. In the eleventh century Pope Leo IX explicitly rejected the idea that clerics should be dismissed from office for occasional acts of mutual masturbation or intercourse where satisfaction was achieved by putting the penis between another man's thighs.[174] In the sixteenth century Pope Julius III was notorious for his sexual relationships with young boys and went so far as to make his seventeen-year-old lover, the street boy Innocenzo, a cardinal. As pope, Julius was to all intents and purposes above the law, but making his lover a cardinal nevertheless caused a scandal among Catholics and glee among Protestants.[175]

Thus, even though the dominant trend in Christianity has clearly been one of condemnation and persecution, history shows that there have always been many Christians who have either not considered homosexuality to be a real issue or have defended it from a Christian point of view. In the case of sex between women, the extent to which it has been ignored or not regarded as real sex shows that it was not considered to be a problem. Christianity, then, provides a good example of the way a religion widely known for its unbending historical hostility to homosexuality has nevertheless always had voices that proclaim something quite different.

Acceptance or Punishment

At the end of the nineteenth century and the beginning of the twentieth, many Western European Christian men attracted to other men took refuge in the Muslim world. In 1894 the French author André Gide lost his virginity in the desert sand as a twenty-four-year-old. He was with Ali, a young Muslim man, and as Gide himself tells us, 'His body was quite hot but to my hands he felt as refreshing as the shade.' Hardly surprisingly, Gide returned to North Africa frequently after this.[176] Oscar Wilde also liked to visit the same regions because of the many sexual possibilities with other men.[177] The British author E. M. Forster found love with Mohammed el Adl, an Egyptian Muslim tram-driver in Alexandria.[178] Right up until the 1950s Tangiers in Morocco was well known as a haven of gay male artists from the West, and their intimate meetings with Muslim men inspired many works of art.[179] The attraction that Muslim countries exerted on cultured European men was certainly influenced by their orientalist fantasies of exotic and erotic Araby, but there is no escaping the fact that these Muslim countries offered them much better opportunities for real sexual experiences with other men without the weight of condemnation attached to such behaviour farther north.

The reason for Muslim countries emerging as homoerotic oases in this way has little to do with Islam taking a fundamentally more tolerant view of male homosexuality than Christianity. In fact, it does not. What Gide, Wilde, Forster and all the rest of these Christians discovered was that the majority of Muslims were more tolerant of sex between men and that homosexual activity was not seen as a great problem *vis à vis* religion. At the same time, most of them discovered that attempts to have exclusive relationships with their Muslim lovers were not so easy: if the Muslim men had not already contracted heterosexual marriages, they had plans to do so.

But Islam is not hostile to homosexuality in any general sense. The Koran does not ban sex between women; indeed, it makes no reference to it. On the other hand, what little there is about sex between men is rather negative. Unlike the Bible, but in accord with various later Jewish and Christian authors, the Koran mainly criticizes the inhabitants of Sodom for sex between men. The male Sodomites, called Lot's people, are criticized for 'lusting after men instead of women'.[180] 'What! Do you come to the males from among the creatures, And leave what your Lord has created for you of your wives? Nay, you are a people exceeding limits.'[181] The fact that men have sex with one another is given theological significance because this means they 'hold the truth to be lies'[182] and are therefore ungodly.[183] It is because of their homosexuality that Allah punishes them with an 'evil' and 'terrifying' rain.[184]

Despite viewing the destruction of Sodom as a punishment for sex between men, the Koran nevertheless proposes a very much milder punishment for homosexuality than the hundred lashes the holy book prescribed for heterosexual adultery.[185] 'And as for the two who are guilty of indecency from among you, give them both a punishment',[186] the Koran states, but does not specify. There is no basis for suggesting that the punishment should be lashes or the death penalty, since this verse follows on immediately after a verse that merely prescribes house arrest for unmarried women guilty of 'indecency'. And there is also a further statement that absolves homosexuals from punishment: if the guilty men 'repent and amend, let them go in peace, for Allah is the most merciful'.[187]

There are some Muslims who believe that homosexuality exists in paradise in spite of the general prohibition voiced in the Koran. The Koranic account of 'eternally young youths' 'as beautiful as pearls' who will serve men in paradise has often been seen as an indication of this. The fact that they figure in the same context as female virgins who are clearly sexually active is often taken as proof that these beautiful youths will also have sex with men in paradise.[188]

The possibility of sex between men in heaven does not, however, make that kind of sex permissible in this life. In the hadiths we find Muhammad demanding more severe punishments for illegal sex than in the Koran: 'If you discover anyone doing what Lot's people did, kill the one doing it and the passive partner.'[189] The clear message is that a man who has anal sex with another man should be stoned,[190] although sometimes it seems that this punishment is reserved for unmarried men.[191]

When we study the hadiths, however, we find that Muhammad pays much less attention to male homosexuality than to heterosexual adultery, in spite of which Muhammad's successors came up with new methods of execution for homosexuals. Abu Bakr, the first caliph, had a wall pushed down on top of a man condemned for homosexuality, and another man was burned alive. Ali, Muhammad's son-in-law, is reported to have ordered a condemned man to be hurled from a minaret.[192]

Initially, then, the Koran proposes milder punishment for sex between men than for heterosexual adultery and Muhammad, too, was more concerned about the latter. But even though Muhammad demanded the death penalty, there is an absence of judicial unity in the traditions: for instance, the Sunni Hanafi school, which is dominant in south Asia, the Balkans, Turkey, Syria and Egypt, does not believe that sex between men is punishable with death.[193]

Just as with illegal heterosexual behaviour, the strict requirement for proof means that sex between men has rarely resulted in significant levels of persecution within Islam. Rather the reverse: same-sex sex has often been tolerated, sometimes even accepted and lauded, in Islamic societies, as many Western homosexuals discovered at the beginning of the last century. Abu Nuwas, who lived around the year 800 and is acknowledged to be one of the great names in classical Arabic poetry, liked to dwell on the love of young men in his poetry.[194] Many male Muslim poets followed in his footsteps and wrote extensively about their erotic desire for young men. A whole series of Muslim rulers, just as was the case with many Christian monarchs, were well known for their predilection for other men – Caliph al-Amin of Baghdad, the caliphs Abd al-Rahman iii and al-Hakam ii of Cordoba, all from the ninth and tenth centuries, are just some of them.[195] In order to wean him from his attraction to boys, al-Amin's mother dressed a group of young girls as male pages for him. This was not only successful in this respect, just as his mother had hoped, but also set a fashion among women that lasted for more than a century.[196]

The popular Tunisian poet Ahmad al-Tifashi, who gave such excellent advice about how to enjoy forbidden sex during the thirteenth century, did not restrict himself to the heterosexual sphere. He gives instructions about how to find and seduce willing boys.Tilfashi also offered practical advice on how to get the most sexual pleasure with hermaphrodites. And although lesbian sex was not forbidden, he also includes a chapter devoted to the ways in which women could enjoy sex with other women.[197]

The Perfumed Garden, written by Sheikh Muhammad al-Nafzawi in the sixteenth century, also contains a chapter devoted to the pleasures of sex between men.[198] It is worth noting in this context that al-Nafzawi was far from being an insignificant figure in religious terms, 'sheikh' being a Muslim religious title. Male followers of Sufism, a tradition of Islamic mysticism, frequently referred to the beauty of beardless young men in their classical verse,[199] and a number of important male Sufists of the twelfth century are known for having had passionate love affairs with one another.[200]

Sex between men is traditionally both widespread and accepted in very many Muslim societies. A number of historical and anthropological studies report of virtually universal homosexual activity between men of different age groups in several Muslim areas from Morocco in the west to Indonesia in the east, from Albania in the north to Zanzibar in the south.[201] The great majority of Muslim men who have sex with men do so without breaking the traditional pattern of entering heterosexual marriage when they have reached a certain age. Since the majority of Islamic countries have strict rules regarding contact between the sexes, homosexuality is particularly widespread among unmarried men.[202] Given that women are so inaccessible, it is hardly surprising that male beauty is emphasized to such an extent. The twelfth-century Hanbalite jurist Ibn al-Jawzi commented on men who look at young boys: 'Anyone who claims that he does not feel some desire is a liar, and if we do believe him then he must be an animal rather than a human being.'[203]

Men who declared their love for other men were often respected and admired.[204] Virtually every Spanish Muslim collection of poetry contains love poems written by men to men.[205] In the early eighteenth-century poem 'Abru', the Indian poet Najmuddin Shah Mubarak writes of young men being courted by other men in the Muslim city of Delhi.[206] Persian and Turkish miniatures from recent centuries depict men in explicitly sexual situations with other men.[207] Relationships between men and young boys were – and still are – socially acceptable in the traditions of the Pashtuns in what is now western Pakistan and southern Afghanistan.[208] The sexually passive partner is, however, often looked down on as behaving in a way that conflicts with the accepted male role. In North Africa the sexually active partners are known to boast of having 'taken' the passive partners, who are thus humiliated.[209]

Many Muslim societies also have a long tradition of men with divergent gender identity having sex with other men.[210] In Java, for instance, it is traditionally acceptable for both male transvestites and young boys who play female roles in the theatre to have sex with other men.[211] The north Sudanese healing cult Zaar is only open to women and to men with divergent gender identity, and many of the latter have sex with other men.[212] Homosexual male transvestites called *mashoga* or *mabasha* are common in the Muslim coastal villages of Kenya and Tanzania.[213] There are clear parallels between this pattern and the so-called *khaniths* in Oman, men who live outside the usual male gender role and have sex with other men.[214] In Muslim South Asia, there are many *hijras* – men who wear women's clothing and have sex with other men – although, historically speaking, the custom seems to have developed within Hinduism.[215] Among the Muslim Hausa people in the Sahel there is a tradition of *k'wazo*, older, masculine and sexually active men, associating with *baja*, younger and more feminine men, and these couples sometimes even live in relationships that resemble marriages.[216] In the Siwa Oasis in Egypt the relationships between men and young boys were institutionalized to the extent that there were weddings and dowries.[217]

Even though the Koran does not ban sex between women, lesbian sex is nevertheless much less visible, probably as a result of the traditional position of Islamic women being much less visible in every respect. The lack of visibility does not, however, mean that sexual relationships between women do not exist. Among Pakistani women, discreet sex is often accepted as long as it does not infringe on the woman's role as wife and mother,[218] and this also seems to be the situation in many other Muslim societies. Twenty-four per cent of Iranian women admit to having had sex with other women although virtually none of them live exclusively lesbian lives.[219] Other patterns of sex between women also exist in the Islamic world. Women who live exclusively lesbian lives are common and traditionally tolerated in the Muslim villages on the coast of East Africa.[220] There are also eighteenth-century references to marriages between Muslim women in India – the partners counted cardamom seeds to decide which of them should 'become the male' in the marriage.[221]

The traditional Muslim attitude to same-sex sexuality is characterized above all by diversity. The fact that sex between women is not banned has not led to any great recognition of the phenomenon whereas, in the case of sex between men, the mild reproofs voiced by the Koran and the harsh punishments proposed by the hadiths have very rarely given rise to active persecution. The regulation that there needs to be either a confession or four male witnesses has meant that legal charges are virtually impossible as long as the perpetrators are discreet.

But the homosexuality that exists in Muslim societies is not necessarily discreet and many Muslims have obviously believed that there are no problems with same-sex sexuality from an Islamic perspective. It would appear that Islam's traditional claim to be a tolerant and merciful religion has had clear and practical consequences in this area. Praise for the beauty of young men is a repeated pattern in Muslim culture – a pattern that has to be seen in the context of the virtual absence of young women from the public space. However, the existence of institutionalized gender variants and marriage-like same-sex relationships in certain Muslim societies serves to demonstrate the extent to which homosexual practices are considered unproblematic in relation to Islam.

Original Ambivalence, Imported Oppression

It is only in the last couple of centuries that it has become possible to view Hinduism as something approaching a unified religion, so it is hardly surprising that there are divergent attitudes to same-sex sexuality within Hindu traditions. Homosexuality is, however, to be found in very many different contexts and the gods themselves were happy to practise it. On one occasion Shiva turned himself into a woman in order to be able to love his wife Parvati better.[222] The god Krishna took on the form of a beautiful young woman in order to seduce and destroy the demon Araka – three days after the wedding Krishna killed his demonic husband.[223] Just as the loving heterosexual couple Shiva and Parvati are often depicted as a single fused being, the god Harihara is a fusion of the male gods Shiva and Vishnu.[224] The almost boundless sexuality frequently exhibited by the gods is often seen as particularly holy, and sometimes even as an example to be followed. It is not insignificant that Vishnu, for example, transforms himself into the temptress Mohini and has a child by Shiva.[225] Homosexuality in itself could be holy, as we can see at a number of temples such as Khajuraho in Madhya Pradesh and Konark in Orissa, where there are depictions of homosexuality among the many varieties of sexual art. Sex between women is a favourite theme in this temple art.

Various mythical narratives show that same-sex sexuality could be directly blessed by the gods. An eleventh-century statue from Orissa shows Kama, the god of love, firing his arrows of love at two women.[226] A number of versions of the medieval text *Padma Purana* tell how the two widows of the childless King Dilipa are advised either by a priest or a god to have sex with one another in order to conceive a child. They do so, with the blessing of the gods, and their child is given the name Bhagiratha since it has been 'born of two vulvas'.[227]

There was no need for any encouragement from the gods, however, for Hindus to practise homosexual sex. The *Kamasutra* describes in detail how men who are concealing their exclusively homo sexual desires have oral sex with other men.[228] The same text includes approving references to the way concubines use various kinds of fruit and vegetables as sexual aids when they lie with one another or with their friends or female servants.[229]

Hijras, the transgender or third gender people, play a particularly prominent role in Hinduism and add variety to the religio-sexual landscape. The goddess Bahuchara, who cut off her own breasts to avoid being raped, is very important to the *hijras*, who see a reflection of their own situation in a legendary male follower of Bahuchara, whom the goddess ordered to castrate himself and wear women's clothes.[230] The *Kamasutra* tells how *hijras* can live as courtesans and enjoy sex with men.[231]

Reincarnation also has its part to play in the Hindu view of same-sex sexuality in that it means that one and the same person may be reborn as a man or as a woman in different lives. Many of the medieval male mystics, for instance, were considered to be reincarnations of Krishna's female lovers.[232] For more ordinary Hindus, however, gender is a boundary that is not normally crossed when an individual is reincarnated,[233] although it is in theory possible to change sex in other ways and thus experience erotic love with people of one's original gender. The legendary Hindu wise man Narada once asked the god Krishna to explain love to him. The god led the wise

Hijras play a prominent role in Hinduism.

man to a miraculous lake brimming with divine nectar and there Narada bathed and was transformed into the beautiful young woman Naradi for a year. Narada – in the form of Naradi – then spent the whole year with Krishna.[234]

There are a number of injunctions in the *Laws of Manu* which, at first sight, seem to suggest a more negative view of sex between women. An unmarried woman who defiles another unmarried woman must pay twice the bride-price and receive ten blows with a cudgel. A married woman who seduces an unmarried woman should be punished even more severely: she is to have her head shaved, two fingers cut off and be forced to ride through the town on an ass.[235] The focus of the *Laws of Manu*, however, is not so much sex between women as such as the importance of protecting unmarried women so that they may be virginal in every respect when they marry. There is consequently absolutely no condemnation of sex between married women like the happy concubines with their vegetables mentioned in the *Kamasutra*.

The *Laws of Manu* also forbids men of the three highest castes to have anal intercourse with other men but it says nothing about other kinds of sex between men. Men of the lowest male caste and men without caste are apparently free to have sex with other men. The punishment for high-caste men who have anal sex with one another is considerably milder than for heterosexual anal sex: where- as a high-caste man only has to take a ritual bath after anal sex with a man,[236] after anal sex with a woman he has to swallow a number of bovine products – urine, dung, milk, sour milk and butter – and then fast for twenty-four hours.[237]

Sex between men was forbidden by law in India right up until 2009, an then again between 2013 and 2018.[238] Before the Supreme Court of India struck down, in September 2018, Section 377 of the Indian Penal Code – a British colonial era law that criminalized sexual acts 'against the order of nature' – homosexual men could, in principle, risk being jailed for life, though in fact the law was a sleeping law. In its origins this law had nothing to do with Hinduism, being a piece of legislation introduced by the British in 1860, modelled directly on the Christian legal tradition in Great Britain. Even though the law had nothing at all to do with Hindu traditions, it nevertheless contributed to the stigmatization of homosexuality among Hindus. Like the Japanese and the Chinese, many Indians adopted European homophobia and made it their own. Mahatma Gandhi called homosexuality and any other sex that could not lead to procreation 'unnatural vice' and in the 1920s and 1930s he led campaigns to remove all positive references to homosexuality and transsexualism in Hinduism. He even sent groups of his supporters round to destroy homoerotic images depicted in medieval Hindu art – especially in temples.[239]

It is difficult to reach firm conclusions about attitudes to homosexuality in the history of Hinduism. Same-sex sexuality may not have been seen as normative but the phenomenon was certainly given a place within the framework of the religion. One of the most striking features of Hinduism is the extent to which factors that originally had nothing to do with the religion contributed to the development of a totally new view of homosexuality during a formative period of its history. Anti-homosexual measures drawn from the British and Christian traditions were not only followed through but were also adopted by Hindus of all classes to the extent that they came to be thought of as elements of their own religion. Though these attitudes were imported they *became* part of Hinduism. The homophobic European colonialists succeeded beyond all expectations: not only did they use the law to stigmatize and suppress sexual behaviour that conflicted with their own religious convictions, but millions of Hindus then went on to accept these things as their religious convictions.

Religion and Homosexuality Today

Same-sex marriage is among the most visible aspects in the current relationship between homosexuality and religion. It is also one of the most significant indicators of the great change in attitude that is taking place, both within religion and in society at general. Most countries in Latin America and the West, all predominantly Christian, have legally recognized same-sex marriage. This is also the case with several other countries and territories on all continents, a couple of them predominantly Buddhist, Hindu, and Muslim. Israel, which only legally accepts domestic marriages when performed by certain religious denominations, recognizes same-sex marriages contracted in other countries (also online) and has thus effectively given it equal status with heterosexual marriage.

These changes have not occurred without opposition from conservative Christians and other believers. In the run-up to the vote on the 2009 marriage law giving homosexual and heterosexual couples the same rights, members of the Norwegian parliament received frequent death threats from pious Christians by telephone, text message and email;[240] the Catholic Church in Spain organized demonstrations involving several hundred thousand participants in 2005;[241] evangelical Christians in California staged a hunger strike for forty days (like Jesus in the desert) to support the bid to abolish same-sex marriage in 2008;[242] Orthodox Jews have often taken a firm stance and criticized other Jews who support same-sex marriage in the USA.[243]

What is particularly interesting about the Christian opposition to same-sex marriage and civil union is its intensity. It is motivated, among other things, by the religious conviction that marriage is an eternal and immutable institution that will be destroyed if it is opened up to new groups. When looked at more closely, it is possible to recognize the same anti-homosexual convictions, the same religious arguments that have been used and are still being used to justify discrimination, a total ban or the death penalty. The debate has not, in fact, added anything very new to the picture.

One of the things that became clear in the debate about the 2009 Norwegian marriage equality law was that there was a significant religious movement in favour of the legalization of same-sex marriage however vocal the religious opposition to it may be. The radical change in attitude that had taken place since the 1993 discussion about the civil union law was particularly remarkable. Whereas almost all religious groups harshly condemned the introduction of the civil union law in 1993, in the discussions about a new marriage law just fifteen years later practically all religious groups *supported* the civil union law, and a significant number even the right to same-sex marriage. A number of Jewish and Christian organizations were supporting the idea of marriage long before legalization was on the agenda. The United Church of Christ in the United States began carrying out marriage ceremonies for same-sex couples as early as 1972.[244] The Union for Reform Judaism pressed for Jewish religious weddings for same-sex couples and for common marriage legislation in 1997.[245] The United Church of Canada, the largest Protestant denomination in the country, introduced homosexual marriage in 2003.[246] In 2009, shortly before it became official church policy, 68 per cent of the ministers of the Church of Sweden – which had earlier been the official state church – stated that they wished to perform marriages for same-sex couples.[247]

In South Africa both the Anglican church and SACC – the joint council of all the churches in the country – took a positive view of the legal acknowledgement of same-sex marriages in the country, although they stressed that their political support did not include religious acknowledgement of such marriages.[248] It was, moreover, religious action – the weddings of Kevin Bourassa to Joe Varnell and of Elaine and Anne Vautour in the Metropolitan Community Church in Toronto on 14 January 2001 – that started the judicial process that led to the legalization of same-sex marriages in Canada.[249]

There is a majority in favour of same-sex marriages in many Catholic and Protestant countries. A survey of European Union countries in 2006 showed this to be the case in the Netherlands, Sweden, Denmark, Belgium, Luxembourg, Spain, Germany and the Czech Republic, with the numbers of those in favour varying between 82 and 52 per cent.[250]

Same-sex marriage has been recognized by law or authority in parts of South and South east Asia. The Supreme Court in Hindu Nepal has ruled that same-sex couples have the right to marry, but the authorities have still not acted on the decision.[251] The Buddhist King Sihanouk of Cambodia has supported same-sex marriage, but there have not been any legislative moves so far.[252]

A whole series of factors seems to have moved developments on to a more gay-positive track. We can point to the arguments that have been put forward on the basis of human rights legislation and its ban on discrimination against gays and lesbians, or to the parallels that have been drawn with other traditionally oppressed groups, or to the focus on such genuine problem areas as the tax, inheritance and social welfare consequences faced by same-sex couples if they are not permitted to marry. The rather imprecise comparison made by the historian John Boswell between same-sex marriage and the way the medieval churches gave its blessing to pairs of same-sex friends also seems to be one of the factors that influenced the debate on same-sex marriage among liberal Christians in the 1990s, at least in North America, where the debate has been going on longest.[253]

The followers of a number of religions in countries where there has not yet been much serious discussion of the topic of equal status for heterosexual and homosexual marriage have taken practical steps to address the issue, or pointed to older traditions. A news paper in Kano in Northern Nigeria that wrote of same-sex marriage as a

Western phenomenon caused the city's gay community to protest and point out that same-sex married couples were common in the Muslim Hausa culture.[254] A number of male couples in Pakistan have been married according to Muslim rites since the 1980s, although the marriages are not formally recognized by the authorities.[255] *Hijras* have sometimes married other men, again according to Muslim rites.[256] Hindu priests in India married a number of same-sex couples with trad itional wedding rituals both in and outside temples during the 1990s and 2000s. The attitudes of family and friends ranged from the totally negative to the fully supportive, and in the latter case they joined in all the traditional wedding celebrations.[257]

Even though positive attitudes towards it have existed in all the major religions at various times in their history, it is still difficult to identify exactly what has led to the levels of tolerance of same-sex sexuality exhibited by major parts of these religions today. Even in relatively gay-friendly religions like Buddhism and Hinduism, the positive attitude was not strong enough to prevent imported homophobia – and, in the case of some countries, imported legal prohibition – from overshadowing a traditionally more liberal view of homosexuality. Traditional Muslim tolerance of discreet homosexuality has similarly been undermined by Christian and Chris tianinfluenced homophobia and by the more recent exclusively gay and lesbian lifestyle that has grown up in the Christian West, which is difficult to combine with more traditional Muslim family life. It is consequently necessary, both in the case of religions that have become more homophobic after contact with Western Christian ideas, and in the case of religions that have always been homo phobic, to examine non-religious factors in order to reach an understanding of why so many people in all these religions have become so tolerant of homosexuality today.

France decriminalized homosexuality, along with all other kinds of consensual sex, in 1791; the reasoning was that bans of this kind created artificial crimes.[258] More than 200 years were to pass before homosexuality was legal across the whole of Europe, but the French decriminalization was enormously important because it showed so clearly that this kind of ban on consensual sex, far from being a legal necessity, had its roots in religious convictions and in the pseudo-religious prejudices held by most people. The legal change had immediate consequences: it was spread by the Napoleonic Wars and then imitated in a number of other Christian countries. Also the predominantly Muslim Ottoman Caliphate, then stretching from Tunisia to Kuwait and from Bosnia to Yemen, abolished its ban on sex between men already in 1858. The underlying logic of the change is also what has been used by gay and lesbian human rights organizations throughout the twentieth and twenty-first centuries. Religion, or prejudices derived from religion, should not be used to forbid or punish relationships that quite clearly belong within the sphere of private life. The same principle has been applied on many occasions by the European Court of Human Rights and the UN Human Rights Council.[259]

The change in religious attitudes to homosexuality during the last two decades also has to be seen in the light of a general shift towards greater freedom and equality in a number of other areas of society. The opposition of religious conservatives to each and every one of these liberation projects is a recurring pattern, irrespective of whether the issue is one of gender equality, racial equality or equal status for heterosexuals and homosexuals. However, very many more liberal religious people of all kinds have been quick to adapt to the liberal currents and to incorporate them into their religious world views. And as more and more gays and lesbians have come out into the open, they too have influenced the religions from within.

Whereas religious arguments were not particularly central to the early struggle to promote acceptance of homosexuality, the opposite was true among those who fought to *uphold* the persecution of and discrimination against gays and lesbians. Conservative interpretations of various religious authorities formed the basis of their arguments. During recent decades it has become more common for them to use different arguments to defend persecution and discrimination, but one still finds that the main opponents of tolerance are religiously conservative individuals and institutions. When the non-religious arguments of such people are examined more closely – statements about human nature, the family as the buttress of society, children's rights vis-à-vis their parents and so on – we usually find that they are almost always aimed exclusively at limiting the rights of gays and lesbians. The non-religious arguments often prove to be merely substitute arguments which are being used because religious control of the lives of others is no longer acceptable in most Christian or Jewish societies. Almost all the efforts to retain, strengthen or reintroduce bans on same-sex sexuality or to discriminate against gays and lesbians will almost invariably be found to be ultimately based on religious opposition.

The same thing holds true of the opposition to homosexuality that has emerged in the last couple of decades in countries where other religions are dominant. Viewed from the perspective of anti-homosexual religious believers, the widespread toleration of open gays and lesbians and gay family arrangements means that it has become impossible for them to see their religious ideals reflected by the society they live in. This, of course, also holds true for the acceptance of other forms of behaviour that are in conflict with conservative religious convictions, but because many conservative faith groups have paid such overwhelming attention to homosexuality, and because of the visibility gays and lesbians have now achieved, the opposition to homosexuality stands out as being particularly pivotal.

Given that all the legal prohibitions against homosexuality have had a direct or indirect religious basis, it comes as no surprise that the opposition to legalization has often been of a strongly religious order, with believers defending their own religious convictions in whatever form they have been codified in the legislation. A number of churches were prominent in their opposition to the process of decriminalization as it spread across Europe. The Calvinistic Church of Scotland supported the continuation of the ban, thus contributing to a significant minority voting against decriminalization in 1980.[260] In Northern Ireland both the Catholic and the Presbyterian churches wished to retain the ban, and homosexuality was only decriminalized there in 1981 after a judgement by the European Court of Human Rights in Strasbourg.[261] Ian Paisley, Presbyterian minister and Unionist leader in a country then suffering what was almost a civil war, argued: 'The crime of sodomy is a crime against God and man and its practice is a terrible step towards the total demoralization of any country and must inevitably lead to the breakdown of all decency within the province.'[262] When the Supreme Court in Eire upheld the ban on homosexuality in 1983, its reasoning was the incorrect claim that homosexuality 'has always been condemned in Christian teaching as morally wrong'.[263] In Romania, the Romanian Orthodox church led the campaign to retain the ban on homosexuality even though the country had pledged to abolish the ban on becoming a member of the Council of Europe in 1993.[264] There was a high level of agreement between the church leadership and the population at large in this case and a survey in 2000 showed that 86 per cent of Roma nians would not want to have gay or lesbian neighbours.[265] In spite of the total opposition of the church, the Romanian parliament repealed the ban in 2000 after the European Union made such a move an absolute condition of membership. The Orthodox Christian student association then mounted a massive campaign against members of parliament, accusing them of atheism and immorality,[266] while the leader of the Orthodox church, Patriarch Teoctist Arapasu, otherwise renowned for his unconditional support for the Communist dictator Ceausescu right to the end, announced that 'evil threatens to take over the world'.[267]

Although many Christians have consistently campaigned for socially liberal measures regarding homosexuality, many other Christians have been trying to introduce new or retain old legal restrictions. When Nicaragua reintroduced a ban on homosexual sex in 1992, the move was driven by conservative Christians and was strongly supported, for instance, by Cardinal Miguel Obando y Bravo.[268] Immediately after the legalization of sex between men in India in 2009, the Mizoram Kohhran Hruaitute Committee – an umbrella organization of churches – demanded that the ban be re-introduced in the federal state of Mizoram.[269] In Poland, the League of Polish Families – a Catholic political party – proposed setting up gay and lesbian re-education camps modelled on the system used during the Chinese cultural revolution.[270] A 2003 opinion poll in the mainly Christian US showed that 37 per cent of the population believed that homosexuality should be made illegal.[271] Several Anglican bishops in Nigeria have proposed the death penalty for homosexuals,[272] and in 2006 Archbishop Peter Akinola supported a proposed law that would not only ban all same-sex sex but also remove human rights from gays and lesbians, ban expressions of gay or lesbian identity and take away the right of assembly; the latter would have made it illegal for two open gays or lesbians to go to the cinema or to a restaurant together.[273] In 2010 the Anglican church in Uganda supported a proposed law that would mean the death sentence for homosexuality in spite of the fact that many other Christians both inside and outside Uganda condemned the proposal.[274] There are some Christians who take a more directly personal view of what they would do. Otto Odongo, a Christian member of parliament in Uganda, declared in 2010 that he would kill his own son if he was homosexual.[275] The American television evangelist Jimmy Swaggart, clearly a spiritual friend of Odongo, had this to tell his audience in 2004: 'I've never seen a man in my life I wanted to marry. And I'm gonna be blunt and plain; if one ever looks at me like that, I'm gonna kill him and tell God he died.' At this point his audience applauded.[276]

Some people in other religions have devoted a similar amount of time and effort to upholding or reintroducing a ban on homosexuality and discrimination against those who practise it. Hindu nationalists in India have actively defended the Victorian ban in the Indian criminal code, arguing on the basis of popular opinion. According to the world view of the Hindu nationalists, which is not a completely accurate one, homosexuality did not exist in original Hinduism but was introduced along with Muslim and Christian imperialism during medieval and modern times.[277]

Islamic fundamentalists have also seized every opportunity open to them to restrict the rights of homosexuals. In Iran, where the otherwise not very democratic regime of the shah allowed gays and lesbians to live openly in peace, the Islamic revolution of 1979 led to a reintroduction of the death penalty and systematic persecution on a scale that is perhaps unmatched in history. Men were hanged for homosexuality in towns all over Iran[278] and others suspected of being homosexual were summarily shot in the street after a short interrogation.[279] The Muslim homosexual organization Al-Fatiha estimates that about 4,000 people have been executed for homosexuality since the revolution, most of them in the early days.[280] It is impossible to come up with an exact figure. Similarly, the reintroduction of sharia law in Afghanistan under the Taliban, in the Sudan and in some Northern Nigerian provinces has led to the death penalty for sex between men. Condemned men in Afghanistan were frequently killed by having a wall collapsed on top of them. Also in the absence of the Taliban, Afghan courts continued to punish homosexuals with prison sentences although they could, in principle, still use the death penalty.

A completely new development that began to emerge at the end of the twentieth century is the constantly growing activism of open gays and lesbians working inside their own religious communities. This activism often takes the form of setting up their own movements and these have had varying levels of impact on the faith communities as a whole. In the US, for instance, gay and lesbian Baptists set up their own organization in 1972, Episcopalians in 1974, Adventists in 1976, Evangelicals in 1975, Anabaptists in 1976 and Mormons in 1977. Now there are also active groups among the Lutherans, Orthodox,

Southern Baptists, Catholics, the Quakers, Unitarians and Christian Scientists.[281] Comparable activism within the Jewish community led gays and lesbians to establish their own synagogues in New York, San Francisco and Los Angeles in the 1970s.[282] Religious homosexual movements of this kind do not, however, guarantee increased acceptance within the religious groups in question. Dignity, the Catholic homosexual group, was allowed to meet in many churches in the US during the 1980s but stricter rulings from the centre put a stop to this.[283]

The Muslim homosexual movement Al-Fatiha was founded in the US in 1998 and has since become established in Great Britain, Canada and South Africa.[284] As well as creating a community and working for human rights in general, the group (together with other liberal Muslims) argues that homosexuality is compatible with Islam, just as liberal Jews and Christians argue in the case of their religions. The existence of homosexual organizations in mainly Muslim countries like Albania, Bangladesh, Bosnia, Indonesia, Kazakhstan, Kosovo, Lebanon, Malaysia, Morocco, Palestine, Senegal and Turkey, as well as gay parades in Istanbul and Sarajevo, bear witness to increased consciousness among gay and lesbian Muslims. They base their arguments on interpretations of the Koran and the hadiths, and point to hundreds of years of Muslim tolerance towards homosexuality.[285] Given the long tradition of tolerance of homosexuality in Muslim countries, many of them argue that the homophobia that is more widespread in the Islamic world these days is as much a result of Western influence as it is of Islamic tradition.[286] Sex between women has never been banned either by the Koran or by tradition, yet many Muslims now rank it alongside sex between men and condemn both. And even when it comes to the issue of living an exclusively homosexual life, there is a whole series of not very well-known traditional parallels to which modern Muslims can point, as we have seen earlier in this chapter.

Even though Hinduism originally took a fairly relaxed view of same-sex sexuality, that is no longer the case. The legal and secular influence exerted by the Christian colonial power has resulted in most Hindus having a negative attitude to homosexuality. Thus homophobia has now become a part of Hindu belief. But there is by no means a consensus. When a reporter from *Hinduism Today* asked a number of priests at the 2004 *kumbha mela* festival about Hindu attitudes to homosexuality and same-sex marriage, he received a range of very different answers. Some thought the whole business was connected to Western influences, others viewed homosexuality as 'unnatural, uncommon and unusual' without offering any further theological backing, others thought it was all up to the individual believer, whereas others again argued in favour of acceptance.[287]

Hindu gay and lesbian activists are increasingly referring to the more gay-friendly, pre-colonial Hindu traditions and are using religious arguments in their criticism of homophobic Hindu nationalists. They are pressing right-wing activists to read Hindu texts and to look more closely at Indian history in order to learn the extent to which present-day Hindu homophobia is largely a result of imported British values, legislation and other more recent historical developments.[288] The reactions that greeted Deep Mehta's 1996 feature film *Fire*, which depicts a love affair between two Hindu sisters-in-law, exemplify the different attitudes. Supporters of the Hindu nationalist Shiv Sena party attacked cinemas and accused the film of being antagonistic to Indian culture. Other Hindus, on the other hand, defended the film precisely on the grounds that it defended the traditional Hindu acceptance of homosexuality.[289]

The more liberal attitudes among modern Hindus are also a result of the international struggle for gay and lesbian human rights, as well as of the recognition by an increasing number of Hindus that homophobia is primarily a result of British influence. In 2007, the Supreme Court in Hindu Nepal, for instance, decided that homosexuality should be legalized and gays and lesbians given equal rights with heterosexuals,[290] and a court judgement in India in 2009 set aside the legal ban on sex between men.[291]

The changes in Hindu attitudes are particularly visible among the middle classes, which is also the situation in other religious communities. A survey of Hindus in southern Florida showed that 20 per cent accepted same-sex relationships, 20 per cent considered them to be 'immoral' and the remaining 60 per cent found them 'personally unacceptable but people should be allowed to do what they want'.[292]

Buddhism, too, has been affected by a variety of recent trends. In Japan, with its mixture of Buddhism and Shintoism, the original acceptance of homosexuality has grown again after disappearing during the period when the country was modernizing. This is mainly a result of the general international struggle for gay and lesbian human rights that started in the Western world, but there is also an increasing awareness of their own, older gay-friendly attitudes. Colourful and exuberant gay and lesbian parades have become more and more popular in Thailand and Cambodia, and Thailand has become something of a tourist paradise for homosexuals because of its traditionally relaxed attitudes and because of the way it has integrated the more recent pattern of people living exclusively homosexual lifestyles. Better economic circumstances combined with a consciousness of the modern gay and lesbian lifestyle have led more and more people to want to live more independently from the traditional family structures. Thailand, Japan and Taiwan, as well as a number of other countries, have developed their own gay and lesbian organizations. Western Buddhism is usually very tolerant and some of the very earliest AIDS hospices were established by Zen Buddhists in San Francisco.[293]

In rather the same way as the modernization of Japan led to the introduction of homophobia, opposition to homosexuality has begun to emerge elsewhere in recent years. It would appear, for instance, that the Dalai Lama, the exiled Tibetan god-king, forgot how homosexual behaviour is traditionally common among Tibetan monks when he claimed on a number of occasions that homosexuality conflicts with Buddhist teaching because the vagina is the only orifice that should be used for sexual purposes. Despite this, the Dalai Lama does make a clear distinction between what he believes to be the right sexual behaviour for Buddhists and the human rights that protect gays and lesbians and their private lives. While the god-king believes that Buddhist teaching prohibits homosexual behaviour, he has no desire to see this incorporated into the legislation of any country.[294]

A number of specifically Buddhist homosexual groups have also been established in the West. A short search of the Internet reveals that in the major Western countries alone there are specific gay and lesbian groups associated with many different branches of Buddhism.

The majority of liberal Jews are tolerant of homosexuality these days. Open homosexuals were accepted among reformed Jews during the 1980s, both as followers and as rabbis.[295] Conservative Jews agreed in 2006 to accept two different positions. The first position, which has been the standard stance of Rabbinic Judaism for several centuries, is an overall rejection of all homosexuality. The second position gives equal status to heterosexuals and gays and lesbians with regard to marriage and the right to become rabbis. This position is, however, based on an absolutely literal reading of the Torah and it accepts homosexuality while excluding anal sex between men, that being the only activity specifically forbidden by the Hebrew Bible.[296] Even Orthodox Jews show signs of moving towards increased tolerance and the 2001 film *Trembling before G-d*, which deals with Orthodox Jewish gays and lesbians, was shown in a number of Orthodox communities. Both liberal and conservative Jewish organizations in the US have made official statements supporting human rights for gays and lesbians and condemning any violence directed at them.[297] During recent years Israel has become by far the most gay-friendly country in the Middle East in terms of legislation and public attitudes; it is also the country with the most thriving gay community in the region.

Judaism is, however, still home to some very forceful voices condemning homosexuality. Nissim Ze'ev, for instance, an Ultra-Orthodox rabbi and member of the Israeli parliament, proposed in 2007 that all gays and lesbians should be forcibly sent to specially built rehabilitation centres.[298] Three participants in the gay and lesbian parade in Jerusalem in 2005 were stabbed by a Jewish extremist and many others had urine and excrement hurled at them by radical Jewish counter-demonstrators.[299] In 2006 Jewish extremists distributed flyers promising a bounty of about £3,000 to anyone who killed a gay or lesbian in the parade. The flyer also had practical instructions on how to make Molotov cocktails to throw at the marchers.[300]

As is the case with other religions, more and more Muslims living in the West or living in a middle-class environment in Muslim countries are choosing to live exclusively as homosexuals. In Western countries in particular, and in the larger cities in Muslim countries, there are Muslims with a gay or lesbian identity and in the documentary film *A Jihad for Love* many of these people discuss their own situation and talk about both the increased level of tolerance and about growing opposition to open homosexuality.[301] Even in Muslim societies like the East African coastal villages, where there has traditionally been greater tolerance of people living exclusively as homosexuals lives, there is a tendency for the traditional same-sex categories to be supplanted or replaced by a more Western understanding of homosexuality.[302] The anonymity of large cities, in which social controls are lower, means that even less affluent men can live together as couples; this is often the case in large Pakistani cities although, in many cases, the men would not consider themselves to be gay.[303]

Muslims who are exclusively homosexual are nevertheless still a minority among those Muslims who practise homosexual sex, just as is the case with other groups. The general picture in mainly Muslim countries has been less affected by modern thinking and the more traditional pattern remains in force: that is, as long as the man does not deviate from the public male norm of being the active man, and as long as he keeps his sexuality strictly private, there is no problem with being sexually active. Because of the strict rules about contact between the sexes in Muslim Pakistan, it is easier for unmarried men to bring younger male lovers back to their flat than to bring female guests.[304] Even in countries like Iran where sex between men is punishable with death, it is far from unusual and 16 per cent of Iranian men say they have had homosexual experiences.[305] The gay American anthropologist Jerry Zarit, who makes no secret of his own promiscuity, has the following to say about the four years he spent in Tehran in the years around 1990: 'Iran was for me, and for others like me, a sexual paradise. In terms of both quantity and quality it was the most exciting period of my life.'[306] In southern Afghanistan, unmarried men who have sex with other men point out that women are not only completely inaccessible but also completely covered: 'We can't see whether the women are beautiful. But we can see the boys and see which of them is beautiful.'[307] Most of the men who have sex with men are nevertheless married, or will get married, as we saw in the case of the Pakistani lorry drivers.[308] Even men who sell sex to other men are traditionally not uncommon in some Muslim countries.[309] Even though it is not condemned in the Koran or in the hadiths, the position of lesbian sex, on the other hand, is as it always has been – discreet and rather more invisible.[310]

Muslim opposition to the practice of homosexuality is usually directed more at the newer, Western lifestyle of people being exclusively homosexual rather than at the sexual practice itself – as long as the latter runs parallel with the traditional pattern of family life. But there are changes taking place here too. Many Muslim families accept their gay and lesbian children and, increasingly, discreet gay meeting places are tolerated. In Norway, the Muslim and Conservative Party politician Afshan Rafiq criticizes her fellow believers for not condemning the discrimination, bullying and punishment of gays and lesbians: 'If you are of a gay disposition, that is between you and God . . . only God . . . can judge us.'[311] In Turkey a political alliance has formed between transvestite gay men and pious Muslim women who want the right to wear the hijab in public.[312]

When young Muslims tell their families that they do not wish to be part of a traditional heterosexual family structure, the private condemnation can sometimes be even stronger if they live in countries where homosexuality is more generally accepted. Young British Muslim gays and lesbians, for instance, may experience threats, compulsion and even serious violence from members of their own families.[313] There can also be great variations in Muslim attitudes to homosexuality between one Western country and another. A survey in 2008 showed that only 4 per cent of Muslims in London thought homosexuality was 'morally acceptable', although in Paris the figure was 18 per cent and in Berlin 26 per cent.[314]

The religious regime in Shia Muslim Iran has created a unique situation for some homosexuals. In spite of the fact that there is a death penalty for sex between men, Ayatollah Khomeini issued an authoritative fatwa in 1979 recognizing the right of diagnosed transsexuals to have gender corrective surgery. Once this has been done, the individuals are fully acknowledged by law and by religion to be of their new gender and to have the right to marry people who were previously of the same biological and legal sex as themselves.[315] As the 2008 documentary film *Be Like Others* reveals, many gays have undergone the surgery simply to be able to have legal relationships with people of the sex they are attracted to.[316]

The issue of homosexuality has caused major schisms in the Christian world. The Anglican Church provides a good example of the current depth of disunity within Christianity. On the one hand, there are the Nigerian and Ugandan bishops calling for the death penalty and the banning of gays and lesbians from restaurants; on the other there is Gene Robinson, an ordained bishop in New Hampshire who is married to another man. This disunity is reflected among most church members in countries where Anglicanism is widespread.

The fiercest Christian opposition is coming from countries that were until recently missionary fields, particularly those in Africa. Really extreme opposition to homosexuality is, however, fairly rare in most countries and even religious groups that consistently work against equal status for gays and lesbians object to some of the most violent attacks. When Robert Mugabe, the President of Zimbabwe, stated in 1995 that homosexuals are lower than animals, the Catholic Commission for Justice and Peace in Zimbabwe protested and argued that the right to respect for the private life of the individual also applied to gays and lesbians.[317]

There are times when the Christian arguments actually parallel the arguments that were formerly used by Christian supporters of racial segregation in the US: for instance, the claim that black demands for equal rights were irrelevant since they already had equal rights thanks to segregation. The fundamentalist lobbying group Focus on the Family, along with other conservative American Christians, maintain that they are not against homosexuals having the same rights as heterosexuals, but merely object to them having 'special rights'. By 'special rights' they mean such things as the same right to marry, to be taxed in the same way, to be protected by antidiscrimination legislation, to have an end to direct discrimination in the armed forces and for individual states to repeal their laws banning sex between men.[318]

Although Christianity has argued in favour of vigorous and violent persecution of men who have sex with men for the better part of its history, arguments for continued discrimination are seldom used these days. Indeed, the majority of Christian homophobes shut their eyes to this bloody history. Since people in mainly Christian countries no longer accept that punishments such as burning, strangulation and drowning are appropriate punishments for consensual sex, it has become all the more important for them to make a disconnection between earlier persecutions and current persecution – even though it is the same few passages in the Bible that form the basis for both.

There is considerable disagreement between Christians about the few verses in the Bible that deal with homosexuality. St Paul's condemnation of sex between men as being against 'natural use' is a particular area of disagreement,[319] since many people do not believe he is condemning monogamous homosexual relationships and believe it should be read in the light of Paul's more general message about love. It is relatively rare these days for people to point explicitly to the ban on sex between men in the Pentateuch, partly because it is part of the Old Testament law that Christianity has rejected and partly because it is one of a whole series of parallel prohibitions that the vast majority of Christians no longer find in the least relevant. Although it takes a considerable degree of reinterpretation to make it support Christian homophobia, the story of the creation is used more frequently to justify the condemnation of homosexuality, just as it was often used to condemn sexual relations between people of different colour.

In the case of the Catholic Church, there is frequently a mismatch between the stance taken by the leadership and the attitudes of the majority of Catholics, rather similar to the mismatch in Catholic views on contraception. In many European countries and in America, Catholics are among the most liberal sections of the population in terms of their attitude to homosexuality. Even within the Catholic hierarchy itself, the accord between life and doctrine is less than perfect since a significant number of priests are gay: various studies put the proportion of gay clerics at somewhere between 25 and 50 per cent.[320] And there are a number of very senior figures within the Catholic church who are strongly opposed to official policy. José Policarpo, the Portuguese cardinal and archbishop, not only voiced his support for some legal rights for homosexual couples but was also accused of having made a 'pact of silence' with the Portuguese government when it legalized same-sex marriage in 2010.[321]

In many largely Christian countries, the attitudinal changes towards homosexuality have reached a point where acceptance and tolerance seem to be quite natural to the great majority of people. A few leading Christian conservatives like Espen Ottosen of the Norwegian Lutheran Mission express their concern – probably with good reason – that those who condemn homosexuality run the risk of being harassed for doing so.[322] There are parallels here with the position of religious racists, who quite clearly are no longer able to propound their beliefs without stirring up a negative response.

As recently as the 1980s gays and lesbians were effectively non-existent in the public and private space in Christian countries. Since then, however, there has been a rolling and self-reinforcing cycle whereby, as more gays and lesbians come out, tolerance and natural acceptance among their friends and acquaintances grows, which leads in turn to more gays and lesbians coming out. We should not overlook the way this has influenced Christian attitudes: when those one condemns are no longer abstract figures but one's own neighbours, friends, children and siblings, it is not so easy to accept the traditional Christian condemnation.

Attitudes to homosexuality are influenced by a whole series of religio-sexual rules. The primary reason for condemning homosexuality often has nothing to do with the fact that the sex is between two people of the same sex but because the sex is non-procreative or because, by definition, the sex is often extramarital. In those religions that are more hostile to procreation, a more positive view of homosexuality is usually visible. In other cases again, only certain kinds of homosexual behaviour are condemned because, for instance, they fall within the scope of general rules defining which orifices may be used for sexual purposes. There are many occasions when it is difficult to identify which religio-sexual rules apply specifically to homosexuality – occasions when it would be more accurate to say that the rules apply to male and female sexuality in a wider sense. It would also appear that the use of creation narratives and other religious myths either to justify or to condemn certain kinds of sexuality can have both positive and negative outcomes in terms of any given religion's attitude to homosexuality.

Given on the one hand the religious acceptance of same-sex marriage and the liberalization of society, and on the other the continued demands for the death penalty and the constant focus on the retention of homophobic discrimination, the overall picture of the current religious attitudes towards homosexuality is a complex one. Most of the fundamental attitudes to homosexuality that existed in the various religions still survive in those religions. But even those people who live in the most conservative religious circles have had to relate to the more recent and more liberal attitudes, if for no other reason than the fact that their own faiths include other believers with a more liberal view of homosexuality. At the same time, however, we have witnessed the growth of an interpretation of homosexuality that sees it as the single greatest threat to the religious world view: the intense, almost obsessive focus on homosexuality in many religious circles represents something new. Traditionally, homosexuality was a non-issue in most conservative religious circles. It was not that this implied acceptance – it was simply something that should not be talked about. Nowadays, however, the conservative religious media contains far more material about homosexuality than is to be found anywhere else outside the explicitly gay media.

The range of religious attitudes to homosexuality is wider today than it has ever been. While many people consider that their religion accepts this sort of sex completely, others interpret their sources differently and create a view of homosexuality so negative as to be virtually unparalleled in the history of religion. What is a new phenomenon is the fact that homosexuality now occupies a unique position in the world view of many religions – despite the many religious claims to the contrary. For many people it is an important *article of faith* that their particular religions have always viewed homosexuality as *the* form of sexual behaviour to be opposed above all others. There is, as we have seen, nothing in religion as a phenomenon that states that it must be hostile to homosexuality – it can just as well be positive in its attitude, or even see homosexuality as superior to heterosexuality. In the end, the only conclusion to be drawn is that there is no such thing as a view of homosexuality that cannot be defended from a religious standpoint.

6

Religio-Sexual Racism and Religious Discrimination

Harry S. Truman, the man who as president abolished racial segregation in the American army, was asked by a journalist in 1963 whether he believed that marriage between people of different colours would become widespread in the US. The ex-president answered: 'I hope not. I don't believe in it. Would you want your daughter to marry a Negro?' Truman's conviction had a deeper basis: he believed that interracial marriage ran counter to the teachings of the Bible. Sexual segregation of the races was a fundamental Christian truth as far as he was concerned, as he explained: 'The Lord created it that way. You read your Bible, and you'll find out.'[1]

Most people are only too aware of the fact that racism is a widespread phenomenon; fewer people, however, recognize the central role that religions, particularly Christianity and Hinduism, have played in the history of racism. In the same way as religions tend to categorize people by their sex, the classification of people according to colour and ethnicity is an important element in the world view of many religions. Religious classification of this kind is a major contributory factor to the common belief that it is 'natural' for one race to be superior to another, just as many people hold a religious conviction that homosexuality is not 'natural'.

Sexual racism, the conviction that people of different colour or ethnicity should not have sex with one another, has often proved to be one of the most persistent aspects of religious racism. Since sex is the most intimate way in which people can interact with one another, it is not difficult to understand why this is so. If there were no rules governing whether ethnic or religious groups should abstain from sex with those of different ethnicities or religions, procreation would inevitably lead to an irreversible mixing of identities that would be catastrophic in the eyes of adherents of a racist world view. Given that the regulation of sexual behaviour is one of the most effective methods of controlling human society, it is hardly surprising that sex is an absolutely central element in religious racism.

The boundaries between religio-sexual racism and restrictions on having sex with people of other religions is sometimes fluid. There are times when, as was the case in Islam originally, the restrictions refer solely to religious adherence – if you change your religious adherence, you automatically move from one category to another in terms of whom you can have sex with.

Religious opposition to homosexuality has diminished as a result of a greater degree of tolerance of homosexuality in society in general; similarly, and to an even greater extent, religio-sexual racism has diminished because racism is generally less acceptable in the modern world than in the past. We have perhaps become less conscious of sexual racism because so much of the current religio-sexual debate focuses on homosexuality, but we should not overlook it, and the importance it has and has had in the lives of millions of people.

What God has put asunder, let no man join together

Although most present-day Christians would disagree with Truman's religious conviction that the races should not mix, the great majority of American Christians at the time would have shared his opinion. In 1968 73 per cent of Americans held the same view, in 1958, 94 per cent.[2] Religious racism has played a central part in the regulation of sexual life for thousands of years and remains a factor today. Truman's claim that the Bible prohibited mixed-race sex did not merely reflect the Christian understanding of his time; there is a solid basis for it in the Bible itself. God is constantly forbidding the Israelites to take marital partners from neighbouring peoples.[3] The children of mixed marriages shall not have entry into the congregation of the Lord 'even to his tenth generation'.[4] This is obviously connected with a fear that the Jews will adopt the gods of their neighbours, but there is also a directly racist element involved in that the descendants of mixed marriages are not even to be permitted to worship Jehovah. A prohibition of this kind reflects a demand that the 'holy seed' should be kept pure from outside blood.[5]

Unlike many of the other prohibitions in the Pentateuch, the rules governing sex and race are followed up in many other parts of the Bible. When the prophet Nehemiah saw that some 'Jews . . . had married wives of Ashdod, of Ammon, and of Moab', he chided and cursed them and indeed, 'smote certain of them, and plucked off their hair'.[6] Nehemiah also drove out a priest with a non-Jewish wife because he had 'defiled the priesthood, and the covenant of the priesthood, and of the Levites'.[7] When the prophet Ezra heard that Jewish men in Babylon had been marrying non-Jewish women 'so that the holy seed have mingled themselves with the people of those lands', he despaired: 'And when I heard this thing, I rent my garment, and my mantle, and plucked off the hair of my head and of my beard.'[8] Ezra had good reason to be upset since the 'trespasses' against God represented by these marriages might well have caused God to 'be angry with us [until he had] consumed us'.[9] A solution to this potential tragedy is, however, provided by the men deciding to 'make a covenant with our God to put away all the wives, and such as are born of them'.[10] Ezra then commanded all the other Jewish men who had entered mixed marriages to 'make confession unto the Lord God' and to separate immediately from their foreign wives.[11] There are times, then, when divorce is not just a possibility, but a religious necessity.

An interesting aspect of this prohibition against mixed marriage is that it only seems to be operative in the case of marriages entered into in the usual peaceful manner. Other rules operate 'when thou goest forth to war against thine enemies': if you see 'among the captives a beautiful woman, and hast a desire unto her, that thou wouldest have her to thy wife; then thou shalt bring her home to thine house; and she shall shave her head, and pare her nails; And she shall put the raiment of her captivity from off her, and shall remain in thine house, and bewail her father and her mother a full month.' You are nevertheless permitted to have sex with her during that time: 'thou shalt go in unto her, and be her husband, and she shall be thy wife'. If, however, you eventually get tired of your booty, you should just let her go free and not sell her, 'because thou hast humbled her'.[12]

From time to time the various authors of the Bible overlook these sexual prohibitions and write as if they do not exist. In the Book of Ruth, Jewish men do not only marry Moabite women without any suggestion that it is a problem,[13] but Ruth, the Moabite protagonist, becomes one of the ancestors of the famous King David.[14] A number of other mixed marriages are mentioned almost in passing.[15] Really powerful people effectively did what they wanted. Moses marries Zipporah, a Cushite woman from the land of Midian.[16]

When Aaron and Miriam, Moses's brother and sister, reprimand him for his mixed-race marriage, God himself comes to his support, castigating the brother and sister and making Miriam a leper.[17] King David, too, had a non-Jewish wife,[18] and his son Solomon took wives from Egypt, Moab, Ammon, Edom, Sidon and the land of the Hittites.[19]

Throughout history the Jews have to a great extent married each other; indeed, the Christian and Muslim societies in which they lived frequently gave them no other choice. In India too it was impossible for Jews to marry outside their own ranks, but they also operated with their own racial limitations from at least the sixteenth century on: Indian Jews with a lighter skin colour refused to recognize darker-skinned Jews as full Jews and banned marriage with them.[20]

At the present time Jews outside Israel are perhaps the religious group most likely to marry people of other faiths – about 50 per cent of Jews in the US do so. At the same time, however, many Jews are deeply disapproving of the general acceptance of mixed marriage, not least because the rule is that only children with a Jewish mother may be considered Jews by birth. Many Orthodox and Zionist Jews in Israel and the US define the high frequency of mixed marriages as self-inflicted genocide and refer to it as 'the silent holocaust'.[21]

There is little in the New Testament that can be interpreted as supporting the divinely inspired sexual racism of the Old Testament and both Jesus and his disciples insisted on associating with people of different ethnicities. But this has not prevented many Christians from continuing to believe that God demands them to restrict themselves sexually to those of their own colour, ethnicity or at least religion. And there is nothing in the New Testament that rescinds the sexually racist prohibitions of the Old Testament. The exhortation to associate with people of other ethnicities does not go beyond general courtesy, helpfulness and hospitality. Not even St Paul's forceful statement that 'there is neither Jew nor Greek . . . for ye are all one in Christ Jesus' can be seen as rescinding the Old Testament prohibitions; if it did so, we should have to see his parallel statement 'there is neither male nor female' as a direct exhortation to homosexuality – and there are virtually no Christians who understand Paul this way.[22]

Sexual relations between Christians and non-Christians in the Middle Ages often led to severe punishments. Several Christian women and Muslim or Jewish men who had sex with one another were condemned to death. It was less common for Christian men to be punished for having sex with non-Christian women.[23] The principle was, nevertheless, the important point, as demonstrated by the English law from the end of the thirteenth century which states that 'Those who have [sexual] dealings with Jews or Jewesses . . . are to be buried alive.'[24] This was a prohibition that often went deeper than just the fear of mixing religions. In 1268 Pope Clement IV reprimanded King Alphonso III of Portugal for permitting Christian men to marry Christian women of Saracen (Arabic) or Jewish *descent*.[25] Sex between Christians and Jews – even Jews who had converted to Christianity – was punishable by death in twelfth-century Aragon.[26] The medieval reader of romances could read of a marvellous racist miracle in this context. In the English romance *The King of Tars*, a Muslim sultan converts to Christianity after marrying a Christian princess. When he is baptized, God arranges for his skin to change from black to white so that the readers no longer have to worry about the theological complications of a marriage between individuals of different colours.[27]

New rules arose at the time of the Reformation. It became a general rule that a princess who was given in marriage to a crown prince of a different confession would change her faith. Among the population in general, however, such marriages were not so straightforward. In 1631 the Lutheran city council in Strasbourg decided that any man who married a Calvinist would have to pay a fine. A Lutheran woman would lose her citizenship if she married a Calvinist man.[28]

Just as Christians in Spain were not permitted to marry Jews or Muslims, the basic prohibition on marriage between Christians and non-Christians was also brought to Spanish America.[29] Once again, religion was not the only problem: the European expansion led to widespread sexual contact between white men and non-white women. This was condemned by many Christian missionaries, who did their best to convince the colonial authorities to forbid such relations.[30]

Christian authorities were, in any case, more than happy to introduce laws of this kind without any encouragement from missionaries. The Protestant Dutch authorities in South Africa banned marriage between those of different colours as early as 1685,[31] and the Catholic authorities in Brazil introduced a similar ban in 1726.[32]

In the Dano-Norwegian colony of Tranquebar in India, the Lutheran church attempted to discourage sex between white men and Indian women by refusing to baptize their children. The practical effect of this was that the mothers had their children baptized in a not quite so racist Catholic church farther down the street.[33]

German missionaries in German South-west Africa around 1900 were divided in their view of sex racism: some of them argued that marriage between blacks and whites was a 'sin against racial consciousness', whereas others were more pragmatic and thought that marriage was preferable to widespread extramarital sex between white men and black women.[34] Christian missionaries in Australia tended to condemn all sex between whites and Aborigines.[35]

The US offers one of the most complete and long-lasting examples of sexual racism. The first American laws against sex between those of different colours were introduced in Virginia in 1662,[36] and the ban on marriages across colour lines was supported by the majority of churches in America. In practice, however, a slave owner had the right to use his black slaves sexually and neither civil nor religious authorities opposed this.[37] The rape of black female slaves by their white owners was not covered by any law and was therefore not illegal.[38] The large number of slaves with white blood in their veins was in itself proof of this practice.[39] Slaves with a lighter skin colour also fetched a better price on the market[40] and the laws in Virginia, to give one example, supported the economically profitable practice of white slave owners begetting their own slave children. The children of a black woman and a white man would be 'slaves or free solely based on the status of the mother'.[41]

Before the abolition of slavery the widespread opposition to sex between people of a different colour has to be seen in the context of the Christian defence of slavery as an institution supported by both Old and New Testaments. In addition to that, many white Christians argued strongly that black people were the descendants of Cain, whom God had cursed,[42] or of Ham, whose father Noah had cursed and condemned him to be a servant 'unto his brethren' for ever.[43]

The focus changed somewhat after the abolition of slavery. During the slave period, slaves did not normally have the right to marry but, with slavery gone, there was a greater judicial need to prevent whites and blacks from marrying each other.[44] In the years after the Civil War there was some decline in the number of states where mixed marriages were banned, but the number increased again between 1897 and 1913, by which point mixed marriages were illegal in thirty of the states of the union. The arguments the authorities used to justify the ban on mixed marriage continued to be of a theological nature. The Supreme Court in Georgia in 1869 stated that mixed marriage was impossible in the eyes of God and that 'no human law' could change that fact.[45] In upholding its ban on marriages between people of different colours, the Supreme Court in Tennessee in 1871 pointed to the Old Testament prohibition of mixed marriage.[46] The Texas Supreme Court in 1877 argued that since marriage is 'a public institution established by God', marriage between people of different colours could not be permitted.[47] A unanimous decision of the Supreme Court of the northern state of Indiana stated in 1871: 'The natural law, which forbids their intermarriage and that amalgamation which leads to a corruption of races, is as clearly divine as that which imparted to them different natures.'[48]

Segregation, particularly in schools, was important from a religio-sexual point of view in order to prevent children thinking that racial discrimination was odd and wrong-headed.[49] In practical terms, the ban was aimed primarily at sex between black men and white women and against any *legal* acknowledgement of relationships between people of different colour. Just as white slave owners had had free access to their black slave women, white men continued to enjoy the possibility of sex with their black house servants.[50] Thus Christian religio-racial convictions were less than strictly consistent.

Even though it was frequently argued that sexual relationships that crossed colour lines were no good for any of the races involved, it is clear that the Christian regulation of mixed sex focused on ensuring the purity of the white race. The mere fact that an individual had a small admixture of black blood in his or her veins was sufficient for that individual to be defined as black from a Christian and from a Christian-influenced legal standpoint. It was, after all, black skin that was the mark of God's curse on Cain and Ham.

The conviction that God desired to keep the races separate survived with undiminished force and as late as 1958 94 per cent of the population of the United States was still opposed to marriage between people of different colours.[51] When Barack Obama was born in Hawaii in 1961, his parents' marriage would still have been considered a crime in twenty-two of the states of the union.

The black and white couple Mildred and Richard Loving got married in 1959 and were sentenced to a year in jail or twenty-five years' exile from Virginia. The judge offered the following theological explanation of the judgement: 'Almighty God created the races white, black, yellow, malay and red, and he placed them on separate continents . . . The fact that he separated the races shows that he did not intend for the races to mix.' It was precisely this Christian argument that the United States Supreme Court declared irrelevant when, in 1967, it ruled that the ban on racially mixed marriages that still existed in sixteen states was unconstitutional.[52] This was by no means a popular decision. In 1968, a year after the Supreme Court ruling, 73 per cent of all Americans were still opposed to the legalization of mixed marriages. Not until sixteen years after the ruling did the opposition to mixed marriages fall below 50 per cent,[53] the same percentage nationally as those who were against same-sex marriage when that became legal in an American state for the first time in 2004.[54] There is still significant opposition to marriage across the colour line: in 1994 37 per cent of Americans were against marriages between blacks and whites,[55] and 20 per cent were still opposing it as recently as 2009.[56]

Many Christians saw and still see sexual racism as a fundamental issue for their religion. The Southern Baptist Convention, the largest denomination in the US, was founded in 1845 following a disagreement with northern Baptists on the question of the central importance of racism in their Christian faith. Up until the year 2000, the leaders of the Southern Baptists continued to use mainly theological arguments in their struggle to maintain racial segregation in different areas of society.[57] Even Baptists who were otherwise liberal, along with many other Christians who were in favour of ethnic equality, were still of the opinion that God did not wish there to be sex between blacks and whites.[58] In a letter to all the Presbyterian churches in the US in 1965, the influential Presbyterian theologian John Edwards Richards stated: 'Let those that would erase the racial diversity of God's creation beware lest the consequences of their evil be visited upon their children.'[59] And when the children's book *The Rabbits' Wedding*, which told the story of the wedding of a black rabbit and a white rabbit, appeared in 1958, it led to Christian protests against such a perversion of the work of the Creator.[60]

Partly because the ban on mixed marriage was so important to many believers, a number of states chose to retain the ban in their own law codes even after the Supreme Court ruling of 1967, although there was no longer any possibility of putting it into operation. It was not until 1998 and 2000 that the last two states – South Carolina and Alabama – removed the prohibition after holding referenda. Even then there was still significant opposition: 38 per cent in South Carolina voted to retain the ban in 1998 and 41 per cent in Alabama still wanted to keep it in 2000. Bearing in mind that both these states have a large African-American population (30 per cent and 26 per cent respectively), and that African-Americans oppose legalized sex racism much more strongly than whites, the opposition to lifting the ban was clearly very strong indeed among the white voters in these two southern states.[61]

Religious convictions still form the basis of American sex racism and some believers recognize this more clearly than others. Lanny Littlejohn, a representative in the South Carolina State Legislature and one of those who voted to retain the ban in 1998, had this to say about the proposal to remove it: 'That's not what God intended when he separated the peoples back in the Babylonian day.'[62] His justification for racial segregation in marriage was thus the story in Genesis that tells how God separated the peoples at the Tower of Babel.[63] Littlejohn also revealed the roots of his conviction: 'I have been raised a Baptist all my life, and I guess that's exactly where it comes from. My family taught me that over the years.' Kenneth Wayne Hagin, a central figure in the American Pentecostalist movement and son of the founder of the Rhema Bible Centres in fifteen countries, has this to say about sex between people of different colours: 'We're friends. We play. We go together as a group, but we don't date one another . . . I don't think we ought to mix any of the races.'[64] In 1998 Bob Jones University, a Christian fundamentalist institution and the largest private university in South Carolina, gave the following formal answer to a white applicant married to a black woman: 'Bob Jones University does, however, have a rule prohibiting interracial dating among its students. God has separated people for His own purpose. . . . Although there is no verse in the Bible that dogmatically says that races should not intermarry, the whole plan of God as He has dealt with the races down through the ages indicates that interracial marriage is not best for man.' By 'down through the ages' the university also meant biblical history and was pointing to the story of the Tower of Babel as a prime example of God's plan to keep the races separate.[65]

The Church of Jesus Christ of Latter-day Saints (LDS), which came into existence in the middle of the nineteenth century, also reflected the Christian racism of that time and sexual racism was a core element of its teachings. In 1863 the Mormon prophet Brigham Young explained 'the law of God in regard to the African race': 'If the white man who belongs to the chosen seed mixes his blood with the seed of Cain, the penalty, under the law of God, is death on the spot.'[66] During his migration westwards from Illinois in 1847, Young heard that a black male member of the church had married a white woman in Massachusetts; he stated that he would have had the couple killed if he had been close enough to do so.[67] Since the Mormons consider themselves to be the new chosen people, they trace their ban on racial mixing directly to God's command that the Israelites should practise sexual racism. In 1954 one of the leading members of the church claimed that whites having sex with blacks was equivalent to 'spiritual death'. It is essential for white people to be on their guard because 'the negro seeks absorbtion with the white race. He will not be satisfied until he achieves it by intermarriage.'[68] The fundamental racism of the LDS Church was not abolished until Spencer W. Kimball, then its president, received a divine revelation in 1978.[69]

Although Adolf Hitler's anti-Semitism rested on a foundation of centuries of Christian prejudice against the Jews, his ideas of racial purity were at least in part directly inspired by American legislation – which in itself was a result of American Christian racism.[70] In addition to banning sex between people of different ethnicities and preventing people with disabilities from breeding, many Nazis believed their notion of racial purity to be fully in accordance with Christianity, even when it entailed the systematic use of mass murder. Christian Nazis argued that God's law meant that they had to fight against all forms of miscegenation and bastardization.[71] The prevention of breeding by those they considered to be inferior beings was regarded as an expression of 'the highest respect for the God-given natural laws'.[72]

The Dutch Reformed Church in South Africa also used biblical arguments to defend both sexual separation of the races and apartheid in general. The divine separation of the races was compared to the way God had separated light from darkness or the waters from the land. For people of different colours to mix was tantamount to rebelling against creation itself – had not God separated the races when mankind tried to build the Tower of Babel?[73] It was not only from the US that the Christian racists of South Africa received support: several free church organizations in Sweden defended apartheid during the 1960s precisely because sexual relations between blacks and whites were considered an abomination.[74]

The widespread condemnation of racism by society today is the only thing that makes sexual racism on religious grounds stand out as a rather odd religio-sexual phenomenon. In reality it should rather be seen as a typical example of how religious rules for living are based on the way a religion categorizes and ranks human beings. A religious rule defining who may have sex with whom is one of the most powerful means of reinforcing particular identities.

Christian sexual racism is, however, a fairly unique phenomenon in another sense: having once been both so central and self-evident, it has quickly been completely marginalized and almost forgotten. The change has been so complete over just a few decades that many people no longer realize how important such racist perceptions were for many centuries and – in many parts of Christendom – until less than a generation ago.

Christians who are sexual racists are just as much parts of the Christian religion as those who are not racist: both sides base their religious beliefs on the same scriptures and on the same tradition. The situation is exactly the same when it comes to the Christian view of homosexuality: the majority of the biblical passages that deal with interracial sex condemn it, yet there are also narratives that point in a very different direction. If we look at church history we can see the same constant swing of the pendulum between more and less homophobia and more and less sexual racism – with a fairly marked negative turn from the Middle Ages on. And when we examine the way both sexual racism and homophobia have gradually lost ground in Christendom, we can see that Christian homophobia waned even more rapidly than racism once homophobia was seriously problematized. Both of these viewpoints have had – and still have – strong support, and it is perhaps the speed at which Christian homophobia has ceased to be regarded as utterly natural and self-evident which has given the defence of that position such a high profile. But the defence of sexual racism has been strong and notably tenacious, too, and has also been based on biblical principles.

Sticking to your own caste

In New Delhi in 2010 a nineteen-year-old girl called Aisha Saini fell in love with Yogesh Kumar, a twenty-year-old neighbour. When her family found out they had fallen in love, they did everything they could to put a stop to it. Yogesh was completely unacceptable as a partner because his family was of a lower caste than Aisha's. Aisha was immediately promised in marriage to a man of the proper caste in a neighbouring village, but since she refused to give way she was sent off to stay with her uncle. When Aisha still remained in contact with Yogesh, her family invited Yogesh to come to the uncle's house to discuss the situation. Once there, both Aisha and Yogesh were tied up and beaten for several hours with iron rods before finally being electrocuted.[75]

For a family to do what the Saini family did and kill a daughter and her lover because the lover is of a different caste is by no means unusual in Hindu society. In the month of May 2008 alone, five double murders of this kind were reported in the states of Haryana, Punjab and Uttar Pradesh.[76] Every day scores of young couples turn to the High Court in the states of Punjab and Haryana alone for protection against their own families.[77] Preventing young people of different castes from inter-marrying is a matter of considerable importance in large parts of South Asia. What makes the case of Aisha and Yogesh special, however, is the way the family publicly defends the crime. Aisha's uncle, who emerges as the individual most responsible for the deed, declared, 'I have no regrets . . . I would punish them all over again if given another chance.' Neither did Aisha's father have any regrets about his involvement in the killing of his daughter. A cousin commented: 'What will any parent do if they see their daughter in a compromising position with a man? What would you do if you were in the same situation? That's why my uncles killed them.' Another uncle, who was not directly involved in the murder, also defended it: 'How can we marry outside the caste? This cannot be tolerated . . . the killings were justified.' The murders were justified, in particular, as a way of forestalling other breaches of caste rules within the family: if the family had not killed Aisha and Yogesh, it 'would have set a bad precedent for the other children in the family. They would have done the same . . . This is better.' Even Yogesh's family understood Aisha's family's desire to punish their daughter for bringing shame on her family: 'If they wanted to kill their daughter, that's okay. But they shouldn't have killed our boy.'[78]

The right to do whatever is necessary to uphold caste rules on sex is often viewed as a matter of central religious importance. When the Supreme Court of India ruled in 2007 that parents do not have the right to beat, threaten or lock up daughters over eighteen if they wish to marry without parental consent, it led to an indignant outcry and claims that it was a serious blow to Indian culture. The point at issue is that many of the daughters who marry against their parents' wishes choose to marry men of castes different to their own.[79] It is not only marriage across caste boundaries that is taboo: many Hindu couples have been killed because they married within the same sub-caste or *gotra*. Many of the killings of this kind are carried out on the orders of traditional *khap* or clan courts in northern India. In 2010 five members of a court of this kind were sentenced to death for the killing of Manoj and Babli Banwal.

The reaction of the clan court was far from being remorseful. On the contrary, they started a political lobby to get the Hindu Marriage Act – the Indian marriage laws for Hindus – changed and their action was quickly supported by many conservative politicians and regional parties.[80]

The original Hindu caste system shows obvious parallels with other kinds of religious racism in that the population is permanently divided into different groups that neither can nor should mix. No one has any chance of escaping the caste he or she is born into. There are also deep-seated perceptions that people of different castes are physically different from one another, including in terms of skin colour. Traditionally, the prohibition of marriage across caste boundaries in Hinduism is absolute. Men are not permitted to have sex with women of a higher caste than themselves, but high-caste men are allowed to have sex with low-caste women so long as they do not marry them.[81] In the eleventh-century literary compilation *Kathasaritsagara*, we can read the tragic story of a low-caste man who falls in love with a princess. The man despairs because his love is utterly unattainable and contrary to nature – it is as though a crow were to desire to join in union with a swan. In his desperation the man decides to burn himself alive, but before climbing on to the pyre he prays to the gods that he and the princess will be reincarnated in the same caste so that they may be man and wife in the next life.[82]

The ancient *Laws of Manu* not only refer in general to the command to marry within one's own caste, they also demonstrate the consequences of not doing so. A man from the three highest castes who marries a *sudra* woman – that is, a woman from the lowest of the four main castes – drags both his family and his children down to that low level.[83] A Brahmin who marries a *sudra* woman will end up in hell.[84] The *Laws of Manu*, just to be on the safe side, recommend that a man from the higher castes should not even marry a woman with a low-caste name. Similarly, a woman whose father is unknown should also be avoided.[85] Generally speaking, both men and women risked losing their caste status if they married people of a lower caste. In some parts of India, however, a high-caste woman who had a child by a man of lower caste could regain her original high-caste status if she gave away the child.[86] In southern India, marriage was also permissible for couples from different sub-castes as long as these were at the same level.[87]

Even though the caste system itself is primarily an expression of the Hindu conviction that people are born to the position in life they have earned by their deeds in earlier incarnations, there are many examples of the caste system being retained even after people have converted to other religions. The Buddhist text *Kalacakratantra*, probably from around the time of Christ, considers love between high-caste men and low-caste women as being on the same level as murder, lying, theft and adultery.[88] Many Muslims in South Asia, as well as their descendants in Europe, North America and other areas, have supported the caste system and taken the ban on sexual relations across caste boundaries as an ideal. Among South Asian Muslims and other groups, however, there is a growing tendency for there to be less emphasis on caste in selecting a marital partner and more emphasis on wealth, education and social status.[89]

Catholic converts in Portuguese India retained the caste system, including the ban on marrying across caste boundaries, while more traditional members of the Syriac Churches in southern India have not intermarried with converts from lower castes. In so far as marriage across caste boundaries is increasing among the Christians of today, it occurs mainly between people who are positioned close together within the Christian caste system.[90] Hindu untouchables who convert to Christianity complain that other Indian Christians discriminate against them in just the same way as they are discriminated against by Hindus.[91] Many Catholics in Sri Lanka also operate with the caste system, but they do accept sex across caste boundaries and any children produced by such liaisons will be of the same caste as the father.[92]

The general ban on marriage across caste boundaries remains strong in present-day Hinduism. Given the increased levels of geographical mobility, it has also become obvious that Hindus prefer not to marry outside their own ethnic group,[93] something that is also linked with caste in the sense that many of the castes are ethnically limited. The desire to avoid inter-caste marriage is also visible in new ways – in, for instance, the personal ads in the newspapers and on the Internet, which are used by Hindu singles and their parents to locate suitable partners within their particular castes.[94] The fact that a number of more liberal South Asians, particularly those in the middle class and in emigrant communities, now take a less rigid view of this does not imply any specific opposition to the sexual prohibition so much as a more relaxed attitude to the caste system as a whole.[95] Many of those who have more liberal views themselves are nevertheless prepared to fall into line with stricter family demands: a survey of young people of South Asian origin in London, for instance, revealed that the number who took a positive view of mixed marriage was much greater than the number who would not enter such a relationship without the blessing of their family.[96] It has also become more common to marry across caste boundaries when the particular castes are close to one another in terms of status – and income, wealth and education have grown in importance as factors of choice.[97] In some of the poorer and newer emigrant communities where there are very few South Asian partners to choose from, caste is more often ignored – the most important thing in this situation is not to marry someone from a different ethnic background.[98] And there are times when the voice of money speaks louder than the rules of caste: since economic mobility has become less dependent on caste membership, it is often much more tempting to marry one's children to affluent members of another caste than to marry them off to poor members of one's own caste.

In terms of practice, there is a parallel here with white Christian racism in that it is less acceptable for high-caste women to have sex with low-caste men than vice versa. Whereas extremely discreet relationships between high-caste women and their low-caste male servants may tacitly be accepted,[99] high-caste men frequently go quite openly to low-caste prostitutes. Nor is it unusual for high-caste men to rape low-caste women in order to humiliate low-caste people in general.[100]

Regulating sex by means of the caste system provides a good example of how a feature that began as a clear prohibition is watered down when it becomes possible to evade it or when more important factors come into play. The prohibition has been reinterpreted so that it applies mainly to open and religion-sanctioned sex: it is above all in the case of marriage that the old caste rules must be adhered to, the rules being viewed with some degree of laxity when the sex is discreet and extramarital. When the issue is one of prostitution or systematic rape, the purchase of sex from, or the rape of, lower-caste women serves to humiliate the lower caste sexually, and such sexual humiliation of socially and religiously inferior individuals helps to emphasize caste differences, thereby making the practice more acceptable to those who are at the top of the caste system.

The way in which the caste system and its sexual rules have been transferred into certain parts of Buddhism, Christianity and Islam gives some indication of how important and attractive many people still find such attitudes. They represent deep structures which are difficult to move away from. We should not underestimate the security and self-confidence that often result from being able to define other human beings as inferior just because of who they are or who they have sex with.

Sex with True Believers and with those who are not

The Bible, as we have seen, consistently condemned sex with other races, and during the Christian Middle Ages Jewish men and Christian women were likely to be burnt if they had sex with each other. While it is often difficult in the case of Judaism or Christianity to distinguish between sexual prohibitions based on religion, ethnicity or colour, Islam operates with rules that make an effort to regulate sexual behaviour solely on the basis of religious affiliation.

The Koran offers clear guidelines in this respect. Neither men nor women should marry idolaters, but if those same idolaters convert to Islam they are automatically classified as Muslims and immediately become acceptable marriage partners.[101] In addition to that, Muslim men may marry chaste women from 'those who have been given the Book before you', that is, Jews and Christians.[102] Women did not originally have an equivalent right, something that has to be seen in the context of men being defined as women's protectors or maintainers, *qawwamun*.[103] If a Muslim woman were permitted to marry a non-Muslim man it would lead to the problematic situation of a Muslim being subordinate to a non-Muslim. Nevertheless, many Muslims do believe that Muslim women also have the right to marry Christian or Jewish men.

The debate about how Muslims should relate sexually to non-believers has sometimes taken more peculiar forms. The early Muslim poet Abu Nuwas and a number of jurists of the Maliki school were of the view that the penetration of Christian and Jewish men by Muslims was a way of demonstrating the superiority of Islam – and therefore could be considered more of a duty than a sin.[104] In practice, however, the erotic relationships of Muslim men went in more than one direction: Muslim men often wrote love poems to young Jewish and Christian boys, but Jewish men also wrote tenderly to young Muslim boys.[105]

The number of marriages between Muslims and non-Muslims has increased along with the growing levels of integration. Mixed marriages were not at all uncommon in the former Yugoslavia, and the number of Muslims marrying non-Muslims in the US increases with each new generation that grows up in that country. The number of American Muslims married to non-Muslims in 2001 was 21 per cent, a proportion identical to that of American Catholics married to non-Catholics.[106]

Many countries still prohibit Muslim women from marrying non-Muslim men, while in Israel Muslim men may only marry non-Muslim women in Muslim wedding ceremonies, not Jewish ones. All interfaith marriages are, however, recognized by the Israeli authorities if they are entered into abroad, even through live zooming. In Malaysia any non-Muslim, male or female, wishing to marry a Muslim must convert.[107] The fact that people of all religious affiliations tend to marry people of their own faith is not, however, solely due to explicit and traditional religious restrictions. Social networks, particularly among people who des cribe themselves as having strong religious convictions, are frequently defined precisely by the fact that their members share a religious affiliation, so it is hardly surprising that people find marital partners of the same faith as themselves. And there are, of course, people for whom religion is so important that the idea of living life with someone who does not share their faith is simply not a viable alternative.

The religious proscriptions against having sex with people of other faiths brings us back to the starting-point of our discussion of sexual rules. If your sex life is subject to regulation, who you associate with on all kinds of levels is also regulated – including who your children and grandchildren will be. If you have sex with people of other religions, particularly if you marry someone of a different faith, not only will you be at very close quarters with people of a different religion in your daily life, but you are also likely to be confronted in your sexual life by quite different rules to those your own religion has set for you. One central dilemma is the decision about which faith the children should be raised in. There is also the problem of what happens after death, since so many religions believe that marriage and family relationships continue after death: what will happen then if your spouse and children are not of the same true faith as yourself?

Even though religious rules about the beliefs of one's sex partners share much the same historical origin as religio-sexual racism – not least because many religions have an ethnic basis – they simultaneously represent something quite different. Whereas religio-sexual regulation according to religious affiliation is based on clear differences between people's ways of life, religio-sexual racism is only based on a particular religion's understanding of human identities.

The religious rules defining who may have sex with whom, whether based on gender, colour, ethnicity, caste or religion, all have one thing in common: they reinforce the fundamental rule, important to many religions, that there are differences between people, that there should be differences between people, and that a different value is attached to different people depending on who they are (or are defined as being). Gender, colour, ethnicity, caste and religion are all factors that define people's worth within a religious world view. Sex rules contribute to the upholding of these definitions. Those who defy the rules are consequently not only violating these sacred distinctions between people but are also defining themselves as being out of the whole system by breaking the boundaries of the identity assigned to them.

7
Sex Beyond the Mortal Sphere

In Greek antiquity the Trojan prince Ganymede was known for his beauty; he was universally acknowledged to have been 'born the most beautiful of mortal men'. One day he vanished. Everyone searched for him and his father was inconsolable until the god Hermes appeared and explained that there was no reason to despair – Ganymede had become immortal and been given eternal youth. This is only half the story, however. Zeus, the supreme god, had kidnapped Ganymede 'because of his beauty'.[1] Tradition varies as to whether Zeus took the form of an eagle in order to kidnap Ganymede or whether he appeared as his usual middle-aged male self. Whichever it was, the enamoured supreme god had not only brought Ganymede to Olympus to act as cup-bearer to the gods at their divine feasts – Sophocles puts it rather bluntly when he talks of the young Trojan 'inflaming the royalty of Zeus with his thighs'.[2]

Gods, angels and demons, all living at various distances from mankind, are not to be overlooked in any discussion of the religions. Many such supernatural creatures are sexually active in different ways, whether with one another or with ordinary mortals, as Zeus was in the case of Ganymede. The supernatural spheres in which the gods and their like normally exist, and where we ourselves may end up when we die, are not regions where sex is excluded. The fact that sex exists in these superhuman contexts is not, however, the only reason for looking more closely at them in relation to sex and religion. How the gods behave sexually, and the rules that are valid in such spheres, may often be seen as the ultimate and essential formulation of the religio-sexual rules that operate in life on earth. Additionally, there are often particular rules as to how a human being should behave when first confronted sexually by these superhuman beings: gods, angels and demons are, when all is said and done, not like ordinary people.

Sex between Gods

In many of the non-monotheistic religions the very creation of the world was the result of sexual activity. In the Egyptian, Mesopotamian, Greek and other creation narratives, the world is created by various divine couples indulging in sex and having children, who become the various elements. Even when there is only one god in the beginning, sex is often still seen as part of the process, as in the Egyptian Heliopolitan narrative of Re-Atum, who creates his descendants by masturbating: 'Before I had spit out Shu, before I had expectorated Tephnut . . . I am the one who masturbated with my fist, I stimulated with my hand.'[3] But many gods did not restrict themselves to procreative sex; they were sexually highly active in a more general sense.

Though the deeds of the Greek gods are perhaps most familiar to the Western world, the sexuality of the Hindu gods provides us with what are undoubtedly the most important examples of sexually active deities among religions that are extant today. Most of the gods live in heterosexual relationships with one another, although it can be difficult to offer a complete overview of who is with whom because this can vary from source to source and because, among other factors, some of the gods have rather fluid identities. Just as the gods surpass human beings in most activities, they also do so in the sexual sphere. Sex between gods can be sensational: the first sexual intercourse between Shiva and Parvati is a good example – it lasts an eternity and is so intense that the whole cosmos trembles and the other gods are terrified.[4] The divine heterosexual couple making love is often portrayed as a single merged being.[5]

The fact that the gods of a particular religion have sex generally implies that that religion takes a positive view of sex. But the many and various sexual deeds of the gods do not automatically provide models for human beings. When goddesses like Aphrodite and Parvati were sexually unfaithful to their husbands this was not regarded as exemplary behaviour: they were seen as examples of divine transgression.[6] The unfaithfulness of so many male gods to their marital partners, though not ideal, was usually seen as less of a problem. It equates to the way male sexuality in the human world is so often allowed more freedom than female sexuality. While the incestuous relationship of Isis and Osiris was mirrored by the marriages of the pharaohs and, in Hellenic times at least, served as a model for wealthier Egyptian families,[7] the equally incestuous unions entered into by the numerous primordial gods of many other religions were not usually seen as examples to be followed. The incestuous sibling marriage of the important Greek gods Zeus and Hera was not something that people in general were meant to imitate and, in fact, it was sometimes even criticized precisely because it fell so far short of the ideal.

Even though there are numerous gods and goddesses who remain virgins, the Judaic-Christian-Muslim God is rather exceptional in his asexuality. Since these are monotheistic faiths, he is the only God in his universe and his sexual abstinence means that there are no sexually active gods in this universe. There are, however, some episodes in which God finds himself in situations that could easily have been sexual but, on closer examination, these episodes merely serve to underline God's absolute abstinence. Sperm is among the ingredients God uses to create human beings in the Koran, but this act is not presented as being at all sexual. Sperm appears to be a necessary substance for the creation of human beings, but the sperm is not even God's sperm: it is something he extracts from clay.[8] In Christianity, the nearest God comes to sex is not with another divine being but with a mortal woman, Mary. As she is told in Luke's Gospel: 'The Holy Ghost shall come upon thee, and the power of the Highest shall overshadow thee.'[9] The point remains, however, that this is *not* a sexual act: God makes Mary pregnant without having sex with her.

The asexuality of the monotheistic God is an example of how the same fundamental ideas can lead to totally different consequences. In Jewish and Islamic contexts the eternal virginity of God is something that *distinguishes* God from mankind since mankind is meant to be sexually active; in Christianity, however, God's abstinence is seen as an *ideal* to be followed. The asexuality of the Christian God is further reinforced in that he, in the form of his incarnate son Jesus, is also sexually abstinent. Seen in this light, there is a parallel between the abstinent divine figures of Christianity and the sexually active gods of the Hindus, ancient Greeks and other more traditional religions: in all these cases, the sexual behaviour of their gods provides a model for their mortal followers.

Sex between Humans and Supernatural Beings

Though the Christian God refrained from sex even while making Mary pregnant, innumerable other gods have had sexual relations with human beings. Many gods are notably active in their efforts to seduce men and women. This has never been an everyday feature of any religion but it does reveal a very different dimension of sexuality: sex with gods can be a part of human religious reality.

The story of the relationship between the god Zeus and the handsome lad Ganymede is by no means unique. Greek religion offers a host of stories of gods and humans having sex with each other. Several goddesses and almost all the male gods were well-known for constantly trying to seduce ordinary men and women. The surest proof of this was the large number of heroes and heroines who were the result of relations between divine beings and mortal men and women. The fact that such a large number of people in mythological times had a god or goddess as one of their parents was also associated with the idea that the sexual potency of the gods was such that every time one of them had heterosexual intercourse with a human being it resulted in conception. Zeus sometimes took on the form of an animal when he wanted to have sex with a human being, something that in itself gives us a good example of divine transgression, since human beings should not normally have sexual relations with animals. When Zeus wanted to seduce the princess Europa he turned himself into a bull,[10] and he took on the form of a swan in order to have sex with the princess Leda. Some ancient depictions of the scene show the excited bird virtually raping Leda.[11]

It is important to understand that the Greeks believed these mythical heroic figures to be genuinely historical persons. Even though there was little agreement about precisely what Hercules, Odysseus and Helen of Troy had actually done, few people doubted their historical existence.[12] One of the ideas that was generally accepted as authentic was that many of these figures we now consider mythical had been involved in sex with the gods. Julius Caesar, for instance, made great play of the fact that according to Greek sources his family was the result of an affair between the Trojan warrior Anchises and the goddess Aphrodite – Venus to the Romans. And since the gods had been sexually active with human beings in the historical period, there was no reason to doubt that they had also been active in the most distant past. The mother of Alexander the Great, for example, insisted that she had been made pregnant by Zeus in the shape of a snake.[13] Possibly because the Emperor Augustus did not want to appear any less important than his Macedonian role model, rumours circulated that his mother had been made pregnant by Apollo in the shape of a snake.[14] Many people thought that gods in the form of snakes were also the fathers of the Messenian tyrant Aristomenes[15] and the Sicyon general Aratus,[16] whereas Euthymus of Locri, who was Olympic boxing champion in 427 BC, was reputed to be the son of the river god Caecinus.[17] Although there were many who doubted her, there were also many people who believed a Pontian woman in the fourth century bc when she claimed she had become pregnant after sleeping with the god Apollo.[18]

Hinduism, too, has many instances of erotic love between gods and humans, the best known of which is perhaps the relationship between Krishna and the many *gopis*, the beautiful cowherd girls. This relationship tends to be portrayed in Hindu art with the blue god playing the flute while the girls listen enraptured. Once, according to the *Bhagavatam Purana*, things go beyond this, and Krishna makes love to every single one of them: 'he pleasures the young women

Leda and the Swan, *c.* 1512–17, by Il Sodoma (Giovanni Antonio Bazzi).

with embraces, stroking them with his hand and giving loving looks and great smiles'. He multiplies himself into as many forms as there are *gopis* so that each and every one of them can be satisfied.[19] The sources disagree about how many *gopis* Krishna makes love to, but there is a tendency for the number to rise with every retelling of the story, reaching 900,000 in some versions.

On another occasion Krishna marries 16,000 virgins he has saved from imprisonment by the demon Bhauma.[20] On yet another occasion Krishna transforms himself into a woman so that he can marry Arjuna's son Aravan, who has promised to sacrifice himself to the goddess Kali the following day;[21] Tamil *hijras* regard this episode as a divine model for their own lives.[22]

In these narratives of consummated love between gods and human beings we can see that Hinduism does not always make a clear distinction between the human and the divine. In mythical times there is constant close contact between gods and men and even today some ordinary people are considered to be incarnations of gods. The great differences between people are sometimes understood to parallel the differences between gods and men. In the *Kamasutra*, for instance, women are exhorted to treat their husbands like gods.[23]

Even if the God of Abraham abstains from sex, that does not mean that Jews, Christians and Muslims miss out on the chance of having sex with supernatural beings. Genesis tells that 'the sons of God saw the daughters of men that they were fair; and they took them wives of all which they chose . . . and they bear children to them'.[24] These 'sons of God' are usually identified as being angels of the less moral variety and the sexual contact between human beings and divine creatures was definitely not a good thing. Both Jewish and Christian sources considered that unnatural sex of this kind was the cause of Noah's Flood,[25] and other similar relationships were linked to other catastrophes. In a number of Jewish and Christian texts the primary sin of the Sodomites lay in their desire to have sex with the visiting angels as *angels* – humans should not have sex with superhuman beings.[26]

Some Muslims believe that djinns are interested in having sex with people. Djinns are supernatural creatures, neither humans nor gods, the most famous of which is probably the genie in the lamp in the story of Aladdin. The Koran, for example, makes reference to virgins whom neither human beings nor djinns have touched.[27] There have been Muslim disputes about whether women were permitted to marry djinns, the most frequent conclusion being that it was permissible since there was no specific ban on it.[28] Djinns no longer play a central role in modern Islam but ideas about sexually active djinns still exist, among women in Egypt, for instance.[29] Islamic devils can also have sex with human beings whereas angels are abstemious.[30]

According to Christian tradition, angels left people in peace after the time of the Old Testament. But there were other superhuman temptations that were quite dangerous enough. Immediately after Anthony the Great had begun his ascetic career in the third century AD but before he went out into the desert, the Devil attempted to tempt the steadfast man. One night the Devil took on the form of a beautiful woman and imitated all of her amorous tricks in order to seduce Anthony.[31] The Devil then seems to have thought that women might not be Anthony's thing, so he adopted the guise of a handsome young black boy instead.[32] That also failed to tempt the ascetic. When Anthony went out into the desert the demons became even more active and according to later tradition much of the demonic activity involved sexual temptations. Anthony, however, did not fall for any of these demonic attempts to lead him away from a life of asceticism.

Given that the control of sex played a central part in Christianity, it is not surprising that many Christians believed that supernatural enemies of God were using sex to lead men into perdition. History shows that not every Christian had the strength of Anthony when it came to resisting demonic temptation. And the dangers were not to be scorned. In his great work *The City of God* Augustine links the biblical stories of angels having sex with mortal women to the traditional Greek and Roman beliefs about people having sex with fauns, satyrs and sylvans, these half-animal, half-human creatures that traditionally populated the ancient wilderness. He calls these un-Christian creatures *incubi*, thus giving a name to the sexually active demons that would continue to have sex with Christian people right up to modern times.[33] The active incubi-demons were soon joined by succubi-demons, who were sexually passive but no less dangerous for that. In the thirteenth century the Cistercian monk Caesarius of Heisterbach is able to tell us that female succubi-demons sexually abused monks to the extent that some of the monks died as a result.[34] At about the same time Thomas Aquinas explained how the demons used their human sexual partners in order to have demon children. First of all the demon takes on the form of a woman and steals the seed of a man by lying with him. Then the demon changes into a man's body and lies with a woman and makes her pregnant.[35] The fifteenth-century Castilian theologian and bishop Alonso Tostado thought that demons also used simpler methods: they simply collected the seed from men who masturbated and made women pregnant with what they had collected.[36] These kinds of scholarly speculations were not for everyone, however: in the 1520s Giovanni Francesco Pico della Mirandola interrogated a woman who talked enthusiastically about how demons gave her much greater sexual satisfaction than her husband had ever done.[37]

In his 1487 *Malleus Maleficarum* (The Hammer of Witches), the most influential Christian work on witchcraft, the inquisitor and Dominican monk Heinrich Kramer gave an account of the ideas about women who had sex with demons.[38] Kramer knew his Bible and associated the demonic sex of his day with the sons of God having sex with the daughters of men before the Flood.[39] In Kramer's view, God's destruction of Sodom was also a result of the inhabitants having had sex with demons.[40] Kramer believed that the reason St Paul insisted that a woman should 'have power on her head because of the angels'[41] was to ensure that evil angels would not be tempted as they had been in Old Testament times.[42] Kramer also went along with Thomas Aquinas' theories about how demons impregnated women, but he pointed out at the same time that these children were actually the children of the men whose seed had been used. Nevertheless, the demonic insemination procedure meant that the demons had had the opportunity to infect the children's bodies and souls.[43] According to *Malleus Maleficarum*, however, it was only female witches who had sex with demons.[44] The traditional view had been that incubi-demons, in their lust, also penetrated men anally,[45] but Kramer did not only claim that demons restricted themselves to women: he also insisted that they refrained from everything apart from vaginal sex.[46]

Using the 'powers of the air', the demons transformed themselves into the most dashing and energetic of lovers. But if you wanted to have demonic sex you had to stick to certain rules. Kramer tells of a young virgin who was looking forward to having sex with a group of demons who had taken on the guise of hearty young men, but their bodies dissolved the moment she made the sign of the cross.[47] Kramer did not base his ideas about sex between women and demons solely on the speculations of earlier writers: he also relied on what he considered to be 'eye-witnesses, reports and the statements of reliable witnesses' from a number of legal cases undertaken by the inquisitor in Como in 1485 (which led to the burning of forty-one witches).[48] Kramer's views were supported by the top echelons of the Catholic church and as early as 1484 Pope Innocent VIII issued a bull stating that he 'ha[d] recently been made aware that . . . in some parts of northern Germany, as well as in the provinces, towns, territories, districts and dioceses of Mainz, Cologne, Trier, Salzburg, and Bremen, many people of both sexes, with no thought of their own salvation and that they are straying from the Catholic faith, have delivered themselves to devils, incubi and succubi.'[49]

Others are reported to have had sex with the Devil himself. The affair between the Devil and Walpurga Hausmännin, a day labourer from Dillingen outside Augsburg, began when she arranged to meet for sex with a man she had worked with. They met that night at the pre-arranged location and Walpurga realized that she had been having sex with the Devil as soon as she saw that one of his feet was a hoof and one of his hands seemed to be made of wood. When she uttered the name of Jesus the Devil disappeared immediately. Walpurga must nevertheless have been smitten by the Devil's charms since she continued to have sex with him on later occasions, and she also gave herself to him spiritually. Bearing such things on her conscience, Walpurga was finally burnt on 20 September 1587.[50]

Whereas Walpurga seems to have allowed herself to be seduced quite voluntarily, there were others who ended up in more complicated situations. In 1628 a certain Johannes Junius admitted to having had sex with a demon who at first appeared to be an ordinary woman. After the moments of bliss the beautiful woman suddenly changed form and became a talking goat, which threatened to break Johannes' back unless he denied God. Even though he had been both tricked and threatened by the demon, Johannes was executed in Bamberg in Bavaria.[51]

A number of modern Satanists have tried to reawaken the belief that it is possible to have sex with demons but their point of departure is a rather positive one: not only will you have unbelievably good sex but demons 'are fantastic when it comes to listening to all your worries, troubles and problems and can often help by punishing your enemies and fixing things for you.'[52] Demons are quite simply perfect lovers. This is obviously a wonderful starting point but we do have to ask whether texts such as this reflect genuine conviction rather than wishful thinking.

Possibly the closest modern parallel to the earlier widespread belief in demonic and divine sex is provided by the many people who are convinced they have had sex with extra-terrestrial beings, usually aboard UFOs. When, for example, the French UFO prophet Raël visited the distant planet Elohim, he was entertained by naked dancers, who were also sexually available.[53] Rather more unpleasant than this are the repeated reports of people being abducted by extra-terrestrials and subjected to rape or sexual experiments.[54]

Contact with divine beings is a central concern of many religions, and believers actively strive to achieve it by means of prayers, sacrifices and incantations. The gods respond in various ways. They speak to us directly, reveal themselves to us in person or bring us good fortune or adversity by manipulating our fates or the forces of nature. In the worst case, if they are particularly provoked, they strike us down and kill us. Given that all this may be the case, sex with these supernatural beings makes good sense.

The fact that the notion of humans having sex with gods and demons is no longer as widespread as it was has little to do with changing views of sexuality. It is primarily a result of religion having become more spiritual and of fewer people believing that gods, demons and similar beings intervene directly and physically in our lives. Their interventions are generally more indirect, more sensitive. Consequently the idea that human beings can have sex with these beings is no longer so convincing.

Confirmation of this connection between supernatural sex and the general understanding of religion is provided by the only form of religion where many followers still believe in sex between supernatural creatures and humans: in the UFO religions the deities have been made part of a scientific world picture and consequently there is nothing to prevent them from having sex with us.

Sex for Eternity

Testimonies from people who willingly or unwillingly have had sex with demons, gods or other supernatural beings are often very dramatic. Nevertheless, it is and always will be exceptional. Sex of that kind will never be something that affects most people directly even though ideas about it have sometimes played a major role in public debate. What happens to us after death is something that affects us in a quite different way. All believers can relate to the idea of post-mortal sex, irrespective of whether it implies eternal abstinence or unlimited sex for the whole of eternity.

The Islamic view is that there is no reason for sex to come to an end simply because of death. The Koran promises Muslim men that wide-eyed, voluptuous virgins will keep them company in paradise.[55] These are the houris, women God has created just for paradise and who have never lived on earth, and it is emphasized that they have never been touched either by men or by djinns.[56] According to tradition the houris are waiting impatiently for the husbands they have been promised and Ridwan, the chief angel, sometimes takes them to the top of paradise so that they can look expectantly down at their husbands on earth.[57]

In the hadiths Muhammad explains in more detail how no man will be without a wife in paradise: indeed, each man will have two wives.[58] These women will be virgins with big eyes, and both men and women will be 27 metres tall.[59] Since pious spouses will also be reunited in paradise,[60] some of these women will have originally been ordinary Muslim women who have regained their youth on entering paradise.[61] The Syrian Koranic scholar Ismail ibn Kathir stated in the fourteenth century that all the women in paradise would automatically become virgins again after every sexual intercourse.[62] And in any case, Kathir thought, every man would have sex with a hundred virgins every day. This would be physically possible because every man would have the strength of a hundred men.[63] In a hadith that Islamic scholars are more sceptical about, it is claimed that Muhammad held out the promise of 72 wives for every man in paradise.[64]

The Koranic account of 'eternally young youths' 'beautiful as pearls' who will serve the most wondrous drinks in beautiful goblets has sometimes been seen in the Islamic tradition as an indication that sex between men will also exist in paradise, particularly since they are frequently presented side by side with the many very sexually active virgins and just as much stress is placed on their beauty and willingness to serve.[65] This is still a current question and at the start of the 1990s in Egypt there was a wide-ranging debate, involving some of the most prominent scholars in the country, as to whether homosexuality and eternal erections existed in paradise.[66]

The Christian view of the blessings of paradise is considerably more moderate than the Islamic. As Jesus explains: 'they which shall be accounted worthy to obtain that world, and the resurrection from the dead, neither marry, nor are given in marriage . . . for they are equal unto the angels.'[67] Given that sexual abstinence is the original Christian ideal, we will not be surprised that the general rule states that there will be no sex in heaven either. Not all Christians agree on this, however: the Mormons, for instance, who put a great deal of weight on salvation by what they call celestial marriage, are firm in their belief that marital sex will last for all eternity.[68]

With the general Christian position on sex being a negative one, it is hardly surprising that sex figures fairly frequently in hell, which is not to say that the sinners in hell will enjoy themselves in the same way as they did on earth. Quite the opposite. Sexual activity in hell is only used as punishment. The many very detailed medieval and renaissance depictions of hell and the Day of Judgment frequently show devils inflicting sexual torture on their victims. Anal penetration, either using objects or parts of the demonic body, seems to be particularly popular. Since torture is traditionally the only kind of sexual activity to be portrayed in the Christian perception of eternity, the generally negative message about sex is further reinforced. In an ideal state sex is and remains something that humanity should abstain from totally; anyone who believes anything different may well end up experiencing for eternity how truly terrifying sex can be.

The lack of prominence given to sex beyond this life in the religious discourse of today probably reflects the fact that religious beliefs have become less material. This is not dissimilar to the decline in belief in human beings having sex with gods and demons. Sex is primarily a physical activity and if eternity is spiritual it becomes more difficult to have an understanding of how sex may exist in such a sphere.

It is, however, not possible to explain the increased absence of sex in the afterlife just by pointing out that religion has become more spiritual – religious notions of sex are, after all, not limited by what we can do with our physical bodies. The fact that so many believers scarcely associate sex with our existence after death is not just a matter of course. When sex is something that does *not* exist in the eternal ideal condition of those fortunate enough to be chosen, it means that a particular religious conviction is being maintained:

the fact that, for example, Christian eternity is consistently presented as a sexless condition points to an unequivocal view that sex has no place in any sort of ideal human condition. Sex is and remains a matter not fully worthy of a place in this religious picture. Sex belongs to our imperfect condition as mortal and transient beings and when we become perfect we will neither practise nor miss sex. Seen in this light, the religious depictions of the relationship between sex, the gods and life after death tell us more than a little about the relationship between sex and religion in general.

8
Because You're Worth It

According to the American Westboro Baptist Church, God is angry with Sweden and has visited his wrath upon the Swedes in a variety of ways. The main reason for God's displeasure is that 'Sweden embraces [homosexuality] so that it is considered to be one of the most "gay-friendly" countries in Europe and maybe even the world.' The legalization of homosexuality in 1944, the anti-discrimination regulations of 1987, the civil union law of 1995, the right of gays and lesbians to be considered as adoptive parents from 2002 and the annual Stockholm gay parade are all factors that are said to have angered God. The fact that Sweden has one of the world's highest divorce rates has also contributed to God being against the Swedes, and he will certainly not have been pleased when they decided to permit same-sex marriage in 2009. The consequences of the 'evil' Swedish government and the acceptance by the Swedish people of all this 'sinful' sexuality are obvious – according to the Westboro Baptist Church. The tsunami in December 2004 that took the lives of over 500 Swedes was God's punishment on this sinful nation, as were the storm of August 2008 that cut off electricity to 11,000 Swedish homes, the storm on the west coast in January 2007 that killed six people, the storm in January 2005 that took seven lives, the 1998 discotheque fire in Gothenburg that claimed 63 lives and the 1994 sinking of the ferry *Estonia*, which resulted in 501 Swedes being drowned.[1]

Even though the other Nordic countries – Norway, Denmark, and Iceland – take more or less the same view of same-sex sexuality as Sweden, this particular American congregation has not targeted them in the same way. Using the same logic, however, various floods, landslides, volcanic eruptions, conflagrations and other disasters that have befallen these countries should also be considered God's punishment for their liberal attitudes to homosexuality. The Westboro

Baptist Church believes that even the US, with its considerably lower level of official acceptance of gays and lesbians, has provoked God's wrath for the same reasons. One result was that 'God sent the planes' that crashed into the World Trade Center on 11 September 2001. Hurricane Katrina and the disastrous war in Iraq are also punishments from God.[2] In order to make Americans aware of how bad things are, members of the church travel round the US and demonstrate at the funerals of soldiers killed in Iraq with placards saying 'God hates fags', 'God hates America' and 'Thank God for 9-11!'

Westboro Baptist Church is a small church, although it has an enormously successful media strategy. The way in which it perceives logical connections between unacceptable sex and various disasters, natural catastrophes and other serious events is, however, far from unique. Given the extent to which the various religions focus on sex, it is unsurprising that in all the religions that have rules on sex, sex has consequences, at the very least in the sense that it defines whether or not you are the sort of person who abides by the basic principles of your religion. Since there is scarcely a single religion that does not have some regulations about sexual conduct, sex has consequences in virtually every religion. The Westboro Baptist Church's conviction that torrential floods, storms and wars result from improper sex does not represent a radical qualitative difference from other religions, merely a difference of degree. Whereas some people think that your sexual behaviour defines you as a proper Jew, Christian or Hindu, the pious little Baptist church goes a step further and also believes that your sexual behaviour has consequences in the physical world, sometimes in the form of natural disasters or of world events. The main distinction between this Baptist church and many other denominations is not the belief that sex has consequences but the conviction that natural phenomena and the course of history may be counted among the phenomena that are governed directly by divine powers.

The Posthumous Consequences of Sex

It is not very common for the religious consequences of our sexual behaviour to feature on the weather report or the six o'clock news. Most beliefs regarding the consequences of sex are concerned with what is beyond this life: our sexual behaviour is closely connected to whether we will achieve salvation or redemption, or, for those who believe in reincarnation, a better existence the next time we are reborn. Existence after death is an area about which no religious ideas have yet been disproven (or, for that matter, proven), so it is not surprising that it also reflects some of the same religio-sexual ideas that various faiths insist on. If sex were not to have consequences in an area over which the divine powers are generally understood to have full control, what would be the point of all the religious ordi nances designed to regulate our sex lives?

The conviction that sex will have consequences that will last for eternity is particularly important in Christianity. Jesus himself pointed out that the divorced and all those who have sex before or outside marriage will end up in hell: 'And if thy right eye offend thee, pluck it out, and cast it from thee: for it is profitable for thee that one of thy members should perish, and not that thy whole body should be cast into hell.'[3] According to Jesus, then, it is a tiny and ever-shrinking proportion of the world's population – not least in the Western world – that has any kind of chance of getting to heaven. St Paul states empha tically (and predictably) that 'fornicators' are among those who will not inherit God's kingdom.[4] The Revelation of John is a little more explicit and explains how the 'whoremongers' will under go a 'second death' after the Resurrection, together with the fearful, the murderers, the sorcerers, idolaters and liars: they will all have 'their part in the lake which burneth with fire and brimstone'.[5] They will suffer this for all eternity.

All of this implies that people who live in monogamous heterosexual marriages can look forward to eternity with hope (as long as they are not cowardly, tell lies, commit murder or dabble in religions other than Christianity). But as so often in Christian contexts, the Revelation of John shows that *not* indulging in sex at all is by far the best option: the first to be assured of eternal salvation will be 144,000 men 'which were not *defiled* with women'.[6]

With the passing of time, however, quite specific punishments arose for different sexual misdemeanours. The text known as the Apocalypse of Peter from the second century AD, which was certainly not composed by St Peter, presents us with a selection of the punishments of hell. Along with those who are being punished for murder, miserliness and usury we find men and women who have committed adultery, hanging by their hair or by their feet respectively over a lake of boiling mud.[7] Men who have had passive homosexual experience and women who have had active lesbian sex are being repeatedly chased up a precipice and then hurled from it.[8] Men who have taken the active role in homosexual activity and women who have had passive lesbian sex are not, however, mentioned, so it is possible they are not in hell at all.

Throughout the whole history of Christianity both church art and popular stories have built on the notion that there are special punishments for specific sexual sins. One of the most influential works of this kind is Dante's *Divine Comedy*, in which sexual behaviour is a decisive factor in determining whether people end up in Heaven, Hell or Purgatory. People who have allowed themselves to be overcome by heterosexual lust before or outside marriage are to be found in the Second Circle of Hell, where their souls are blown around by violent winds without the lovers ever being able to come in contact with each other.[9] In the Seventh Circle, below heretics, murderers and suicides, we find sodomites being punished by an eternal rain of fire.[10] Seducers, people who have used sex or love to cheat others, are to be found even further down, in the Eighth Circle of Hell.[11] Those who have committed mild sexual sins, however, are located just below heaven, on the Seventh (and uppermost) Terrace of Purgatory.[12]

Implicit in all this is the idea that people will be rewarded in the eternal afterlife for *not* indulging in improper sex. Indeed, witnessing the punishment of others can be part of the reward. When the pious saint Bernardino of Siena saw the enthusiasm of the spectators at the burning of a sodomite in Venice at the start of the fifteenth century, he compared them to the 'blessed spirits of paradise [who] blissfully glory in witnessing the justice of God' when they see sinners being punished in hell for eternity.[13] In other words, God-fearing people with a taste for snuff movies and public torture have a good deal to look forward to.

The notion that people will end up in hell because of unacceptable sexuality has remained present in Christianity. When twenty-one-year-old Matthew Shepard died in 1998 after two men had subjected him to brutal torture just because he was gay and then left him to die tied to a fence in a lonely part of Wyoming, many Christians knew whose fault his fate really was. Not all of them expressed it as clearly as the members of Westboro Baptist Church who, in their desire to save others from sin, turned up at Shepard's funeral bearing placards proclaiming 'Matt Shepard rots in Hell!' It may be less common

The Lover's Whirlwind: Francesca da Rimini and Paolo Malatesta. A scene from Dante's *Divine Comedy*, in a watercolour by William Blake, 1824–27.

to say such things in public now but the Westboro Baptist Church is certainly not alone. Emmanuel Chukwuma, Anglican Bishop of Enugu in Nigeria, publicly tells gay priests that they will end up in hell[14] and a quick search of the Internet will reveal many well-known people saying similar things. John Hagee, the prominent American TV evangelist, takes a more theological approach and is of the opinion that Antichrist will be 'homosexual' and 'partially Jewish'.[15]

Another currently fashionable attempt to inspire proper Christian sexuality is represented by the Hell Houses, as they are known, organized by evangelical churches all over the United States and in a number of other countries. Working on the same principle as the haunted houses at fairgrounds, the Hell Houses invite children and young people to come in and take a tour of a series of tableaux illustrating a variety of 'sinful' situations, alongside which are depictions of hell not unlike those in the Apocalypse of Peter or Dante's *Divine Comedy*. Hell Houses are often set up by buying a package deal on the Internet ($299, excluding tax).[16] In the standard presentation we meet, for instance, Steve the homosexual, writhing in eternal agony in hell after dying of AIDS.[17] More surprising, perhaps, are a girl who is a victim of incest and a teenager who is raped after getting drunk – both in hell after committing suicide. The degree of violence and suffering in these hell scenes is so graphic that a number of psychologists have described them as disturbing.[18] But as a Texas priest who set up a Hell House along with his congregation points out, the degree of horror and suffering is necessary to emphasize the message that certain actions can have certain consequences in 'a real place called hell'.[19]

For the majority of Christians, however, there is always the possibility of being forgiven by God if they repent. It is rarely too late to save yourself from the sufferings of hell. Even if you recognize yourself in one of the 'sinful' situations depicted in the Hell House, there is still hope if you repent. Ole Kristian Hallesby, the theology professor who sparked off a major debate in Norway about hell in 1953 when he wondered how anyone 'who has not repented' can go to bed 'and sleep peacefully at night' when 'they don't know whether they will wake up in bed in the morning or in hell' – insisted that someone 'sitting there with a sin as red as blood' could still be saved from hell if he or she repented.[20]

Discussions about hell no longer play the same central role as they used to in mainstream Christian debate, but hell nevertheless tends to turn up in not quite such public contexts in many circles. Gays and lesbians growing up in conservative surroundings are often confronted with the risks of hell. When Arnfinn Nordbø, who occupied an important position in Christian conservative circles in Norway as a hymn singer, came out as gay, many pious Christians let him know where they thought he was headed. 'No one [in the Christian conservative circles I grew up in] gave me any support though one or two people omitted to mention hell,' Nordbø said. 'The general message in all the many reactions was: we are just as fond of you as we were before but you are living in sin and must repent – otherwise you will end up in hell.'[21]

The increasing focus on equality and human rights has meant that many heterosexuals have put their own salvation at risk simply by supporting homosexual rights. In Norway, for instance, the debate about the 2009 marriage law that covers both heterosexuals and homosexuals has shown that simply being in favour of equality can have eternal consequences. The members of parliament who supported the law received letters, emails and telephone calls warning them of what the future held for them. The most common content of the messages consisted of death threats and statements that they would end up in hell.[22] Even the business of documenting homosexuality can put your soul at risk. Pious Christians warned those responsible for mounting an exhibition at the Oslo Natural History Museum in 2006 that the flames of hell awaited them: the exhibition was about same-sex sexuality among animals.[23]

The conviction that hell awaits those who have sex with people of the same sex is often internalized and can lead to anxiety and profound self-contempt, sometimes to such an extent that gay and lesbian Christians would rather take their own lives than live with the risk of eternal damnation. Research shows that attempting to solve such dilemmas by making contact with censorious religious circles further increases the risk of suicide.[24] There are many examples of personal tragedy and Trond Winterkjær and Jan Dalchow's 2000 film *Dirty, Sinful Me* gives us a rare insight into how this can turn out. In the film we meet the parents, siblings and friends of Bjørn Erik, a young Christian who disappeared without trace in 1992. His letter of farewell to his family points to him having taken his own life. Told in his own words, we can hear Bjørn Erik's spiritual agonising about his homosexuality, his despair and his hopelessness. 'Dirty, Sinful Me' is how Bjørn Erik thought of himself, a self-image that reflects much of the conservative Christian teaching of the time.[25]

Islam has had a more positive attitude to sex than Christianity from the start but there are still parallels between Islamic and Christian views of eternity. The idea that heaven and hell are constructed on a series of levels, for instance, can be found in Islamic descriptions that pre-date Dante and may have influenced the Italian poet.[26] According to the Koran the Islamic hell is above all a place of unbelief, a place for those who put barriers in the way of Islam, but that does not mean that sexual transgressors will only be punished in this life. The Koran points out that 'the punishment shall be doubled on the day of resurrection' for people who commit adultery, though it also stresses the fact that God will forgive those who do penance.[27] It is rarely too late: even at the moment of death there is time to honour God, and then to slip straight into paradise.[28] The fact that God's mercy is greater than his wrath is a recurring theme in Islam – a theme that is symbolized by heaven having eight doors whereas hell has only seven.[29]

Since Islamic religious authorities generally adhere faithfully to their texts, the ideas in these writings as to the eternal consequences of particular sexual activities for the individual are still very relevant. This is also reflected among the majority of Muslims in rather the same way as concepts of heaven and hell are still central in many Christian circles. Young British Pakistani Muslims, for instance, talk about how they have been brought up to believe (and do believe) that they will end up in hell if they break various Islamic rules, including sexual rules.[30]

The ancient Hindu *Laws of Manu* state that sexually abstinent Brahmin men will go to heaven even if they do not have any sons, as will widows who refrain from sex after the death of their husbands. Women who have sex after becoming widows automatically lose their place in heaven.[31] But men must be careful as well: a man of the highest caste who marries a woman of the lowest caste will go straight to hell.[32] Hinduism also reveals that our current life situations can often be explained by our sexual behaviour in earlier lives. The *Laws of Manu* state that women who are unfaithful will be reborn as diseased jackals – according to the same text, however, unfaithful men have less to worry about.[33] High-caste men who sleep with women of the very lowest castes will be reborn as tormented spirits;[34] men who sleep with the wives of their gurus will be reborn a hundred times as various plants and beasts of prey before they can be reborn as a human being again.[35] The epic *Mahabharata* tells of the karmic consequences of various sexual practices. Promiscuous men who have intercourse with women of a higher caste than their own, or who sleep with the wives of their teachers, will be impotent in the next life. People who are blind deserve to be so, having been reborn that way because they looked lustfully at other men's wives in earlier lives. The mere fact that a man looks at naked women leads to the whole of his next life being one long illness.[36] Recalling how modern Hindu homophobia seems to be primarily a result of Christian colonial politics, it is worth noticing that none of the classical Hindu writings specifically refers to same-sex sexuality as leading to bad karma.[37]

Buddhism and Jainism take a similar view to Hinduism as to the way our sexual behaviour in this life will have consequences both for reincarnation and for our consciousness when dead. Sexual abstinence is the key to better karma in Jainism: it can lead to longer life, enlightenment, an existence in heaven and better reincarnation.[38] Buddha himself pointed out that all heterosexuality could result in ending up in hell.[39] As far as Buddhism is concerned, the worst consequences after this life will be the result of various forms of heterosexual behaviour: men who have intercourse with other men's wives or who use impermissible parts of the body will be punished by being reborn as women.[40] When the daughter of the eighth-century Tibetan king Trisong Detsen died at only eight years of age, the legendary monk Padmasambhava explained that this was because she had been a male monk in an earlier life and had been so aroused by the sight of two dogs copulating that he had sex with a married woman. That, together with the fact that she (as a monk, that is) killed one of the dogs and himself/herself, meant that she would be reincarnated as a woman 500 times in addition to suffering many other misfortunes.[41] In other words, when the eight-year-old girl died she was simply getting what she deserved.

Being reincarnated as a woman does not, however, signal the end of all hope because, if she is of good morality and suppresses her sexual lusts, a woman might be fortunate enough to be reborn as a man.[42] The very fact that being reborn as a woman is regarded as a punishment obviously tells us something about women's place in the Buddhist system, but there are also other undesirable fates that can be explained by sex in an earlier existence: if, for instance, one has coarse and improper sex with a female relation one might end up as an effeminate man.[43]

Buddhist men who sleep with other men's wives take the risk of ending up in hell, where they will be forced to climb repeatedly up a tree covered in thorns with a woman at its top.[44] The thorns will dig so deep into the man's flesh as he climbs that he never reaches the woman. This was witnessed by the famous Thai monk Phra Malai, who visited both heaven and hell and came back to tell us about them.[45] The edifying thorn tree and its unfortunate climbers can also be seen depicted in temple art over large parts of the Buddhist world.

According to traditional Chinese Buddhism, a man who commits incest with his mother will be punished in seven different hells. The consequences are not so severe, however, if he lies with his sister.[46] In order to be reincarnated, many Buddhists will have to spend a certain amount of time in heaven or in hell depending on the extent to which they have followed Buddhist rules, and sexual prescriptions are of particular importance.

When sexual behaviour can lead to consequences after death, it means that we are operating completely within a religious world view. But the fact that proper or improper sex can lead to salvation or damnation does not mean that sex is in a class of its own – a whole host of other activities can have similar consequences. The fact that current Christian discourse about hell seems to be particularly concerned with certain kinds of sex is not because there is a special connection between sex and eternity; rather, it has to do with the increased level of attention given to sexuality by these believers. This also reveals something about the motivation behind some of the most extreme religious agitation against certain kinds of sex: as a result of their own convictions, believers are simply trying to save others from hell – even when they have to kill those others to do so.

The conviction that certain kinds of sex will inevitably lead to eternal damnation consequently represents an extreme form of the general religious condemnation of such acts. Changes in the perception of the eternal consequences of sex therefore mirror changes in the overall religio-sexual landscape: if many believers are less condemnatory of improper kinds of heterosexual behaviour in this world, these will no longer have the same major consequences in eternity. The emphasis that many groups currently put on homosexuality as the quintessential improper sex is reflected in those same groups' view of its religio-sexual consequences in hell.

By and large, however, given the greater levels of acceptance of consensual sex in general, the whole idea that sex is a decisive factor in the hereafter has lost ground among believers of all kinds.

The Consequences of Sex in this World

We do not always need to wait until after death to discover how the divine powers react to different kinds of sex. That sex can lead to sexually transmitted diseases is an incontrovertible fact but it does not preclude many religious people from seeing the spread of venereal disease as evidence of a stern divine hand at work. AIDS is, of course, the example *par excellence* in modern times, but in 1980, even before the AIDS epidemic, the General Assembly of the Free Church of Scotland was warning that 'the increased incidence of certain sexually transmitted diseases bears witness to the reality of God's just judgment.'[47] So gonorrhoea and chlamydia can also be seen as punishments sent by God. Jerry Falwell, the influential American evangelist and leader of the conservative Christian lobbying organization

Moral Majority, explicitly stated that herpes is 'the judgment of God upon the society that has forgotten Him'.[48]

These current ideas about painful but non-fatal sexually transmitted diseases are nevertheless quite moderate when we compare them with the sweeping claims of divine retribution for sin that were heard in the early days of the AIDS epidemic.[49] According to an official pronouncement from the leadership of the Church of Jesus Christ of Latter-day Saints in 1988, the homosexual AIDS sufferer was something quite different from what it called the 'innocent victim, including unsuspected marriage partners, babies, and those who have received infected blood'.[50] Men who have sex with men were, in other words, *guilty* victims. Jerry Falwell, for his part, made his view clear in 1987 when he called AIDS 'God's judgment upon America, for endorsing immorality':[51] it was a consequence of the sexual revolution and 'an appropriate punishment' for homosexuality.[52]

A survey in 1991 showed that 70 per cent of American Protestants and 54 per cent of American Catholics thought that all HIV-positive individuals should wear visible tokens, not unlike the yellow stars Jews wore during the Nazi period.[53] Among Orthodox Jews AIDS was frequently seen as a direct consequence of a morally unacceptable lifestyle.[54] John O'Connor, the Catholic cardinal in New York, declared that it was a disease people caught because they 'broke the teachings of the church'.[55] Moral Majority opposed the use of public funds in the search for a cure for AIDS since it was a disease that primarily afflicted gay men:[56] they deserved to die, as indeed they did in their tens of thousands. Attitudes of this kind contributed to the fact that little or nothing was done by the authorities to control the epidemic among gay men in the US before 1986. This, however, does not give the whole picture. Many Christian and Jewish congregations eventually began to oppose claims of this kind, pointing out that AIDS in no way could be viewed as God's punishment, and many religious organizations opened hospices for the victims of AIDS.[57]

The wrong kind of sex does not only lead to individuals suffering from divinely inflicted sexual disease. In the Middle Ages, for example, leprosy was often seen as a result of individual sexual sin.[58] The same pattern is to be found in other religions. According to the traditional Yoruba religion of south-west Nigeria, people who commit adultery must be punished. If adultery is not punished by society, gods and spirits will inflict disease, infertility and death on the perpetrators since adultery is an insult to the gods and ancestors who have vouched for the marriage.[59]

In some circumstances it is the perpetrator's nearest and dearest who are most at risk. According to the traditional Sudanese Azande religion, a woman's unfaithfulness might lead to the death of her husband in war or when out hunting.[60] In Chinese Buddhism a man who is unfaithful risks losing his wives, children and grandchildren. Even though this is obviously a misfortune for the wives and children, it is nevertheless the husband who is being punished by the divine powers, in this case because the absence of wives and descendants means that there is no one to perform the necessary sacrifices to the ancestors on his behalf when he dies.[61]

But if the wrong sexual behaviour can lead to death and misery for an individual in this life, the correct sexual behaviour can have positive results. In medieval China the Taoist view of sexuality was influenced by the concept of the cultivation of yin and yang on what were virtually alchemistic principles. By cultivating *fangzhong shu*, the 'arts of the bedchamber', you learned how to manage your sexuality most effectively in order to achieve the highest physical and spiritual benefit from orgasm.[62] Since a man can increase his yang force by having intercourse with one woman, he will increase it even more if he has intercourse with many – three, nine and eleven are particularly auspicious numbers. In this way a man's skin will gleam, his body feel light, his eyes will be bright and his life-force will be strong and flourishing. The right sex can make old men like twenty-year-olds.[63] If a man can perfect the way he controls and nourishes his yin and yang through intercourse, he can become immortal, like the legendary Yellow Emperor after he had enjoyed intercourse with 1,200 women.

Nevertheless, this is above all a question of having the right religious knowledge – of quality, not quantity. If you do not know exactly how to have the correct sex, having sex with even one woman could be the death of you,[64] so Taoist sex manuals give practical advice on how to go about it. The man is recommended to collect as much of the woman's yin force as possible without giving away any of his yang force. He might, for example, keep his penis in the woman while she has an orgasm and then withdraw it before he himself ejaculates. And he is not the only one who will profit from this technique: if he has intercourse with five or six concubines in this way before he has intercourse with his wife in order to make her pregnant, the child they conceive will be that much better.[65] Similarly, a woman can become stronger by letting young men ejaculate inside her without her having an orgasm.[66]

These Taoist notions of the positive consequences of sex were strongly criticized by both Buddhists and Confucians.[67] Thanks to their administrative power in China, the Confucians were able to have Taoist sex manuals branded as evil and degenerate, and had many of them destroyed.[68] More orthodox Taoists also condemned this extremely positive view of sex.[69] And with the decline of Taoist yin and yang sex, no one has since managed to achieve immortality through sex.

That your sex life contributes to your individual salvation or perdition remains a widespread religious idea; that you will be punished already in this world, however, has become a more marginal belief, in the same way that fewer people are now convinced that the gods physically intervene in our lives. The idea of gods who punish or reward human beings at their own discretion is a general religious conviction which, of course, is not limited to the sphere of sexual behaviour. But, given the central position occupied by sex in many religions, if we first believe in the ability of the gods to intervene directly in our existence it follows quite logically that our sexuality can lead to good fortune or misfortune in this life.

When whole Societies are Punished

The Westboro Baptist Church insists that the consequences of the wrong kind of sex can also afflict the whole of society, and in this view they are by no means alone. Many people, both Christians and Jews, believed that Noah's Flood – when God drowned everyone apart from Noah and his family – was the direct result of sinful sexual relationships between angels and humans.[70] Rabbinic texts explain the Flood as the result of more general fornication;[71] the Council of Paris in AD 829 put it down to sex between men;[72] and the strictly Catholic Jansenites at the end of the seventeenth century simply stated that it was caused by lust in the marital bed – good Christians should not allow desire to govern their marital sex lives and they should only do what was absolutely necessary for the future of the species.[73]

Even though it originally seems to have been a breach of the laws of hospitality that caused God to rain fire and brimstone down on Sodom and Gomorrah and kill all the inhabitants of the cities,[74] a firm belief developed over time that God was punishing the inhabitants for their sexual preferences. The sexual crime was initially identified as being the Sodomites' desire to have sex with angels *qua* angels, but later centuries usually identified it as being the male citizens' desire to have sex with their male visitors *qua* men.

The Bible tells us that correct sexuality was an absolute condition God demanded of the Israelites in exchange for his continued protection. During this period God was particularly keen on preventing sex across ethnic boundaries. When Moses was leading the people through the desert, for example, God slew 24,000 of them with plague because the Israelites had sex with Moabite women. What finally appeased the wrath of God was that the son of a priest killed an Israelite who brought a Midianite woman home with him. The priest's son 'went after the man of Israel into the tent, and thrust both of them through, the man of Israel, and the woman through her belly'. As God then explained to Moses: 'Phineas, the son of Eleazar, the son of Aaron the priest, hath turned my wrath away from the children of Israel, while he was zealous for my sake among them.'[75] It is not enough, then, for you as an individual to abstain from forbidden sex: if you silently accept *others* doing it, that is sufficient for God's punishment to apply to you too. As the priest's son's exemplary double murder demonstrates, in order to placate God it is sometimes necessary to take particular action against those who break his sexual rules.

The prophet Ezra states that ethnically mixed marriages make God so angry that there would be no end to his wrath until he had 'consumed us, so that there should be no remnant nor escaping.'[76] Only immediate divorce would appease him.[77]

Nor is it only the failure to practise sexual racism that can lead to serious consequences. In the Pentateuch we learn that bestiality and incest, as well as sex with menstruating women and with in-laws, all contribute to making the Promised Land unclean. 'Whosoever shall commit any of these abominations . . . shall be cut off from among their people.' And if the Israelites themselves fail to kill anyone who commits 'one of these abominable customs', they need to take care 'that the *land* spue not you out also, when ye defile it, as it spued out the nations that were before you.'[78] The Promised Land itself operates in such a way that people who have the wrong kind of sex – or fail to kill those who do so – will automatically be driven from it.

The conviction that the wrong kind of sex can easily lead to horrendous catastrophes is a prime reason why believers of different kinds have put so much energy into regulating other people's sex lives. If society does not ensure that its members' sexual behaviour is as it should be, society as a whole will be punished directly or indirectly. The whole social structure might be shattered by divine wrath.

Christianity took over this fundamental biblical belief that God might punish the whole of society for indulging in sex of the wrong kind. In AD 538 the Emperor Justinian linked the fate of Sodom and Gomorrah to the serious 'famines, earthquakes and plagues' of his own times. It was the generally ungodly conduct and deplorable sexual behaviour – 'in conflict with nature' – of the Christian Romans that was the root cause of all the disasters that struck Justinian's empire.[79] Alfonso the Wise of Castile had his own good reasons for ordering the public castration and execution of men who had sex with men: 'our Lord God sends upon the land where they do [such things], famine, pestilence, storms, and many other ills that cannot be counted.'[80] Benedict Levita, who forged Charlemagne's law in the ninth century to make it prescribe the death penalty for homosexuality, naturally also had good reasons for doing what he did: otherwise 'the Saracens', that is the Muslims, would come and subjugate us.[81]

The Black Death and other outbreaks of plague were seen by many as God's punishment for adultery, sodomy, sexually active priests and various other sexual abominations.[82] If we are to believe pious Christian spokesmen from this period, a number of indecent fashions – such as figure-hugging clothing for women, feminine clothing for men and garments that reputedly hardly covered the sexual organs – not only led to outbreaks of plague in fourteenth-century England but also caused violent storms and destroyed the crops.[83] Many people learned the lessons of these disasters. In the fifteenth century, for example, the authorities in Florence instituted a whole series of new regulations aimed at warding off the plague, and among them were various measures against sexual immorality such as prostitution and sex between men.[84]

Even though the outbreaks of plague diminished, disasters of one sort or another continued to afflict parts of the Christian world, so there was good reason to keep a watchful eye open. When Thomas Granger was condemned to death in Plymouth, Massachusetts, in 1643 for having had sex with 'a mare, a cow, two goats, five sheep, two calves and a turkey', it was quite clear that this was a crime that threatened the whole of society because of its impurity and revolt against the laws of God.[85] The perpetrator was, of course, doomed to perdition, but unless society also saw to it that he was punished appropriately in this world, society itself would be guilty of tolerating ungodly deeds and might consequently be punished by God. Even the sexually abused animals represented a threat and would also need to be eradicated as insurance against the wrath of God. Unfortunately, the authorities had some difficulty in identifying the five guilty sheep so five animals were picked out of the flock at random. Thomas Granger then had to witness all the animals he had had sex with, including the five unfortunate sheep, being burned in a pit, after which he was hanged.[86]

The mass persecution of men who had sex with men in the Netherlands in 1730 and 1731 was also justified by the danger of incurring the wrath of God. The judges in the village of Faan referred to the Pentateuch and its warnings that any acceptance of wrong sexuality would cause God to 'punish the iniquity of our land with his terrible judgments, and spew forth the land and its inhabitants'.[87] The authorities in the province of Holland were convinced that homosexuality represented 'transgressions of God's most sacred laws, whereby his just wrath towards our dear Fatherland has been inflamed time and again'. As they went on to explain: 'Many of our subjects have turned so far from any fear of God as audaciously to commit crimes which should never be heard of, on account of which God Almighty had in earlier times overturned, destroyed, and laid waste Sodom and Gomorrah.'[88]

This fear of God's impending wrath did not just come out of thin air. It was based on what the Dutch considered to be sound and relevant evidence that provided parallels going right back to the Flood and the improper sex that had caused it. A series of major floods in 1728, a fall on the Amsterdam stock exchange and a special kind of wood-eating maggot that caused many dykes to break in the winter of 1731 all seemed to point to and underline the connection between homosexuality and God's punishment. Priests took particular pains in their sermons to stress the connection between sexual morality and the dyke-destroying maggot sent by God.[89]

Not all illicit sex was equally dangerous. When a Dutch woman called Mayken Joosten was accused in 1606 of having married and had sex with another woman, the prosecution argued that this was at least as dangerous to society at large as sex between men. This type of crime, the prosecution argued, called down 'the anger of God upon cities and countries' and they demanded that Joosten should be tied in a sack and hurled into the water. The court was not, however, convinced that lesbian sex could provoke the same disastrous consequences as male homosexuality, so Joosten was just given a whipping and expelled.[90]

Even though the logical connection between incorrect sex and a wide range of disasters is no longer a central part of the public debate, that particular religious model remains in constant use as a way of explaining events. The evangelist David Wilkerson made a name for himself in 1973 by prophesying that sexual promiscuity, topless women on television, a high divorce rate and increasing tolerance of homosexuality would lead to disasters such as financial crises, earthquakes, flooding, hurricanes, famine, nuclear war and disobedient children.[91] Many conservative Christians believed that the financial crisis of 2008 was the final proof that Wilkerson was right. Nuclear war is the only thing we are still waiting for and there is no guarantee that it will not happen sooner rather than later. To many conservative Christians in the future, the words of the fundamentalist television evangelist Pat Robertson will no doubt sound like an exact prophecy: speaking in June 1998, he said that the acceptance of homosexuality would lead to the destruction of the US through terrorist bombs, earthquakes, tornadoes and meteors. Well, there has not yet been much meteor damage in the US but there has been plenty of the rest.[92]

Whereas Westboro Baptist Church believes that 'God sent the planes that brought down the New York towers and killed 3,000 on 9/11',[93] the Moral Majority leader Jerry Falwell had earlier stated that tolerance of homosexuality, feminism and abortion may have 'caused God to lift the veil of protection which has allowed no one to attack America on our soil since 1812'.[94] Pastor John Hagee, a Christian fundamentalist and prominent supporter of the Republican presidential candidate John McCain, explains how a planned gay parade in New Orleans led to God punishing the city with Hurricane Katrina in 2005: 'All hurricanes are acts of God, because God controls the heavens.'[95] Graham Dow, the Anglican Bishop of Carlisle in England, felt competent to inform us in 2007 that the many floods then afflicting Britain were caused by God because of the country's support for gay rights.[96]

Ivar Kristianslund, the leader of the fundamentalist Christian Unity Party, suggests that Norway is facing similar dangers. He considers that 'the new marriage law [covering both opposite-sex and same-sex couples] is a revolt against the living God' and consequently represents 'a security risk both for the individual and for the Norwegian people'. This sexual 'parliamentary criminality . . . will call down the wrath of the Lord' and put 'the security of Norway at risk'.[97] Since the new, common marriage law was approved with a two-thirds majority in the Norwegian parliament in 2008, we can assume that any disasters that have afflicted Norway since then are punishments sent by God.

Islam and Judaism, too, have retained the biblical concept that the wrong kind of sex can have consequences that go far beyond the individual. The prominent Saudi Arabian cleric Fawzan Al-Fawzan declared that the tsunami of Christmas 2004 was 'God's punishment' for the way 'immoral and corrupt people from all over the world gathered together to practise immorality and sexual perversions'.[98] The repeated earthquakes in Iran can be explained from a Muslim perspective by the deficient adherence to the formal dress codes in the country, including women letting their hair show under the hijab or wearing fully covering clothes that are too close fitting.[99] The earthquakes in Indonesia were set off by immoral television programmes, according to the Muslim information minister in 2009.[100] Similarly, the kabbalistic leader of Magen David Yeshiva, Rabbi David Basri, explained the outbreak of bird flu in Israel in 2006 as being the result of the authorities recognizing same-sex marriages.[101] A powerful earthquake in the eastern Mediterranean in February 2008 was caused by Israel's defence of homosexuality, according to Shlomo Benizri, an Israeli member of parliament. The earthquake should not have come as a surprise to anyone since Nissim Ze'ev, another member of the Knesset, had already warned a few weeks earlier that 'homolesbianism' would lead to the 'self-destruction' of the state of Israel.[102]

The religious belief that sex of the wrong kind can cause plagues, earthquakes and floods gives us a good idea of how significant sexual matters may be in a religious world view. 'Correct' sex emerges as one of the most important ways we humans can relate to divine reality. The centrality of such ideas in some places and periods of religious history shows us how they have contributed to the religious fervour for regulating other people's sex lives. If people are allowed to do anything they like, it may lead to the downfall of the whole of society.

Nevertheless, even though a conviction that natural forces may be triggered by our sexual behaviour is genuine enough in those who still believe in such things, it is really something of a curiosity in the modern religious landscape. It is no longer a widespread belief, not because there is any fading of the focus on sex but rather because of the growing recognition that there is a fundamental difference between the divine world and the physical world. There are fewer people now who believe that gods or other supernatural beings intervene directly and wield the forces of nature for their own gratification. Irrespective of what each one of us may think about divorce, miscegenation, homosexuality, premarital sex and all the other sexual varieties from a religious point of view, we will have to wait until this life is over before having the chance to see these kinds of behaviour getting their divine deserts – whatever they may be.

9
Sacred Sex, Ritual Sex

A phenomenon common among certain Læstadian congregations in northern Sweden in the middle of the 1930s was for members of the congregation to expose their sexual organs to each other during the service. Then one of the congregation members, usually a woman, went round and combed the believers' pubic hair. Much of the rest of the service was given over to extramarital intercourse, normally performed quite openly. The practice was voluntary and not everyone took part sexually, but everyone was free to watch.

The combing of pubic hair and extramarital sex in a Christian context in church is an idea this group of Læstadians had come up with while waiting for God to send a new Ark to take them to the heavenly Jerusalem. It started when Sigurd Siikavaar, their revealed prophet, became convinced that he represented Jesus Christ and thus had the power to cleanse all believers of their sins. The reason for the congregation committing what they believed to be the worst of sins was their belief that it would speed the arrival of God's Ark. Irrespective of what they did, these believers remained the holiest people on earth because their prophet could absolve them from all their sins.[1] All this sex, even though they themselves viewed it as sinful, was thus a way of ensuring salvation for the pious Christian Læstadians.

Most, perhaps all, religions use sex for religious ends by the mere fact that they have rules about sex. Every religious prohibition or injunction about sex means that sex is clearly being used for religious purposes. By regulating sex, religions ensure respect, contempt or annihilation in this life, and salvation or damnation in the next. Seen in this light, the Læstadian sexual exposure and intercourse in church does not represent anything uniquely different from what happens in other religions – it is a difference of degree rather than of essence. At the heart of all these religious world views lies the same fundamental belief, which is that sex can signify a good deal more than pleasure, procreation and sexually transmitted diseases.

But the direct use of sex in a religious context – the idea that it can be seen as a religious ritual – seems more than a little alien to many believers. Yet whereas the Christian combing of pubic hair is probably unique in the history of religion, the systematic use of sex is not. There have been many believers throughout history who have been convinced that this sort of direct linkage of sex and religious ritual is a good way of winning the favour of the gods.

The Sacred Use of Sex

Just as the Læstadians used sex to demonstrate that they could transcend all the sin of the world by their own freedom from sin, ritual sex is usually believed to have many, and more significant, consequences.

Tantra originated in India in the first century AD, but has never constituted a unified movement. In Western discourse tantra is often presented as an unlimited sanctification of all kinds of sex, something approaching a basic course in how to combine sexual and religious ecstasy. This view is widespread mainly because of the way Joseph Campbell and other New Age religious figures have presented tantrism. Tantra is also often confused with the *Kamasutra*, which offers a more general overview of sexual variations.

What is often overlooked is that one of the most important principles of tantra is transgression. Sexual transgression is just one of many different kinds of transgression that can be undertaken within the framework of strictly controlled and secret rituals. Tantrism was not originally intended to be a way of spicing up the everyday or of undermining existing norms. Instead, it placed transgressive acts into a system precisely in order to affirm and reinforce gender roles and other social boundaries.[2] Accepted structures are divinely reinforced by breaking them systematically through strictly controlled rituals. The seriousness of some of the boundaries breached, such as boundaries of caste or of what can be eaten, cannot be truly understood unless these rules have been completely internalized. The fact that Hindu tantrism focuses primarily on the male Brahmin, the highest human level in the caste system, once again emphasizes the extent to which boundaries are being crossed. The lower an individual is in the caste system, the fewer the rules there are to limit that individual's behaviour in respect of what is damaging to his karma. Brahmins,

Preparation of Noble Tantrik Lady before Intercourse, from Rajasthan, 18th century.

who are not only at the top of the system but also have a central role in the Hindu world view as a whole, must comply with rules that are a good deal stricter. When these Brahmin rules are breached, formally and in a ritual context, the forces that are released are perceived as particularly powerful.

Within the framework of religion, tantric sex can be understood in many ways. One fundamental Hindu understanding of tantra is that heterosexual intercourse mirrors the eternal union of Shiva and Shakti, the primordial masculine and feminine, the passive and active principles that underlie all reality. For Buddhist tantrists, heterosexual intercourse symbolizes the union of passive wisdom (*prajña*) and the active quality (*upaya*), which taken together are the essence of perfect liberation.[3] Tantric sex can also be compared to the ritual of sacrifice.[4] There is, however, disagreement about a whole series of aspects: for example, should the man ejaculate his seed into the woman or should he allow it to be sublimated and absorbed into his body? Other questions concern such things as whether the pleasure of the orgasm is merely incidental or the actual essence of the ritual, and whether or not one should consume the bodily fluids.[5] These questions are also related to a perception of the bodily fluids as ultimate sources of power.[6] The sixteenth-century Bengali text *Brihat tantrasura* by Krishnananda Agamavagisha, the most influential manual of ritual in north-eastern India, is one of the sources that stresses that one must consume the bodily fluids during the tantric ritual; if one does so *outside* the ritual, however, one will go straight to hell.[7]

In a number of New Age versions of tantra, the fundamental emphasis on transgression as a means of upholding social structures is replaced by the idea that tantra offers an all-round liberation from social structures. The guru Bhagwan Shree Rajneesh and his Osho movement put great stress on free sex. As he explained in 1968: 'The more wholeheartedly you accept sex, the freer you will become of it . . . The total acceptance of life, of all that is natural in life, I call religiousness. And it is this religiousness that liberates a person.'[8] After many of his followers died of AIDS, the guru denied that he had ever promulgated free sex and claimed he had merely stressed the sanctity of sex.[9] The movement still does not call for monogamy, which is perhaps why anyone now wishing to enter the ashram in Pune must take an AIDS test.

Swami Muktananda, the guru who led the Siddha Yoga Dham of America, was the advocate of a particular form of tantrism. He believed that he had transformed his own sexual frustrations and desires into spiritual power.[10] Among the ways he demonstrated his sacred self-control was by putting his non-erect penis into the virginal vagina of female followers and remaining like that for some hours while talking of his childhood.[11]

The Tibetan guru Chögyam Trungpa also had great success in the West with his tantric principles, which included such things as being carried around naked by equally naked devotees. Trungpa, who also had a taste for Mercedes cars, expensive clothes and various stimulants, died of alcohol-related disease in 1987.[12] He was succeeded by Ösel Tendzin, originally Thomas Rich Jr, who infected many of his followers with HIV before dying of AIDS in 1990.[13]

The majority of tantric handbooks to be found in bookshops these days usually contain little but tantric exercises aimed at increasing sexual pleasure and they have little to do with original tantrism. This does not, however preclude these books from having a genuinely religious dimension for many people. New niches have developed within tantrism in the West, including S&M tantra and gay tantra, both of which are rapidly growing movements.[14]

A number of other religions also use what might be seen as extraordinary sex in extraordinary circumstances. In some traditional religions, sexual rituals are particularly common as elements of rites of passage, as we have already seen in the case of the North American Sauks and Meskwaki, whose young men have to have sex with one of the two-spirit men before they are acknowledged as men.[15] There is a widespread belief in some of the religions of New Guinea and the neighbouring islands that young boys must receive the seed of grown men either orally or anally in order to become men themselves.[16] When a boy of the Kaluli people is about ten or eleven he finds, either himself or with the help of his father, a grown man to act as seed-inseminator. They will then have sex together for some months or years, and the practice is ritualized by having its own ceremony. The transfer of seed is considered to be particularly important because men who 'have too much to do with women' are likely to frighten away wild prey.[17] Another people in New Guinea, anonymized within anthropology as the Sambia people, believes that girls become women of their own accord whereas boys will not become men without ritual homosexuality, partly because they will be held back by the women's sphere in which they grew up. The initiation includes the boy sucking the penis of a slightly older youth in order to swallow the seed. This happens on a daily basis over a period of several years.[18]

The transition from life to death also makes a religious use of sex, as we can see, for instance, in Norse religion. In the description of a Norse chieftain's burial by the River Volga, written by Ibn Fadlan of Baghdad in 922 and generally considered to be authentic,[19] we see that sex may be an element in the funeral rites of powerful Norse individuals. After the death of a chieftain one of his female thralls was sent around the camp from tent to tent and the most powerful man in each tent lay with her to show his devotion to his dead chieftain. After she had looked over a ritual door-frame three times into the land of the dead, she was accompanied into the ship where the dead chieftain was lying. There she was given intoxicating drink to make her drunk and six other men had intercourse with her. Then she was placed by the side of the corpse, strangled and stabbed with a knife between her ribs. Finally the ship was set alight and both the chieftain and the thrall woman were burned.[20]

Sex as part of a funeral celebration is not just a historical phenomenon. In Taiwan, where most people are either Buddhists or Taoists or both, women striptease artistes have become part of burial ceremonies for men in the last few decades. The custom has spread to the mainland of southern China, although the authorities there have actively tried to stamp it out. The connection between this sexual display and the funeral ritual itself is, however, rather less direct than at the Norse chieftain's ceremony. Since the number of people attending a funeral is a measure of the respect for the dead man, having female striptease artistes dancing round the coffin for a few minutes is an effective way of increasing the number of mourners.[21]

Several more recent religious movements have based some of their practices on the ritual use of sex in older religions. More often than not these New Age practices are based on perceptions that have a less than solid basis in historical fact. There are a number of reasons for this, among them being a widespread conviction that any religion repressed by Christianity and its anti-sex attitudes must have had a quite different and pro-sex set of beliefs. Since the sources we have for many of the older religions are not always very sound, this has opened the way both for historians with a taste for a good story and for New Age adherents with a taste for religious sex to assume the presence of ritual sex where it may not have existed.

The influential British occultist Aleister Crowley created what he called a Gnostic mass for his movement Ordo Templi Orientis (OTO). Among other things, it included the priest penetrating the priestess's vagina with his 'sacred lance'; that is, his erect penis. Cowley's mass was largely a corruption of the Roman Catholic mass along with various ideas about the reversal of Catholic rituals.[22] Crowley's ritual use of heterosexuality did not, however, mark the limit to his use of sexuality – he stressed that both homosexuality and masturbation were excellent ways to unleash powerful magic forces.[23] He was fond of making reference to tantrism and to Greek and Egyptian beliefs in order to support his ideas of sacred sex, though on the whole his references tend to demonstrate that his insight into these traditions was fairly limited.[24]

If Crowley was inspired by the notion of the reverse mass or black Catholic mass, Anton LaVey and his Church of Satan took it the whole way. We need to recognize, however, that although there were many beliefs about sexual activity between witches and demons, the sexualized black mass is primarily based on a tradition of Christian horror visions from the nineteenth century on.[25] There is just one isolated earlier episode: in 1673, in her desperation to retain the affections of Louis XIV, his mistress Madame de Montespan is supposed to have taken part in a black mass which involved among other things a naked woman and the blood of a sacrificed baby.[26] But it is not until LaVey that we can prove that black masses with ritual sex took the step from fantasy to reality. LaVey's emphasis on sacred sex was inspired by what he saw as the fundamentally hypocritical attitude to sex taken by Christianity. He referred, for instance, to the way Christian men lusted after the half-naked women at the circuses he had worked in over a long period, although the same men put on pious faces at the Sunday services when they prayed to God to forgive them and to free them from the lusts of the flesh.[27]

Gerald Gardner, who was involved in founding the new religious witchcraft movement Wicca, worked with what he called 'the great rite', part of which took the form of ritual heterosexual intercourse with the man's 'lance' being put into the woman's 'grail'. As he wrote in his *Book of Shadows*: 'And ye shall be free from slavery, and as a sign that ye be really free, ye shall be naked in your rites, and ye shall dance, sing, feast, make music and love.' Gardner claimed to have been initiated himself by a witch called Old Dorothy, who was said to be a member of a witch cult that was many centuries old.[28] In reality, however, this religious sexual ritual is based more on old ideas about sexual orgies at the witches' sabbath than on any genuine pre-Christian practice in Western Europe.[29] Marion Zimmer Bradley's literary descriptions of ritual heterosexuality among fictitious goddess worshippers in Arthurian Britain in her 1983 novel *Mists of Avalon* have had considerable influence on new religious notions of the importance of sex in religious contexts. The myth of what they term the sacred marriage between the Goddess and The Horned God plays a central role in the Wicca movement and heterosexuality is often seen as a recreation of the divine intercourse.[30] This focus on the sexual polarity between men and women has also given rise to some feminist and queer criticism within the movement, on the grounds that it is both heterosexist and unnecessary.[31]

There are few limits to what can be involved in religious rituals: eating, drinking, killing, animal sacrifice, song, dance, sport, reading and silence, to name but a few. The ritual use of sex does not make sex unique in this religious context. In terms of the history of religion, however, sexual rituals have not played a particularly important part. This is mainly because of the dominance of the three great monotheistic religions, especially because of the dominant Christian tendency to exclude the sexual from any definition of the religious. This means that the idea of sex being a part of religious ritual seems alien to many people.

At the same time, we can see that many of the sex rituals that do exist involve practising the sort of sex that is otherwise forbidden, rather than the sort that is acceptable within the world view of the particular religions, It is precisely the fact that it is forbidden or excluded that makes sex of this kind so powerful.

Religious Sex Specialists

When sex is being used in this direct manner in religious contexts, it is natural that control is usually in the hands of ordinary religious leaders. The religious sex specialist, however, is not such a widespread phenomenon. The notion of a religious sex specialist whose primary function is to deal with sexual matters perhaps figures most prominently in erotic fantasies about ancient religions in far-off countries. But even if religious sex specialists do not exist to the extent that many people might like, they are by no means completely absent.

The Hebrew Bible contains a number of references to sacred prostitutes in temples. Since such references consist largely of condemnations of behaviour that – it is claimed – typify neighbouring peoples,[32] we cannot see them as proof that prostitutes actually existed in these other religions. The primary sources relating to various religions in the ancient Middle East do not support either Greek or biblical claims that sacred prostitution was widespread.[33] The biblical statements are therefore likely to be yet another example of the Israelites ascribing customs to their neighbours that they themselves considered to be ungodly. There were, however, non-prostitute religious sex experts: the priestesses in ancient Babylonia, for example, played a sexual role when they took the part of the goddess Inanna in a sacred marriage with the king.[34]

Yet the fact that there is little basis for assuming the existence of sacred prostitution among the religions of the Israelites' neighbours is not the end of the story. The specific prohibition against Israelites becoming either male or female temple prostitutes[35] suggests that the phenomenon was perhaps not unknown in Israelite religion itself. The Bible tells us, for example, that temple prostitutes were introduced to the temple in Jerusalem under King Rehoboam, the son of Solomon.[36] Since there are repeated references to those who practised temple prostitution being driven from the land, the practice may be linked with Israelite religiosity.[37] And interestingly enough, there are a number of occasions when the references are only to the expulsion of male prostitutes,[38] which may indicate that female prostitutes were allowed to remain. The sources do not, however, provide a basis for drawing any firm conclusions about how the Israelites practised their religion with regard to ritual sex.

If the Middle Eastern accounts of temple prostitutes are very ambiguous, there are more obvious examples of religious sex experts elsewhere. The devadasis, women attached to some Hindu temples, often have a specialized sexual role to play in Hindu worship. Even though devadasis are no longer so widespread, they do still exist in the Indian states of Andhra Pradesh, Karnataka, and Maharashtra. Their primary duty is to be temple dancers and, although the devadasis in the most sacred parts of the temple should be virgins, sex is a part of the religious function of other devadasis.[39] Among their traditional duties, for instance, is having sex with local princes and with Brahmin priests, and they are frequently available to other local men of the three highest castes. They cannot, however, be called temple prostitutes, since as a matter of principle they do not receive payment for sex.[40] With their sexual services, the devadasis in the temples play the role of the heavenly courtesans, the *swargabesya* or *apsaras*, who belong to the court of Indra, king of the gods, and who provide sexual pleasure for the gods.[41] The sexual intercourse practised by the devadasis is a positive force with a beneficial effect on society as a whole.[42] They are also more directly linked with the gods in that they are frequently formally dedicated to particular Hindu deities – often Shiva or Krishna[43] – and some are actually dedicated to goddesses, such as the goddess Yellamma in the state of Karnataka. In such cases, the devadasis like to refer to the goddess as their husband.[44]

Just as younger religions have found new ways of using sex in religious contexts, they have also come up with a completely new kind of sex specialist. When Jesus called on Peter and his brother Andrew to become his disciples he used the words 'Come ye after me, and I will make you to become fishers of men.'[45] Traditionally speaking, this has been seen as a general exhortation to missionary activity. In the 1970s David Berg, founder and leader of the new religious movement The Family (also known as the Children of God or The Family International), came up with a rather original interpretation of Jesus's exhortation to become 'fishers of men'. Young female Family members were sent out to convert men by using sex. 'The "fish" can't understand the crucifixion, they can't understand Jesus. But they can understand the ultimate creation of God, a woman . . . Every one of you girls who spreads out your arms and legs on the bed for those men are just like Jesus, exactly like Jesus', Berg explained.[46] This sexual missionary work was called 'flirty fishing' and the 'hookers for Jesus' (as they were called) had to go through a long training process before being allowed to start their sexual missionary activity.[47] The 'hookers for Jesus' also used sex as a way of winning the favour of influential men in politics and business for the Family. According to the painstaking records kept by the movement, exactly 223,311 men were given carnal knowledge of the holy message in this way.[48] In spite of these pious intentions, the practice was discontinued in 1987 because of the risk of AIDS.[49]

One of the most important reasons why there are not more religious sex specialists is that their existence might imply a religious sanctioning and regulating of sex in contexts where marriage does not come into the picture. And since this type of sex often exists on the fringes of what is religiously acceptable, the religious sex specialist is an impossible figure in many religions – which is perhaps precisely why sex specialists often figure in exotic perceptions of what goes on in *other* religions. But even if they are rare, religious sex specialists do nevertheless belong to the sexual landscape of religion. Where they do exist, they are honoured, and they bear witness to the fact that there is nothing in religion as a phenomenon that completely excludes the possibility of ritual sex.

Sacred Sexual Symbolism

It is no exaggeration to say that eroticism becomes utterly tangible during *kanamara matsuri*, an annual Shinto festival in Kawasaki in Japan. Phalluses several metres long, some black, some bright pink, are carried around in sacred procession. Enormous wooden phalluses are placed at the Kanayama temple so that small girls can ride on them and ensure that they will become fruitful brides in the future. Even adult women are keen to ride on them or at least to touch them.[50] Impotent men also believe they will be helped by touching the giant penises.[51] Happy women dressed in festive costumes carry around dildos the size of babies and pious believers can buy lollipop

The Shinto Kanamura Matsuri (Phallus Festival), in Kawasaki, Japan.

dildos for their children to suck. People looking for more nourishing sustenance can buy Chinese cabbages and other vegetables shaped like penises.[52] At a similar festival at the Ogata-jinja shrine in Inuyama, people process around the town with floats on which there are enormous male and female sexual organs, while at the nearby Tagata-jinja shrine huge red phalluses are carried around.[53]

What is eroticism to one is pornography to another, so it is not easy to decide how to categorize extremely explicit portrayals of religious sex like these. This religious eroticism is nevertheless visible evidence of how great the differences are between different religions' attitudes to sex. The general hostility to sex in Christianity means that erotic representations of this kind are usually absent unless hell and demons are part of the scene. Even the older Christian depictions of half-naked saints and of the Virgin Mary miraculously giving the breast to male saints like Bernard of Clairvaux were not intended to be erotically loaded, even though they may seem like that today. Nor was Jesus's foreskin, supposedly preserved until 1421 in the monastic church at Coulombs near Chartres (and at other churches, too), presented as an erotic relic, although it was supposed to have the miraculous power to increase fertility.[54] Similarly, when the Christian Herrnhuter sang hymns about Jesus's penis and Mary's breasts and womb in the sixteenth century, they denied that there was any erotic connotation: their explanation was that any shame about the sexual organs of Jesus and Mary implied a denial of the human nature of Jesus Christ.[55]

Religio-erotic representations are often not just connected with the central role of sex within religion, but with more specific aspects. The Shinto phallus cult celebrated in temples all over Japan is particularly associated with the idea that the gods may increase the fertility of believers if they use erotic symbols in their religious rites. And the assistance of the gods against impotence and childlessness are only one element in these festivals of the sex organs – agriculture and business are also miraculously boosted by these rituals.[56] The power of divine fertility is also a positive force in general: phalluses, often to be found in temples or at the side of country roads, are thus there not only to ensure all kinds of fertility but also as a protection against evil forces.

Shinto eroticism also provides examples of religious symbolism being used directly in sexual activity, as if to ensure a divine blessing on it. From the seventeenth century on, for instance, dildos have often been carved in the image of Otafuku, the goddess of joy, or of Benten, the popular goddess of love.[57] The latter is still a popular image on the dildos used in Japanese strip bars.[58]

Divine phalluses and vulvas are by no means restricted to Shintoism and there are many other religions that focus on the reproductive organs in a similar manner. In Hinduism, the sacred *lingam* is a phallic symbol of the god Shiva. Shrines to Shiva normally have a large *lingam* in a central position, often so stylized in form that the uninitiated might easily assume that they are looking at nothing more than a large, long, highly polished stone.

Shiva *lingams* are carefully tended religious objects, washed with holy water, wiped with milk, butter and honey, and garlanded with flowers. Some of them are much more sensational than others: the priests at the Tilabhandeshwar temple in Varanasi inform visitors that the temple *lingam* is constantly growing, and sooner or later they will have to raise the height of the ceiling.

As counterparts to the *lingams* in Hindu temples there are symbolic depictions of female reproductive organs. These *yonis* come in many different sizes and are usually associated with various goddesses. Shiva's *lingam* is frequently positioned in the middle of a *yoni*, as if growing out of it.

It is not only stylized reproductive organs that play a central role in the religious symbolism of Hinduism. The Khajuraho temples in Madhya Pradesh and the Konark temple in Orissa are almost completely covered in depictions of a variety of sexual activities, and similar depictions on a lesser scale are to be found on temples from the same period all over India. Similar erotic temple art, but of a later period, can also be found in many temples in Nepal. Most of the images present a very wide variety of heterosexual and lesbian activity. Sex between men is less common, though it does exist, along with more marginal sexual phenomena. Khajuraho, for instance, has a depiction of an apparently happy horse being taken from behind by one man while another man is offering his erect penis to the horse's mouth. At Konark, too, there are portrayals of sex with animals, as there are at a number of temples in Bhuvanesvar,[59] whereas at Bhaktapur in Nepal we can see animals having sex with each other alongside depictions of various human sexual constellations. Exactly

A brass lingam cover.

Seventeenth-century sculptures showing humans having sex alongside animals at the Jagannath temple in Kathmandu, Nepal. These depictions may reflect examples of sexual transgressions performed in Tantric rituals.

how these erotic images should be interpreted is uncertain, but it is not at all improbable that these depictions of sacred sex, which are quite clearly separate from the ideal of marriage, represent something similar to the systematic transgression that lies at the heart of Hindu tantrism.[60]

Like Hinduism, Greek religion was fascinated by divine sexual organs: the image posterity sometimes has of a religion eternally focused on elevated speculation and philosophical thought is not quite correct. Erect penises were present on all sides. *Hermai*, pillars with the head of Hermes and erect penises, stood at virtually every front door and were also placed at the frontiers of the city states.[61] Huge phalluses were carried around Athens during the annual feast of Dionysus and the unveiling of a phallus was a core element of the Dionysian mysteries.

Sacred penises were an equally central element in Roman religion. Phalluses decorated everyday articles and were worn around the neck as powerful amulets – even small children wore these potent articles for protection.[62] In Greek and Roman religion, then, the religious significance of the phallus was associated with more than fertility and seems to represent a mighty, divine protective power

A Greek herm, a copy of an original by Polyeuktos, *c.* 280 BC, depicting the statesman Demosthenes.

that was particularly concentrated on people in vulnerable situations, or who were undergoing physical transitions.

Some of the most explicit religio-sexual depictions we know of are, unfortunately, so detached from their original context that we have little more to go on than the images themselves. Archaeological material from the Moche culture that flourished on the north coast of Peru in AD 100–800 reveals repeated representations of heterosexual intercourse in what appear to be ritual contexts. Vaginal sex, however, is in a minority and most of the depictions are of anal sex.[63] What heterosexual activity they do portray is not always fully human: the women depicted also have sex with animals and with various supernatural creatures, often humanoid creatures with great claws.[64] In some of the images the male partner seems to be a prisoner of war, who is then sacrificed to the gods.[65] Some of the images show heterosexual anal sex in the context of funeral rituals.[66] Others portray people coming with grave offerings at the same time as having sex.[67] The connection between sex and death rituals is further reinforced by the many images of women having sex with creatures that look like living corpses, and by the placing of sexually explicit objects in the grave along with the corpse.[68]

The Moche images point to what seems to have been an extremely sexualized series of rituals, but exactly what part these erotic images played in the religion is difficult to say, apart from the fact that they appear to be important ritual funerary gifts. The very explicit sexual images are not, however, unique to the Moche culture and can also be found in a number of other Andean cultures, though unfortunately that does not help us to reach any definite conclusions.[69] Nevertheless, of all the material we have from the Moche culture, the very high proportion that consists of figures of this kind points to a religion with a religio-sexual understanding that is very different from anything found among religions extant today.

Divine sexual organs also had an important role in Norse religion and 56 phallus stones from the Norse period have been found in Norway. It is difficult to state the significance of these stones since they all come from a period – AD 400–600 – with virtually no documentary sources. Twenty-one of these stones were found on graves and three close to grave mounds, which might suggest they had something to do with a cult of the dead. A number of smaller stone phalluses have also been found with the body in the grave itself.[70] A few people consider that cup marks – small, round, bowl-shaped hollows cut into stone – are symbols of the womb, but the material does not enable us to say whether this is so. Fifteen of the phallus stones discovered so far also have cup marks cut into them.[71]

According to Adam of Bremen in the eleventh century, the fertility god Freyr was depicted with a large phallus at his shrine in Uppsala.[72] From Viking Age Sweden there is a small figure of a sitting man with an oversized erect penis and that, too, is usually considered to be Freyr.[73] The idea that a god in a state of sexual excitement might be embarrassing was clearly alien to people at the time; indeed, the powerful sexuality of the gods appears rather to have been one more aspect of their generally superhuman nature.

In the *Völsa þáttr*, a story preserved in the fourteenth-century Icelandic manuscript *Flateyjarbók*, we are told how Olaf Haraldsson, the Norwegian king and saint, witnesses a heathen sacrificial rite. Every evening on a farm in the far north of Norway a woman takes out a *völsa*, the penis of a slaughtered horse, which is kept rolled up in a piece of linen and onions. This is then passed from hand to hand around the table and various ritual stanzas are said over it. Among other things, the people pray that the *mornir*, the divine giant *jotun* women, will accept this offering. The linen and the onions in which the horse phallus is wrapped also have a symbolic value of their own and probably point to a very ancient tradition. On a fifth-century bone scraper found on the Fløksand farm in northern Hordaland there is an inscription *línalaukar*, 'linen and onions'.[74] Unfortunately, we have little idea of the rationale behind these ancient religio-sexual rituals. As a pious and not very tolerant Christian saint, the Olaf of *Völsa þáttr* was not particularly interested in finding out and he gave the sacred phallus to the farm dog as a titbit.

There was a modern echo of the Christian struggle against the Norse phallus cult in the Dønna district on the coast of Helgeland in northern Norway in 1993. In connection with an old phallus stone being returned to the district by the Bergen Museum, every newborn child was given a gift of a silver phallus and the marketing opportunity was used to start a fertility play. Conservative Christians mounted strong opposition to these moves, arguing that they represented heathen, occult and inappropriate demonic activity. Reactions were particularly strong against giving the newborn phallic jewellery – what they needed was a cross.[75]

Sacred sex symbolism, then, is by no means just a historical phenomenon. The mainly Muslim government in Indonesia discovered this in 2008 when they introduced an anti-pornography law. The law, which forbids all public displays, sounds or gestures that may be obscene, sexual or 'violate moral ethics in the community', was not received with joy by all the religious groups in the country. Whereas individual Muslim members of parliament rejoiced and proclaimed 'God is great' when they passed the law, Balinese Hindus and followers of various traditional religions in Papua were enraged. As they pointed out, this was a law that could place serious restrictions on their traditional religious practices, since erotic display frequently figured in these.[76]

The walls of many houses in modern Bhutan have erect penises painted on them. These enormous penises, usually depicted at the moment of ejaculation and sometimes with a helping hand drawn in, are fairly specifically associated with the 'divine madman', Drukpa Kunley, who demonstrated his religious insight around the year 1500 by referring to his own organ as a 'flaming thunderbolt of wisdom'.[77] According to the Bhutanese themselves, the penises protect the houses against evil spirits.

Religious depictions of sexual symbols and situations do not only represent the opposite extreme to those religious movements that are hostile to sex, they move the whole religio-sexual sphere onto a very different level. The sacred images mean that believers must relate to their particular religion's view of sex as a core sacred phenomenon whether they like it or not. Seen in this light, there are parallels between this and the various religious forms of duty sex.

Sacred sexual symbolism – or the absence of it – often represents the extreme formulation of a particular religion's view of sex. When different religions come into contact with one another, the spotlight is often turned on sexual symbolism in particular, and when followers of the more sexually repressive religions are brought face to face with this explicit emphasis on sacred sexuality in certain other religions, the contrast tends only to buttress their condemnation of the religion in question.

10
Religio-Sexual Priorities

The religio-sexual landscape is, as we have seen, characterized more than anything else by variety and change. But if we look more closely at sacred injunctions and prohibitions in relation to one another and to other religious decrees, it emerges that the changes often involve various injunctions or prohibitions constantly being upgraded or downgraded in relation to others. Both ordinary believers and religious leaders often choose, explicitly or implicitly, to ignore certain clear and absolute religious rules when they feel that other injunctions and prohibitions are more important. Religio-sexual guidelines may be set aside in order to promote other kinds of regulations, or they may be prioritized at the expense of other religio-sexual rules.

A further pattern that emerges is that not all religio-sexual guidelines are given the same emphasis. While certain injunctions and prohibitions are repeatedly stressed as being fundamental to the faith, others may be completely overlooked – often without us being able to discern any clear logic about the prioritization.

The Downgrading of Religious Sex Rules

Ever since the 1970s news headlines in the Western world have been reporting the sexual abuse of children and young people by Catholic priests, although it was not until 2009 that the public aspects of this scandal began to affect the Vatican directly. There can be very few people who believe that this scandal tells us much about Catholic doctrines as such. There is nothing in Catholicism to suggest that their priests have the right to abuse their flock – quite the reverse. All sex outside marriage is strictly forbidden and the vast majority of Catholic priests are committed to being unmarried and to living in a state of celibacy. Priests who abuse boys and young men are also breaking the Catholic Church's total ban on homosexual sex. What makes the abuse of the young by priests an even more serious matter from a Catholic perspective is that actions of this kind have nothing to do with voluntary sexual choice; they involve individuals in authority violating the young.

Even though the abuse conflicts with all Catholic teaching, the way the Catholic Church has chosen to handle the matter demonstrates how a religious institution can in certain circumstances disregard its most central sexual rules for reasons of religio-sexual prioritization. The reactions of the Vatican and the rest of the Catholic leadership to the abuse do not involve changes to theological principles, but they do reveal the priorities of the Church in dealing with priests who have acted so flagrantly against Catholic teachings on sex. These priests, of course, are not just a problem for the Church in that they have broken the sexual rules and abused the innocent, they were also official representatives of the Church while doing so. Thus clerical abuse threatens the reputation of the Church as a whole.

Every religion has to balance one consideration against another. In this context the Catholic Church was faced with a threefold challenge: it had to find ways to protect the reputation of the Church itself; it had to ensure clerical celibacy; and protect innocent children. The Vatican made a clear decision about its priorities in these matters as early as 1962. The line they took is to be found in an official but highly confidential document sent out to all bishops. The document, which only became known to the public when it was published in the *Guardian* in 2003, deals with sexual solicitation on the part of a priest,[1] sexual acts directed at animals and 'a person of his own sex',[2] and direct abuse of 'youths of either sex'.[3] The Church stated that the most important thing in all such cases 'is to observe the strictest *secrecy*'. When bishops pursue cases of this kind, they are to be 'restrained by a perpetual *silence*'.[4] Even the victims, those who have accused priests of abuse, must swear to complete secrecy.[5] All those involved in dealing with these cases must sign a form pledging themselves not to 'commit anything against this fidelity to the secret' . . . 'even for the most urgent and serious cause' or 'for the purpose of a greater good'. The only way an individual can be absolved from the duty of secrecy is if 'dispensation has been expressively given [me] by the Supreme Pontiff'.[6] Anyone breaking this call for absolute silence does so at the risk of excommunication, which means both being excluded from the Church and endangering one's salvation.[7] This applies as much to the victim as to the accused.

Priests who admit their guilt are to be forgiven and a special form for the forgiveness of the priest's sin was part of the document sent out in 1962.[8] Priests found guilty by the Church can be transferred or dismissed.[9] The sexual abuse in itself does not lead to excommunication – only those who talk about their transgressions to anyone *outside* the church hierarchy are at risk of excommunication. The Church thus places the victims on the same level as the offenders, since the victims are equally at risk of excommunication if they discuss what they have been subjected to with anyone apart from Church leaders.[10]

In this official document from 1962, then, the Vatican stated that its absolutely top priority in dealing with the problem was to protect the reputation of the Church. But this implies a good deal more than avoiding a bad image. If the reputation of what the Vatican believes to be God's own institution on earth is sullied, it could lead to fewer converts, more people leaving the Church and more people turning away from the leadership of the Church. Ultimately, the salvation of millions of people is at stake. Seen from that perspective, it is not really so strange that the sexual morality of the servants of the Church was given less priority.

Since the importance of keeping the image of the Church unblemished was absolute, calling in the police or the normal judicial system to deal with the abuse was not an option. Before 2000, this meant that when the police and authorities actually did become involved – such as when a large number of children were sexually abused by Catholic priests in Newfoundland at the end of the 1970s – the Church systematically put pressure on the police and judicial authorities not to proceed against the guilty parties. Instead, the priests involved were relocated to other congregations.[11]

One of the problems with the measures the Vatican introduced is that none of them – forgiveness, relocation or dismissal – prevented the priests involved from committing further sexual crimes. The fact that the public image of the Catholic Church was given absolutely top priority in dealing with the behaviour of the priests meant that the safety of the children in their care was the lowest priority. It has been common knowledge for decades that the priests the Church ignored, forgave or transferred consistently continued to commit further offences within the framework of the institutional care of the Church. An examination of legal documents, published reports, interviews and church documents shows that about two-thirds of Catholic bishops in the US allowed priests to continue working even after they had been accused.[12] The lack of will to follow up its own rules for investigation seems to have gone right to the top of the Church. In 2010 the Austrian cardinal Christoph Schönborn criticized the former cardinal state secretary of the Vatican for having blocked a Church investigation of widespread sexual abuse in Austria that came to light in 1995.[13] Even Pope John Paul II has been accused of covering up a string of abuse cases and of protecting perpetrators high in the church hierarchy.[14] In cases where the Church had dismissed priests for sexual abuse without contacting the police or judicial authorities, it proceeded to wash its hands of the matter if those priests then went on to commit offences *outside* the Church. This systemic toleration of widespread sexual abuse has meant that the Catholic Church has had to pay out hundreds of millions of pounds to victims who have taken the Church into ordinary courts of law.

The willingness of the Church to tolerate its priests seriously transgressing against the most fundamental tenets of its sexual morality in order to preserve its facade – and thus its ability to save millions of souls – is a typical example of the way a religion may choose to close its eyes to its own religio-sexual doctrines when other more important religious aspects come into play. The Vatican consistently condemns all heterosexual behaviour outside marriage and absolutely all homosexual acts, yet it was prepared for decades to tacitly accept both of these things within its own organization – including the widespread sexual abuse of children and young people – so that the sacred reputation of the Church would not be destroyed. Now, following the flood of revelations since 2009, the leadership of the Catholic Church is battling for its reputation. It is interesting to hear how Pope Benedict explains the events. At the same time as voicing a belated prayer for forgiveness, he has said that the 'enemy', that is, the Devil himself, was behind the whole scandal because he desired to see 'God driven out of the world'.[15] So the real problem is not the abuse of all the children, nor the systematic cover-up, but the fact that the Devil has used these things to damage the reputation of the Church.

We can see the same kind of radical shift of priorities among Orthodox Jews in the United States. Even though the secular media have uncovered a series of cases in which children and young people have been abused by rabbis and other prominent Orthodox Jews, the Jewish media have consistently paid little attention to them. In other words, much of the Orthodox Jewish community seems to believe, like the Vatican, that it is better to pass over these things in silence rather than to sully the reputations of prominent religious figures because to do so would undermine the religion as a whole.[16] The fact that the sexual abuse of children quite clearly conflicts with all Jewish teachings is secondary: the good name of prominent Orthodox Jews, and consequently of the religion itself, is more important than fundamental sexual prohibitions and the welfare of the children. But this is still not an unambiguous situation. Just as the struggle against the Catholic Church's systematic cover-up of clerical abuse has been headed by other Catholics, Orthodox Jews have been prominent in the criticism of such Orthodox cover-up practices.

It is often the case that forbidden actions in themselves present less of a problem than people talking about them. The Vatican's handling of sexual abuse by priests and the Orthodox Jewish attempt to ignore similar abuse are clear examples of this. The same principle was in operation in Egypt in 2005 when a young unmarried costume designer, Hind el-Hinnawy, filed a paternity suit against the actor Ahmed el-Fishaway. The scandal was not so much that she had become pregnant outside marriage and thus broken fundamental Muslim sexual rules, but that she had then failed to behave in the usual way for young Egyptian upper-class women who get pregnant before marriage: to have an abortion and have her hymen reconstructed.[17] This case does not, of course, give any full and representative picture of Islam, but it does offer a good example of the way a clear breach of Islamic sexual rules may be tolerated as long as the unlawful sex is passed over in silence. In Hinduism, too, discreet sexual relationships between married high-caste women and their lower-caste male servants is fairly widespread without becoming a major issue within the Hindu community: the religious and religiously inspired social sanctions only become operative when, because of indiscretion, pregnancy or the couple eloping together, such relationships become public.[18]

There is, course, another pattern that can also be discerned in the way Catholic priests and prominent Orthodox Jews have effectively been allowed to get away with breaking religio-sexual rules. Powerful and important religious figures are more often in a position to set aside religio-sexual restrictions than ordinary people: we have already seen how Christian and Muslim monarchs, who have always played a central role in religion, could to a large extent do what they wanted.

Some of the most central figures in the religious world seem to have been able to live in conflict with their own laws. Abraham and his many wives have been the cause of some theological debate, even though polygamy was not in conflict with biblical law. Fewer people have commented on the fact that he was married to his half-sister Sarah. Abraham himself points this out: 'And yet indeed she is my sister; she is the daughter of my father, but not the daughter of my mother.'[19] Even though the law of Moses postdates the lifetime of Abraham, the ban on incest is one of the most important laws of Judaism. God himself commands: 'And if a man shall take his sister, his father's daughter, or his mother's daughter, and see her nakedness, and she see his nakedness; it is a wicked thing; and they shall be cut off in the sight of their people.'[20] In the case of Moses, who broke the racist sex rules of the Pentateuch by marrying a non-Jewish woman, God himself came to his defence and punished the woman who criticized Moses by giving her leprosy.[21] So Abraham and Moses, the mythic ancestors of three religions, are elevated above all criticism even when they do what others may be executed for doing.

There are times when religious sex regulations are set aside deliberately or broken quite openly for what are considered to be more important religious considerations. The story of Sodom is an interesting example of a sexual prohibition being set aside in order to uphold a different religious rule that has nothing to do with sex. When the male inhabitants of Sodom demand that Lot, Abraham's nephew, should hand over the angels who are his guests, Lot was clearly concerned that the angry Sodomites will break into his house and take his guests by force. This would represent an absolute violation of the sacred duty of hospitality. Lot came up with an original suggestion to save the situation, and he says to the multitude: 'Behold now, I have two daughters which have not known man; let me, I pray you, bring them out unto you, and do ye to them as is good in your eyes.'[22] Even if we ignore what the daughters themselves were to think about this, which was anyway irrelevant as they had to obey their father, there are still problematic aspects to Lot's offer. Given that Lot's daughters were engaged to be married, their being raped by the Sodomite mob meant that Lot's future sons-in-law would have their honour violated.[23] As women engaged to be married having sex within the city walls, their rape would in principle also mean that the daughters should be stoned to death afterwards.

The Sodomites reject Lot's offer to rape his daughters and consequently we never learn whether he thought the prescribed execution of his daughters ought to be carried out. Irrespective of that, however, Lot is quite clear that a violation of one of the most fundamental sexual prohibitions is defensible in order to uphold the more important law of hospitality. As Lot proclaims to the inhospitable Sodomites: 'only unto these men do nothing; for therefore came they under the shadow of my roof.'[24] This story of Lot has a relevance that goes well beyond those directly involved, since Lot's insistence on doing whatever is necessary to protect his guests has been held up as exemplary behaviour in both Jewish and Christian tradition.

Among many believers of all kinds we can also see a quite different kind of downgrading of the numerous religio-sexual prescriptions and proscriptions. The more traditional religio-sexual rules are increasingly seen to be of little relevance. Premarital sex or homosexuality or divorce are no longer thought to be among the most important religious criteria. For the great majority of Christians and Jews this is now the case. The more or less general acceptance of premarital sex, of divorce and, to a somewhat lesser extent, of homosexuality, demonstrates that most people now believe that behaviour that was once utterly condemned by Jews and Christians is fully compatible with modern Jewish and Christian beliefs. And similar attitudes are to be found among many Muslims, Hindus and Buddhists.

Sexual prescriptions and proscriptions are thus being viewed as less important aspects of religion whereas things like the individual's level of religious activity, honesty, contentment, solidarity and much else are considered more important in his or her relationship with religion. Even in the case of adultery, which is still less than acceptable, it is clear that the sexual aspect has been downgraded. The sex act that actually constitutes the adultery no longer always lies at the heart of our condemnation as it once did, the most morally objectionable element now being the fundamental dishonesty that lies behind the physical act: the sex itself is seen as a symptom of this dishonesty.

The enormous attitudinal changes among the majority of believers to issues such as premarital sex, same-sex relationships and divorce have left religious leaders and institutions with an awkward set of problems. How are they to react to so many of their followers no longer behaving as their faiths have traditionally demanded, and worse, no longer *believing* what their authorities tell them?

There are essentially four strategies available to leaders wishing to create conformity between religio-sexual directives and what the faithful actually do. First, the rules themselves can be changed completely to say that premarital sex (to take just one example) is perfectly acceptable. Suggestions in this category vary greatly depending on what kind of sex is being discussed. Sometimes the rules *have* already changed to such an extent that even religious leaders now consider the new views to have been natural right from the start. We can see this, for instance, in present-day Christian attitudes to the biblical sexual racism that characterized much of the Christian world right up until our own times. On the other hand, if we consider the issue of committed same-sex relationships, many people today will defend this from a religious perspective, although very few people believe that these represent a form of sexual behaviour that Christianity, Judaism or whichever religion it may be has *originally* supported.

In the second strategy, religious leaders and others who adhere to traditional rules attempt to coerce their flocks into doing what their religion traditionally prescribed. Many leaders have attempted to impose this solution and, indeed, gone a step further and tried to compel the whole of society, irrespective of religious faith, to follow their particular rules of sexual behaviour. This was by far the most common strategy in the past and there are still a few countries that stick to this principle very rigidly. Elsewhere, as we have seen, attempts are made to control sexual morality more indirectly, for instance by redefining sex education or trying to prevent access to contraceptive measures. The problem with this coercive approach is that it conflicts with human rights, since both the European Court of Human Rights and the UN Human Rights Committee have affirmed that adults have the right to partake in consensual and private sex without interference. Even group sex in private is protected by human rights.[25] Religious leaders are free to threaten their followers and everyone else with damnation, hell, excommunication and other religious sanctions, but the moment legal punishment or discrimination is imposed on people in terms of employment, social benefits or respect for their private lives, fundamental human rights are violated.

The third possible strategy is for religious institutions to *expel* all those who break their various sex rules. The dilemma here is a simple one – the majority of religious communities would have to expel the majority of their followers.

A fourth and very different strategy is simply to *ignore* the discrepancies between doctrine and behaviour. The leadership would continue to proclaim the approved principles, and perhaps to ensure that the priesthood does what it is supposed to do, while leaving the great majority of followers to do what they like. This is the solution that many major faith communities have tacitly chosen with regard to issues like contraception and premarital sex. The drawback with such a strategy is that it can erode the essence of the religion and the authority of the religious leadership. When believers think they no longer need to believe in or obey certain fundamental religious principles, many of them will soon begin to question other beliefs. If religious authorities are prepared to allow them to behave as they like in one area, why not in another?

Any tacit acceptance of a disconnection between the religious elite and ordinary believers also means that every faith community will have at least two different truths in every single area, however small. Since people usually look to their religious institutions and leaders to furnish them with religious truths, who will then be in a position to say to an individual Muslim, Catholic, Jew or Hindu that he or she is not a true member of their faith because he or she believes something quite different? If the religious leadership is not prepared to repudiate them because of their beliefs and way of life, who can do so? What is the *real* position of a religious leadership that says one thing and silently accepts that many of its followers are doing something quite different?

The religious downgrading of sex consequently poses a challenge to many of the parties involved but particularly to the religious leadership. When dealing with the danger to the reputation of a faith community caused by the sexual transgressions of clerics, and when facing the fact that many believers no longer pay any attention to many of the religio-sexual injunctions, religious leaders have to decide whether to adhere to their religio-sexual principles or to ignore and even downgrade those principles in order to support other principles they believe to be more vital.

The Upgrading of Religious Sex Rules

At Christmas 2008 Pope Benedict XVI declared that heterosexuality is just as worthy of protection as the rainforest. The protection of heterosexuality, in the pope's view, implies things like accepting a legal ban on homosexuality, discrimination against gays and lesbians and, indeed, their persecution.[26] The policies of the Vatican at that time revealed that saving the rainforest was in fact *less* important than the battle against homosexuality. The protection of the natural environment may be high on the theological agenda for many modern Christians but as far as Catholicism before Pope Francis was concerned, this issue was pushed down the agenda by the much more important struggle to defeat homosexuality.

While many believers are happy to downgrade religio-sexual rules in order to promote other issues, there are situations where the reverse is true. Time and again we see religious people and institutions downgrading or setting aside other issues of faith – sometimes even central issues of faith – because they stand in the way of the promotion of what they believe to be more important religio-sexual truths.

If you want to be declared a saint in the Christian world, it is usually an advantage not to have had sex. This is obviously connected to the fundamental traditional Christian view that the best thing is to have no sex at all. There are occasions when fighting hard to retain your virginity is in itself sufficient reason to be canonized. One day in July 1902 Maria Goretti, an eleven- or twelve-year-old Italian girl, was at home alone when she was attacked by a young man called Alessandro Serenelli who threatened to kill her if she would not have sex with him. Maria refused and Serenelli stabbed her repeatedly. The girl died the following day, but not before she had told people what had happened. Serenelli was found guilty of murder and sentenced to thirty years in prison. While he was in prison, Maria Goretti appeared to him in a vision and forgave him. After his release Sere nelli entered a monastery and when Maria was canonized in 1950, he was present along with Maria's mother and the rest of her family.[27]

Maria seems to have been a nice, kind girl, but not all nice, kind Catholic girls who die young become saints. One thing is certain: if the girl had been raped rather than killed when resisting the sexually aroused young man, she would never have been canonized. The moral of this, to push the point to the extreme, is that a really good Catholic should prefer death to premarital sex.

Young Maria Goretti is one of many other female saints who have died rather than lose their virginity. The early church father Tertullian summed it up succinctly when he said that it was worse to condemn a Christian woman to prostitution than to feed her to wild animals.[28]

Since it is almost invariably young women who are canonized for dying for their virginity, we can see yet again that female virginity is considered more precious than male virginity. There are male saints who died because they would not have sex but, not surprisingly, we are no longer talking about heterosexual sex. The young Christian Pelagius, who was executed after rejecting the sexual approaches of the Spanish caliph Abd al-Rahman in the tenth century, immediately became a popular Christian saint.[29] It may not be so important for Christian men to preserve their virginity in general, but it is still better to die than to have sex with other men.

Exhortations to die rather than have sex are important in underlining the Christian message about the value of virginity, but they have never led to a host of imitators. A rather more current example of the way many Christians believe a ban on certain kinds of sex is more important than saving lives can be found in the repeated lies claiming that condoms do not prevent the spread of AIDS. Cardinal Alfonso Lopez Trujillo, head of the Pontifical Council for the Family, claimed in 2003 that the HIV virus easily passes through condoms.[30] In 2007 Archbishop Francisco Chimoio of Maputo in Mozambique declared that condoms are infected with HIV.[31] Pope Benedict XVI initially did nothing to correct statements of this kind. On the other hand, during his first visit to Africa he stated that AIDS is 'a tragedy . . . that cannot be overcome through the distribution of condoms, which can even increase the problem.'[32] Statements of this sort from church leaders demonstrate that their opposition to contraception is more important than telling the truth or preventing people dying of a fatal disease. The strong and repeated critique of this official Catholic position, both within and outside the church, seems nevertheless to have made a certain impact on the Pope, as he indicated in 2010 that 'in certain cases' condoms may be used to prevent HIV infection.[33]

We can see the particular importance of religio-sexual morality to the three Abrahamic religions in the emphasis they put on punishment. All three religions condemn murder in one way or another but the punishment for impermissible sex is often as strict or stricter than the punishment for taking life. The Pentateuch usually calls for the death penalty both for murder and for some kinds of consensual sex, such as sex during menstruation, male anal sex and female adultery. The fact that engaged women who are raped in a town and married women who are raped anywhere should be stoned to death[34] is one of the clearest demonstrations of how absolutely central the rules on correct sex were in the religion of the Israelites.

Islam does not give the same clear-cut high priority to what it considers to be impermissible sex. The Koran demands the death penalty for murder[35] but not for forbidden sex. In the hadiths, however, Muhammad demands the death penalty for both heterosexual adultery and sex between men.

Within Christianity we have to fall back on tradition to see how murder and impermissible sex were weighed against each other. Both were often punishable by death and can thus be viewed as equally serious. Castration of the condemned man before his execution or the destruction of his body after death normally occurred only if the man had been condemned for sex with other men. The gradation of punishments had been set even before Christians had the judicial right to execute one another, and the Christian Council of Elvira, held in Spain at the beginning of the fourth century, provides an interesting overview of how various transgressions can be ranked from a Christian perspective. A woman who leaves her husband for another man should be refused communion for the rest of her life, which means that she is excluded from all hope of salvation. A man who knows of his wife's adultery and does not leave her should not be allowed to take communion either. If, however, a woman intentionally kills a servant, she is only to be refused communion for seven years.[36]

The high priority given to religio-sexual rules compared with other religious ordinances can have fatal consequences even without the death penalty and direct persecution. When a fire broke out in a girls' school in Mecca in 2002, the Saudi Arabian religious police prevented some of the girls from escaping from the burning building because, according to the strict religious dress code, they were not decently dressed. The result was that fifteen girls were locked in and died in the fire.[37] When Rick Perry, the Republican governor of Texas, introduced a major programme to vaccinate schoolgirls against the sexually transmitted papilloma virus that is the cause of about 70 per cent of cases of cervical cancer, the programme met with strong opposition from many conservative Christians. 'The Governor's decision seems to mean that God's moral laws about sex outside marriage can be broken without any consequences,' said Rick Scarborough of the conservative Christian lobby group Vision America. In other words, it is better for women to die of cervical cancer than to allow them to have sex with several partners without having to worry about that particular possibility.[38]

Opposition to homosexuality sometimes brings together people prepared to put aside their other – often fundamental – religious disagreements for a while. In Jerusalem, where in other respects religious splits are severe, Jewish, Muslim and Christian authorities stand shoulder to shoulder in their condemnation of organized gay parades in the city. They have persistently lobbied the civil authorities to ban the parades, and while leading Muslims have threatened that the lives of those who take part 'will be in danger',[39] Jewish activists – as we have seen – have promised a reward to anyone who kills participants in the march.[40] The 2006 gay parade in Moscow was condemned in very violent terms by Patriarch Alexei ii, head of the whole Russian Orthodox Church, and Russian Muslim leaders called for 'violent mass demonstrations' against the march. The counter demonstrations brought together neo-Nazis and more traditional Orthodox believers bearing icons.[41]

There are times when the call to focus on sex stands out particularly clearly. In response to the increased attention Christians were paying to environmental issues, the leading American Christian fundamentalist Jerry Falwell claimed in 2007 that global warming was 'Satan's attempt to change the primary focus of the church'.[42] Among the much more important things Christians should focus on, according to Falwell, was the struggle against same-sex marriage and homosexuality in general. Falwell himself devoted much time and effort to condemning the British children's programme *The Teletubbies* because one of the characters, being the colour lavender and having a triangle on his head, could be interpreted as gay.

Although the Catholic Church tolerated sexual abuse by many of its own priests for decades, it still maintains that the fight against homosexuality is more important than many other issues. The fight to preserve the rainforest is not the only thing to be pushed down the agenda by the Church's war on homosexuality. Before the changes introduced with Pope Francis, the Vatican argued that we should exclude gays and lesbians from the protection provided by human rights legislation in such areas as the right to respect for the individual's private life, the right not to be discriminated against and the right to free speech.[43] But excluding gays and lesbians from their human rights has consequences that go far beyond the sexual minorities themselves, since it would mean that human rights are being relativized in a manner that opens the way for anyone to exclude other groups they do not like – Jews, women, people with disabilities or, indeed, Catholics. So the Catholic Church at this time clearly considers it more important to campaign for discrimination against those who live gay and lesbian lives than to work towards ensuring the survival of human rights as a system.

The religious opposition to same-sex sexuality is without doubt *the* issue that has caused most religious people today to downgrade their other religious prescriptions and proscriptions. The huge opposition to homosexuality is more or less unique when viewed in a historical context. The great majority of believers have changed their views completely about many other rules that used to be given high priority within Christianity. At other times they have agreed to disagree about the issues. Even though many of the faithful have become more sympathetic to gays and lesbians in recent decades, the focus on homo sexuality has simultaneously become much stronger and more negative. Whereas the Anglican Church managed to survive disagreements about slavery, abortion, divorce and women priests, the international Anglican communion is in the process of splitting because of disagreement on the issue of gay bishops. Desmond Tutu, South African archbishop and winner of the Nobel Peace Prize, accuses his own church of being obsessed by homosexuality. 'God is weeping,' says Tutu, to see the church using all its energy on homosexuality and ignoring important issues such as poverty.[44] The same priority is to be seen in other churches. When the bishop Walter C. Righter was formally charged with heresy by the Anglican Episcopal Church in the United States in 1995 after he had ordained an openly gay mini ster and supported a call for gay and lesbian clerics, he was only the second bishop in the Episcopal Church to have ever been charged with heresy.[45] When the internal Episcopal court acquitted the bishop, many prominent American Lutherans felt that this was such a serious issue that all church cooperation between the Lutheran and Anglican churches should be discontinued.[46]

When so many believers insist that a particular sex rule is one of the most important elements in their religion, this normally represents a radical reinterpretation of the particular religious tradition. A change in religious priorities of this kind simultaneously presents a challenge to society at large since many active believers then go on to demand that the sex rules they have prioritized should be vigorously introduced in all parts of society, simply because they are 'so central' to their religion.

One Religious Sex Rule rather than Another

The way in which the ban on homosexuality has come to occupy such a uniquely central role in many religious value systems leads us on to the third kind of religio-sexual prioritization: the internal ranking order of different religio-sexual prescriptions and proscriptions. Very often there is a clear-cut priority stating which of the rules are the most important. Many religious campaigns for or against one or the other form of sexuality tend to ignore other sexual prescriptions and proscriptions which, if the logic in the arguments of the most zealous religious activists was followed through, should have been just as important or even more important.

In certain Islamic countries – Iran, for instance – the ban on sex between men is not enforced any more strictly than the ban on heterosexual adultery; in some western countries, on the other hand, many Muslims have clearly reprioritized the traditional religious injunctions. The Koran considers heterosexual adultery to be worse than sex between men and in the hadiths Muhammad pays more attention to heterosexual adultery than to sex between men even though he considers that both qualify for the death penalty. Nevertheless, when the Norwegian Islamic Council, for example, asked the European Council for Fatwa and Research to consider whether Islam should uphold the traditional death penalty for forbidden sex, they omitted all mention of heterosexual adultery and only asked whether the death penalty should be the punishment for homosexual behaviour.[47] Their focus on homosexuality was so dominant that they did not even distinguish between male homosexual acts, which according to the hadiths should be punished with death in the same way as heterosexual adultery, and sex between women, which is not forbidden either in the Koran or in the hadiths. This strange change of priorities in parts of Western Islamic thinking seems to have very little basis in Muslim sources. It is worth considering whether this new and one-sided Muslim focus on homosexuality actually has more to do with the severe condemnation of homosexuality by very many conservative Christians than with anything within Islam itself.

Christian attitudes to homosexuality provide us with one of the very best examples of a religion changing its sexual priorities. Same-sex sexuality is one of the many areas that Jesus did not deal with. St Paul merely listed sex between men along with a whole series of other things that can prevent an individual's entry to the Kingdom of God. According to the New Testament, however, there are other sexual prohibitions that are much stricter. Jesus pointed out that adultery automatically condemns an individual to hell, and divorce is completely forbidden both for men and for women. When we compare the modern Christian conservative obsession with homosexuality with the lack of attention paid to divorce – indeed, the general *acceptance* of divorce – we can see that a religio-sexual change of priorities has occurred that is difficult to explain on the basis of the Christian sources usually used to condemn homosexuality.

From a purely religio-sexual standpoint, it is not easy to understand why the enormous opposition to homosexuality among conservative Christians has been able to screen out so many other things that were originally considered much worse, and we may well have to use non-religious models in order to explain it.

The tendency for particular groups of people to construct and reinforce their identity by persecuting and demonizing other groups is a familiar historical and sociological phenomenon. It is in this area that we can find the fundamental rationale for racism and for the persecution of religious, ethnic or social minorities which differ in some way from the majority. We need perhaps to use a model of this kind to explain why conservative Christians prioritize the ban on homosexuality rather than other sexual prohibitions that were originally more important.

Unlike, for instance, people who are divorced or those who have sex before or outside marriage, present-day gays and lesbians stand out as a distinct and clearly identifiable social group. It is not strange that the growing visibility of gays and lesbians is seen as a serious provocation by many conservative Christians, and by focusing their religio-sexual opposition on homosexuality, conservative Christians are thus identifying a quite clearly defined segment of the population as their opponents. The battle against 'the homosexuals' provides a cause around which many Christians can unite in the same way as people can unite in their opposition to people of other religious groups or to people of a different colour. Even though modern Western societies are on the whole less accepting of the systematic condemnation and persecution of particular sectors of the population, Christian conservatives use the religious bans on same-sex sexuality to legitimatize their prejudices and their constant demands for discrimination.

There is nothing new about God supposedly giving his blessing to the condemnation of a particular group of people; it is in fact a feature typical of many of the religious persecutions of ethnic, religious or otherwise different social groups. Thus, when we look at the way in which many conservative Christians violently condemn gays and lesbians, we can see just the same social mechanisms at work as in racism; all the techniques groups use to condemn other groups and thus portray themselves in a better light are functioning in complete accord with the standard model.

The religious proscriptions regulating the heterosexual behaviour of women are discussed less frequently these days than the prohibition of homosexuality, although they have a considerably longer history. They are much stricter than those covering the behaviour of men and they are also subject to a greater degree of enforcement. This has been the case in all the major religions right from the start. In the oldest sources we have for Judaism, Islam, Hinduism, Buddhism and, to some extent, Christianity, we repeatedly find that the primary religious focus is on men, which means among many other things that the sexuality of women is mainly defined in relation to men. Whereas men tend to have access to several women both inside and outside marriage, the main religious rule is that a woman is limited sexually to *one* man – not always for life, but certainly not more than one at a time. This is evidenced by the generally stricter sanctions applicable to female premarital sex and by the way that adultery is so often defined by whether the woman is married or not: whether a man is married or not is irrelevant.

Homosexuality is the only area in which more emphasis – both positive and negative – is placed on the regulation of male rather than female sexuality. The simple fact that lesbian relationships do not involve men has undoubtedly contributed to lesbian sex frequently being ignored or considered as irrelevant.

We have to be cautious not to reach over-confident conclusions about the reasons for the widespread religious conviction that it is more important to regulate female heterosexuality than male. Nevertheless, the main tendency is clear and, for the most part, still holds in the majority of religions. It is daughters, not sons, who are taken to Christian fundamentalist purity balls; it is daughters, not sons, who continue to be the victims of so-called honour killings because of their heterosexual behaviour; it is women, not men, who have to take care that their clothing covers enough of the their bodies in conservative Muslim countries; and it is women, not men, who get beaten up by ultra-Orthodox Jews if they sit in the wrong part of the bus.

The consistently different treatment of men's and women's sexuality by the various religions lies at the very heart of religious regulation of sexuality. Since heterosexual activity involves both a man and a woman, the effect of the difference is that the punishment for a particular misdemeanour varies depending on who commits it. This absolute lack of logic in the system of prioritizing the religio-sexual prohibitions on women's sexuality fundamentally undermines the legitimacy of all religio-sexual regulation.

Some Concluding Thoughts

As far back as we can trace, we find that human sexuality has been so tightly interwoven with religious convictions that it is difficult to identify any sexual regulations that are completely independent of religion. The relationship between religion and sex also remains one of the strongest and most important forms of religious expression. The extent to which you follow the religio-sexual doctrines of your religion will decide your religious situation in this life, your fate after death, and sometimes even the relationship between the gods, your country and your people. Regardless of whether you believe in them yourself, religio-sexual regulations govern large parts of your private life, your family structures and other close social relationships. To a great extent these rules govern your entire society, not least because of the way they often survive as apparently natural truths, detached from the religious convictions that once created them.

We live in societies in which various forces are constantly trying to use their religio-sexual convictions to influence our lives, whether by compulsion or by persuasion. Simultaneously, however, religio-sexual ideas are always shifting ground and changing. The constant state of flux of religio-sexuality, the uncountable multiplicity of religio-sexual ideas, and the numberless array of different religio-sexual truths – all these things tell us that we are not dealing with final and ultimate religious, human or natural truths.

It is impossible to find any truly common norms for the huge variety of religio-sexual behaviours and beliefs. What one religion worships as sacred sex, another demands the death penalty for; certain kinds of sex that some find central to their whole religious world view represent demonic forces to others. Therefore no one religion can impose its religio-sexual truths without simultaneously violating the religio-sexual truths of other religions.

It is therefore not possible for present-day societies to regulate human sexuality in accordance with religio-sexual prescriptions unless they set aside both individual freedom and the religious freedom of those who differ in their religio-sexual beliefs. In the final instance, we must perhaps look outside the sphere of religion if we wish to devise ultimately tenable guidelines for the way we live our sexuality. We must perhaps look instead to the rules that govern the border zones that lie both between religions and between religion and society in general. We must look to democratic values, human rights and respect for the individual's own choice. If we do that we may settle on three fundamental principles to guide not only religio-sexual ideas but all human sexuality: free will, consent and respect. Every individual must have the right to decide the extent to which he or she wishes to abide by or not abide by various religio-sexual codes of behaviour; the individual sexuality of every human being must be a matter of that individual's choice; and everyone must respect the consensual choice of others when it comes to living their sex lives.

Many believers will find the very idea of free will, consent and respect difficult to accept because their own religio-sexual beliefs are so strong that they feel an overwhelming need to control the sex lives of others. As such, homophobia, sexual racism, the conviction that the sexuality of women must be governed by special regulations, objections to premarital sex and contempt for other varieties of consensual sex, are all one and the same thing: the reflection of a belief in religio-sexual regulation. But perhaps we should ask those who want to regulate the lives of others according to their own religio-sexual beliefs how *they* would feel if *they* were forced to live their lives according to religio-sexual rules *others* believe in. Then they will recognize, perhaps, that free will, consent and respect are not such terrible concepts after all.

REFERENCES

Introduction

1 The story of Hippolytus is best known from Euripides's tragedy (428 BC): *Hippolytus*. The quotations are from lines 13 and 14.

2 *BBC* 2005a.

1 Defining Sex and Religion

1 Lefkovits 2007.

2 *BBC* 2008a.

3 *VG* 2008.

4 *Image Nepal* vol. 23:3, January–February 2010:12.

5 2010a.

6 Matthew 5.28.

7 Thomas Aquinas *Summa Theologica* 2-2.154.4.

8 Wiesner-Hanks 2000:156.

9 Imam Bukhari *Sahih Bukhari* 8.74.260, 8.77.609; Muslim Ibn al-Hajjaj *Sahih Muslim* 33.6421–22.

10 Muslim Ibn al-Hajjaj *Sahih Muslim* 33.6422.

11 Faure 1998:17.

12 Genesis 3.7.

13 Genesis 9. 21–27.

14 Athanasius *Vita Antonii* 47.2–3.

15 Bullough 1976:442.

16 *365gay* 2008b.

17 Bouhdiba [1975]:165–67.

18 Koran 24.31.

19 McCarthy 2009.

20 Imam Malik *Muwatta* 48.4.7.

21 Bouhdiba [1975]:36.

22 *BBC* 2008b.

23 Brooks 1995:107–8.

24 Akst 2003.

25 Røthing 1998:13, cf. 166–7, 176, 182–7.

26 Røthing 1998:183.

27 Røthing 1998:184.
28 Røthing 1998:13.
29 Revd Bill McGinnis, 'A study of Christian sexuality' at *LoveAllPeople.org*, http://www.loveallpeople.org/pearl-christiansexuality.html.
30 Røthing 1998:15, my italics.
31 *American Family Association* 'Disney using ABC to sell homosexual vision to nation's television viewers' in *American Family Association Journal* 21.2, March 1997. http://www.despatch.cth.com.au/Misc/disney.html
32 Eron 1993:119–20.
33 Benkov 2001:105–6.
34 Monter 1990:281–82.
35 Blanc & Way 1998.

2 No Sex, Thank You

1 *Parajika* 4, 1.
2 Wilson 2003:140.
3 Faure 1998:29.
4 Faure 1998:33.
5 *Samyutta Nikaya* 4.3.5, cf. *Sutta Nipata* 4.9.
6 Parrinder 1996:48–9.
7 Faure 1998:189.
8 Wilson 2003:168.
9 Faure 1998:136.
10 Guan Yin was originally the male Indian bodhisattva Avalokiteshvara, but was normally portrayed as female in China from the time of the Sung dynasty (960–1127) on (Reed 1992:164).
11 Reed 1992:164–5.
12 Reed 1992:166.
13 1 Corinthians 7.7.
14 1 Corinthians 7.8–9.
15 1 Corinthians 7.2.
16 Mark 3.31–35, Matthew 12.46–50, Luke 8.19–21.
17 Luke 14.26.
18 Romans 1.3–4.
19 Matthew 1.1–17.
20 Matthew 1.18, 1.1–17.
21 Luke 1.35
22 *Harris Poll* 2007.
23 'Wherefore, as by one man sin entered into the world, and death by sin; and so death passed upon all men, for that all have sinned' (Romans 5.12).
24 Augustine *On Marriage and Concupiscence* 1.1.
25 Augustine *On Marriage and Concupiscence* 1.27.
26 Augustine *On Marriage and Concupiscence* 1.35.
27 Mark 2.19, Matthew 9.15, Luke 5.34–5.
28 Tertullian *On the Veiling of Virgins* 26.

29 Evans 2003:59.
30 Ambrose *Concerning Virginity* 2.2.16.
31 Endsjø 2008a:82–83.
32 Pseudo-Matthew 7.3.
33 Acts of Thomas 12, 51.
34 Teague 1989:130; Lamberts 1998:21.
35 Bullough 1976:5, 392.
36 Wiesner-Hanks 2000:161.
37 Parrinder 1996:220.
38 Bullough 1976:320.
39 Bullough 1976:327.
40 Evans 2003:91.
41 Council of Carthage (AD 419), Canon 4.
42 Bullough 1976:320.
43 Wiesner-Hanks 2000:118.
44 Bullough & Bullough 1987:129.
45 Bullough 1976:430–31.
46 Fox 1995:182.
47 Cavendish 2003:223.
48 *Dutch News* 2010.
49 Foster 1984:25, 46.
50 Foster 1984:25, 32, cf. 39.
51 Josephus *The Jewish War* 2.8.2.
52 Philo *De Vita Contemplativa*.
53 Evans 2003:3.
54 Plutarch *Numa Pompilus* 10.1–7.
55 Koran 19.19–24.
56 Hidayatullah 2003:273.
57 *Laws of Manu* 5.159.
58 Khandelwal 2001:157–58.
59 Khandelwal 2001:158.

3 Solitary Sex

1 Gardella 1985:44; Bullough & Bullough 1977:70; J. H. Kellogg *Plain facts for old and young. Embracing the natural history of hygiene of organic life*. Burlington: I. F. Segner & Co. 1892: 295–6.
2 Genesis 38.9–10.
3 Unterman 1996:134; Leviticus 15.16–18.
4 Genesis 38.9; Isaiah 57.5; Noonan 1986:50.
5 Gold 1992:195; cf. Isaiah 1.15.
6 Gittelsohn 1989:111.
7 Brundage 1987:108–9.
8 Thomas Aquinas *Summa Theologica* 2.2.154.1, 2.2.154.11.
9 *Congregation for the Doctrine of the Faith* 'Persona humana. Declaration on certain questions concerning sexual ethics', 24 December 1975, §9.

10 James Dobson *Preparing for adolescence. Straight talk to teens and parents.* Ventura: Regal 1979:83.
11 Bennett & Rosario 1995:2.
12 Koran 23.5–7.
13 Koran 70.29–31.
14 Imam Bukhari *Sahih Bukhari* 7.62.4.
15 Sheikh Mustafa Az-Zarqa, 'Fatwa on masturbation'. http://www.islamonline.net/servlet/Satellite?pagename=IslamOnline-English-Ask_Scholar/FatwaE/FatwaE&cid=1119503545922.
16 Faure 1998:84.
17 Faure 1998:88; Powers 2008:206.
18 Jaffrelot 1996:35–6.
19 Olivelle 2008:163.
20 Demaitre 1937:39.
21 Alexander & Fisher 2003.
22 *UKGayNews* 2009.
23 Laumann, Gagnon, Michael & Michaels 1994:fig. 3.1.
24 Laumann & Mahay 2002:fig. 5.
25 Kinsey, Pomeroy & Martin 1948:499; Kinsey, Pomeroy, Martin & Gebhard 1953:142.
26 Laumann, Gagnon, Michael and Michaels, 1994:fig. 3.1. The percentage figures for weekly masturbations among men are 37.6 for non-believers, 28.2 for moderate Protestants, 24.9 for Catholics and 19.5 for fundamentalist Protestants. The figures for women are 13.8 for non-believers, 7.4 for moderate Protestants, 6.6 for Catholics and 5.5 for fundamentalist Protestants.

4 The Blessings and Curses of Heterosexuality

1 Greenhouse 1988; *Le Monde* 1988; Chebel d'Appollonia 1998:390.
2 The film was formally charged with blasphemy but was found not guilty (Bald 1998:148). Nikos Kazantzakis, who had written the book on which the film was based in 1953, was excommunicated by the Greek Orthodox church the following year, and the Catholic church included the book in its index of forbidden books (Bald 1998:147).
3 Banerjee 2008.
4 Brückner & Bearman 2005:271.
5 Brückner & Bearman 2005:275.
6 1 Corinthians 6.9–10.
7 Deuteronomy 22.22–34.
8 Deuteronomy 22.24.
9 Deuteronomy 22.13–28–9; Exodus 22.16–17.
10 Deuteronomy 22.23–27.
11 Deuteronomy 22.13–21.
12 Broyde 2005:96–99, 88.
13 Broyde 2005:97.
14 Dorff 2005:217.

15 Wiesner-Hanks 2000:46.
16 Bullough & Bullough 1987:143; Wiesner-Hanks 2000:86.
17 Wiesner-Hanks 2000:87.
18 Eder, Hall & Hekma 1999:12.
19 Wiesner-Hanks 2000:234.
20 Phayer 1977:25.
21 Phayer 1977:24.
22 Player 1977:25. At the same time, there were few if any births out of wedlock among the upper-classes in Germany. The middle-classes filled the legal vacuum with new rules that preserved traditional sexual morality.
23 Fahey 1999:62.
24 Klein 2006:6.
25 Klein 2006:17; Rosenbaum 2009.
26 Klein 2006:17.
27 Røthing 1998:113.
28 Røthing 1998:186, cf. 175.
29 Røthing 1998:208–9.
30 *Durex* 2005:13.
31 *Eurostat* 2005:67.
32 Kyi 2005:5. The figures for Georgia refer to 2003.
33 Ventura & Bachrach 2000:2–3.
34 Thomson 2008.
35 *Gallup* 1997.
36 Finer 2007:73.
37 *Gallup* 1997.
38 Koran 24.2.
39 Koran 4.15.
40 Koran 4.16.
41 Koran 24.3.
42 Imam Malik *Muwatta* 41.1.6, 41.2.12–13, 41.3.14; Muslim Ibn al-Hajjaj *Sahih Muslim* 17.4191–93, 17.4209, cf. Imam Malik *Muwatta* 41.2.13, 41.3.15, 41.3.16.
43 Imam Malik *Muwatta* 41.3.14; Muslim Ibn al-Hajjaj *Sahih Muslim* 17.4219, 17.4221, 17.4223, cf. Muslim Ibn al-Hajjaj *Sahih Muslim* 17.4222.
44 Bouhdiba [1975]:105.
45 Koran 24.33.
46 Abu Dawud *Sunan Abi Dawud* 12.2257.
47 Bouhdiba [1975]:189–92.
48 Bouhdiba [1975]:194.
49 Bouhdiba [1975]:192–3.
50 Seliktar 2000:135–36.
51 Thorenfeldt 2006.
52 Meland 2006.
53 Esposito 2002:147.
54 Halstead & Reiss 2003:101.
55 Fleishman & Hassan 2009; 'Buy for ladies: Virginity hymen' på *www.gigmo.com*, http://www.gigimo.com/main/browse/For,Ladies_Virginity,Hymen,79.php?cat=79.

56 Foster 2002:102.
57 *Durex* 2005:13.
58 Rheault & Mogahed 2008.
59 Foster 2002:99.
60 Pelham 2000.
61 Vivekananthan 2005.
62 Worth 2008; *UNIFEM* 2007:3.
63 Khalaf 2006:187.
64 Khalaf 2006:190.
65 Iqbal & Lund 2010.
66 Pelham 2000.
67 Hazaimeh 2009.
68 Brooks 1995:49.
69 Brooke 1991.
70 *BBC* 2003.
71 Parrinder 1996:23.
72 Olivelle 2008:159.
73 Jaffrelot 1996:35–6.
74 Mishra 2000:182.
75 Mishra 2000:184.
76 Mishra 2000:182.
77 *Times of India* 2010.
78 Reynolds & Tanner 1995:153.
79 Virdi 1972:33–4.
80 Hawley 1994:6–10.
81 Olivelle 2008:159.
82 Olivelle 2008:161.
83 cf. *Laws of Manu* 5.159–61.
84 Khandelwal 2001:158, cf. Virdi 1972:220.
85 Suwanbubbha 2003:147.
86 Tiyavanich 2007:16.
87 *Book of Common Prayer*, 'The Form of Solemnization of Matrimony'.
88 *Congregation for the Doctrine of the Faith* 'Considerations regarding proposals to give legal recognition to unions between homosexual persons', 3 June 2003, §§4, 8.
89 Pagels 1988:xix.
90 *European Convention on Human Rights* §12; *United Nations Convention on Civil and Political Rights* §23.
91 Exodus 20.17.
92 1 Corinthians 11.3.
93 Augustine *On Marriage and Concupiscence* 1.1.
94 Koran 4.34
95 *UNIFEM* 2003:40.
96 Barden 1987.
97 Bullough 1976:385.
98 Johnson & Jordan 2006:84.
99 Weeks 1981:24.
100 *Congregation for the Doctrine of the Faith* 'Considerations regarding proposals to give

legal recognition to unions between homosexual persons', 3 June 2003, §§4, 8.

101 Council of Carthage (AD 419), Canon 4.
102 *DNA* 2007.
103 *MSNBC* 2007.
104 Nelson 2009.
105 *Economist* 2007b.
106 Keown 2005:57.
107 See, for instance, http://www.rockyresort.co.m/weddings/samui_buddhist_weddings.php
108 Koran 4.24
109 Muslim Ibn al-Hajjaj *Sahih Muslim* 8.3248–50.
110 Shahine 1999.
111 Miyahiro Sadao *Kokueki honron* 1831, translated in LaFleur 1992:111.
112 Miyahiro Sadao *Nihon shiso taikei*, translated in Hanootunian 1988:300.
113 Miyahiro Sadao *Kokueki honron* 1831, translated in LaFleur 1992:111.
114 Bornoff [1991]:241.
115 Judges 11.30–37.
116 Genesis 1.28.
117 Genesis 9.1.
118 Psalms 127.2–4.
119 Genesis 12.2.
120 Deuteronomy 7.14.
121 Jeremiah 16.1–7.
122 Genesis 38.6–26.
123 *Mishnah, Yevamot* 61b, 64a, 63b, 65b.
124 Maimonides *Mishneh Torah, Sefer Nashim, Ishut* 14.8; cf. Berger 2005c:149–50.
125 *Zohar* 1.12–13, refers to Isaiah 66.24.
126 Joseph ben Ephraim Caro & Moses Isserles, *Shulhan Aruch Even ha-ezer* 1.1. Isserles quotes from Proverbs 18.22.
127 1 Corinthians 7.5, my italics.
128 1 Corinthians 7.3–4.
129 Bullough 1976:385.
130 Weir 2000:8–9.
131 Canon Law of the Catholic Church, Canon 1084, §1.
132 Fontes 2001.
133 *New York Times* 1982a; *New York Times* 1982b.
134 Sommer 2000:101–4.
135 Hutton [1909]:301.
136 Dr. Frank Kaufmann, executive director *Inter-Religious Federation for World Peace* [movement associated with Pastor Moon's Unification Church] 'A portrait' in Beversluis 2000:109–10.
137 Koran 24.32.
138 Imam Malik *Muwatta* 29.27.74–5.
139 Imam Malik *Muwatta* 29.5.17–19.
140 Virdi 1972:6.
141 Lidke 2003:109.
142 *Laws of Manu* 3.45, cf. Parrinder 1996:20.

143 *Laws of Manu* 9.4.
144 *Laws of Manu* 5.159.
145 *Congregation for the Doctrine of the Faith* 'Considerations regarding proposals to give legal recognition to unions between homosexual persons', 3 June 2003, §7.
146 Genesis 38.6–9.
147 Noonan 1986:10–11.
148 Noonan 1986:50–51.
149 Alpert 2003:194.
150 Utnerman 1996:146.
151 Augustine *On Marriage and Concupiscence* 1.1.
152 Augustine *Of the Good of Marriage* 5.
153 Augustine *Against Faustus* 15.7.
154 Augustine *On the Morals of the Manichaeans* 18.65.
155 McLaren 1990:53–4.
156 Pope Gregory 9 *Decretalium compilatio* 5.12.5.
157 Gudorf 2003:62.
158 Pope Pius 11 'Casti Connubii' 31 December 1930, §56, cf. §54.
159 Pope Pius 12 'Address to midwives' 29 October 1951.
160 Fox 1995:59.
161 Fox 1995:52.
162 Oosterhuis 1999:80.
163 Parrinder 1996:240.
164 Fox 1995:77–81.
165 Parrinder 1996:238.
166 Greeley 1989:52.
167 D'Antonio, Davidson, Hoge & Meyer 2001:76.
168 Pope John Paul 2 'Veritatis Splendor' 6 August 1993, §80.
169 Ertelt 2008.
170 *Congregation for the Doctrine of the Faith* 'Considerations regarding proposals to give legal recognition to unions between homosexual persons', 3 June 2003, §7.
171 Cavendish 2003:218.
172 Jain 2003a:241.
173 Noonan 1986:409.
174 Noonan 1986:490.
175 Røthing 1998:203.
176 Røthing 1998:205.
177 Hoel 2010.
178 Imam Malik *Muwatta* 29.32.95.
179 Shaikh 2003:115.
180 Shaikh 2003:116.
181 Jain 2003a:241.
182 Hegna 2008.
183 Shaikh 2003:105.
184 Jain 2003b:136.
185 Jain 2003b:138.
186 Jain 2003a:241.
187 Reynolds & Tanner 1995:67.

188 Kumar 2003.
189 Jeffrey & Jeffrey 1997:216.
190 Puttick 1997:108.
191 Suwanbubbha 2003:148.
192 Reynolds & Tanner 1995:67.
193 Reynolds & Tanner 1995:67.
194 *Catholic Online* 2003; Johannessen 2007.
195 Martin Luther in a letter to the Chancellor of Saxony, Gregor Brück, 13 January 1524, in de Wette 1826:459.
196 Martin Luther in a letter to Philip of Hesse, 10 December 1539, in de Wette 1856:238–44.
197 Parrinder 1996:202.
198 Augustine *Of the Good of Marriage* 33.
199 Exodus 21.10.
200 Deuteronomy 21.15–17.
201 Deuteronomy 17.17.
202 Berger 2005b:119.
203 Sabry 2008.
204 Koran 4.2–3.
205 Koran 4.3, 4.129.
206 Koran 24.33.
207 Bouhdiba [1975]:105.
208 Bouhdiba [1975]:107.
209 Boudhiba [1975]:107–8.
210 Toledano 1998:29.
211 Toledano 1998:31.
212 Sykes 2008.
213 *Kamasutra* 4.2.
214 Parrinder 1996:63.
215 Parrinder 1996:72.
216 *Hindu Marriage Act* (1955) §5.1; *Parsee Marriage and Divorce Act* (1936) §4.1; *Indian Christian Marriage Act* (1872) §60.2.
217 *The Muslim Personal Law (Shariat) Application Act* (1937) §2.
218 Parrinder 1996:48.
219 Yao 2003:86.
220 Childs 2004:42.
221 Zeitzen 2008:180.
222 Parrinder 1996:215.
223 Westoff, Blanc & Nyblade 1994.
224 Cf. *European Convention on Human Rights* §14; *United Nations Convention on Civil and Political Rights* §§2, 24 & 26.
225 Wiesner-Hanks 2000:157.
226 Wiesner-Hanks 2000:158.
227 Steinsland 2005:374–75.
228 Wiesner-Hanks 2000:66.
229 Foster 1984:107–8.
230 Daynes 2001:26.

231 Daynes 2001:76.
232 Daynes 2001:76–8.
233 Abanes 2003:419.
234 Daynes 2001:79.
235 *Morill Anti-Bigamy Act*, adopted 1 July 1862.
236 *Edmunds-Tucker Act*, adopted 1887; cf. Gordon 2002:180–81.
237 Daynes 2001:175.
238 Gordon 2002:181.
239 Wilford Woodruff 'Official declaration – 1. (The manifesto)' 24 September 1890, http://scriptures.lds.org/en/od/1; cf. Gordon 2002:220.
240 Hardy 1992:206–11.
241 Joseph F. Smith 'Official declaration (The second manifesto)' 6 April 1904, http://www.mormon-polygamy.org/second_manifesto.
242 Quinn 2001:371–2.
243 CNN 2007.
244 Zeitzen 2008:171.
245 *BBC* 2007b. Mokkarrameh Ebrahimi, the woman Kiani had had sex with, was also condemned to death, but she was reprieved and freed in March 2008.
246 Deuteronomy 22.13, cf. Leviticus 20.10.
247 *Laws of Hammurabi* 129.
248 Whereas it is made clear that engaged virgins should not be stoned if they were raped outside the city but only if they were raped in the city, there were no such limitations on the death penalty for married women who had sex with someone other than their husband. A married woman, raped by someone other than her husband, should be stoned together with her rapist (Deuteronomy 22.22–7). If she is raped by her husband, however, there is no legal involvement at all.
249 Alpert 2003:181.
250 Exodus 20.14.
251 Deuteronomy 22.13–28; Leviticus 20.10.
252 Imam Malik *Muwatta* 41.1.8; Muslim Ibn al-Hajjaj *Sahih Muslim* 17.4194.
253 Koran 17.32.
254 Koran 24.2.
255 Imam Malik *Muwatta* 41.1.1, 41.1.2, 41.1.4, 41.1.5, 41.1.6; Imam Bukhari *Sahih Bukhari* 8.23.413; Muslim Ibn al-Hajjaj *Sahih Muslim* 17.4191–201, 17.4205–14, 17.4216; Abu Dawud *Sunan Abi Dawud* 24.3619, 38.4364.
256 Imam Malik *Muwatta* 41.1.1–2, 41.1.4–6; Muslim Ibn al-Hajjaj *Sahih Muslim* 17.4211, 17.4214; Abu Dawud *Sunan Abi Dawud* 24.3619, cf. Imam Malik *Muwatta* 41.1.8, 41.1.9, 41.1.10, 41.1.11.
257 Muslim Ibn al-Hajjaj *Sahih Muslim* 17.4211; Imam Malik *Muwatta* 41.1.1, cf. Imam Bukhari *Sahih Bukhari* 2.23.413; Muslim Ibn al-Hajjaj *Sahih Muslim* 17.4212–13, 17.4216.
258 Muslim Ibn al-Haijaj *Sahih Muslim* 17.4191–93, cf. Koran 24.2.
259 Imam Malik *Muwatta* 41.1.5; Muslim Ibn al-Hajjaj *Sahih Muslim* 17.4206; cf. Imam Malik *Muwatta* 41.1.11.
260 Imam Bukhari *Sahih Bukhari* 2.23.329; Muslim Ibn al-Hajjaj *Sahih Muslim* 1.171, 1.172.
261 Koran 4.15, 24.4; Imam Malik *Muwatta* 41.1.7.

262 Imam Malik *Muwatta* 41.1.7; Muslim Ibn al-Hajjaj *Sahíh Muslim* 9.3569–72.
263 Muslim Ibn al-Hajjaj *Sahíh Muslim* 15.4090.
264 Koran 24.4.
265 Bouhdiba [1975]:143.
266 Bouhdiba [1975]:105.
267 *UNODC* 2007:21.
268 *BBC* 2006b.
269 Kon 1995:167.
270 Waris Shah *Heer Ranjha*. See English summary at http://www.apnaorg.co./poetry/heercomp/heerenglish.html and Vanita 2005:103.
271 John 8.3–11.
272 Matthew 5.27–30.
273 1 Corinthians 6.9–10.
274 Ephesians 5.6.
275 Hebrews 13.4. My italics.
276 Bullough & Bullough 1987:118.
277 Augustine *De ordine* 2.4; Thomas Aquinas *Summa Theologiae* 2–2.0.11.
278 Bullough & Bullough 1987:141.
279 Kon 1995:16.
280 Katz 1995:37.
281 Wiesner–Hanks 2000:78.
282 Parrinder 1996:26.
283 *Kamasutra* 1.5.
284 Parrinder 1996:57.
285 Parrinder 1996:21.
286 *Laws of Manu* 9.30, 5.164.
287 *Kamasutra* 4.1.
288 *Laws of Manu* 12.58.
289 Parrinder 1996:30.
290 Fleeman 2010.
291 *Sutta Nipata* 2.14.
292 Harvey 2000:71.
293 *BBC* 2007a.
294 *ENI* 2007.
295 Dickerson 2007.
296 Turley 2004.
297 Drummond 2008.
298 *Durex* 2005:15; cf. Druckerman 2007:*passim*.
299 Atkin, Baucom & Jacobson 2001:746.
300 cf. *European Convention on Human Rights* §8; *United Nations Convention on Civil and Political Rights* §17; *Toonen v. Australia*, decision of the UN Human Rights Committee, 4 April 1994, §8.2; *A.D.T. v. United Kingdom*, judgement in the European Court of Human Rights, 31 July 2000, §26.
301 Basar 2004; *Turkish Daily News* 2004.
302 Zuria 2004.
303 Deuteronomy 24.1.
304 Deuteronomy 24.2–3.

305 Deuteronomy 22.28–9.
306 Judges 19.1–2.
307 *Mishnah, Yevamot* 112b.
308 Unterman 1996:148–9.
309 Berger 2005a:5; Broyde 2005:93.
310 Berger 2005a:9; Broyde 2005:93–4.
311 Unterman 1996:148.
312 Berger 2005a:12.
313 Koran 65.1.
314 Imam Malik *Muwatta* 29.5.17–18.
315 Koran 65.2.
316 Koran 65.6–7.
317 Esposito 2002:108.
318 Barakat 1993:115.
319 Harter 2004.
320 Esposito 2002:108.
321 Eickelman & Piscatori 2004:93.
322 Mir-Hosseini 2000:65.
323 Harter 2004.
324 Matthew 5.27–32; cf. Parrinder 1996:208.
325 Mark 10.2–12; Matthew 19.3–9; Luke 16.18, cf. Deuteronomy 24.1.
326 1 Corinthians 6.15.
327 Bjørke 2009; Eikeland 2009; Henriksen 2009.
328 Phillips 1992:9–10.
329 Tertullian *On Exhortation to Chastity* 9.
330 *Council of Elvira*, Canon 65.
331 Wiesner-Hanks 2000:50.
332 Wiesner-Hanks 2000:34.
333 Wiesner-Hanks 2000:79.
334 Wiesner-Hanks 2000:78.
335 *U.S. Department of Health and Human Services* 2009.
336 Cleminson & Amezúa 1999:187, 192.
337 Wanrooij 1999:125.
338 Jacobsen 2008.
339 *Eurostat* 2007: fig. 1.20.
340 Dewaraja 1981.
341 Harvey 2000:103.
342 Harvey 2000:497.
343 Faure 2003:46–7.
344 Faure 2003:45–7.
345 Virdi 1972:33.
346 Derrett 1963:167.
347 Derrett 1963:166.
348 Derrett 1963:167.
349 Derrett 1963:165; Virdi 1972:246, cf. 229.
350 Virdi 1972:33.
351 *Hindu Marriage Act* (1955) §§12–13.

352 Virdi 1972:39–49.
353 *Hindu Marriage Act* §13b.
354 Leviticus 20.18.
355 Leviticus 15.19–24.
356 Leviticus 15.1.
357 Leviticus 11.1–47, 20.25.
358 Leviticus 12.1–14.57.
359 Leviticus 15.15–18.
360 Leviticus 18.1–30, 20.1–27.
361 Leviticus 20.26.
362 Leviticus 18.27–8.
363 Alpert 2003:182.
364 Koran 2.222.
365 Brundage 1987:156, 242.
366 Bullough 1976:360.
367 Brundage 1987:242.
368 *Laws of Manu* 3.46.
369 *Laws of Manu* 11.174.
370 *Laws of Manu* 11.213.
371 *Laws of Manu* 11.175.
372 Ovid *Metamorphoses* 10.681–707, cf. Pseudo-Apollodorus *Bibl.* 3.9.2; Pseudo-Hyginus *Fabulae* 185.
373 Deuteronomy 23.17.
374 1 Samuel 2.22, 2.34, 4.11.
375 Ruggiero 1985:119.
376 Monter 1990:285, 294.
377 Blanc & Way 1998.
378 Alpert 2003:181.
379 Muslim Ibn al-Hajjaj *Sahih Muslim* 8.3365.
380 Schmitt 1992:15.
381 Brundage 1987:108.
382 Akst 2003; Røthing 1998:13,182–7.
383 Augustine *Of the Good of Marriage* 12.
384 Brundage 1987:241.
385 Brundage 1987:322.
386 *Congregation for the Doctrine of the Faith* 'Considerations regarding proposals to give legal recognition to unions between homosexual persons', 3 June 2003, §7.
387 Lawrence et al. v. Texas, 26 June 2003.
388 *Durex* 2005:15.

5 Homosexuality: Expected, Compulsory, Condemned

1 Mitsuo Sadatomos *Kobo Daishi's Book*, translated extracts and summary in Schalow 1992:216.
2 Smith, Rissel, Richters, Grulich & de Visser 2007:138, 141.
3 *Durex* 2005:15.
4 Jansen 2003.

5 Agha 2000:tab. 1; cf. Khan & Hyder 1998.
6 *UKGayNews* 2009.
7 Kinsey, Pomeroy & Martin 1948:656; Kinsey, Pomeroy, Martin & Gebhard 1953:488.
8 Kon 1995:45.
9 Melikian 1967:173.
10 Schalow 1992:227.
11 Schalow 1992:215.
12 Wilson 2003:166.
13 Schalow 1992:222.
14 Kitamura Kigin *Rock azaleas*, translated in Schalow 1992:222.
15 Ihara Saikaku *The mirror of manly love* 1.1.
16 Ihara Saikaku *The mirror of manly love* 1.1.
17 Ihara Saikaku *The mirror of manly love* 2.5, 1.1.
18 Watanabe & Iwata 1989:121; Hawkins 2000: 37.
19 Ha Fei Zi *Ha Feizi* 12; Hinsch 1990:20–22.
20 Bullough 1976:303; Crompton 2003:218.
21 Bullough 1976:303; Crompton 2003:218.
22 Crompton 2003:220.
23 Hinsch 1990:53; Wawrytko 1993:200.
24 Wawrytko 1993:202.
25 Hinsch 1990:163.
26 Baird 2001:65.
27 Kitamura Kigin *Rock azaleas*, translated in Schalow 1992:222.
28 Zwilling 1992:204–8; Wilson 2003:162–3.
29 Zwilling 1992:207.
30 Goldstein 1964:134; Murray 2002:62–3.
31 Goldstein 1964:134; Murray 2002:62–5; Wilson 2003:167–8.
32 Conner & Donaldson 1990:169.
33 Parrinder 1996:48.
34 Zwilling 1992:209.
35 Faure 1998:98.
36 Faure 1998:82.
37 Dover [1978]:91–100.
38 Pindar according to Athenaeus 13.564e.
39 Bullough 1976:101.
40 *Inscriptiones Graecae* 12.3.537a and 537b.
41 Endsjø 2008b.
42 Xenophon *Constitution of the Lacedaemonians* 2.12.
43 Plutarch *Pelopidas* 18.
44 Aelianus Tacticus 3.12; Plutarch *Lycurgus* 18.4.
45 Strabo *Geografi* 10.19–21.
46 Dio Cassius 11.3; *Hist. Aug. Hadr.* 14.5–6; Sext. Aur. *Caesarib.* 14.8; Cf. Endsjø 2009:96.
47 Lambert 1988:166, 180, 184–85, 191–95, cf. Pausanias *Descr.* 8.9.7–8; 8.10.1.
48 Origen *Contra Celsum* 3.36, 5.63.
49 Athanasius *Contr. Gent.* 9; Athenagoras *Leg. pro Christ.* 30; Hegesippus according to

Eusebius *Hist. Eccl.* 4.8.2; Origenes Origen *Cantra Celsum* 3.36–38.
50 Cf. Brooten 2002:78–9.
51 Sappho, Fragment 1, according to Dion. H. *Comp* 23.
52 Ovid *Metamorphoses* 9.715–97.
53 Baum 1993:10.
54 Baum 1993:10.
55 Baum 1993:15.
56 Baum 1993:13, 16–17.
57 Baum 1993:12.
58 Baum 1993:12.
59 Baum 1993:12.
60 Baum 1993:13.
61 Murray & Roscoe 1998:99.
62 Murray & Roscoe 1998:101.
63 Murray & Roscoe 1998:93.
64 Murray & Roscoe 1998:98.
65 Baum 1993:39; Murray & Roscoe 1998:147–8.
66 Murray & Roscoe 1998:280.
67 Murray & Roscoe 1998:37.
68 McAlister 2000:132.
69 McAlister 2000:135.
70 Murray & Roscoe 1998:xv.
71 Bandlien 2001:57–9.
72 Bandlien 2001:54.
73 Snorri *The Saga of Harald Finehair* 35.
74 Noordam 1995:273–5.
75 Van der Meer 2004:80.
76 Leviticus 20.13.
77 Leviticus 20.10,18; Deuteronomy 22.23–4.
78 Leviticus 20.23.
79 Deuteronomy 22.5.
80 Leviticus 19.19; Deuteronomy 22.9–11.
81 Leviticus 20.13.
82 Leviticus 20.9.
83 Numbers 35.16–18, 26–27; Deuteronomy 19.10, 21.8.
84 Leviticus 20.10–12, 15–16.
85 Leviticus 20.27.
86 1 Samuel 18.1.
87 1 Samuel 20.16.
88 2 Samuel 20.41.
89 2 Samuel 1.26.
90 Romans 1.25–7.
91 Romans 1.27.
92 Romans 1.29.
93 John 8.11.
94 Matthew 8.5–13.
95 Luke 7.10.

96 Cf. Stuart 1995:160.
97 Genesis 19.5.
98 Ezekiel 16.48–50; Zephania 2.8–9.
99 Jubilees 20.5; Test. Naph. 3.4–5; 2 Peter 2.4, 6–8.
100 Deuteronomy 29.22.28; Jeremiah 50.38–40; Amos 4.11.
101 Isaiah 3.8–9; Jeremiah 23.14, 49.16–18; Lamentations 3.61–4.4.
102 Judges 19.22–5.
103 Matthew 10.14–15; Luke 10.10–12.
104 Matthew 11.20–24.
105 Philo *De Abr.* 135; cf. Philo *Quaest. et Solut. in Gen.* 4.31, 4.37.
106 Josephus *Ant.* 1.11.3; Clement of Alexandria *Paed.* 3; Augustine *De civitate Dei* 16.30.
107 Maimonides *Mishneh Torah, Sefer Kedushah, Issurei Bi'ah* 1.14.
108 Unterman 1996:134.
109 Joseph ben Ephraim Caro & Moses Isserles *Shulhan Aruch Even ha-ezer* 24.
110 Unterman 1996:134–5.
111 N. Roth 1982:29–51; Crompton 2003:169.
112 Eron 1993:113; *Sefer ha-Hinuch* 209; Rashi on Leviticus 20.13; cf. *Mishnah, Yevamot* 55b; Maimonides *Mishneh Torah, Sefer Kedushah, Issurei Bi'ah* 1.10, 1.14, 1.19.
113 Sarah [1993]:95–7.
114 Maimonides *Mishneh Torah, Sefer Kedushah, Issurei Bi'ah* 21.8; reference to Leviticus 18.3.
115 Eron 1993:119–20.
116 Alpert 2003:188.
117 *Council of Elvira* Canon 71.
118 Theodosius the Great's law against homosexual sex is to be found in the law collection of his grandson Theodosius II, *Codex Theodusianus* 9.7.6.
119 Justinian *Novella* 77.
120 Crompton 2003:155.
121 Crompton 2003:155.
122 Crompton 2003:152.
123 *Lex Visigothorum* 3.5.5–6.
124 *Concilium Parisiense* 34, translated in Crompton 2003:158.
125 Boswell [1980]:177 n. 30; Crompton 2003:159–60.
126 Cf. Rian 2001:32.
127 *El fuero real* 4.9.2; cf. translation in Crompton 2003:200.
128 *Fleta* 37.3.
129 *Li livres de jostice et de plet* 18.24.22; cf. Crompton 2003:202.
130 Labalme 1984, 238–45.
131 Monter 1990:280.
132 Crompton 2003:190, 245.
133 Crompton 2003:189–90.
134 Monter 1990:288.
135 *Li livres de jostice et de plet* 18.24.22; cf. Crompton 2003:202.
136 Crompton 2003:246–7.
137 Crompton 2003:299.
138 Ludovico Maria Sinistrati *De delictis et poenis* §24, translated in Crompton 2003:473.

139 Rian 2001:33; cf. Stephens 2002:332.
140 Monter 1990:280.
141 Romans 1.25–7.
142 Justinian *Novella* 77.
143 Basil *Sermo asceticus* 2.321.
144 Katz 1995:38–40.
145 Crompton 2003:366.
146 Katz 1995:38; Crompton 2003:391.
147 Bullough 1976:522.
148 Long, Brown & Cooper 2003:262.
149 Plant 1986:61.
150 Adolf Hitler 'Speech to the Reichstag' 23 March 1933, http://hitler.org/speeches/03-23-33.html.
151 Roos 2005:83.
152 Herzog 2005:13.
153 *Deutsche Allgemeine Zeitung* 6. april 1933 in Grau [1993]:30.
154 Opposition to homosexuality also provided a good excuse to dispose of a man Hitler was coming to see as a dangerous rival. Homosexuality was one of the justifications for the liquidation of Röhm and other SA leaders during the so-called Night of the Long Knives on 30 June 1934.
155 Plant 1986:110.
156 Timm 2005:233.
157 Plant 1986:117.
158 Plant 1986:118.
159 Crompton 2003:467; van der Meer 2004:79.
160 Boon 1989:244–5; Crompton 2003:467.
161 Kon 1995:15.
162 Kon 1995:17.
163 Kon 1995:46.
164 Weeks 1981:109.
165 Murray & Roscoe 1998:22.
166 Monter 1990:175.
167 Michel de Montaigne *Journal de voyage en Italie par la Suisse et L'Allemagne en 1580 et 1581. Tome premier.* Paris: Garnier Frères 1774:120; Antonio Tiepolo 2 August 1578 in Fabio Mutinelli (ed.) *Storia arcana ed aneddotica d'Italia racontata dai Veneti ambasciatori. Vol I.* Venice: Pietro Naratovich 1855:121; cf. Boswell 1994:264–5; Crompton 2003:286.
168 Bates 2004:73.
169 Gardiner 1883:98; Bullough 1976:475.
170 Crompton 2003:344; Elisabeth Charlotte in letters from Paris, 1721, quoted in Wormeley 1899:174–5.
171 Kennedy 1997:67.
172 Crompton 2003:250, 345.
173 Bullough 1976:484.
174 Crompton 2003:177.
175 Schleiner 1994:44; Crompton 2003:322–3.
176 Aldrich 2003:336.

177 Boone 2001:44; Aldrich 2003:337.
178 Copley 2006:131.
179 Aldrich 2003:398.
180 Koran 7.81, cf. Koran 27.56, 29.28.
181 Koran 26.165–6.
182 Koran 50.13.
183 Koran 21.74, 29.33.
184 Koran 26.172–3, cf. Koran 7.84, 27.59, 53.54.
185 Koran 24.2.
186 Koran 4.16.
187 Koran 4.16.
188 Koran 52.24, 56.17–18, 76.19; cf. Miller 1996:26–7; Wafer 1997:90.
189 Abu Dawud *Sunan Abi Dawud* 28.4447.
190 Imam Malik *Muwatta* 41.1.11.
191 Abu Dawud *Sunan Abi Dawud* 28.4448.
192 Bosworth, van Donzel, Lewis & Pellat 1986:77.
193 Wafer 1997:89.
194 Kennedy 1997:16–17.
195 Murray 1997a:23–4; Crompton 1997:150.
196 Bosworth, van Donzel, Lewis & Pellat 1986:777; Murray 1997a:24.
197 Bouhdiba [1975]:143.
198 Parrinder 1996:169. The chapter on sex between men is unfortunately omitted from most European translations.
199 Hidayatullah 2003:274.
200 Duran 1993:196.
201 De Martino 1992; Eppink 1992; Khan 1992; MacDonald 1992; Murray 1997b; Murray 1997c; Murray 1997d.
202 Duran 1993:185; Bouhdiba [1975]:200.
203 Schmitt 1992:5.
204 Crompton 2003:172.
205 Crompton 2003:167.
206 Vanita 2005:9.
207 Murray 1997a.
208 Khan 1997:276; Bromark & Herbjørnsrud 2002:220–22, 226.
209 Duran 1993:188.
210 Murray 1997a:28.
211 Murray 1997d:257–8.
212 Murray & Roscoe 1998:25.
213 Murray & Roscoe 1998:30–34; Amory 1998.
214 Amory 1998:74, 84; Wikan 1977.
215 Naqvi & Mujtaba 1997:264–6.
216 Murray & Roscoe 1998:97–8; Gaudio 1998:116–28.
217 Murray 1997a:37–40.
218 Khan 1997:283–4.
219 *UKGayNews* 2009.
220 Murray & Roscoe 1998:34–5, 39; Amory 1998:75–6.
221 Vanita 2005:187.

222 *Ramayana* 7.87.
223 Pattanaik 2001:83.
224 Vanita 2005:74.
225 *Brahmanda Purana* 4.10.
226 Vanita 2005:9.
227 Vanita 2005:145–9.
228 *Kamasutra* 2.9.
229 *Kamasutra* 5.6.
230 Vanita 2005:75.
231 *Kamasutra* 2.9.
232 Vanita 2005:84.
233 Vanita 2005:78.
234 *Padma Purana* 5.75.
235 *Laws of Manu* 8.369–70.
236 *Laws of Manu* 1.175.
237 *Laws of Manu* 1.174.
238 Timmons & Kumar 2009; *Penal Code* (1860) §377.
239 Mahatma Gandhi in *Young India* 26. July 1929, in Vanita & Kidwai [2000]:255–6; Baird 2001:61–2.
240 Fuglehaug 2008; Udjus 2008.
241 *BBC* 2005a.
242 *365gay* 2008c.
243 Rabbi Tzvi Hersh Weinreb 'Orthodox response to same-sex marriage' 5 June 2006, http://www.ou.org/public_affairs/article/ou_resp:same_sex_marrrage/.
244 Holben 1999:182.
245 *General Assembly Union of American Hebrew Congregation* 'Civil marriage for gay and lesbian Jewish couples', 2 November 1997, http://urj.org/Articles/index.cfm?id=7214&pge_prg_id=29601&pge_id=4590.
246 Cline 2003.
247 *Svenska Dagbladet* 2009a; *Svenska Dagbladet* 2009b.
248 *Afrol News* 2005.
249 Thompson 2003.
250 *Angus Reid* 2006.
251 *365gay* 2008d.
252 Vanita 2005:233.
253 Boswell 1994.
254 Murray & Roscoe 1998:97–8.
255 Vanita 2005:60; *BBC* 2005b.
256 Naqvi & Mujtaba 1997:264–6.
257 Vanita 2005:1, 5, 6, 23, 37, 64, 68, 100, 162, 234–7.
258 Sibalis 1996:82.
259 In, for instance, the European Court of Human Rights in the cases of *Dudgeon v. United Kingdom*, 22 October 1981, *Norris v. Ireland*, 26 October 1988, *Modinos v. Cyprus*, 22 April 1993, *Smith & Grady v. United Kingdom*, 27 September 1999, and *S.L. v. Austria*, 9 January 2003. Also in the UN Human Rights Committee in the case of *Toonen v. Australia*, 4 April 1994.
260 Davis 2006:152–3.

261 *Dudgeon v. United Kingdom*, judgment in the European Court of Human Rights, 22 October 1981, §25.
262 Davis 2006:154.
263 *Norris v. Ireland*, judgement in the European Court of Human Rights, 26 October 1988.
264 Ramet 2006b:167.
265 Ramet 2006b:168.
266 Stan & Turcescu 2007:177.
267 Ramet 2006b:171.
268 *Envío Team* 1992.
269 Hmar 2010.
270 Ramet 2006a:127.
271 Newport 2003.
272 Bates 2004:137; Pritchard 2007.
273 Osodi 2006. Partly as a result of strong international pressure the proposal was put on ice in 2007.
274 Archbishop Henry Luke Orombi 'Church of Uganda's position on the antihomosexuality bill 2009', 9 February 2010, http://churchofuganda.org/wp-content/uploads/2010/02/COU-official-position-on-the-Anti-Homosexuality-Bill-2009..pdf.
275 Garcia 2010.
276 *Canadian Broadcast Standards Council. Ontario Panel* 2005.
277 Kapur 2005:84.
278 Seliktar 2000:135–6.
279 Millett 1982:109.
280 Baird 2001:68.
281 Wilcox 2003:337–8.
282 Alpert 2003:189.
283 Holben 1999:112.
284 Goldman 1999.
285 See, for instance, Manum 2007.
286 AbuKhalil 1993:32.
287 Malik 2004.
288 Vanita 2005:30.
289 Vanita 2005:29.
290 *BBC* 2007c.
291 Timmons & Kumar 2009.
292 Mishra 2000:184.
293 Cabezón 1993:94.
294 Wilson 2003:167; Conkin 1998.
295 Alpert 2003:189.
296 Spence 2006.
297 Dorff 2005:226.
298 Meranda 2007.
299 Peters 2005.
300 *365gay* 2006b.
301 Sharma 2007.

302 Amory 1998:86.
303 Mujtaba 1997:270.
304 Mujtaba 1997:273.
305 *UKGayNews* 2009.
306 Zarit 1992:55.
307 Reynolds 2002.
308 Agha 2000:tab. 1, cf. Khan & Hyder 1998.
309 Mujtaba 1997:267–68.
310 DeMartino 1992:25, 27; Schmitt 1992:7; Murray 1997a:16–17; Eder, Hall & Hekma 1999:7–8.
311 Afshan Rafiq & Bente Bakken *Utfordringer og muligheter*. Oslo: Cappelen Damm 2008:118.
312 *Economist* 2008.
313 Taneja 2010.
314 Rheault & Mogahed 2008.
315 Harrison 2005; Eshaghian 2008.
316 Eshaghian 2008.
317 Murray & Roscoe 1998:249.
318 Holben 1999:78–79.
319 Romans 1.26–7, cf. Ellison 1993:158–9.
320 Fox 1995:176.
321 Hoffman 2010.
322 Gillesvik 2008.

6 Religio-Sexual Racism and Religious Discrimination

1 Zabel 2000:54; Leuchtenburg 2005:223.
2 Carroll 2007.
3 Exodus 34.15–16; Deuteronomy 7.2–4; Joshua 23.12–13, 1 Kings 11.2; Ezra 9.12, cf. Judges 3.6–7.
4 Deuteronomy 23.2.
5 Ezra 9.2.
6 Nehemiah 13.23–5.
7 Nehemiah 13.28–29
8 Ezra 9.2–3.
9 Ezra 9.14.
10 Ezra 10.3.
11 Ezra 10.11, cf. Ezra 10.16–44.
12 Deuteronomy 21.10–14.
13 Ruth 1.4, 4.10.
14 Ruth 4.13–22.
15 2 Samuel 11.3; 1 Kings 7.13–14; 1 Chronicles 2.17.
16 Exodus 2.15–21.
17 Numbers 12.1–15.
18 2 Samuel 3.2–3.
19 1 Kings 3.1, 11.1.

20 Israel 1984:34–35.
21 Brook 2006:311; Shapiro 2006:125.
22 Galatians 3.28
23 Wiesner–Hanks 2000:41.
24 *Fleta* 37.3.
25 Kruger 1997:169.
26 Kruger 1997:169.
27 Kruger 1997:164.
28 Wiesner–Hanks 2000:75.
29 Wiesner–Hanks 2000:149.
30 Scammel 1989:183–89.
31 Samson 2005:22.
32 Wiesner–Hanks 2000:150–51.
33 Wiesner–Hanks 2000:208.
34 Walther 2002:41.
35 Johnston 2003:18; Kociumbas 2004:98.
36 Johnson 2006:10.
37 Bullough 1976:518.
38 Higginbotham & Kopytoff 2000:82; Nagel 2003:102.
39 Bullough 1976:518.
40 Nagel 2003:107.
41 Nagel 2003:107.
42 Genesis 4.11–15.
43 Genesis 9.24–7.
44 Wiesner–Hanks 2000:234.
45 *Scott v. State* in Georgia, 1869.
46 *Lonas v. State* in Tennessee, 1871.
47 *Frasher v. State* in Texas, 1877.
48 *State v. Gibson* in Indiana, 1871.
49 Ross 2002:268–69.
50 Ross 2002:260.
51 Carroll 2007.
52 *Loving et ux. v. Virgina*, 12 June 1967.
53 Carroll 2007.
54 *Harris Poll* 2004.
55 Carroll 2007.
56 *Princeton Survey Research Associates* 2009.
57 Leonard 1999; Manis 1999.
58 Willis 2004:160.
59 Snoke 2004.
60 Clapp 1972:319–21.
61 Altman & Klinkner 2006.
62 Martin 1999.
63 Genesis 11.1–9.
64 Lowery-Smith 2003:69.
65 Jonathan Pait, Coordinator of Communications, Bob Jones University, 'Letter to James Landrith', 31 August 1998, in Martin 1999.

66 Brigham Young 'The persecutions of the Saints. Their loyalty to the Constitution. The Mormon battalion. The laws of God relative to the African race. Remarks by President Brigham Young, made in the Tabernacle, Great Salt Lake City. Reported by G. D. Watt', 8 March 1863, http://journalofdiscourses.org/Vol_10/refJDvol10-24.html.
67 Quinn 1997:246–7.
68 Elder Mark E. Peterson 'Race problems. As they affect the Church', 27 August 1954.
69 Embry 2005:60.
70 Kühl 1994: *passim*.
71 Montagu 1997:53.
72 Kühl 1994: *passim*.
73 Montagu 1997:206, cf. Genesis 11.1–9.
74 Sellström 1999:221–3.
75 Ghosh 2010; Pandey 2010.
76 Overdorf 2008.
77 Sengupta & Siwach 2010.
78 Pandey 2010.
79 Johri 2007.
80 *Indo-Asian News Service* 2010.
81 *Kamasutra* 1.5.
82 *Kathasaritsagara* 112, cf. Vanita 2005:109.
83 *Laws of Manu* 3.15.
84 *Laws of Manu* 3.17.
85 *Laws of Manu* 3.6–11.
86 Böck & Rao 2001:17.
87 Den Uyl 2005:143.
88 Broido 1993:71.
89 Werbner 2001:421–3.
90 Robinson 2003:78–9.
91 *Times of India* 2007.
92 Stirrat 1982:14–15.
93 Mani [1993]:932; Rye [1993]:732.
94 Therborn 2004:108–9.
95 Hollup 2001:221.
96 Baumann 1996:151–2.
97 Hollup 2001:231.
98 Mani [1993]:932.
99 Kannabiran & Kannabiran 2002:66.
100 *BBC* 2004; Nelson & Hasnain 2006.
101 Koran 2.221.
102 Koran 5.5.
103 Koran 4.34.
104 Murray & Roscoe 1997:304.
105 N. Roth 1982:29–30, 44–45; Crompton 2003:169.
106 K. McCarthy 2007:134.
107 'Marriage procedures between Muslim and Non-Muslim' on *www.malaysia.gov.my*,

http://www.malaysia.gov.my/EN/Relevant%20Topics/Society%20and%20Life/Citizen/Family/Marriage/ProcedureMarriageMuslimandNonMuslim/Pages/MarriageBetweenMuslimandNonMuslim.aspx.

7 Sex Beyond the Mortal Sphere

1 *The Homeric Hymn to Aphrodite*, 5.206–14; *Iliad*, 20.232–5.
2 Sophocles, according to Athenaeus, *Deipn.* 3.602e, cf. *Iliad* 20.232–35; *Homeric Hymn to Aphrodite* 5.202–6; Pindar, *Ol.* 1.43–45; Ps-Lucian, *Charidemus* 7; various painted vases.
3 The Bremner-Rhind-Papyrus, *British Museum* 10188.
4 Kinsley 1988:43.
5 Vanita 2005:74.
6 Doniger O'Flaherty 1981:150; *Odyssey* 8.266–366.
7 Scheidel [2004]:93.
8 Koran 22.5, 23.12–14.
9 Luke 1.35, cf. Matthew 1.18.
10 Ps-Apollodorus *Bibl.* 3.1.1.
11 Euripides *Helen* 16–19; Pausanias *Descr.* 3.16.1; Ps-Apollodorus *Bibl.* 3.10.7.
12 Veyne [1983]:112.
13 Arrian *Anabasis* 151, cf. Plutarch *Alexander* 2.4.
14 Suetonius 94.4.
15 Pausanias *Descr.* 4.14.7.
16 Pausanias *Descr.* 2.10.3.
17 Pausanias *Descr.* 6.6.4.
18 Plutarch *Lysander* 26.1–4.
19 *Bhagavatam Purana* 10.33.
20 *Bhagavatam Purana* 10.59.
21 In Tamil versions of the *Mahabharata*. See Vanita 2005:75.
22 Vanita 2005:75–6.
23 *Kamasutra* 4.1.
24 Genesis 6.2, 6.4.
25 Jubilees 7.20–21; 2 Peter 2.4–5.
26 Jubilees 20.5; Test. Naph. 3.4–5; 2 Peter 2.4, 2.6–8, cf. Genesis 19.5; Bailey 1955:12–13, 16.
27 Koran 55.56, 55.74.
28 Bouhdiba [1975]:69.
29 Sengers 2003:243.
30 Bouhdiba [1975]:58.
31 Athanasius *Vita Antonii* 5.5.
32 Athanasius *Vita Antonii* 6.1.
33 Augustine *De civitate Dei* 15.23.
34 Elliott 1997:14–15.
35 Thomas Aquinas *Summa Theologiae* 1.51.3.
36 Stephens 2002:69–70.
37 Stephens 2002:106.

38 In order to boost the reputation of his book, Kramer cited Jacob Sprenger, head of the Catholic inquisition in Germany, as his co-author.
39 Heinrich Kramer & Jacob Sprenger *Malleus Maleficarum* 1.3 , cf. Genesis 6.2, 6.4.
40 Heinrich Kramer & Jacob Sprenger *Malleus Maleficarum* 1.4.
41 1 Corinthians 11.10.
42 Heinrich Kramer & Jacob Sprenger *Malleus Maleficarum* 1.3.
43 Heinrich Kramer & Jacob Sprenger *Malleus Maleficarum* 1.3.
44 Heinrich Kramer & Jacob Sprenger *Malleus Maleficarum* 1.6.
45 Stephens 2002:54.
46 Heinrich Kramer & Jacob Sprenger *Malleus Maleficarum* 1.4.
47 Heinrich Kramer & Jacob Sprenger *Malleus Maleficarum* 2.1.4.
48 Heinrich Kramer & Jacob Sprenger *Malleus Maleficarum* 2.1.4.
49 Pope Innocent 8 'Summis desiderantes', 5 December 1484.
50 Stephens 2002:2.
51 Stephens 2002:5.
52 *Joy of Satan Ministries*, http://www.angelfire.com/empire/serpentis666/Incubus.html.
53 Chryssides 2003:54.
54 Denzler 2003:304–5; Partridge 2003:28; Rothstein 2003:269.
55 Koran 37.40–49, 44.54, 52.17–20, 55.56–8, 55.72–6, 56.22–40, 78.31–4.
56 Koran 55.56, 55.74.
57 Bouhdiba [1975]:85.
58 Muslim Ibn al-Hajjaj *Sahih Muslim* 40.6793, 40.6707.
59 Muslim Ibn al-Hajjaj *Sahih Muslim* 40.6795–96.
60 Koran 13.23, 40.8.
61 Tirmidhi *Sunan* 1.35.6.
62 Ibn Kathir *Tafsir* in his commentary to Koran 56.
63 Ibn Kathir *Tafsir* in his commentary to Koran 56.
64 Tirmidhi *Sunan* 4.21.2687.
65 Koran 52.24, 56.17–18, 76.19, cf. Wafer 1997:90.
66 Miller 1996:26–7.
67 Luke 20.35; Mark 12.25; Matthew 22.30.
68 Forrest 1999:31.

8 Because You're Worth It

1 Westboro Baptist Church 'God hates Sweden' on http://www.godhatessweden.com/sweden/godswrath.html and http://www.godhatessweden.com/sweden/government.html.
2 Sermon by Fred Phelps, head of the Westboro Baptist Church, 16 March 2008, at http://www.westborobaptistchurch.com/written/sermons/outlines/Sermon_20080316.pdf.
3 Matthew 5.27–32.
4 Galatians 5.19–21.
5 Revelation 21.8.
6 Revelation 14.4, my italics.

7 Apocalypse of Peter 23.
8 Apocalypse of Peter 31.
9 Dante Alighieri *Inferno* 5.
10 Dante Alighieri *Inferno* 15.
11 Dante Alighieri *Inferno* 18.
12 Dante Alighieri *Purgatorio* 25–7.
13 Bernardino of Siena *Del vizione dei sodomiti*, Translated in Crompton 2003:254.
14 Bates 2004:137.
15 Blumenthal 2008.
16 Kennedy & Cianciotto 2006:2.
17 Kennedy & Cianciotto 2006:4.
18 Kennedy & Cianciotto 2006:5.
19 Yardley 1999.
20 Ole Kristian Hallesby on NRK (Norwegian Radio), 25 January 1953.
21 Holbek 2008, my italics.
22 Fuglehaug 2008.
23 Søderlind 2006.
24 Kjær 2002:17.
25 Winterkjær & Dalchow 2000.
26 Palacios [1919]:92, *passim*.
27 Koran 25.68–70.
28 Imam Bukhari *Sahih Bukhari* 2.23.329; Muslim Ibn al-Hajjaj *Sahih Muslim* 1.171, 1.172.
29 Schimmel 1994:80.
30 Jacobson 1998:106.
31 *Laws of Manu* 5.159–61.
32 *Laws of Manu* 3.17.
33 *Laws of Manu* 9.30, 5.164.
34 *Laws of Manu* 12.59.
35 *Laws of Manu* 12.58.
36 *Mahabharata* 13.145.
37 Pattanaik 2001:8.
38 Dundas 2008:194.
39 *Parajika* 4.
40 Young 2004:203.
41 Young 2004:206.
42 Young 2004:203.
43 Young 2004:205.
44 *Sattisimbalivana Jataka* 5.453.
45 Cf. Ginsburg 2003:147:fig. 3.
46 Bullough 1976:294.
47 'Reports to the General Assembly of the Free Church of Scotland,' cited in Davidson 2001:225.
48 Harding 2000:160.
49 *National Research Council* 1993:130.
50 'First Presidency Statement on AIDS,' July 1988, my italics. http://www.lds.org/ldsorg/v/index.jsp?vgnextoid=2354fccf2b7db010VgnVCM100

0004d82620aRCRD&locale=0&sourceId=7f12d7630a27b010VgnVCM1000004d82620a____&hideNav=1.

51 Harding 2000:160.

52 Shelp 1994:322.

53 Greeley 1991.

54 Gold 1992:158.

55 Allen 2002:143.

56 *National Research Council* 1993:131.

57 *National Research Council* 1993:129–31, 135, 138–49; Allen 2002:152–3.

58 Bullough 1976:393.

59 Conner 2003:17.

60 Baum 1993:24.

61 Bullough 1976:294.

62 Yao 2003:87.

63 Bullough 1976:288.

64 Yao 2003:85–6.

65 Bullough 1976:288.

66 Bullough 1976:290.

67 Yao 2003:86.

68 Yao 2003:87–8.

69 Yao 2003:90.

70 Jubilees 7.20–21; 2 Peter 2.4–5.

71 Eron 1993:111.

72 *Concilium Parisiense* 34, translated in Crompton 2003:158.

73 Wiesner–Hanks 2000:109.

74 Genesis 19.24.25.

75 Numbers 25.1–11.

76 Ezra 9.12.

77 Ezra 10.14.

78 Leviticus 18.1–29, my italics.

79 Justinian *Novella* 77.

80 *Las Sietes Partidas* 7.21, translated in Crompton 2003:200.

81 *Patrologia Latina* 97.909c-d; Crompton 2003:160.

82 Horrox 1994:116, 127, 141–2, 145–6, 193; Byrne 2004:41.

83 Horrox 1994:131–4.

84 Byrne 2004:117.

85 Castronovo 2001:145.

86 Bullough 1976:521.

87 Crompton 2003:463, reference to Leviticus 18.28.

88 Crompton 2003:463.

89 Boon 1989:241–42; Crompton 2003:464.

90 Dekker & van de Pol 1989:60, 79–80.

91 Boyer 1994:234.

92 Burack 2008:113.

93 Sermon by Fred Phelps, head of the Westboro Baptist Church, 16 March 2008, at http://www.westborobaptistchurch.com/written/sermons/outlines/Sermon_20080316.pdf

94 *CNN* 2001.
95 Z. Roth 2008.
96 *365gay* 2007.
97 Ivar Kristianslund, 'Norway's Security in Danger!', at *Ivar Kristianlund's Net News-sheet*, 23 June 2008, http://www.ikrist.com/cgi-bin/npublish/search.cgi?keyword=kaldeernes
98 *365gay* 2005a.
99 *BBC* 2010b.
100 *BBC* 2009b.
101 *365gay* 2006a.
102 *365gay* 2008a.

9 Sacred Sex, Ritual Sex

1 Berglund 2001:4.
2 Urban 2006:105.
3 Urban 2003:40.
4 Urban 2006:89.
5 Urban 2003:41.
6 Urban 2006:89.
7 Urban 2006:90.
8 Osho *From sex to superconsciousness*. Pune: Thomson Press 1973:35.
9 Urban 2003:242.
10 Urban 2003:245–6.
11 Urban 2003:147.
12 Urban 2003:231–5.
13 Puttick 1997:60.
14 Urban 2003:261.
15 Baum 1993:13.
16 Elliston 1999:136.
17 Schieffelin 1982:162, 177, 149.
18 Herdt 1984:171–3; Herdt 1981:2.
19 Steinsland 2005:411–12.
20 Ibn Fadlan *Risala* 89–91.
21 Curry 1997:79; *BBC* 2006a.
22 Urban 2006:25, 121.
23 Urban 2006:11, 109–10.
24 Urban 2006:125.
25 Russell 1972:253.
26 Russell 1972:253; Urban 2006:195.
27 Urban 2006:202.
28 Gerald Gardner *The Gardnerian Book of Shadows*. Forgotten Books 2008 [1950]:54.
29 Urban 2006:25.
30 Puttick 1997:121.
31 Puttick 1997:120.
32 Deuteronomy 23.17; 1 Kings 14.22–4, 15.12, 22.47; 2 Kings 23.7.

33 Budin 2006:83–4; M. T. Roth 2006:23–4.
34 M. T. Roth 2006:23.
35 Deuteronomy 23.17.
36 1 Kings 14.24.
37 1 Kings 15.12, 22.47; 2 Kings 23.7.
38 1 Kings 15.12; 2 Kings 23.7.
39 Marglin 1985:95.
40 Marglin 1985:90.
41 Marglin 1985:91.
42 Marglin 1985:98.
43 Marglin 1985:96; Vanita 2005:77.
44 Vanita 2005:77.
45 Mark 1.16; Matthew 4.19, cf. Luke 5.11.
46 Father David [Berg] 'You *are* the love of god!' 5 June 1978. http://www.xfamily.org/index.php/You_Are_The_Love_of_God!
47 Puttick 1997:79.
48 'FF stats', 1 October 1988, http://xfamily.org/images/a/a8/FF-Stats-1988-10-01.jpg.
49 Puttick 1997:52.
50 Bornoff [1991]:384–85.
51 Lee 1995:84.
52 Grove 2008.
53 Bornoff [1991]:148.
54 Glick 2003:97.
55 Wiesner-Hanks 2000:66.
56 Lee 1995:84.
57 Bornoff [1991]:242.
58 Bornoff [1991]:156, 468.
59 Bullough 1976:266.
60 White 1998:269–70.
61 Dover 2002:20.
62 Pliny *Hist. Nat.* 28.7.39.
63 Bourget 2006:66.
64 Bourget 2006:65:figs. 1.46, 2.1–10, 2.13–14, 2.17–20, 2.32, 2.34–45, 2.50–60, 2.67, 2.71–4, 2.88, 2.101, 2.120, 2.124, 2.126–7, 2.129–31, 2.134–36, 2.140–41, 2.144–5, 3.1–2, 3.4, 4.43.
65 Bourget 2006:figs. 2.140–41, 2.144–45, 4.43.
66 Bourget 2006:180–82, figs. 3.1–2.
67 Bourget 2006:fig. 3.4.
68 Bourget 2006:178.
69 Bourget 2006:65.
70 Solli 2005:50; Steinsland 2005:150.
71 Solli 2005:50.
72 Adam of Bremen 4.26.
73 Steinsland 2005:152.
74 Steinsland 2005:350–51.
75 Gilhus 2004:177, 180–82.

76 Khalik 2008; Suriyani & Nathalia 2008.

77 Carpenter & Carpenter 2002:132.

10 Religio-Sexual Priorities

1 *The Supreme and Holy Congregation of The Holy Office* 'Instruction on the manner of proceeding in cases of solicitation' 1962, in the *Guardian* 17 August 2003 (http://image.guardian.co.uk/sys-files/Observer/documents/2003/08/16/Criminales.pdf); 1.

2 *Ibid.* 15–16.

3 *Ibid.* 16.

4 *Ibid.* 3, my italics.

5 *Ibid.* 4.

6 *Ibid.* 7.

7 *Ibid.* 3.

8 *Ibid.* 18.

9 *Ibid.* 2.

10 *Ibid.* 3.

11 Barrie 2002:69.

12 Egerton & Dunklin 2002.

13 Pullella 2010.

14 Pancevski & Follain 2010.

15 Gentile 2010.

16 Neustein & Lesher 2002:80–81; *Associated Press* 2008.

17 MacFarquhar 2005.

18 Kannabiran & Kannabiran 2002:66.

19 Genesis 20.12.

20 Leviticus 20.17.

21 Numbers 12.1–15.

22 Genesis 19.1–9, 19.14.

23 Deuteronomy 22.23–24.

24 Genesis 19.18.

25 *A.D.T. v. United Kingdom*, judgement of the European Court of Human Rights, 31 July 2000, §§26, 38–39.

26 Pope Benedict 16 'Address of his Holiness Benedict XVI to the members of the Roman Curia for the traditional exchange of Christmas greetings', 22 December 2008.

27 Young 1995:279–80.

28 Tertullian *Apology* 50.

29 Bosworth, van Donzel, Lewis & Pellat 1986:777; Crompton 1997:150.

30 *Catholic Online* 2003.

31 Johannessen 2007.

32 *BBC* 2009a.

33 Kington & Quinn 2010.

34 Deuteronomy 5.22–3.

35 Koran 2.178.

36 Council of Elvira, Canons 8, 65, 5.

37 *BBC* 2002.

38 *Economist* 2007a.

39 *365gay* 2005b.

40 *365gay* 2006b.

41 Thornberry 2006.

42 Hellemann 2007.

43 *Congregation for the Doctrine of the Faith* 'Some considerations concerning the response to legislative proposals on the non-discrimination of homosexual persons', 22 July 1992, §§1, 10–13 (www.ewtn.com/library/CURIA/CDFHOMOL.HTM); *Congregation for the Doctrine of the Faith* 'Considerations regarding proposals to give legal recognition to unions between homosexual persons', 3 June 2003, §§4–5 (www.vatican.va/roman_curia/congregations/cfaith/documents/rc_con_cfaith_doc_20030731_homosexual-unions_en.html); Pope John Paul 2 'Message of the Holy Father John Paul II for the 38th World Communications Day', 23 January 2004, §§3–4 (www.vatican.va/holy_father/john_paul_ii/messages/communications/documents/hf_jp-ii_mes_20040124_world-communications-day_en.html). Cf. Endsjø 2005; Endsjø 2008c.

44 Pigott 2008.

45 Nebuhr 1995.

46 Rogers 1999:30–31.

47 Letvik 2007.

BIBLIOGRAPHY

365gay 2008a. 'Demands for censure after gay earthquake remark' at *www.365gay.com*, 21 February 2008, http://365gay.com/Newscon08/02/022108shake.htm.

365gay 2008b. 'Mormon excommunicated for sexy male calendar' at *www.365gay.com*, 14 Jul 2008, http://365gay.com/Newscon08/07/071408cal.htm.

365gay 2008c. 'Religious leaders call for fast in support of gay marriage ban' at *www.365gay.com*, 25 September 2008, http://www.365gay.com/news/religious-leaders-call-for-fast-in-support-of-gay-marriage-ban/.

365gay 2008d. 'Nepal Supreme Court orders full LGBT rights' at *www.365gay.com*, 19 November 2008, http://www.365gay.com/news/nepal-supreme-court-orders-full-lgbt-rights/.

365gay 2007. 'Bishop: Gays, permissible society responsible for disasters' at *www.365gay.com*, 1 July 2007, http://365gay.com/Newscon07/07/070107bishop.htm.

365gay 2006a. 'Rabbi: Gays responsible for bird flu' at *www.365gay.com*, 21 March 2006, http://365gay.com/Newscon06/03/032106israel.htm.

365gay 2006b. '"Bounty" for killing gays at world pride' at *www.365gay.com*, 11 July 2006, http://365gay.com/Newscon06/07/071106jerusalem.htm.

365gay 2005a. 'Gays responsible for tsunami Muslim cleric charges' at *www.365gay.com*, 5 January 2005, http://www.365gay.com/newscon05/01/010505gayDisaster.htm.

365gay 2005b. 'Religious leaders demand cancellation of World Pride' at *www.365gay.com*, 30 January 2005, http://www.365gay.com/newscon05/01/013005jerusalem.htm.

Abanes, Richard 2003. *One nation under gods. A history of the Mormon Church.* New York: Four Walls Eight Windows.

AbuKhalil, As'as 1993. 'A note on the study of homosexuality in the Arab/Islamic civilization' in *Arab Studies Journal* 1:32–4.

Afrol News 2005. 'Church, ANC welcome same-sex marriage ruling' in *Afrol News*, 2 December 2005, http://afrol.com/articles/17515.

Agha, Sohail 2000. 'Potential for HIV transmission among truck drivers in Pakistan' in *AIDS* 4:2404–6.

Akst, Leslie 2003. 'Abstinence pledges usually broken' at *MedicineNet.com*, 21 October 2003, http://www.medicinenet.com/script/main/art.asp?articlekey=37696.

Aldrich, Robert 2003. *Colonialism and homosexuality.* London and New York: Routledge.

Alexander, Michele G. and Terri D. Fisher 2003. 'Truth and consequences. Using the bogus pipeline to examine sex differences in self-reported sexuality' in *Journal of Sex Research* 40:27–35.

Allen, Peter Lewis 2002. *The wages of sin. Sex and disease, past and present.* Chicago: University of Chicago Press.

Alpert, Rebecca 2003. 'Sex in Jewish law and culture' in David W. Machacek and Melissa M. Wilcox (eds) *Sexuality and the world's religions.* Santa Barbara, Denver and Oxford: ABC-CLIO: 177–202.

Altman, Micah and Philip A. Klinkner 2006. 'Measuring the difference between white voting and polling on interracial marriage' in *Du Bois Review. Social Science Research on Race* 3: 299–315.

Amory, Deborah P. 1998. '*Mashoga, mabasha,* and *magai.* "Homosexuality" on the East African coast' in Stephen O. Murray and Will Roscoe. *Boy-wives and female husbands. Studies of African homosexualities.* Basingstoke: Macmillan: 67–87.

Angus Reid Global Monitor 2006. 'Eight EU countries back same-sex marriage' in *Angus Reid Global Monitor*, 24 December 2006, http://www.angus-reid.com/polls/view/eight_eu_countries_back_same_sex_marriage/.

Associated Press 2008. 'US: Child sex abuse claims divide Orthodox community' in *Associated Press* 24 November 2008, http://www.ynetnews.com/articles/0,7340,L-3627632,00.html.

Atkins, David C., Donald H. Baucom and Neil S. Jacobson 2001. 'Understanding infidelity. Correlates in a national random sample' in *Journal of Family Psychology* 15:735-49.

Bailey, Derrick Sherwin 1955. *Homosexuality and the western Christian tradition.* London: Longmans.

Baird, Vanessa 2001. *The no-nonsense guide to sexual diversity.* Oxford: New International Publications.

Bald, Margaret 1998. *Banned books. Literature suppressed on religious grounds.* New York: Facts on File.

Bandlien, Bjørn 2001. 'Å være ragr. Liminalt kjønn i norrøn mytologi' in *Din. Tidsskrift for religion og kultur* nr. 2–3, 2001:53–60.

Banerjee, Neela 2008. 'Dancing the night away, with a higher purpose' in *New York Times*, 19 May 2008, http://www.nytimes.com/2008/05/19/us/19purity.html?_r=1andoref=slogin.

Barakat, Halim 1993. *The Arab world. Society, culture, and state.* Berkeley: University of California Press.

Barden, J. C. 1987. 'Marital rape. Drive for tougher laws is pressed' in *New York Times*, 13 May 1987, http://www.nytimes.com/1987/05/13/us/marital-rape-drive-for-tougher-laws-is-pressed.html.

Barrie, Iain A. G. 2002. 'A broken trust: Canadian priests, brothers, pedophilia, and the media' in Dane S. Claussen (ed.) *Sex, religion, media.* Lanham: Rowman and Littlefield: 65–77.

Basar, Nejat 2004. 'Why adultery?' in *Turkish Daily News*, 15 September 2004, http://www.turkishdailynews.com.tr/archives.php?id=37664.

Bates, Stephen 2004. *A church at war. Anglicans and homosexuality.* London and New York: I. B. Tauris.

Baum, Robert M. 1993. 'Homosexuality and the traditional religions of the Americas and Africa' in Arlene Swidler (ed.) *Homosexuality and world religions.* Valley Forge: Trinity Press International: 1–46.

Baumann, Gerd 1996. *Contesting culture. Discourses of identity in multi-ethnic London.* Cambridge: Cambridge University Press.

BBC 2010a. 'Valentine attackers held in India' at *news.bbc.co.uk*, 14 February 2010, http://news.bbc.co.uk/2/hi/south_asia/7890457.stm.

BBC 2010b. 'Iranian cleric "blames quakes on promiscuous women"' at *news.bbc.co.uk*, 20 April 2010, http://news.bbc.co.uk/2/hi/middle_east/8631775.stm.

BBC 2009a. 'Pope tells Africa "condoms wrong"' at *news.bbc.co.uk*, 17 March 2009. http://news.bbc.co.uk/2/hi/7947460.stm

BBC 2009b. 'Indonesia minister says immorality causes disasters' at *news.bbc.co.uk*, 28 November 2009, http://news.bbc.co.uk/2/hi/asia-pacific/8384827.stm.

BBC 2008a. 'Saudi men arrested for "flirting"' at *news.bbc.co.uk*, 23 February 2008, http://news.bbc.co.uk/2/hi/middle_east/7260314.stm.

BBC 2008b. 'Saudi judge condemns "immoral TV"' at *news.bbc.co.uk*, 12 September 2008, http://news.bbc.co.uk/2/hi/middle_east/7613575.stm.

BBC 2007a. 'Ugandan adultery law "too sexist"' at *news.bbc.co.uk*, 5 April 2007, http://news.bbc.co.uk/2/hi/africa/6528869.stm.

BBC 2007b. 'Iran "adulterer" stoned to death' at *news.bbc.co.uk*, 10 July 2007, http://news.bbc.co.uk/2/hi/middle_east/6288156.stm.

BBC 2007c. 'Nepal court rules on gay rights' at *news.bbc.co.uk*, 21 December 2007, http://news.bbc.co.uk/2/hi/south_asia/7156577.stm.

BBC 2006a. 'China acts on funeral strippers' at *news.bbc.co.uk*, 23 August 2006, http://news.bbc.co.uk/2/hi/asia-pacific/5280312.stm.

BBC 2006b. 'Islamists debate rape law moves' at *news.bbc.co.uk*, 16 November 2006, http://news.bbc.co.uk/2/hi/south_asia/6153994.stm.

BBC 2005a. 'Spain in same-sex marriage rally' at *news.bbc.co.uk*, 18 June 2005, http://news.bbc.co.uk/2/hi/europe/4106890.stm.

BBC 2005b. 'First gay "marriage" in Pakistan' at *news.bbc.co.uk*, 5 October 2005, http://news.bbc.co.uk/2/hi/south_asia/4313210.stm.

BBC 2004. 'Men held over "caste gang-rape"' at *news.bbc.co.uk*, 10 July 2004, http://news.bbc.co.uk/2/hi/south_asia/3882833.stm.

BBC 2003. '"Honour killings" law blocked' at *news.bbc.co.uk*, 8 September 2003. http://news.bbc.co.uk/2/hi/middle_east/3088828.stm.

BBC 2002. 'Saudi police "stopped" fire rescue' at *news.bbc.co.uk*, 15 March 2002, http://news.bbc.co.uk/2/hi/middle_east.1874471.stm.

Benkov, Edith 2001. 'The erased lesbian. Sodomy and the legal tradition in medieval Europe' in Francesca Canadé Sautman and Pamela Sheingorn (eds) *Same sex love and desire among women in the Middle Ages*. New York and Houndmills: Palgrave: 101–22.

Bennett, Paula and Vernon A. Rosario II 1995. 'Introduction: The politics of solitary pleasures' in Paula Bennett and Vernon A. Rosario II (eds) *Solitary pleasures. The historical, literary, and artistic discourse of autoeroticism*. New York and London: Routledge: 1–17.

Berger, Michael S. 2005a. 'Marriage, sex, and family in the Jewish tradition. A historical overview' in Michael J. Broyde and Michael Ausubel (eds) *Marriage, sex, and family in Judaism*. Lanham and Oxford: Rowman and Littlefield Publishers: 1–14.

Berger, Michael S. 2005b. 'Two models of medieval Jewish marriage. A preliminary study' in Michael J. Broyde and Michael Ausubel (eds) *Marriage, sex, and family in Judaism*. Lanham and Oxford: Rowman and Littlefield Publishers: 116–48.

Berger, Michael 2005c. 'Maimonides on sex and marriage' in Michael J. Broyde and Michael Ausubel (eds) *Marriage, sex, and family in Judaism*. Lanham and Oxford: Rowman and Littlefield Publishers: 149–91.

Berglund, Torjer 2001. '*Babylonin portto helvittiin*. Om en læstadiansk vekkelse, kjønnshår og sex' in *Din. Tidsskrift for religion og kultur* nr. 2–3, 2001:2–8.

Beversluis, Joel (ed.) 2000. *Sourcebook of the world's religions. An interfaith guide to religion and spirituality*. Novato: New World Library.

Bjørke, Christian Nicolai 2009. '– Trekk deg Kjølaas' in *Vårt Land*, 17 January 2009, http://www.vl.no/kristenliv/article4057260.ece.

Blanc, Ann K. and Ann A. Way 1998. 'Sexual behaviour and contraceptive knowledge and use among adolescents in developing countries' in *Studies in Family Planning* 29:106–16.

Blumenthal, Max 2008. 'Pastor Hagee: The Antichrist is gay, "partially Jewish, as was Adolph Hitler" (Paging Joe Lieberman!)' at *www.huffingtonpost.com*, 2 June 2008. http://www.huffingtonpost.com/max-blumenthal/pastor-hagee-the-antichri_b_104608.html

Boon, L. J. 1989 'Those damned sodomites. Public images of sodomy in the eighteenth century Netherlands' in Kent Gerrard and Gert Hekma (eds) *The pursuit of sodomy. Male homosexuality in renaissance and enlightenment Europe.* New York and London: Haworth Press: 237–48.

Boone, Joseph 2001. 'Vacation cruises, or, the homoerotics of orientalism' in John Charles Hawley (ed.) *Postcolonial queer. Theoretical intersections.* Albany: State University of New York Press: 48–78.

Bornoff, Nicholas [1991]. *Pink samurai. Love, marriage and sex in contemporary Japan.* London: HarperCollins 1994.

Boswell, John 1994. *Same sex unions in pre-modern Europe.* New York: Villiard Books.

Boswell, John [1980]. *Christianity, social tolerance, and homosexuality.* Chicago and London: The University of Chicago Press 1981.

Bosworth, C. E., E. van Donzel, B. Lewis and Ch. Pellat 1986. 'Liwat' in C. E. Bosworth, E. van Donzel, B. Lewis and Ch. Pellat (eds) *The encyclopedia of Islam. New Edition. Volume 5.* Leiden: E. J. Brill: 776–9.

Bouhdiba, Abdelwahab [1975]. *Sexuality in Islam.* London: Routledge and Kegan Paul 1985.

Bourget, Steve 2006. *Sex, death, and sacrifice in Moche religion and visual culture.* Austin: University of Texas Press.

Boyer, Paul 1994. *When time shall be no more. Prophecy belief in modern American culture.* Cambridge, Mass.: Harvard University Press.

Broido, Michael M. 1993. 'Killing, lying, stealing, and adultery. A problem of interpretation in the Tantras' in Donald S. Lopez Jr (ed.) *Buddhist hermeneutics.* Delhi: Motilal Banarsidass: 71–118.

Bromark, Stian and Dag Herbjørnsrud 2002. *Blanke løgner, skitne sannheter. En kritikk av det nye verdensbildet.* Oslo: Tiden Norsk Forlag.

Brook, Vincent 2006. '"Y'all killed him, we didn't!" Jewish self-hatred and *The Larry Sanders Show*' in Vincent Brook (ed.) *You should see yourself. Jewish identity in postmodern American culture.* New Brunswick, New Jersey: Rutgers University Press: 298–318.

Brooke, James 1991. '"Honor" killing of wives is outlawed in Brazil' in the *New York Times*, 29 March 1991. http://www.nytimes.com/1991/03/29/us/honor-killing-of-wives-is-outlawed-in-brazil.html?pagewanted=1?pagewanted=1

Brooks, Geraldine 1995. *Nine parts of desire. The hidden world of Islamic women.* New York: Anchor Books Doubleday.

Brooten, Bernadette J. 2002. 'Naturen, loven og det alminnelige' in Halvor Moxnes, Jostein Børtnes and Dag Øistein Endsjø (eds) *Naturlig sex? Seksualitet og kjønn i den kristne antikken.* Oslo: Gyldendal Akademisk: 73–98.

Broyde, Michael J. 2005. 'Jewish law and the abandonment of marriage. Diverse models of sexuality and reproduction in the Jewish view, and the return to monogamy in the modern era' in Michael J. Broyde and Michael Ausubel (eds) *Marriage, sex, and family in Judaism.* Lanham and Oxford: Rowman and Littlefield Publishers: 88–115.

Brundage, James A. 1987. *Law, sex, and Christian society in medieval Europe.* Chicago: The University of Chicago Press.

Brückner, Hannah and Peter Bearman 2005. 'After the promise: The STD consequences of adolescent virginity pledges' in *Journal of Adolescent Health* 36:271–78, http://www.yale.edu/ciqle/PUBLICATIONS/AfterThePromise.pdf.

Budin, Stephanie L. 2006. 'Sacred prostitution in the first person' in Christopher A. Faraone and Laura K. McClure (eds) *Prostitutes and courtesans in the ancient world*. Madison: University of Wisconsin Press: 77–91.

Bullough, Vern L. 1976. *Sexual variance in society and history*. Chicago: The University of Chicago Press.

Bullough, Vern L. and Bonnie 1987. *Women and prostitution. A social history*. Buffalo: Prometheus Books.

Bullough, Vern L. and Bonnie 1977. *Sin, sickness, and sanity. A history of sexual attitudes*. New York and London: Garland Publishing.

Burack, Cynthia 2008. *Sin, sex, and democracy. Antigay rhetoric and the Christian right*. Albany: SUNY Press.

Byrne, Joseph P. 2004. *The Black Death*. Westport: Greenwood Publishing Group.

Böck, Monika and Aparna Rao 2001. 'Introduction. Indigeneous models and kinship theories. An introduction to a South Asian perspective' in Monika Böck and Aparna Rao (eds) *Culture, creation, and procreation. Concept of kinship in South Asian practice*. New York and Oxford: Berghahn Books: 1–51.

Cabezón, José Ignacio 1993. 'Homosexuality and Buddhism' in Arlene Swidler (ed.) *Homosexuality and world religions*. Valley Forge: Trinity Press International: 81–101.

Canadian Broadcast Standards Council. Ontario Panel 2005. 'OMNI.1 re an episode of the *Jimmy Swaggart Telecast*' at *www.cbsc.ca* 19 April 2005. http://www.cbsc.ca/english/decisions/2005/050614a.php.

Carpenter, Russ and Blyth Carpenter 2002. *The blessings of Bhutan*. Honolulu: University of Hawai'i Press.

Carroll, Joseph 2007. 'Most Americans approve of interracial marriages' at *Gallup News Service*, 16 August 2007, http://www.gallup.com/poll/28417/Most-Americans-Approve-Interracial-Marriages.aspx.

Castronovo, Russ 2001. 'Enslaving passions. White male sexuality and the evasion of race' in Tracy Fessenden, Nicholas F. Radel and Magdalena J. Zaborowska (eds) *The Puritan origins of American sex. Religion, sexuality, and national identity in American literature*. New York and London: Routledge: 145–68.

Catholic Online 2003. 'Cardinal Lopez Trujillo on ineffectiveness of condoms to curb AIDS' at *Catholic Online*, 12 November 2003, http://www.catholic.org/featured/headline.php?ID=488.

Cavendish, James C. 2003. 'The Vatican and the laity. Diverging paths in Catholic understanding of sexuality' in David W. Machacek and Melissa M. Wilcox (eds) *Sexuality and the world's religions*. Santa Barbara, Denver and Oxford: ABC-CLIO: 202–29.

Chebel d'Appollonia, Ariane 1998. *L'extrême-droite en France. Du Maurras à Le Pen*. Brüssel: Editions Complexe.

Childs, Geoff H. 2004. *Tibetan diary. From birth to death and beyond in a Himalayan valley of Nepal*. Berkeley: University of California Press.

Chryssides, George D. 2003. 'Scientific creationism. A study of the Raëlian Church' in Christopher Hugh Partridge (ed.) *UFO religions*. London and New York: Routledge: 45–61.

Clapp, Jane 1972. *Art censorship. A chronology of proscribed and prescribed art*. Metuchen: The Scarecrow Press.

Cleminson, Richard M. and Efigenio Amezúa 1999. 'Spain. The political and social context of sex reform in the late nineteenth and early twentieth century' in Franz X. Eder, Lesley A. Hall and Gert Hekma (eds) *Sexual cultures in Europe. National histories*. Manchester and New York: Manchester University Press: 173–96.

Cline, Austin 2003. 'Canada's largest church endorses same-sex marriage' at *about.com*, 22 August 2003, http://atheism.about.com/b/2003/08/22/canadas-largest-church-endorses-same-sex-marriage.htm.

CNN 2007. 'Utah polygamist released from prison on parole after serving 6 years' at *cnn.com*,7 August 2007, http://edition.cnn.com/2007/US/08/07/polygamist.ap/index.html.

CNN 2001. 'Falwell apologizes to gays, feminists, lesbians' at *cnn.com*, 14 September 2001, http://archives.cnn.com/2001/US/09/14/Falwell.apology/.

Conkin, Dennis 1998. 'The Dalai Lama and gay love' in Winston Leyland (ed.) *Queer dharma. Voices of gay Buddhists. Vol. 1.* New York: Garland Press: 168–71.

Conner, Randy P. 2003. 'Sexuality and gender in African spiritual traditions' in David W. Machacek and Melissa M. Wilcox (eds) *Sexuality and the world's religions.* Santa Barbara, Denver and Oxford: ABC-CLIO: 3–30.

Conner, Randy and Stephen Donaldson 1990. 'Buddhism' in Wayne Dynes (ed.) *Encyclopedia of homosexuality. Vol. 1.* New York: Garland Press: 168–71.

Copley, Antony 2006. *A spiritual Bloomsbury. Hinduism and homosexuality in the lives and writings of Edward Carpenter, E. M. Forster, and Christopher Isherwood.* Lanham: Lexington Books.

Crompton, Louis 2003. *Homosexuality and civilization*. Cambridge, Mass. and London: The Belnap Press.

Crompton, Louis 1997. 'Male love and Islamic law in Arab Spain' in Stephen Murray and Will Roscoe (eds) *Islamic homosexualities. Culture, history, and literature*. New York: New York University Press: 142–57.

Curry, Jeffrey 1997. *Passport Taiwan.* San Rafael: World Trade Press.

D'Antonio, Willam V., James D. Davidson, Dean R. Hoge and Katherine Meyer 2001. *American Catholics. Gender, generation, and commitment.* Walnut Creek: Altamira Press.

Davidson, Roger 2001. '"The price of the permissive society". The epidemology and control of VD and STDs in late-twentieth-century Scotland' in Roger Davidson and Lesley A. Hall (eds) *Sex, sin and suffering. Venereal disease and European society since 1870*. London and New York: Routledge: 220–36.

Davis, Christie 2006. *The strange death of moral Britain*. New Brunswick, New Jersey and London: Transaction Publishers.

Daynes, Kathryn M. 2001. *More wives than one. Transformation of the Mormon marriage system 1840–1910*. Urbana: University of Illinois Press.

Dekker, Rudolf M. and Lotte C. van de Pol 1989. *The tradition of female tranvestisism in early modern Europe*. New York: St Martin's Press.

Demaitre, Edmond 1937. *The Yogis of India*. London: G. Bias.

De Martino, Gianni 1992. 'An Italian in Morocco' in Arno Schmitt and Jehoeda Sofer (eds) *Sexuality and eroticism among males in Moslem societies*. New York: Harrington Park Press: 25–32.

Denzler, Brenda 2003. 'Attitudes towards religion and science in the UFO movement in the United States' in Christopher Hugh Partridge (ed.) *UFO religions*. London and New York: Routledge: 201–13.

Derrett, John Duncan Martin 1963. 'Divorce by caste custom' in *The Bombay Law Reporter* 65: 161–70.

Dewaraja, L. S. 1981. *The position of women in Buddhism*. Kandy: Buddhist Publication Society.

Dickerson, Brian 2007. 'Adultery could mean life, court finds' in *Detroit Free Press*, 15 January 2007, http://web.archive.org/web/20070206173058/http://freep.com/apps/pbcs.dll/article?AID=/20070115/COL04/701150333.

DNA 2007. 'Man "marries" hill to end Maoist menace' in *Daily News and Analysis* 29 December 2007, http://www.dnaindia.com/report.asp?newsid=1142123.

Doniger O'Flaherty, Wendy 1981. *Siva. The erotic ascetic*. Oxford: Oxford University Press.

Dorff, Elliot N. 2005. 'The Jewish family in America. Contemporary challenges and traditional resources' in Michael J. Broyde and Michael Ausubel (eds) *Marriage, sex, and family in Judaism*. Lanham and Oxford: Rowman and Littlefield Publishers: 214–43.

Dover, K. J. 2002. 'Classical Greek attitudes to sexual behaviour' in Laura McClure (ed.) *Sexuality and gender in the classical world. Readings and sources*. Oxford: Blackwell: 19–33.

Dover, K. J. [1978]. *Greek homosexuality*. London: Duckworth 1979.

Druckerman, Pamela 2007. *Lust in translation. The rules of infidelity from Tokyo to Tennessee*. London: Penguin Books.

Drummond, Andrew 2008. 'British man facing jail over his "adultery" with a Filipino woman asks. "Why won't the Foreign Office help us?"' in *Daily Mail*, 24 February 2008, http://www.dailymail.co.uk/femail/article-517821/British-man-facing-jail-adultery-Filipino-woman-asks-Why-wont-Foreign-Office-help-us.html.

Dundas, Paul 2008, 'Sthulabhadra's lodgings. Sexual restraint in Jainism' in Carl Olson (ed.) *Celibacy and religious traditions*. New York: Oxford University Press: 181–99.

Duran, Khalid 1993. 'Homosexuality and Islam' in Arlene Swidler (ed.) *Homosexuality and world religions*. Valley Forge: Trinity Press International: 181–97.

Durex 2005. *Give and receive. 2005 Global Sex Survey results*. London: Durex.

Dutch News 2010. 'Gay man on ChristienUnie MP list, because he's celibate' at *www.dutchnews.nl*, 3 June 2010, http://www.dutchnews.nl/news/archives/2010/06/gay_man_on_christenunie_mp_lis.php.

Economist 2008. 'Transvestites in Turkey. Gender-benders' in *The Economist*, 8 November 2008.

Economist 2007a. 'God, sex, drugs and politics' in *The Economist*, 10 February 2007.

Economist 2007b. 'China's corpse brides. Wet goods and dry goods' in *The Economist*, 28 July 2007.

Eder, Franz X., Lesley A. Hall and Gert Hekma 1999. 'Introduction' in Franz X. Eder, Lesley A. Hall and Gert Hekma (eds) *Sexual cultures in Europe. National histories*. Manchester and New York: Manchester University Press: 1–26.

Egerton, Brooks and Reese Dunklin 2002. 'Special report. Catholic bishops and sex abuse' in *Dallas Morning News*, 12 June 2002, http://www.dallasnews.com/cgi-bin/bi/dallas/2002/priests.cgi.

Eickelman, Dale F. and James Piscatori 2004. *Muslim politics*. Princeton: Princeton University Press.

Eikeland, Martin 2009. 'Skjevesland: Fullt mulig å være skilt biskop' in *Vårt Land*, 17 January 2009, http://www.vl.no/kristenliv/article4052800.ece.

Elliott, Dyan 1997. 'Pollution, illusion, and masculine disarray. Nocturnal emission and the sexuality of the clergy' in Karma Lochrie, Peggy McCracken and James A. Schulz (eds) *Constructing medieval sexuality*. Minneapolis: University of Minnesota Press: 1–23.

Ellison, Marvin M. 1993. 'Homosexuality and Protestantism' in Arlene Swidler (ed.) *Homosexuality and world religions.* Valley Forge: Trinity Press International: 149–79.

Elliston, Deborah A. 1999. 'Erotic anthropology. "Ritualized homosexuality" in Melanesia and beyond' in Morton Klass and Maxine Weisgrau (eds) *Across the boundaries of belief. Contemporary issues in the anthropology of religion.* Boulder and Oxford: Westview Press: 133–58.

Embry, Jessie L. 2005. 'Spanning the Priesthood Revelation (1978). Two multigenerational case studies' in Newell G. Bringhurst and Darron T. Smith (eds) *Black and Mormon.* Urbana: University of Illinois Press: 60–81.

Endsjø, Dag Øistein 2009. *Greek resurrection beliefs and the success of Christianity.* New York: Palgrave Macmillan.

Endsjø, Dag Øistein 2008a. *Primordial landscapes, incorruptible bodies. Desert asceticism and the Christian appropriation of Greek ideas on geography, bodies, and immortality.* New York: Peter Lang.

Endsjø, Dag Øistein 2008b. 'The queer periphery. Sexual deviancy and the cultural understanding of space' in *Journal of Homosexuality* 54:9–20.

Endsjø, Dag Øistein 2008c. 'Sex, nattverd og menneskerettigheter. Nye utfordringer for Den katolske kirke' in Tomas Hägg (ed.) *Kjetterne og kirken. Fra antikken til i dag.* Oslo: Scandinavian Academic Press 2008:209–22.

Endsjø, Dag Øistein 2005. 'Lesbian, gay, bisexual and transgender rights and the religious relativism of human rights' in *Human Rights Review*, 6:102–10.

ENI 2007. 'Ugandan church leaders concerned after old adultery law scrapped' in *Ecumenical News International*, 31 April 2007, www.eni.ch/highlights/news/shtml?2007/04.

Envio Team 1992. 'New legislation. A crime to be gay' in *Envio Digital* 133, www.envio.org.ni/articulo/2539.

Eppink, Andreas 1992. 'Moroccan boys and sex' in Arno Schmitt and Jehoeda Sofer (eds) *Sexuality and eroticism among males in Moslem societies.* New York: Harrington Park Press: 33–42.

Eron, John Lewis 1993. 'Homosexuality and Judaism' in Arlene Swidler (ed.) *Homosexuality and world religions.* Valley Forge: Trinity Press International: 103–34.

Ertelt, Steven 2008. 'Pope Benedict renews Catholic opposition to birth control contraception' at *LifeNews.com*, 3 October 2008, www.lifenews.com/int947.html.

Eshaghian, Tanaz 2008. *Be like others.* Documentary film. USA, Canada and Iran.

Esposito, John L. 2002. *What everyone needs to know about Islam.* New York and Oxford: Oxford University Press.

Eurostat 2007. *Europe in figures. Eurostat yearbook 2006–07.* Luxemburg: Office for Official Publications of the European Communities.

Eurostat 2005. *Europe in figures. Eurostat yearbook 2005.* Luxemburg: Office for Official Publications of the European Communities.

Evans, Roger Steven 2003. *Sex and salvation. Virginity as a soteriological paradigm in ancient Christianity.* Lanham and Oxford: University Press of America.

Fahey, Tony 1999. 'Religion and sexual culture in Ireland' in Franz X. Eder, Lesley A. Hall and Gert Hekma (eds) *Sexual cultures in Europe. National histories.* Manchester and New York: Manchester University Press: 53–70.

Faure, Bernard 2003. *The power of denial. Buddhism, purity, and gender.* Princeton: Princeton University Press.

Faure, Bernard 1998. *The red thread. Buddhist approaches to sexuality.* Princeton: Princeton University Press.

Finer, Lawrence B. 2007. 'Trends in premarital sex in the United States: 1954–2003' in *Public Health Reports* 122:73–78.

Finley, M.I.N. 2002. 'The silent women of Rome' in Laura McClure (ed.) *Sexuality and gender in the classical world. Readings and sources*. Oxford: Blackwell: 147–56.

Fleeman, Mike 2010. 'Dalai Lama: Who's Tiger Woods?' at *www.people.com*, 22 February 2010, www.people.com/people/article/0,,20346109,00.html?cnn=yes.

Fleishman, Jeffrey and Amro Hassan 2009. 'Gadget to help women feign virginity angers many in Egypt' in *Los Angeles Times*, 7 October 2009, www.latimes.com/news/nationworld/world/la-fg-fake-hymen7-2009oct07,0,6868813.story.

Fontes, Flavia 2001. *Forbidden wedding*. Documentary film. USA.

Forrest, Jeannie 1999. 'Sources and characters of religious values. Church of Jesus Christ of Latter-Day Saints' in Robert T. Francoeur, Patricia Barthalow Koch and David L. Weis (eds) *Sexuality in America. Understanding our values and sexual behavior*. New York: Continuum: 29–41.

Foster, Angel 2002. 'Women's sexuality in Tunisia. The health consequences of misinformation among university students' in Donna Lee Bowen and Evelyn A. Early (eds) *Everyday life in the Muslim Middle East. Second edition*. Bloomington: Indiana University Press: 98–110.

Foster, Lawrence 1984. *Religion and sexuality. The Shakers, the Mormons, and the Oneida Community*. Urbana and Chicago: University of Illinois Press.

Fox, Thomas C. 1995. *Sexuality and Catholicism*. New York: George Braziller.

Fuglehaug, Wenche 2008. '"Grava di er klargjort"' in *Aftenposten*, 6 March 2008, www.aftenposten.no/nyheter/iriks/article2296426.ece.

Gallup 1997. 'Family values differ sharply around the world' at *Gallup News Service*, 7 November 1997, www.gallup.com/poll/4315/Family-Values-Differ-Sharply-Around-World.aspx.

Garcia, Michelle 2010. 'Ugandan MP would kill his own son' at *www.advocate.com*, 19 February 2010, www.advocate.com/News/Daily_News/2010/02/19/Ugandan_MP_Would_Kill_Son_if_He_Were_Gay/

Gardella, Peter 1985. *Innocent ecstasy. How Christianity gave America an ethic of sexual pleasure*. New York and Oxford: Oxford University Press.

Gardiner, Samuel Rawson 1883. *History of England from the accession of James I to the outbreak of the Civil War, 1603–1642. Volume 3, 1616–1621*. London: Longmans, Green and Co.

Gaudio, Rudolf P. 1998. 'Male lesbians and other queer notions in Hausa' in Stephen O. Murray and Will Roscoe. *Boy-wives and female husbands. Studies of African homosexualities*. Basingstoke: Macmillan: 116–28.

Gentile, Tony 2010. 'Pope pleads for forgiveness over abuse' in *New York Times*, 11 June 2010, www.nytimes.com/2010/06/12/world/europe/12pope.html?hp.

Ghosh, Dwaipayan 2010. 'Family tortures, kills daughter and lover' in *Times of India*, 15 June 2010, http://timesofindia.indiatimes.com/city/delhi/Family-tortures-kills-daughter-lover/articleshow/6048315.cms.

Gilhus, Ingvild Sælid 2004. 'Kampen om Dønnafallosen' in Jostein Børtnes, Siv-Ellen Kraft and Lisbeth Mikaelsson (eds) *Kampen om kroppen. Kulturanalytiske blikk på kropp, helse, kjønn og seksualitet*. Kristiansand: Høyskoleforlaget: 173–87.

Gillesvik, Kjetil 2008. 'Tror homobråk skaper mobbing' in *Vårt Land*, 20 September 2008, www.vl.no/kristenliv/article3797291.ece.

Ginsburg, Henry 2003. 'A monk travels to Heaven and Hell' in Nigel Allan (ed.) *Pearls of the Orient. Asian treasures from the Wellcome Library*. London: Serindia Publications: 45–60.

Gittelsohn, Roland B. 1989. *How do I decide? A contemporary Jewish approach to what's right and what's wrong*. West Orange: Behrman House.

Glick, Leonard B. 2003. *Marked in your flesh. Circumcision from ancient Judea to modern America*. New York and Oxford: Oxford University Press.

Gold, Michael 1992. *Does God belong in the bedroom?* Philadelphia: Jewish Publication Society.

Goldman, David 1999. 'Gay Muslims' in *Southern Voice*, 19 August 1999, www.amboyz.org/articles/Fatiha.html.

Goldstein, Melvyn C. 1964. 'A study of the Ldab Ldob' in *Central Asiatic Journal* 9:123–41.

Gordon, Sarah Barringer 2002. *The Mormon question. Polygamy and constitutional conflict in nineteenth century America.* Chapel Hill: The University of North Carolina Press.

Grau, Günter [1993]. *Hidden Holocaust? Gay and lesbian persecution in Germany 1933–45*. London: Cassell 1995.

Greeley, Andrew M. 1989. *Religious change in America.* Cambridge, Mass.: Harvard University Press.

Greeley, Andrew M. 1991. 'Religion and attitudes towards AIDS policy' in *Social Science Research* 75:126–30.

Greenhouse, Steven 1988. 'Police suspect arson in fire at Paris theater' in *New York Times*, 25 October 1988, www.nytimes.com/1988/10/25/movies/police-suspect-arson-in-fire-at-paris-theater.html.

Grove, Steve 2008. 'Kanamara Matsuri festival. Festival of the Steel Phallus' at *2camels.com*, http://www.2camels.com/kanamara-matsuri-festival.php.

Gudorf, Christine E. 2003. 'Contraception and abortion in Roman Catholicism' in Daniel C. Maguire (ed.) *Sacred rights. The case for contraception and abortion in world religions.* New York and Oxford: Oxford University Press: 55–78.

Halstead, J. Mark and Michael Jonathan Reiss 2003. *Values in sex education. From principles to practice.* London and New York: Routledge Falmer.

Hanootunian, H. D. 1988. *Things seen and unseen. Discourse and ideology in Tokugawa nativism.* Chicago and London: The University of Chicago Press.

Harding, Susan Friend 2000. *The book of Jerry Falwell. Fundamentalist language and politics*. Princeton: Princeton University Press.

Hardy, B. Carmon 1992. *Solemn covenant. The Mormon polygamous passage.* Urbana: University of Illinois Press.

Harris Poll 2007. 'The religious and other beliefs of Americans' in *The Harris Poll*, 29 November 2007, www.harrisinteractive.com/harris_poll/index.asp?PID=838.

Harris Poll 2004. 'Strong opposition to same-sex marriage, but those who approve have increased substantially' in *The Harris Poll* 14 April 2004, www.harrisinteractive.com/harris_poll/index.asp?PID=454.

Harrison, Frances 2005. 'Iran's sex-change operations' at *news.bbc.co.uk*, 5 January 2005, http://news.bbc.co.uk/2/hi/programmes/newsnight/4115535.stm.

Harter, Pascale 2004. 'Divorce divide Morocoo and W Sahara' at *news.bbc.co.uk*, 4 August 2004, http://news.bbc.co.uk/2/hi/africa/3532612.stm.

Harvey, Peter 2000. *An introduction to Buddhist ethics.* Cambridge: Cambridge University Press.

Hawkins, Joseph R. 2000. 'Japan's journey into homophobia' in *The Gay and Lesbian Review* 7:36–9.

Hawley, John Stratton 1994. 'Introduction' in John Stratton Hawley (ed.) *Sati. The blessing and the curse. The burning of wives in India.* New York: Oxford University Press: 3–36.

Hazaimeh, Hani 2009. 'No legal exemption for "honour crimes"' in *Jordan Times*, 10 July 2009, www.jordantimes.com/index.php?news=18296andsearchFor=honor%20killings.

Hegna, Kjetil 2008. 'Prevensjon på muslimsk vis' in *Utrop*, 2 June 2008, www.utrop.no/art.html?artid=14529andcatid=189.

Hellemann, John 2007. 'God Dem' in *New York Magazine* 21 May 2007, http://nymag.com/news/politics/powergrid/32119/.

Henriksen, Thor Harald 2009. 'Biskop skilles. Første gang i Norge' in *Vårt Land*, 17 January 2009, www.vl.no/nyheter/innenriks/artikkel.php?artid=539817.

Herdt, Gilbert H 1984. 'Semen transaction in Sambia culture' in Gilbert H. Herdt (ed.) *Ritualized homosexuality in Melanesia*. Berkeley: University of California Press: 1–82.

Herdt, Gilbert H. 1981. *Guardians of the flutes. Idioms of masculinity*. New York: McGraw-Hill.

Herzog, Dagmar 2005. 'Hubris and hypocrisy, incitement and disavowal. Sexuality and German fascism' in Dagmar Herzog (ed.) *Sexuality and German fascism*. New York and Oxford: Berghahn Books: 1–21.

Hidayatullah, Aysha 2003. 'Islamic conceptions of sexuality' in David W. Machacek and Melissa M. Wilcox (eds) *Sexuality and the world's religions*. Santa Barbara, Denver and Oxford: ABC-CLIO: 255–92.

Higginbotham, A. Leon Jr. and Barbara K. Kopytoff 2000. 'Racial purity and interracial sex in the law of colonial and antebellum Virginia' in Werner Sollors (ed.) *Interracialism. Black-white intermarriage in American history, literature, and law*. New York and Oxford: Oxford University Press: 81–139.

Hinsch, Bret 1990. *Passions of the cut sleeve. The male homosexual tradition in China*. Berkeley: University of California Press.

Hmar, Sangzuala 2010. 'Mizo church talks tough on gays' in *Sunday Times of India*, 14 March 2010, http://timesofindia.indiatimes.com/city/kolkata-/Mizo-church-talks-tough-on-gays/articleshow/5681443.cms.

Hoel, Per Anders 2010, 'KrF vil strø om seg med prevensjon' in *Vårt Land*, 20 April 2010, www.vl.no/samfunn/article21867.zrm.

Hoffman, Matthew Cullinan 2010. 'Cardinal Archbishop of Lisbon accused of "pact of silence" with Portuguese government as country lurches towards "gay marriage"' at *www.lifesitenews.com* 7 January 2010, www.lifesitenews.com/ldn/2010/jan/10010714.html.

Holbek, Jan Arild 2008. 'Bedehuskjendis sto fram' in *Vårt Land*, 21 May 2008, www.vl.no/kristenliv/article3555202.ece.

Holben, L. R. 1999. *What Christians think about homosexuality. Six representative viewpoints*. North Richland Hills: Bibal Press.

Hollup, Oddvar 2001. 'Kinship and marriage in the construction of identity and group boundaries among Indians in Mauritius' in Monika Böck and Aparna Rao (eds) *Culture, creation, and procreation. Concept of kinship in South Asian practice*. New York and Oxford: Berghahn Books: 219–41.

Horrox, Rosemary 1994. *The Black Death*. Manchester: Manchester University Press.

Hutton, J. E. [1909]. *History of the Moravian Church*. Whitefish: Kessinger Publishing 2004.

Indo-Asian News Service 2010. 'Naveen Jindal backs khap's marriage diktat' at *www.ndtv.com* 10 May 2010, www.ndtv.com/news/india/naveen-jindal-backs-khaps-marriage-diktat-24532.php.

Iqbal, Samaria and Francis Lundh 2010. '– Døden er bedre enn vanære' in VG, 9 March 2010, www.vg.no/nyheter/innenriks/artikkel.php?artid=598323.

Israel, Benjamin J. 1984. *The Bene Israel of India. Some studies.* Delhi: Orient Longman.

Jacobsen, Magnus W. 2008. 'Skiller seg med ritual' in *Vårt Land*, 30 June 2008, www.vl.no/kristenliv/article3641140.ece.

Jacobson, Jessica 1998. *Islam in transition. Religion and identity among British Pakistani youth.* London: Routledge.

Jaffrelot, Christophe 1996. *The Hindu nationalist movement and Indian politics 1925 to the 1990s.* London: Hurst and Company.

Jain, Anrudh 2003a. 'Religion, state, and population growth' in Daniel C. Maguire (ed.) *Sacred rights. The case for contraception and abortion in world religions.* New York and Oxford: Oxford University Press: 237–54.

Jain, Anrudh 2003b. 'The right to family planning, contraception, and abortion. The Hindu view' in Daniel C. Maguire (ed.) *Sacred rights. The case for contraception and abortion in world religions.* New York: Oxford University Press: 129–43.

Jansen, Martin 2003. 'Unge sier ja til sex med samme kjønn' in *Dagsavisen*, 4 February 2003.

Jeffrey, Roger and Patricia Jeffrey 1997. *Population, gender and politics. Demographic change in rural north India.* Cambridge: Cambridge University Press.

Johannessen, Randi 2007. '– De vil gjøre ende på det afrikanske folk' in *Aftenposten* 27 September 2007, www.aftenposten.no/nyheter/uriks/article2018233.ece.

Johnson, Luke Timothy and Mark D. Jordan 2006. 'Christianity' in Don S. Browning, M. Christian Green and John Witte jr. (eds) *Sex, marriage, and family in world religions.* New York: Columbia University Press: 77–149.

Johnson, William Stacy 2006. *A time to embrace. Same-gender relationships in religion, law and politics.* Grand Rapids and Cambridge: William B. Eerdmans Publishing Company.

Johnston, Anna 2003. *Missionary writing and empire, 1800–1860.* Cambridge: Cambridge University Press.

Johri, Sanjay M. 'Will SC's decision on elopement increase runaway marriages' in *Merinews*, 8 December 2007, www.merinews.com/catFull.jsp?articleID=128413.

Kafi, Hélène 1992. 'Tehran. Dangerous love' in Arno Schmitt and Jehoeda Sofer (eds) *Sexuality and eroticism among males in Moslem societies.* New York: Harrington Park Press: 67–69.

Kannabiran, Kalpana and Vasanth 2002. *De-eroticizing assault. Essays on modesty, honour and power.* Calcutta: Stree.

Kapur, Ratna 2005. *Erotic justice. Law and the new politics of postcolonialism.* London: Glosshouse Press.

Katz, Jonathan Ned 1995. *The invention of heterosexuality.* Penguin: New York.

Kendall 1998. '"When a woman loves a woman" in Lesotho. Love, sex, and the (western) construction of homophobia' in Stephen O. Murray and Will Roscoe. *Boy-wives and female husbands. Studies of African homosexualities.* Basingstoke: Macmillan: 223–41.

Kennedy, Philip F. 1997. *The wine song in classical Arabic poetry. Abu Nuwas and the literary tradition.* Oxford: Clarendon Press.

Kennedy, Sarah and Jason Cianciotto 2006. *Homophobia at 'Hell houses'. Literally demonizing lesbian, gay, bisexual and transgender youth.* New York: National Gay and Lesbian Task Force Policy Institute.

Keown, Damien 2005. *Buddhist ethics. A very short introduction.* Oxford: Oxford University Press.

Khalaf, Roseanne Saad 2006. 'Breaking the silence. What AUB students really think about sex' in Samir Khalaf and John Gagnon (eds) *Sexualities in the Arab world.* London, New York and Beirut: Saqi: 175–98.

Khalik, Abdul 2008. 'Porn bill passed despite protests' in *The Jakarta Post* 31 October 2008, www.thejakartapost.com/news/2008/10/31/porn-bill-passed-despite-protests.html?page=2and%24Version=0and%24Path=/and%24Domain =.thejakartapost.com.

Khan, O. A. and A. A. Hyder 1998. 'HIV / AIDS among men who have sex with men in Pakistan' in *Sex Health Exchange* 2:12–15.

Khan, Badruddin 1997. 'Not-so-gay life in Pakistan in the 1980s and 1990s' in Stephen Murray and Will Roscoe (eds) *Islamic homosexualities. Culture, history, and literature*. New York: New York University Press: 275–96.

Khan, Badruddin 1992. 'Not-so-gay life in Karachi. A view of a Pakistani living in Toronto' in Arno Schmitt and Jehoeda Sofer (eds) *Sexuality and eroticism among males in Moslem societies*. New York: Harrington Park Press: 93–104.

Khandelwal, Meena 2001. 'Sexual fluids, emotions morality. Notes on gendering of brahmacharya' in Elisa J. Sobo and Sandra Bell (eds) *Celibacy, culture, and society. The anthropology of sexual abstinence*. Madison: University of Wisconsin Press: 157–79.

Kington, Tom & Ben Quinn. 'Pope Benedict says that condoms can be used to stop the spread of HIV' in *The Guardian* 21 November 2010. http://www.guardian.co.uk/world/2010/nov/21/pope-benedict-condoms-hiv-infection.

Kinsey, Alfred C., Wardell B. Pomeroy, Clyde E. Martin and Paul H. Gebhard 1953. *Sexual behavior in the human female*. Philadelphia: W.B. Saunders.

Kinsey, Alfred C., Wardell B. Pomeroy and Clyde E. Martin 1948. *Sexual behavior in the human male*. Philadelphia: W.B. Saunders.

Kinsley, David R. 1988. *Hindu goddesses. Visions of the divine feminine in the Hindu religious tradition*. Berkeley: University of California Press.

Kjær, Reidar 2002. 'Anti-homoseksuelle holdninger og selvmord' in *Suicidologi* 7(1):15–17.

Klein, Marty 2006. *America's war on sex. The attack on law, lust and liberty*. Westport: Praeger.

Kociumbas, Jan 2004. 'Genocide and modernity in colonial Australia. 1788–1850' in A. Dirk Moses (ed.) *Genocide and settler society. Frontier violence and stolen indigenous children in Australian history*. New York and Oxford: Berghahn Books: 77–102.

Kon, Igor S. 1995. *The sexual revolution in Russia. From the age of the Czars to today*. New York: Free Press.

Kruger, Steven F. 1997. 'Conversion and medieval sexual, religious, and racial categories' in Karma Lochrie, Peggy McCracken and James A. Schulz (eds) *Constructing medieval sexuality*. Minneapolis: University of Minnesota Press: 158–79.

Kumar, Sampath 2003. 'India rights campaign for infanticide mothers' at *news.bbc.co.uk*, 17 July 2003, http://news.bbc.co.uk/2/hi/south_asia/3071747.stm.

Kühl, Stefan 1994. *The Nazi connection. Eugenics, American racism, and German national socialism*. New York and Oxford: Oxford University Press.

Kyi, Gregor 2005. *Statistics in focus. Population and social conditions. Living conditions and welfare*. Luxemburg: Office for Official Publications of the European Communities.

Labalme, Patricia H. 1984. 'Sodomy and Venetian justice in the renaissance' in *The Legal History Review* 52:217–54.

LaFleur, William R. 1992. *Liquid life. Abortion and Buddhism in Japan*. Princeton: Princeton University Press.

Lambert, Royston 1988. *Beloved and god. The story of Hadrian and Antinous*. Secaucus: Meadowland Book.

Lamberts, Malcolm 1998. *The Cathars*. Oxford: Blackwell.

Laumann, Edward O., John H. Gagnon, Robert T. Michael and Stuart Michaels 1994. *The social organization of sexuality. Sexual practices in the United States.* Chicago and London: The University of Chicago Press.

Laumann, Edward O. and Jenna Mahay 2002. 'The social organization of women's sexuality' in Gina M. Wingood and Ralph J. DiClemente (eds) *Handbook of women's sexual and reproductive health.* New York: Springer: 43–70.

Lee Khoon Choy 1995. *Japan. Between myth and reality.* Singapore: World Scientific.

Lefkovits, Etgar 2007. 'Haredi youths assail woman on bus' in *Jerusalem Post*, 21 October 2007, www.jpost.com/servlet/Satellite?cid=1192380613550andpagename=JPost%2FJPArticle%2FShowFull.

Le Monde 1988. 'Quatorze blessés dans une salle parisienne projetant "la Dernière Tentation du Christ"' in *Le Monde*, 25 October 1988, www.lemonde.fr/cgi-bin/ACHATS/acheter.cgi?offre=ARCHIVESSandtype_item=ART_ARCH_30Jandobjet_id=624183.

Leonard, Bill J. 1999. 'A theology for racism. Southern Fundamentalists and the civil rights movement' in *Baptist History and Heritage Journal* 34:49–68.

Letvik, Tore 2007. 'Ber fatwaråd gi råd om homo-dødsstraff' in *Dagsavisen*, 3 December 2007, www.dagsavisen.no/innenriks/article323752.ece.

Leuchtenburg, William E. 2005. *The White House looks South. Franklin D. Roosevelt, Harry S. Truman, Lyndon B. Johnson.* Baton Rouge: Louisiana State University Press.

Lidke, Jeffrey 2003. 'A union of fire and water. Sexuality and spirituality in Hinduism' in David W. Machacek and Melissa M. Wilcox (eds) *Sexuality and the world's religions.* Santa Barbara, Denver and Oxford: ABC-CLIO: 101–32.

Long, Scott, A. Widney Brown and Gail Cooper 2003. *More than a name. State-sponsored homophobia and its consequences in Southern Africa.* New York: Human Rights Watch.

Lowery-Smith, Darrin 2003. *Handling the truth II: Brothers and white women.* New York: Universe Inc.

McAlister, Elizabeth 2000. 'Love, sex and gender embodied. The spirits of Haitian Vodou' in Joseph Runzo and Nancy N. Martin (eds) *Love, sex, and gender in the world religions.* Oxford: Oneworld: 129–45.

McCarthy, Kate 2007. *Interfaith encounters in America.* New Brunswick, New Jersey: Rutgers University Press.

McCarthy, Rory 2008. 'Hamas patrols beaches in Gaza to enforce conservative dress code' in *The Guardian*, 18 October 2009, www.guardian.co.uk/world/2009/oct/18/hamas-gaza-islamist-dress-code.

MacDonald, Gary B. 1992. 'Among Syrian men' in Arno Schmitt and Jehoeda Sofer (eds) *Sexuality and eroticism among males in Moslem societies.* New York: Harrington Park Press: 43–54.

MacFarquhar, Neil 2005. 'Paternity suit against TV star scandalizes Egyptians' in *New York Times*, 26 January 2005, www.nytimes.com/2005/01/26/international/middleeast/26paternity.html?oref=loginand8hpib.

McLaren, Angus 1990. *A history of contraception from antiquity to the present day.* Oxford and Cambridge, Mass.: Blackwell.

Malik, Rajiv 2004. 'Discussions on dharma' in *Hinduism Today*, October/November/December 2004, www.hinduismtoday.com/archives/2004/10-12/30-31_mela_council.shtml.

Mani, A. [1993]. 'Indians in Thailand' in K. S. Sandhu and A. Mani (eds) *Indian communities in Southeast Asia.* Singapore: Institute of Southeast Asian Studies 2006:910–49.

Manis, Andrew M. 1999. '"Dying from the neck up". Southern Baptist resistance to the civil rights movement' in *Baptist History and Heritage Journal* 34:33–48.

Manum, Olav André 2007. '– Koranen aksepterer homofile' in *Utrop*, 16 November 2007, www.utrop.no/art.html?artid=13621andcatid=1.

Marglin, Frédérique Apffel 1985. *Wives of the god-king. The rituals of the devadasis of Puri*. New Delhi and Oxford: Oxford University Press.

Martin, Phillip W. D. 1999. 'Devoutly dividing us. Opponents of interracial marriage say God is on their side' in *Boston Globe*, 7 November 1999. http://jameslandrith.com/content/view/2909/80/

Meer, Theo van der 2004. 'Premodern origins of modern homophobia and masculinity' in *Sexuality Research and Social Policy. Journal of National Sexuality Resource Center* 1:77–90.

Meland, Astrid 2006. 'Muslimer om kvinner, homofile og sex' in *Dagbladet*, 24 November 2006, www.dagbladet.no/magasinet/2006/11/24/483988.html.

Melikian, Levon H. 1967. 'Social change and sexual behavior of Arab university students' in *Journal of Social Psychology* 73:169–75.

Meranda, Amnon 2007. 'Shas MK proposes "rehab centers" for gays' at *www.ynetnews.com* 21 June 2007, www.ynetnews.com/articles/0,7340,L-3415870,00.html.

Miller, Judith 1996. *God has ninety-nine names. Reporting from a militant Middle East*. New York: Simon and Schuster.

Millett, Kate 1982. *Going to Iran*. New York: Coward, McCann and Geoghegan.

Mir-Hosseini, Ziba 2000. *Marriage on trial. Islamic family law in Iran and Morocco*. London and New York: I.B. Tauris.

Mishra, Anjana Agnihotri 2000. 'Asian Indian Americans in South Florida. Values and identity' Jim Norwine and Jonathan M. Smith (eds) *Worldview flux. Perplexed values among postmodern peoples*. Lanham: Lexington Books: 177–98.

Montagu, Ashley 1997. *Man's most dangerous myth. The fallacy of race. Sixth edition*. Walnut Creek: AltaMira Press.

Monter, William 1990. *Frontiers of heresy. The Spanish Inquisition from the Basque lands to Sicily*. Cambridge: Cambridge University Press.

MSNBC 2007. 'Man in India marries a dog as atonement' at *www.msnbc.com*, 13 November 2007, www.msnbc.msn.com/id/21768663/.

Mujtaba, Hasan 1997. 'The other side of midnight. Pakistani male prostitutes' in Stephen Murray and Will Roscoe (eds) *Islamic homosexualities. Culture, history, and literature*. New York: New York University Press: 267–74.

Murray, Stephen O. 2002. *Homosexualities*. Chicago: The University of Chicago Press.

Murray, Stephen O. 1997a. 'The will not to know. Islamic accommodations of male homosexuality' in Stephen Murray and Will Roscoe (eds) *Islamic homosexualities. Culture, history, and literature*. New York: New York University Press: 14–54.

Murray, Stephen O. 1997b. 'Male homosexuality, inheritance rules, and status of women in medieval Egypt' in Stephen Murray and Will Roscoe (eds) *Islamic homosexualities. Culture, history, and literature*. New York: New York University Press: 161–73.

Murray, Stephen O. 1997c. 'Male homosexuality in Ottoman Albania' in Stephen Murray and Will Roscoe (eds) *Islamic homosexualities. Culture, history, and literature*. New York: New York University Press: 187–96.

Murray, Stephen O. 1997d. 'Male actresses in Islamic parts of Indonesia and the southern Philippines' in Stephen Murray and Will Roscoe (eds) *Islamic homosexualities. Culture, history, and literature*. New York: New York University Press: 256–61.

Murray, Stephen O. and Will Roscoe 1998. *Boy-wives and female husbands. Studies of African homosexualities.* Basingstoke: Macmillan.

Murray, Stephen O. and Will Roscoe 1997. 'Conclusion' in Stephen Murray and Will Roscoe (eds) *Islamic homosexualities. Culture, history, and literature*. New York: New York University Press: 302–19.

Nagel, Joane 2003. *Race, ethnicity, and sexuality. Intimate intersections, forbidden frontiers*. New York and Oxford: Oxford University Press.

Naqvi, Nauman and Hasan Mujtaba 1997. 'Two Baluchi *buggas*, a Sindhi *zenana*, and the status of *hijras* in contemporary Pakistan' in Stephen Murray and Will Roscoe (eds) *Islamic homosexualities. Culture, history, and literature*. New York: New York University Press: 262–66.

National Research Council 1993. *The social impact of AIDS in the United States*. Washington, DC: National Academies Press.

Nebuhr, Gustav 1995. 'Heresy trial is moved after Connecticut Episcopalians protest' in *New York Times*, 17 December 1995, http://query.nytimes.com/gst/fullpage.html?res=9F01E1D71739F934A25751C1A963958260.

Nelson, Dean 2009. 'Seven-year-old Indian girls "marry" frogs' in *The Daily Telegraph*, 19 January 2009, www.telegraph.co.uk/news/newstopics/howaboutthat/4290761/Seven-year-old-Indian-girls-marry-frogs.html.

Nelson, Dean and Ghulam Hasnain 2006. 'Pakistani graduate raped to punish her low-caste family' in *The Sunday Times*, 24 September 2006, www.timesonline.co.uk/tol/news/world/article648817.ece.

Neustein, Amy and Lesher, Michael 2002. 'The silence of the Jewish media on sexual abuse in the Orthodox Jewish community' in Dane S. Claussen (ed.) *Sex, religion, media*. Lanham: Rowman and Littlefield: 79–87.

Newport, Frank 2003. 'Six in 10 Americans agree that gay sex should be legal' at *Gallup News Service* 27 June 2003, http://gallup.com/poll/8722/Six-Americans-Agree-Gay-Sex-Should-Legal.aspx.

New York Times 1982a. 'Paralysis bars a wedding' in *New York Times*, 27 January 1982.

New York Times 1982b. 'Quadriplegic denied wedding by church' in *New York Times*, 5 July 1982, http://query.nytimes.com/gst/fullpage.html?sec=healthandres=9906E1DA133BF936A35754C0A964948260andn=Top%2fReference%2fTimes%20Topics%2fSubjects%2fH%2fHandicapped.

Noonan, John T. Jr 1986. *Contraception. A history of its treatment by the Catholic theologians and canonists. Enlarged edition*. Cambridge, Mass. and London: Harvard University Press.

Noordam, D. J. 1995. *Riskante relaties. Vijf eeuwen homoseksualiteit in Nederland, 1233–1733*. Hilversum: Uitgeverij Verloren.

Olivelle, Patrick 2008. 'Celibacy in classical Hinduism' in Carl Olson (ed.) *Celibacy and religious traditions*. New York: Oxford University Press: 151–64.

Oosterhuis, Harry 1999: 'The Netherlands. Neither prudish nor hedonistic' in Franz X. Eder, Lesley A. Hall and Gert Hekma (eds) *Sexual cultures in Europe. National histories*. Manchester and New York: Manchester University Press: 71–90.

Osodi, George 2006. 'At axis of Episcopal split, an anti-gay Nigerian' in *New York Times*, 25 December 2006, www.nytimes.com/2006/12/25/world/africa/25episcopal.html.

Overdorf, Jason 2008. 'Rebel brides and ex-wives' in *Newsweek*, 26 May 2008, www.newsweek.com/id/137472.

Pagels, Elaine 1988. *Adam, Eve, and the serpent*. New York: Vintage Books.

Palacios, Miguel Asín [1919]. *Islam and the Divine Comedy*. Oxon: Frank Cass and Co. 2006.

Pancevski, Bojan and John Follain 2010. 'John Paul "ignored abuse of 2,000 boys"' in *The Sunday Times*, 4 April 2010, www.timesonline.co.uk/tol/comment/faith/article7086738.ece.

Pandey, Geeta 2010. 'Indian community torn apart by "honour killings"' at *news.bbc.co.uk*, 16 June 2010, http://news.bbc.co.uk/2/hi/world/south_asia/10334529.stm

Parrinder, Geoffrey 1996. *Sexual morality in the world's religions*. Oxford: Oneworld.

Partridge, Hugh Partridge 2003. 'Understanding UFO religions and abduction spiritualities' in Christopher Hugh Partridge (ed.) *UFO religions*. London and New York: Routledge: 3–43.

Pattanaik, Devdutt 2001. *The man who was a woman and other queer tales from Hindu lore*. New York: Haworth Press.

Pelham, Nick 2000. 'Battle of sexualities' at *news.bbc.co.uk*, 26 June 2000, http://news.bbc.co.uk/2/hi/middle_east/806642.stm.

Peters, Rich 2005. 'Jerusalem Pride turns violent' at *www.365gay.com*, 30 June 2005, www.365gay.com/newscon05/06/063005Jerusalem.htm.

Phayer, J. Michael 1977. *Sexual liberation and religion in nineteenth century Europe*. London and Totowa: Croom Helm and Rowman and Littlefield.

Phillips, Roderick 1992. *Untying the knot. A short history of divorce*. Cambridge: Cambridge University Press.

Pigott, Robert 2008. 'Church obsessed with gays – Tutu' at *news.bbc.co.uk*, 7 September 2008, http://news.bbc.co.uk/2/hi/uk_news/7602498.stm.

Plant, Richard 1986. *The pink triangle. The Nazi war against homosexuals*. New York: Henry Holt and Company.

Powers, John 2008. 'Celibacy in Indian and Tibetan Buddhism' in Carl Olson (ed.) *Celibacy and religious traditions*. New York: Oxford University Press: 201–24.

Princeton Survey Research Associates 2009. 'Newsweek poll. The people speak: "Yes, he can"' in *Newsweek* 26 January 2009.

Pritchard, Gemma 2007. 'Anglican bishop calls LGBT people inhuman' at *www.pinknews.co.uk* 11 September 2007, www.pinknews.co.uk/news/articles/2005-5427.html.

Pullella, Philip 2010. 'Cardinal accuses Vatican official of abuse cover-up' at *www.reuters.com*, 9 May 2010, www.reuters.com/article/idUSTRE6481D420100509.

Puttick, Elizabeth 1997. *Women in new religions. In search of community, sexuality and spiritual power*. Houndmills and New York: MacMillan and St Martin's Press.

Quinn, Michael D. 2001. *Same-sex dynamics among nineteenth-century Americans. A Mormon example*. Urbana: University of Illinois Press.

Quinn, Michael D. 1997. *The Mormon hierarchy. Extension of power*. Salt Lake City: Signature Books.

Ramet, Sabrina P. 2006a. 'The way we were – and should be again? European Orthodox churches and the "idyllic past"' in Timothy A. Byrnes and Peter J. Katzenstein (eds) *Religion in expanding Europe*. Cambridge: Cambridge University Press: 148–75.

Ramet, Sabrina P. 2006b. 'Thy will be done. The Catholic Church and politics in Poland since 1989' in Timothy A. Byrnes and Peter J. Katzenstein (eds) *Religion in expanding Europe*. Cambridge: Cambridge University Press: 117–47.

Reed, Barbara E. 1992. 'The gender symbolism of Kuan-yin Bodhisattva' in José Ignacio Cabezón (ed.) *Buddhism, sexuality, and gender*. Albany: State University of New York Press: 159–80.

Reynolds, Maura 2002. 'Kandahar's lightly veiled homosexual habits' in *Los Angeles Times*, 3 April 2002, www.glapn.org/sodomylaws/world/afghanistan/afnews009.htm.

Reynolds, Vernon and Ralph E. S. Tanner 1995. *The social ecology of religion*. New York: Oxford University Press.

Rheault, Magali and Dalia Mogahed 2008. 'Moral issues divide westerners from Muslims i n the West' at *Gallup News Service*, 23 May 2008, http://gallup.com/poll/107512/Moral-Issues-Divide-Westerners-From_Muslims-West.aspx.

Rian, Øystein 2001. 'Mellom straff og forfølgelse. Homoseksualitet i Norge fra vikingtiden til 1930-årene' in Marianne C. Brantsæter, Turid Eikvam, Reidar Kjær and Knut Olav Åmås (eds) *Norsk homoforskning*. Oslo: Universitetsforlaget: 25–56.

Robinson, Rowena 2003. *Christians of India*. London and New Dehli: Sage.

Rogers, Eugene F. Jr 1999. *Sexuality and the Christian body. Their way into the triune God*. Oxford and Malden: Blackwell.

Roos, Julia 2005. 'Backlash against prostitutes' rights. Origins and dynamics of Nazi prostitution politics' in Dagmar Herzog (ed.) *Sexuality and German fascism*. New York and Oxford: Berghahn Books: 67–94.

Rosenbaum, Janet Elise 2009. 'Patient teenagers? A comparison of the sexual behavior of virginity pledgers and matched nonpledgers' in *Pediatrics* 123:110–20.

Ross, Josephine 2002. 'The sexualization of difference. A comparison of mixed-race and same-gender marriage' in *Harvard Civil Rights. Civil Liberties Law Review* 37:255–88.

Roth, Martha T. 2006. 'Marriage, divorce, and the prostitute in ancient Mesopotamia' in Christopher A. Faraone and Laura K. McClure (eds) *Prostitutes and courtesans in the ancient world*. Madison: University of Wisconsin Press: 21–39.

Roth, Norman 1982. '"Deal gently with the young man". Love of boys in medieval Hebrew poetry of Spain' in *Speculum* 57:20-51.

Roth, Zachary 2008. 'The McCain-Hagee connection' in *Columbia Journalism Review*, 7 March 2008, www.cjr.org/campaign_desk/the_mccainhagee_connection_1.php.

Røthing, Åse 1998. *Sex, kjønn og kristentro*. Oslo: Verbum.

Rothstein, Mikael 2003. 'UFO beliefs as syncretistic components' in Christopher Hugh Partridge (ed.) *UFO religions*. London and New York: Routledge: 256–73.

Ruggiero, Guido 1985. *Boundaries of Eros. Sex crime and sexuality in renaissance Venice*. New York and Oxford: Oxford University Press.

Russell, Jeffrey Burton 1972. *Witchcraft in the Middle Ages*. Ithaca: Cornell University Press.

Rye, Ajit Singh [1993]. 'The Indian community in the Philippines' in K. S. Sandhu and A. Mani (eds) *Indian communities in Southeast Asia*. Singapore: Institute of Southeast Asian Studies 2006:707–73.

Sabry, Mohammad 2008. 'No Nigerian death verdict for 86 wives' at *Islam Online*, 22 August 2008, www.islamonline.net/servlet/Satellite?c=Article_Candcid=1219339673209andpagename=Zone-English-News/NWELayout.

Samson, Jane 2005. *Race and empire*. Harlow: Pearson Education.

Sarah, Elizabeth [1993]. 'Judaism and lesbianism. A tale of life on the margins of the text' in Jonathan Margonet (ed.) *Jewish explorations of sexuality*. Providence and Oxford: Berghahn Books 1995:95–101.

Scammell, G. V. 1989. *The first imperial age. European overseas expansion c. 1400–1715*. London and New York: Routledge.

Schalow, Paul Gordon 1992. 'Kukai and the tradition of male love in Japanese Buddhism' in José Ignacio Cabezón (ed.) *Buddhism, sexuality, and gender*. Albany: State University of New York Press: 215–30.

Scheidel, Walter [2004]. 'Ancient Egyptian sibling marriage and the Westermarck effect' in Arthur P. Wolf and William H. Durham (eds) *Inbreeding, incest, and the incest taboo. The state of knowledge at the turn of the century.* Stanford: Stanford University Press 2005:93–108.

Schieffelin, Edward L. 1982. 'The *Baua* ceremonial hunting lodge. An alternative to initiation' in Gilbert H. Herdt (ed.) *Rituals of manhood.* Berkeley: University of California Press: 155–200.

Schimmel, Annemarie 1994. *Deciphering the signs of God. A phenomenological approach to Islam.* Albany: State University of New York Press.

Schleiner, Winfried 1994. '"The matter which ought not to be heard of". Homophobic slurs in renaissance cultural politics' in *Journal of Homosexuality* 26:41–75.

Schmitt, Arno 1992. 'Different approaches to male-male sexuality/eroticism from Morocco to Usbekistan' in Arno Schmitt and Jehoeda Sofer (eds) *Sexuality and eroticism among males in Moslem societies.* New York: Harrington Park Press: 1–24.

Seliktar, Ofira 2000. *Failing the crystal ball test. The Carter administration and the fundamentalist revolution in Iran.* Westport and London: Praeger.

Sellström, Tor 1999. *Sweden and national liberation in Southern Africa. Solidarity and assistance 1970–1994.* Uppsala: Nordic Africa Institute.

Sengers, Gerda 2003. *Women and demons: Cult healing in Islamic Egypt.* Leiden: Brill.

Sengupta, Nandita and Sukhbir Siwach 2010. 'Between life and love' in *Times of India,* 22 June 2010, http://timesofindia.indiatimes.com/india/Between-life-and-love/articleshow/6077052.cms.

Shahine, Gihan 1999. 'Illegitimate, illegal or just ill-advised' in *Al-Ahram* 18 February 1999, http://weekly.ahram.org.eg/1999/417/li1.htm.

Shaikh, Sa'diyya 2003. 'Family planning, contraception and abortion in Islam. Undertaking *Khilafah*' in Daniel C. Maguire (ed.) *Sacred rights. The case for contraception and abortion in world religions.* New York and Oxford: Oxford University Press: 105–28.

Shapiro, Faydra 2006. *Building Jewish roots. The Israel experience.* Montreal and Kingston: McGill-Queen's University Press.

Sharma, Parvez 2007. *A Jihad for love.* Documentary film. USA, Great Britain, France, Germany and Australia.

Shelp, Earl E. 1994. 'AIDS, high-risk behaviors, and moral judgments' in James B. Nelson and Sandra P. Longfellow (eds) *Sexuality and the sacred. Sources for theological reflection.* Louisville: Westminster John Knox Press: 314–25.

Sibalis, Michael David 1996. 'The regulation of male homosexuality in revolutionary and Napoleonic France, 1789–1815' in Jeffrey Merrick and Bryant T. Ragan, Jr (eds) *Homosexuality in modern France.* New York: Oxford University Press: 80–101.

Smith, Anthony M. A., Chris E. Rissel, Juliet Richters, Andrew E. Grulich and Richard O. de Visser 2007. 'Sex in Australia. Sexual identity, sexual attraction and sexual experience among a representative sample of adults' in *Australian and New Zealand Journal of Public Health* 27:2:138–45.

Snoke, David 2004. 'The Southern Presbyterian Church and racism' at *www.cityreformed.org,* www.cityreformed.org/snoke/racism.pdf.

Solli, Britt 2005. 'Norrøn sed og skikk' in Arne Bugge Amundsen (ed.) *Norges religionshistorie.* Oslo: Universitetsforlaget: 16–62.

Sommer, Elisabeth W. 2000. *Serving two masters. Moravian Brethren in Germany and North Carolina 1727–1801.* Lexington: University Press of Kentucky.

Spence, Rebecca 2006. 'Conservative panel votes to permit gay rabbis' at *www.forward.com* 6 December 2006, www.forward.com/articles/9576/.

Stan, Lavinia and Lucian Turcescu 2007. *Religion and politics in post-communist Romania*. New York and Oxford: Oxford University Press.

Steinsland, Gro 2005. *Norrøn religion. Myter, riter, samfunn*. Oslo: Pax.

Stephens, Walter 2002. *Demon lovers. Witchcraft, sex and the crisis of belief*. Chicago and London: The University of Chicago Press.

Stirrat, R. L. 1982. 'Caste conundrums. Views of caste in a Sinhalese Catholic fishing village' in Dennis B. McGilvray (ed.) *Caste ideology and interaction*. Cambridge: Cambridge University Press: 8–33

Stuart, Elizabeth 1995. *Just good friends. Towards a lesbian and gay theology of relationship*. London: Mowbray.

Suriyani, Luh de and Telly Nathalia 2008. 'Indonesians rally, dance to protest anti-porn bill' at *www.reuters.com*, 11 October 2008, www.reuters.com/article/newsMaps/idUSTRE49A1F520081011.

Suwanbubbha, Parichart 2003. 'The right to family planning, contraception, and abortion in Thai Buddhism' in Daniel C. Maguire (ed.) *Sacred rights. The case for contraception and abortion in world religons*. New York: Oxford University Press: 145–65.

Svenska Dagbladet 2009a. 'Många präster vill viga homopar' in *Svenska Dagbladet*, 21 January 2009, www.svd.se/nyheter/inrikes/artikel_2363793.svd.

Svenska Dagbladet 2009b. 'Ja till homovigslar i Svenska kyrkan' in *Svenska Dagbladet*, 22 October 2009, www.svd.se/nyheter/inrikes/artikel_3689859.svd.

Sykes, Hugh 2008. 'Iran rejects easing polygamy law' at *news.bbc.co.uk*, 2 September 2008, http://news.bbc.co.uk/2/hi/middle_east/7594997.stm.

Søderlind, Didrik 2006. 'Homofile dyr skaper strid' at *www.forskning.no* 26 September 2006, www.forskning.no/Artikler/2006/september/1159184941.14/.

Taneja, Poonam 2010. 'Gay Muslims made homeless by family violence' at *news.bbc.co.uk* 11 January 2010, http://news.bbc.co.uk/2/hi/uk_news/england/8446458.stm.

Teague, K. 1989. 'Heresy and its traces. The material results of culture' in Ian Hodder (ed.) *The meaning of things. Material culture and symbolic expressions*. Unwin Hyman: 130–36.

Therborn, Göran 2004. *Between sex and power. Family in the world 1900–2000*. London and New York: Routledge.

Thompson, Ben 2003. 'Gay marriage ban violates right to practice religion minister says' at *www.365gay.com*, 20 February 2003, http://365gay.com/NewsContent/022003mccMarriage.htm.

Thompson, Julia 2008. 'Chile's kids born mostly out of wedlock' in *The Valparaiso Times*, 24 January 2008 www.valparaisotimes.cl/content/view/292/388/

Thorenfeldt, Gunnar 2006. '– Muslimske kvinner har rett til orgasme' in *Dagbladet* 5 November 2006, www.dagbladet.no/nyheter/2006/11/05/481907.html.

Thornberry, Malcolm 2006. 'Mass arrests at Moscow gay, anti-gay marches' at *www.365gay.com*, 22 July 2006, http://365gay.com/Newscon06/05/052706moscow.htm.

Times of India 2010. 'Live in relationship, pre-marital sex not an offence: SC' in *Times of India*, 23 March 2010, http://timesofindia.indiatimes.com/india/Live-in-relationship-pre-marital-sex-not-an-offence-SC/articleshow/5716545.cms.

Times of India 2007. 'Do Christians also practice caste system, asks SC' in *The Times of India* 20 July 2007, http://timesofindia/indiatimes.com/India/Do_Christians_also_practice_caste_system,_asks_SC/articleshow/2218560.cms.

Timm, Annette F. 2005. 'Sex with a purpose. Prostitution, veneral disease, and militarized masculinity in the Third Reich' in Dagmar Herzog (ed.) *Sexuality and German fascism*. New York and Oxford: Berghahn Books: 223–55.

Timmons, Heather and Hari Kumar 2009. 'Indian court overrules gay sex ban' in *New York Times*, 2 July 2009, www.nytimes.com/2009/07/03/world/asia/03india.html.

Tiyavanich, Kamala 2007. *Sons of the Buddha*. Boston: Wisdom Publications.

Toledano, Ehud R. 1998. *Slavery and abolition in the Ottoman Middle East*. Seattle and London: University of Washington Press.

Turkish Daily News 2004. 'Adultery crisis seems over' in *Turkish Daily News* 15 September 2004, www.turkishdailynews.com.tr/archives.php?id=37664.

Turley, Jonathan 2004. 'Of lust and law' in *Washington Post* 5 September 2004, www.washingtonpost.com/wp-dyn/articles/A62581-2004Sep4.html.

Udjus, Vidar 2008. 'Skremt av trusler' in *Fædrelandsvennen* 16 March 2008, www.fvn.no/nyheter/article566842.ece.

UKGayNews 2009. 'Iranian reports on gay, lesbian relationships' at *www.gaynews.org.uk*, 21 January 2009, www.ukgaynews.org.uk/Archive/09/Jan/2103print.htm.

UNIFEM 2007. 'UNIFEM Afghanistan – Fact sheet 2007' at *www.unifem.org*, www.unifem.org/afghanistan/docs/pubs/08/UNIFEM_factsheet_08_EN.pdf.

UNIFEM 2003. *Not a minute more. Ending violence against women*. New York: UNIFEM.

UNODC (United Nations Office on Drugs and Crime) 2007. *Afghanistan. Female prisoners and their social reintegration*. Wien: United Office on Drugs and Crime.

Unterman, Alan 1996. *The Jews. Their religious beliefs and practices*. Brighton and Portland: Sussex Academic Press.

Urban, Hugh B. 2006. *Magia sexualis. Sex, magic, and liberation in modern western esotericism*. Berkeley, Los Angeles and London: University of California Press.

Urban, Hugh B. 2003. *Tantra. Sex, secrecy, politics, and power in the study of religion*. Berkeley, Los Angeles and London: University of California Press.

US Department of Health and Human Services 2009. 'Births, marriages, divorces, and deaths. Provisional data for 2008' *National Vital Statistics Reports* 29 July 2009.

Uyl, Marion den 2005. 'Dowry in India. Respected and modern monstrosity' in Tine Davids and Francien van Driel (eds) *The gender question in globalization*. Aldershot: Ashgate: 143–58.

Vanita, Ruth 2005. *Love's rite. Same-sex marriage in India and the West*. New York: Palgrave Macmillan.

Vanita, Ruth and Saleem Kidwai [2000]. *Same-sex love in India*. New York: Palgrave 2001.

Ventura, Stephanie J. and Christine A. Bachrach 2000. 'Nonmarital childbearing in the United States: 1940–99' in *National Vital Statistics Reports* 18 October 2000, www.cdc.gov/nchs/data/nvsr/nvsr48/nvs48_16.pdf.

Veyne, Paul [1983]. *Did the Greeks believe in their myths? An essay on the constitutive imagination*. Chicago: The University of Chicago Press 1988.

VG 2008. 'Imamer protesterte mot festing i Oslo' in *VG*, 5 October 2008, http://vg.no/nyheter/innenriks/artikkel.php?artid_537599.

Virdi, P. K. 1972. *Grounds for divorce in Hindu and English law*. Dehli: Motilal Banarsidass.

Vivekananthan, Majoran 2005. 'Muslimsk ungdom har minst sex' in *Utrop*, 28 February 2008, www.utrop.no/art.html?artid=7767andcatid=6.

Wafer, Jim 1997. 'Muhammad and male homosexuality' in Stephen Murray and Will Roscoe (eds) *Islamic homosexualities. Culture, history, and literature*. New York: New York University Press: 87–96.

Walther, Daniel Joseph 2002. *Creating Germans abroad. Cultural policies and settler identities in Namibia.* Athens, Ohio: Ohio University Press.

Wanrooij, Bruno P.F. 1999. 'Italy. Sexuality, morality and public authority' in Franz X. Eder, Lesley A. Hall and Gert Hekma (eds) *Sexual cultures in Europe. National histories.* Manchester and New York: Manchester University Press: 114–37.

Watanabe, Tsuneo and Jun'Ichi Iwata 1989. *Love of the samurai. Thousand years of Japanese homosexuality.* London: GMP.

Wawrytko, Sandra A. 1993. 'Homosexuality and Chinese and Japanese religions' in Arlene Swidler (ed.) *Homosexuality and world religions.* Valley Forge: Trinity Press International: 199–230.

Weeks, Jeffrey 1981. *Sex, politics, and society. The regulation of sexuality since 1800.* London and New York: Longman.

Weir, Alison 2000. *The six wives of Henry VIII.* New York: Grove Press.

Werbner, Pnina 2001. 'Global pathways, working class cosmopolitian and the creation of transnational ethnic worlds' in Harry Goulbourne (ed.) *Race and ethnicity. Critical concepts of sociology.* New York: Routledge: 408–29.

Westoff, Charles F., Ann Klimas Blanc and Laura Nyblade 1994. *Marriage and entry into parenthood.* Calverton: Macro International.

de Wette, Wilhelm Martin Leberecht (ed.) 1856. *Dr. Martin Luthers Sendschreiben und Bedenken. Sechster Theil.* Berlin: G. Reimer.

de Wette, Wilhelm Martin Leberecht (ed.) 1826. *Dr. Martin Luthers Sendschreiben und Bedenken. Zweyter Theil.* Berlin: G. Reimer.

White, David Gordon 1998. 'Tantric sects and tantric sex. The flow of secret tantric gnosis' in Elliot R. Wolfson (ed.) *Rending the veil. Concealment and secrecy in the history of religions.* New York: Seven Bridges Press: 249–70.

Wiesner-Hanks, Merry E. 2000. *Christianity and sexuality in the early modern world. Regulating desire, reforming practices.* London and New York: Routledge.

Wikan, Unni 1977. 'Man becomes woman. Transexual in Oman as a key to gender roles' in *Man* 13:304–19.

Willis, Alan Scott 2004. *All according to God's plan. Southern Baptist missions and race 1945–1970.* Lexington: University Press of Kentucky.

Wilson, Liz 2003. 'Buddhist views on gender and desire' in David W. Machacek and Melissa M. Wilcox (eds) *Sexuality and the world's religions.* Santa Barbara, Denver and Oxford: ABC-CLIO: 133–75.

Winterkjær, Trond and Jan Dalchow 2000. *Dirty, Sinful Me (BE—skitne, syndige meg).* Documentary film. Norway.

Wormeley, Katharine Prescott 1899. *The correspondence of Madame, Princess Palatine, Mother of the Regent; of Marie-Adélaïde de Savoie, Duchesse de Bourgogne; and of Madame de Maintenon, in relation to Saint-Cyr.* Boston: Hardy, Pratt and Company.

Worth, Robert F. 2008. 'Tiny voices defy child marriage in Yemen' in *New York Times*, 29 June 2008, www.nytimes.com/2008/06/29/world/middleeast/29marriage.html?_r=1.

Yao, Xinzhong 2003. 'Harmony of yin and yang. Cosmology and sexuality in Daoism' in David W. Machacek and Melissa M. Wilcox (eds) *Sexuality and the world's religions.* Santa Barbara, Denver and Oxford: ABC-CLIO: 65–99.

Yardley, Jim 1999. 'Church's haunted house draws fire' in *New York Times*, 29 October 1999, www.nytimes.com/1999/10/29/us/church-s-haunted-house-draws-fire.html.

Young, Kathleen Zuanich 1995. 'The imperishable virginity of Saint Maria Goretti' in Carol J. Adams and Marie M. Fortune (eds) *Violence against women and children. A Christian theological sourcebook*. New York: Continuum: 279–86.

Young, Serinity 2004. *Courtesans and tantric consorts. Sexualities in Buddhist narratives, iconography and ritual*. New York: Routledge.

Zabel, William 2000. 'Interracial marriage and the law' in Werner Sollors (ed.) *Interracialism. Black-white intermarriage in American history, literature, and law*. New York and Oxford: Oxford University Press: 54–61.

Zarit, Jerry 1992. 'Intimate look on the Iranian male', in Arno Schmitt and Jehoeda Sofer (eds) *Sexuality and eroticism among males in Moslem societies*. New York: Harrington Park Press: 55–60.

Zeitzen, Miriam Koktvedgaard 2008. *Polygamy. A cross-cultural analysis*. Oxford and New York: Berg Publishers.

Zuria, Anat 2004. *Sentenced to marriage / Mekudeshet*. Documentary film. Israel.

Zwilling, Leonard 1992. 'Homosexuality as seen in Indian Buddhist texts' in José Ignacio Cabezón (ed.) *Buddhism, sexuality, and gender*. Albany: State University of New York Press: 203–14.

ACKNOWLEDGEMENTS

Writing a book can be a demanding and strenuous journey, but there are a host of people who have helped me along the way. In particular I would like to thank Knut Olav Åmås, Mia Berner, Ingvild Sælid Gilhus, Hege Gundersen, Bjørn Hatterud, Liv Ingeborg Lied, Kaizad Mehta, Henrik Nordhus, Steinar Opstad, Pål Steiner, Helge Svare and my parents for all their help, support and enthusiasm. I would also like to thank Pål Bjørby, Ole Aastad Bråten, Gina Dahl, Christine Endsjø, Mona Farstad, Roald Fevang, Jonis Forland, Wenche Helstad, Janicke Iversen, Per Thore Lanner, José Martinez, Lisbeth Mikaelsson, Håkan Rydving, Mara Senese, Grigor Simonyan, Michael Stausberg and Arne Veer.

PHOTO ACKNOWLEDGEMENTS

The author and publishers wish to express their thanks to the below sources of illustrative material and/or permission to reproduce it.

© The Trustees of the British Museum, London: pp. 23, 31, 34, 45, 129, 141, 242; Dag Øistein Endsjø: pp. 48, 239, 242; Courtesy of Chad Hardy: p. 24; Library of Congress, Washington, DC: p. 39; North Carolina Museum of Art, Raleigh, NC (Gift of The Samuel H. Kress Foundation, GL.60.17.32): p. 201; Rex Features: p. 53 (Sipa Press); Bibi Saint-Pol: p. 243; Shutterstock: p. 159 (Vishal Shah); University of San Diego, CA: p. 231.

INDEX

ALSO IN SPEAKING TIGER